Friends and Enemies in Penn's Woods

EDITED BY

William A. Pencak and Daniel K. Richter

Friends and Enemies
—— in ——
Penn's Woods

INDIANS, COLONISTS,

AND THE

RACIAL CONSTRUCTION OF PENNSYLVANIA

THE PENNSYLVANIA STATE UNIVERSITY PRESS
UNIVERSITY PARK, PENNSYLVANIA

Library of Congress Cataloging-in-Publication Data

Friends and enemies in Penn's Woods :
Indians, colonists, and the racial construction of Pennsylvania /
edited by William A. Pencak and Daniel K. Richter.
p.   cm.
Includes bibliographical references (p.   ) and index.
ISBN 0-271-02384-8 (cloth : alk. paper)
ISBN 0-271-02385-6 (pbk. : alk. paper)
1. Pennsylvania—History—Colonial period, ca. 1600–1775.
2. Frontier and pioneer life—Pennsylvania. 3. Pennsylvania—Race relations.
4. Pennsylvania—Ethnic relations. 5. Intercultural communication—Pennsylvania—History.
6. Culture conflict—Pennsylvania—History. 7. Colonists—Pennsylvania—History.
8. Indians of North America—Pennsylvania—History. 9. Indians of North
America—Pennsylvania—Government relations.
I. Pencak, William, 1951– . II. Richter, Daniel K.

F152 .F865 2004
974.8′02—dc22
2004006255

Copyright © 2004 The Pennsylvania State University
All rights reserved
Printed in the United States of America
Published by The Pennsylvania State University Press,
University Park, PA 16802–1003
The Pennsylvania State University Press is a member of the
Association of American University Presses.
It is the policy of The Pennsylvania State University Press
to use acid-free paper. Publications on uncoated stock
satisfy the minimum requirements of American National
Standard for Information Sciences—Permanence of Paper
for Printed Library Materials, ANSI Z39.48–1992.

CONTENTS

List of Maps and Figures   vii

Introduction   ix
Daniel K. Richter and William A. Pencak

I. PEOPLES IN CONVERSATION

1 New Sweden, Natives, and Nature   3
Michael Dean Mackintosh

2 Colonialism and the Discursive Antecedents of
Penn's Treaty with the Indians   18
James O'Neil Spady

3 Imagining Peace in Quaker and Native American
Dream Stories   41
Carla Gerona

4 Indian, *Métis,* and Euro-American Women on
Multiple Frontiers   63
Alison Duncan Hirsch

II. FRAGILE STRUCTURES OF COEXISTENCE

5 Female Relationships and Intercultural Bonds in Moravian
Indian Missions   87
Amy C. Schutt

6 The Death of Sawantaeny and the Problem of Justice on
the Frontier   104
John Smolenski

7 Justice, Retribution, and the Case of John Toby   129
Louis M. Waddell

8 The Diplomatic Career of Canasatego   144
William A. Starna

III. TOWARD A WHITE PENNSYLVANIA

9 Delawares and Pennsylvanians After the
   Walking Purchase   167
   Steven C. Harper

10 Squatters, Indians, Proprietary Government,
   and Land in the Susquehanna Valley   180
   David L. Preston

11 Violence, Race, and the Paxton Boys   201
   Krista Camenzind

12 "Real" Indians, "White" Indians, and the Contest
   for the Wyoming Valley   221
   Paul Moyer

13 Whiteness and Warfare on a Revolutionary
   Frontier   238
   Gregory T. Knouff

   Afterword   259
   James H. Merrell

   Abbreviations   269

   Notes   271

   Contributors   325

   Index   329

MAPS AND FIGURES

Maps

1. The greater geographical context   xxii
2. The regional context   xxiii
3. Approximate boundaries of William Penn's purchases from
   the Indians, 1682–84   34
4. Six Nations Iroquois land cessions to Pennsylvania, 1736–92   150

Figures

1. Edward Hicks, *The Peaceable Kingdom*, 1826   xi
2. A Swedish view of American nature, detail of Pehr Lindeström's
   1633 map   12
3. Benjamin West, *William Penn's Treaty with the Indians*, 1771   20
4. Chart of the Delaware prophet Neolin's teachings   59
5. The Great Treaty Wampum Belt   64
6. Detail of *William Penn's Treaty with the Indians*   70
7. Moravian women presented to Christ   91
8. Provincial Secretary James Logan   110
9. Conrad Weiser Homestead   159
10. Deed of Nutimus, Teeshakommen, et al. to John, Thomas, and
    Richard Penn, The "Walking Purchase"   169
11. Provincial Secretary Richard Peters   186
12. Philadelphians mobilize against the Paxton Boys   203
13. King George III shares a feast of his former American subjects   250

To Alden T. Vaughan
and to the memory of Francis Jennings

INTRODUCTION

DANIEL K. RICHTER AND WILLIAM A. PENCAK

Two powerfully contradictory images dominate historical memory of relations between Native Americans and Pennsylvania colonists: Penn's
Treaty, a reverie of harmonious coexistence in 1682; and the Conestoga
massacre, a nightmare of innocents slaughtered in 1763. The two images
are curiously ahistorical, abstracted from real human time. Penn's Treaty
remains frozen in endless variations on Benjamin West's famous painting
and Edward Hicks's allegories of the "Peaceable Kingdom." West, it should
be remembered, composed his work a century after the event he portrayed
and several years after the Paxton Boys did their Conestoga deed; Hicks, a
generation further on, could locate interracial harmony only in a utopian
realm where the lion lies down with the lamb. Conestoga resides in a
darker dystopian corner of the ahistorical national consciousness, but one
all too frequently realized in countless lynchings, Great Swamp Fights, and
Wounded Knees.

Penn's Treaty and Conestoga lie outside historical time in other senses
as well. Despite their bipolar iconic status, they seem to bear no direct
causal or historical relation to each other, posing instead the great historical dilemma of how, in the space of but eighty years, peace could have
given way to bloodlust—how, as James H. Merrell has put it in one of the
few efforts to trace the connection, "Penn's Woods became an abbatoir."[1]
At best we struggle for some moral tale of family decline in which William
Penn—good-hearted father to both his people and the Indians—is replaced by unworthy sons and a future generation more interested in land-
grabbing than treating their fellow human beings with respect. The
Founder, we prefer to believe, bought land from Native Americans fair and
square, inaugurating a remarkable era of peace and honest dealing. Things
only began to go sour in the era of the "Walking Purchase" of 1737, when
his successors swindled the Delawares out of much of what became the
province's northeast corner. In the 1750s, the wrath of the dispossessed
came down upon Pennsylvania during the Seven Years'—or "French and

Indian"—War. Still, in memories of that conflict, Euro-Americans often seem more victims than aggressors, burned out of their homes and hauled off to Indian captivity through no fault of their own, while Quakers in Philadelphia nonetheless tried to keep the peace. Even in a narrative of declension from the Eden of Penn's Treaty, then, the brutal violence of Conestoga finds little connection to the main currents of Pennsylvania's history.

And just as Penn's Treaty and Conestoga stand historically isolated one from the other, each also derives its symbolic power from its seeming disconnection to contexts of its own day. Each seems a historical aberration: Penn's Treaty as a fresh, pacific start, remarkable for its radical disjuncture from a historical norm of conflict; Conestoga as a tragic moment when the inevitable stream of racial incompatibility overflowed to a level of rage unworthy of civilized combatants. And perhaps less obviously, our images of Penn's Treaty and Conestoga are also fundamentally ahistorical in one final way. In each, Euro-Americans tend to be the only real actors, the only bearers of moral messages. William Penn and the Paxton Boys, not the Native people they treated with and murdered, dominate the scenes.

The chapters in this volume provide no easy or definitive answers. But they do attempt to move beyond ahistorical set pieces to frame more subtle contexts for interactions between Euro-Americans and Native Americans in what became known as Pennsylvania. They begin by recognizing as historical problems what have too often been considered historical givens: how Pennsylvania came to be a landscape utterly dominated by Euro-Americans and how those who dominated managed to turn the region's history not only into a story solely about themselves but into a morality tale about their best (William Penn) and worst (Paxton Boys) sides. These chapters also assume that the puzzle of how a significant corner of Native America came to be Penn's Woods reveals something broader about the ways in which Europeans and their descendants, as they constructed a society on territory that once belonged to Native people, simultaneously defined those people as a racial Other and consigned them to the historical past rather than the living present. The construction of Pennsylvania on Native ground was also the construction of a racial order for the new nation.

In exploring the racial construction of Pennsylvania, the essays below vary greatly in approaches and subject matter, but all concentrate less on

Figure 1 Edward Hicks, *The Peaceable Kingdom*, 1826. Abby Aldrich Rockefeller Folk Art Museum, Colonial Williamsburg Foundation, Williamsburg, Virginia.

mundane details of how colonists and Indians negotiated and fought than on how peoples defined themselves, their relationships, and their cultural landscape with reference to others. The first group of chapters, "Peoples in Conversation," examines the ways in which Europeans and Native Americans encountered and tried to make sense of each other initially and through the early eighteenth century. Very real points of congruence between views of the world provided some basis for mutual understanding, but underlying disparities in interests made such understandings—and the possibilities for peaceful coexistence they implied—inherently fragile. Right from the beginning, the intercultural conversation was far from the lovefest enshrined in the Penn's Treaty icon. Michael Dean Mackintosh and James O'Neil Spady discuss relations between the Lenapes and the Swedes and the Dutch during the half-century before William Penn arrived. Misunderstandings abounded concerning land purchases (whether they were perpetual and exclusive, as the Europeans thought, or temporary and shared, as the Indians believed) and the natural world (a resource to be exploited for the Europeans or a realm of powerful spiritual forces for the Indians). Violence broke out intermittently, and tension rather than harmony was the norm. Nor is William Penn's own record as spotless as his admirers have maintained. As Spady shows, the Lenapes had the choice of either submitting to European mores and laws or leaving. Once Penn purchased the land, mutual use was impossible as forests became fields and thousands of Europeans insisting on exclusive possession filled the area around Philadelphia.

"Peoples in Conversation" continues with chapters in which Carla Gerona and Alison Duncan Hirsch explore two types of European–Native American contact that have been relatively neglected: the realm of dreams and the role of women. Quakers, Gerona points out, believed that all human beings, including Indians, had the "inner light" through which God could communicate with them and that dreams could be one medium of encounters with the divine. Similarly, Native American societies placed great stock in the import of nocturnal visions. Dreams do not dictate their own interpretation, however, and Pennsylvania intermediaries were especially apt to point out how Native dreams supposedly mandated peaceful land sessions and coexistence. Only after warfare broke out in the mid-eighteenth century did Quakers begin to consider Indian dreams the work of the devil. On a more material level, Hirsch shows that women were crucial participants in the cultural conversation between Euro-Americans and Native people: large numbers came to councils with their men, they served as go-betweens, they processed and sold skins in the important fur trade, and they provided hospitality for people traveling from one society to another. Hirsch also reads between the lines of colonial texts to show how both contemporaries and later historians minimized women's vital role in preserving the tenuous connections between Pennsylvanians and the people they ultimately displaced. The racial construction of Pennsylvania history required its gendered construction as well.

The chapters in the second section, "Fragile Structures of Coexistence," concentrate on how both the peaceful possibilities and the inherent tensions discussed by Mackintosh, Spady, Gerona, and Hirsch generated social and cultural frameworks that at least some Euro-Americans and Indians managed to inhabit together. Amy C. Schutt examines the interactions between Native and colonial women in Moravian missions. The missionary effort that the *Unitas Fratrum* began in the 1740s possessed a vigor neither the Quakers nor any other Pennsylvania religious group had demonstrated. From their headquarters at Bethlehem, the Moravians granted missionary status to every man and woman who went to convert the inhabitants of the upper Lehigh, Susquehanna, and ultimately Ohio valleys where they concentrated their efforts. Native and European women were especially close, sharing agricultural tasks, childbearing and child rearing, and educational experiences. Many were dear friends who confided their innermost thoughts to each other. Dispossessed from their lands in the Hudson and Delaware Valleys, Mahicans and Delawares found in Moravians confidants who provided spiritual and worldly guidance in their new homes.

Such mutual understanding was rare: much contact between Pennsylvanians and Native Americans consisted of encounters on the border of the two worlds where relatively isolated individuals forged—and smashed—their own personal relationships. As John Smolenski and Louis M. Waddell show, when those relationships went bad, the confusing circumstances and multiple sources of authority on all sides of what was anything but a clearly defined Pennsylvania-Indian frontier led to situations in which the fate of accused criminals was more a matter of compromise and power politics than a standard of justice. Smolenski shows how in two cases involving the murders of Native Americans—Sawantaeny in 1722 and Tacocolie and Quilee in 1728—the Euro-American perpetrators were, respectively, exonerated and hanged based on complicated Native American negotiations with the Pennsylvania authorities who were willing to execute frontiersmen who threatened the peaceful boundary they sought to maintain. Similarly, Waddell details the fascinating case of John Toby, a Nanticoke Indian who sexually assaulted an eight-year-old Euro-American girl in 1751. He was freed from jail after a short time as part of Pennsylvania's effort to keep an increasingly precarious peace with the Nanticokes.

But the Native Americans who Pennsylvania devoted most of its energy to appeasing were the Six Nations of the Haudenosaunee, or the Iroquois League—nations whose core territories lay well to the north and west of Philadelphia, at several layers remove from the Lenapes and other peoples whose lands Euro-Pennsylvanians coveted. This curiously distant emphasis derived from the distinctive historical character of the Native peoples who were actually on the front lines of Penn's Woods' expansion. The Lenapes of the lower Delaware Valley lived in many small, almost entirely autonomous, communities when they first encountered Europeans at the turn of the seventeenth century. These local groups participated in loose regional political groupings that were not so much unified tribes as collections of peoples who shared strong affinities of marriage, trade, and language with each other. Speaking on their behalf were what seemed to Euro-Americans countless "kings"—headmen of various kin groups whose overlapping use rights to territory required colonists to make multiple "purchases" of any single patch of real estate (while providing multiple opportunities for those headmen both to stave off definitive transfers of large tracts and to exploit the Euro-American authorities who had to pay and repay to clear their titles). The Munsee-speakers of the watershed north of the Delaware Water Gap were similarly decentralized, and the social turmoil spawned by the epidemics that devastated both of these peoples in the mid-seventeenth century only compounded the political confusion.[2]

Epidemics, indigenous warfare, and colonial pressures created an even more vexed situation in the Susquehanna River watershed after the 1670s, when the Iroquoian-speaking Susquehannocks, who had controlled much of the mid-Atlantic region's trade in the early and mid-seventeenth century, first relocated to the borders of Maryland and then surrendered to the League Iroquois, who resettled and absorbed most of the survivors. In subsequent decades, an array of refugee groups from all over the Atlantic seaboard—Lenapes, Munsees, and Hudson River valley Mahicans (together the three groups came to be known in the course of their migrations as "Delawares"); Nanticokes, Conoys, and Shawnees from locations to the south; family groups from the Six Nations and from Algonquian New England—created polyglot communities that spread from the Susquehanna and its tributaries westward into the Allegheny, Monongahela, and Ohio countries.[3]

And, as the legal cases discussed by Smolenski and Waddell clearly demonstrate, no one, Native or European, seemed clearly in charge. Blending a variety of political and cultural traditions in potentially unstable ways, each Indian village, and perhaps even each small kin group, was autonomous. And the Penn family—fighting its many battles with Maryland, Virginia, and New York for paper title to Indian lands in the interior while ever-increasing waves of Scots-Irish, German, and English immigrants poured into the contested space—desperately needed a single Indian authority from which they could extract the treaty documents that would give them title to real estate under European law and the right to collect quitrents from Euro-American settlers on the ground. As the work of the late Francis Jennings demonstrated, a faction of Iroquois leaders gladly agreed to satisfy the Pennsylvanians' demand for a single authoritative Native voice.[4] In this marriage of convenience, no single Iroquois diplomat played a more important role than the Onondaga spokesman Canasatego. William A. Starna's essay traces the evolution of the Iroquois as Pennsylvania's putative enforcers through a succession of treaty councils in which Canasatego participated in the years surrounding the Walking Purchase. Starna also points out that the Iroquois courted Pennsylvania more out of desperation than strength: surrounded by stronger British and French colonies and suffering from hunger as they lost their lands to Whites, an alliance with Pennsylvania served the interests of both the Quaker elite and the Iroquois at the expense of the people—both Native and Euro-American—who actually lived on the lands that were sold.

A theme in all of the chapters in the second section is the degree to which the fragile structures of Euro-Indian coexistence rested on personal connections, among religious women, among those who negotiated the thickets of intercultural law, among those who claimed to speak for their people at treaty conferences. When collective stereotypes began to trump personal connections, coexistence became increasingly unlikely. Yet, as the final group of chapters, "Toward a White Pennsylvania," suggests, the process of racial estrangement was neither simple nor direct. Steven C. Harper and David L. Preston demonstrate that the orderly removal and settlement the Pennsylvanians and Iroquois hoped to dictate was being undermined even before it was negotiated. Harper shows that Euro-Americans had been living in the territory conveyed in the Walking Purchase for at least a decade before the treaty and that Native Americans remained in the area long afterwards. In his account, the Walking Purchase emerges more as symbolic ratification of a process of dispossession than a turning point, and also as a symbol of the failure of efforts by outside powers to keep Indians and colonists separate. David Preston tells a similar story for the Susquehanna Valley. Grassroots squatters and Native Americans interacted, sometimes in friendly, sometimes in hostile, ways, despite the efforts of the provincial government and Iroquois to keep them apart. In vain did Pennsylvania authorities, headed by Provincial Secretary Richard Peters, burn squatters' cabins in the early 1750s in an attempt to prevent encounters that would disturb the peace.

Although pockets of friendly mutual interaction would remain, the mixing of Native and European peoples became increasingly parlous by the eve of the Seven Years' War. Krista Camenzind explores how that conflict led many Euro-Americans to brand all Indians as both racially different and evil. Native American attacks against isolated farms challenged men's patriarchal role as protectors of their families and forced them into towns as refugees. There they encountered similar men and vented their frustration by forming mobs, firing guns, and ultimately killing any Indians they could find, refusing to distinguish friend from foe. Eastern Pennsylvanians, too, became targets of the frontiersmen's wrath for protecting Indians and refusing to make such easy racial distinctions. In short, Pennsylvania during the Seven Years' War articulated the myth of heroic yet victimized frontier folk, attacked by Native Americans and neglected by uncomprehending authorities in more settled regions. In Camenzind's account, the Conestoga massacre becomes not an aberration but a logical outgrowth of long-developing historical processes.

The Wyoming Valley in the northeast, as Paul Moyer shows, traced a similar long-term trend toward racialized violence. Native Americans, Pennsylvanians, and Connecticut Yankees struggled with each other throughout the late eighteenth and even into the early nineteenth century before possession of the land was finally established. Not only did some of the Paxton Boys move northward after the massacre of 1763, but they brought with them a style of warfare that colonists began to use in conflict with each other. Frequently disguising themselves as "White Indians," partisans on both sides practiced guerrilla warfare and random killings in an effort to secure control of the region. As Gregory T. Knouff argues, veterans of the American Revolution not only described themselves as "White" in opposition to "Indians" in their early nineteenth-century pension depositions, but they justified the "savage" methods of their scalping raids by claiming that they had reacted defensively to Indians who used the same tactics against White families. With the revolutionary generation, the stark separation of Native and Euro-Americans, practiced by Pennsylvania from the beginning, had finally established itself ideologically in a national consciousness in which White males earned citizenship through ethnic cleansing.

Taken together, then, these chapters trace the collapse of whatever potential may have existed for a Pennsylvania shared by Indians and Europeans and its replacement by a racialized definition that left no room for Native people—except in reassuring memories of the justice of the Founder, and thus presumably of at least some of his Euro-American successors as well. Yet the startling contrast between peaceful beginnings and violent endings should not obscure the possibility that the eras of peace and war shared much in common. As Merrell has recently argued, Pennsylvania may have remained peaceful for so long precisely because it was so successful in uprooting Native Americans from their homelands, while brutal war came despite, and perhaps even because of, close mutual familiarity across cultural lines.[5] In this and many other ways, the experience of how Native America became Penn's Woods suggests fruitful points of both contrast and comparison with patterns of relations between Indians and Europeans elsewhere on the continent.

First, the environment. Despite the different conceptions of nature and land ownership that Mackintosh and Spady explore, outside the fertile southeast, most of the area that became Penn's Woods long retained its seventeenth-century appearance. In this respect, Pennsylvania differed from coastal regions to the north and south where large-scale ecological transformations had almost obliterated the precontact environment by 1800.[6] Although Iroquois and Pennsylvania provincial authorities made great efforts to keep Natives and Europeans separated, squatters, legitimate settlers, and Indians on the frontier engaged in agricultural and economic practices that united diverse peoples.[7] As Harper, Preston, and Moyer show, Native and Euro-American farmers operated side by side, both communally and individually, borrowing each other's methods and establishing friendships as well as animosities.

At the same time, both Native and Euro-American hunters used the river valleys as conduits for the fur trade, leading to the creation of such multiethnic communities as Shamokin.[8] Had the Seven Years' War not occurred, it is possible to imagine a Pennsylvania frontier where Indians and Whites interacted peacefully or solved their differences to general satisfaction, as some of the households described by Smolenski, Waddell, and Starna suggest. Of course, it remains a moot question as to just how powerful these interethnic grassroots ties were and whether they could have survived the joint pressure of the Iroquois and the Pennsylvania government.

Many of these informal ties between Native and Euro-Americans were between women, or involved women interacting with men. As Hirsch and Schutt show, the frontiers of Pennsylvania, like many other regions of cultural contact, enhanced the power of Euro-American women. More sedentary than men, they frequently learned other languages more quickly and established deep friendships. Both the Quakers and the Moravians granted women the right to preach and proselytize along with men.[9] That so much initial intercultural contact occurred peacefully and among women explains why Native American women in this region, unlike those described by Irene Silverblatt in Peru and Karen Anderson in New France, were often at the forefront of cooperation and innovation rather than resistant to economic, religious, and other forms of change.[10]

Alcohol, on the other hand, was an agent of change primarily, although not exclusively, managed by men. In his study of Cherokee anomie, William McLoughlin notes that alcohol abuse tends to be especially prevalent among people who lose their cultural moorings.[11] The Native Americans who traded, treated, and warred with Euro-Pennsylvanians not only endured multiple relocations and recombinations, but rum, along with furs, was a principal item of commerce. Inevitably, both Native Americans in general and those who tried to mediate between Indian and European worlds often turned to liquor for consolation, especially given the obligatory drinking that was a necessary social ritual at many encounters. Liquor cemented ties, but as Smolenski and Waddell show, it also produced (and sometimes at the same time exculpated) crime.[12]

After midcentury, peacekeeping yielded to full-scale race war. As Gregory Evans Dowd's work has demonstrated, Pontiac's War received its spiritual leadership from Neolin, who preached a pan-Indian racial consciousness that demonized Whites and reflected the union the numerous displaced Native groups achieved.[13] The frontiers of Pennsylvania may have been the first place on the continent where "Reds" and "Whites" consciously battled each other as racially defined groups. Studies of how "Whiteness" became the sine qua non of American citizenship have usually attributed this racial consciousness to the need for an insecure group to define itself and cement its ties against "others." They have also debated the extent to which Whiteness as opposed to other factors shaped group self-consciousness and animosities.[14] It seems likely that the sharp Red-White dichotomy Gregory Knouff describes had special explanatory power for both multiethnic Pennsylvania and the multiethnic Indian villages of the Susquehanna and Ohio countries, where both sides had to unite numerous recently dislocated groups to an extent previously unprecedented. By 1800, to be a Pennsylvanian meant to be White. To be a Delaware or a Shawnee meant to be Red—and as Whites saw it, not to be a Pennsylvanian. To a tragic extent, the same remains true to this day. According to the 2000 federal census, among all fifty states and the District of Columbia, Pennsylvania ranks last in the percentage of its population classified as Native American—a mere 0.01 percent, compared to a national average of .9 percent and an average among the original thirteen states of about .04 percent. Moreover, among the original states, only the Keystone lacks both an Indian reservation within its boundaries and any Native groups that (as of this writing) have won legal recognition of their status from state or federal governments.

That Native America thoroughly became Penn's Woods, in demographic as well as political and cultural terms, is thus beyond question. *How* and *why* that racial transformation occurred are the contentious issues that unite the varied chapters in this book. For all their thematic congruencies, the chapters originated separately in the work of a talented group of (mostly) younger scholars. With the exception of the essays by Hirsch, Schutt, and Starna, each began as a submission to *Pennsylvania History*. The work was of such high quality that there appeared to be only two choices: either preempt several issues of the journal while students of other aspects of the state's history gnashed their teeth or collect the work in a single volume. As one of us was then editor of the journal and the other a specialist in relations between Native Americans and Euro-American colonists, a collaboration to pursue the second option seemed natural. The partnership also made sense for another reason: we had known each other (we realized with some alarm) for a quarter-century, since our days as graduate students at Columbia University, where each of us studied with Alden T. Vaughan, to whom this volume is dedicated and whose relentless pursuit of both historical accuracy and good writing we have tried to embrace throughout our careers. His sense of fairness, we trust, will allow him to appreciate our duty also to dedicate this book to Francis Jennings, whose work, more than any other, mapped the complicated, often ugly, historical terrain that Pennsylvanians and Indians created together.

However much these chapters may have initially cohered in theme and approach, essays that originate independently seldom find easy compatibility within the covers of a single volume. Many of our authors made heroic sacrifices in theme, style, and, most bloodily, of pages of cherished prose for the good of a work that—without, we hope, squelching individual voices and interpretive perspectives—can be read profitably from beginning to end. We thank them for their patience, good humor, and remarkable adherence to deadlines set by editors prone to long silences punctuated by frantic bursts of activity. Additional thematic coherence and scholarly collaboration among the authors occurred as the project entered its final stages, when drafts of each chapter were posted on a protected Web site for review and suggestion. This form of virtual scholarly conference prevented several of the inevitable errors of fact or interpretation that slip into the best of work from finding their way into print. The maps, carefully drawn by Adrienne Gruver, similarly profited from the authors' collective review. All of the contributors profited greatly from the enthusiastic support of our editors at Penn State Press, Peter Potter, Patricia Mitchell, and copyeditor Eliza Childs. The Donald Haag Research Fund of the History Department, Penn State University, aided in the cost of preparing the maps. Amy Baxter-Bellamy of the McNeil Center for Early American Studies, as always, helped in numerous ways.

Thanks are also due the volume's authors for their willingness to compromise in difficult matters of terminology. We have attempted to avoid, for instance, the term *backcountry* despite its established use in much of the historiography and in the other work of several of our contributors. As Jennings once said on the floor of an academic conference devoted to the B-word, to the people who lived in contested interior spaces, the territory was "the frontcountry"; moreover, the term can convey an eastern, Eurocentric bias that works against the themes of cultural contestation we are trying to highlight in this volume—a bias that in itself has often been an aspect of a racially constructed past in which Euro-Americans expanded westward into empty lands at the back of the centers of civilization. *Frontier* can be a similarly problematic word—but only if used to convey a sense of empty space. We have tried to use it here with some precision to denote a zone of contestation, of cultural contact between Euro-Americans and Native Americans that was equally "frontier" to all sides. *Settlers,* too, has been used with some care, as a term equally applicable to Natives as well as Euro-Americans who colonized contested frontier spaces.

And, in a work in which the construction of racial categories is a major theme, we have attempted to use *Euro-Americans* and *Indians* or *Native Americans* as convenient collective names for diverse groups who did not necessarily understand each other (or themselves) as "races." *White* and *Red* are used only in contexts where socially constructed racial categorizations were in play as historical phenomena, and the terms are capitalized to emphasize their constructedness. Of course *Pennsylvania*, too, was a construct; we have done our best to use this term to refer primarily to the political entity created by Euro-Americans, not to describe the Native American landscape that eventually became the Keystone State. In all quotations, abbreviations have been silently expanded and antique orthography has been replaced with modern equivalents. No attempt has been made to convert the Old Style (Julian) calendar to the New Style (Gregorian), but dates are given as if the year began on 1 January, and the Quaker practice of referring to months and days of the week by numbers has been silently converted to the modern, pagan form.

"Our own feelings sufficiently prompt us to testify our personal esteem for you," Governor Thomas Mifflin wrote to Alexander McGillivray and the rest of the Creek delegation he led to Philadelphia in July 1790. "As we hope the conduct of Pennsylvania, from the landing of William Penn to this day, has unequivocally proved her love of justice, her disposition for peace, and her respect for the rights and happiness of her neighbors, it is with sincere pleasure that we anticipate . . . the establishment of a lasting harmony between your Nation and the United States of America."[15] Linking Penn's Treaty with the broader history of the United States while ignoring the counter-icon of Conestoga—and defining Native people as, at best, "neighbors" rather than those with a place in his commonwealth's spatial, political, and social order—Mifflin participated deeply in the discursive process by which, in the minds of White Pennsylvanians, Native America became Penn's Woods. We hope the chapters that follow advance understanding not only of Mifflin's era but of the world of more intimate relationships between Euro-American and Native American people that he and his contemporaries sought to erase from historical memory.

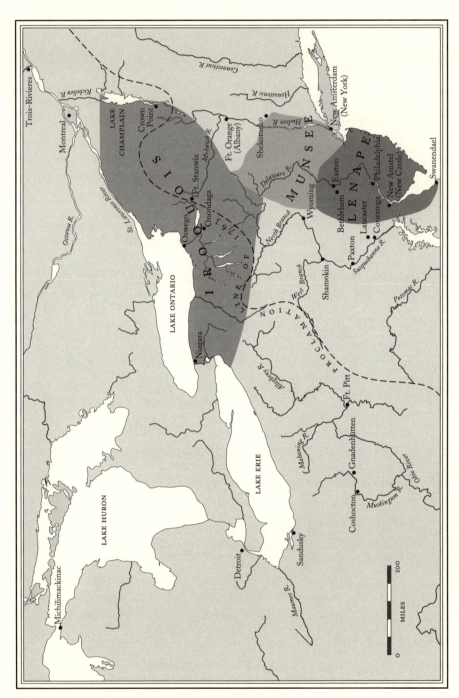

Map 1. The greater geographical context

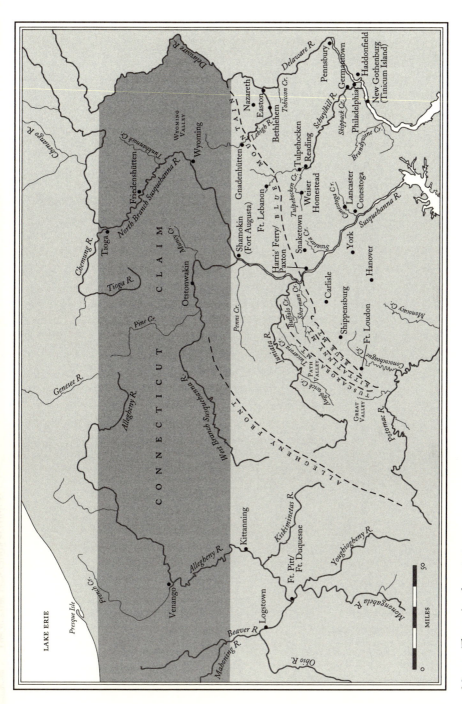

Map 2 The regional context.

I. ❧ PEOPLES IN CONVERSATION

1

❧

NEW SWEDEN, NATIVES, AND NATURE

MICHAEL DEAN MACKINTOSH

According to a story recounted by naturalist Pehr Kalm, "an old Swede once walked with an Indian" in the woods. When they encountered "a red-spotted snake on the road," the colonist "went to seek a stick in order to kill it, but the Indian begged him not to touch it, for it was sacred to him." The Swede might have spared the reptile, "but on hearing that it was the Indian's deity, he took a stick and killed it, in the presence of the Indian, saying 'Because thou believest in it, I think myself obliged to kill it.'"[1] Kalm, who heard the tale while on a 1750 tour of North America, recorded it with no comment. The brutal killing of the snake simply because an Indian "believest in it," seems a clear enough statement on the chasm between Native and colonial worldviews and interests. Yet the picture is complicated by the fact that the Swede and the Indian were, after all, sharing a road, a journey, and a conversation in a common language. Only the appearance of a snake shattered their rapport.

The snake as an emblem of the natural world illustrates how ideas of nature can be powerful historical forces; Raymond Williams has noted that *nature* is "the most complex word in the language" and enticingly suggests that the "idea of nature contains an extraordinary amount of human history."[2] It seems clear, however, that there is no shared, universal view of nature that expresses what Williams describes as "mankind's vision of itself and its place in the world."[3] Instead, ideas about nature are variably under-stood, are complex and contested, and are used (consciously and uncon-sciously) in larger contests over culture and power. Understandings of nature were especially vital, complex, and revealing in places like the Dela-ware Valley in the seventeenth century, where distinct groups that held very different and perhaps incompatible cultural views of the natural world were in contact with one another. Kalm's story was doubtlessly shaded by the darkening climate of Indian-colonial relations in mid-eighteenth-century Pennsylvania. But even from the earliest days of Swedish and Dutch settlement in the Delaware Valley, nature was an important marker of difference, a recurring point of contention, and an issue of critical im-portance in establishing Native and colonial understandings of self and other.

From as early as 1632, more than one hundred years before Kalm would cross the Atlantic Ocean and a half-century before William Penn would establish his colony, nature was critically important in shaping relation-ships between European newcomers and American Natives in the Delaware Valley. In that year, a group of Lenape Indians, angry over a series of misunderstandings with the Dutch inhabitants of a small whaling station on Cape Henlopen at the southern end of the Delaware Bay, crept into the settlement and killed all of the thirty or so colonists there. In retrospect, the events that preceded the outbreak of violence at Swanendael reveal more misunderstanding than malice, and more fear of vulnerability than hatred for the other. According to a Native witness, Dutch settlers painted their coat of arms on a piece of tin and posted it in the woods. A Lenape man removed the tin, "not knowing what he was doing amiss," in order to make tobacco pipes of the metal. The ruckus raised by the Dutch settlers in response to the incident impressed on the Indians that a great wrong had been done, so a contingent of them slew the offender and brought a token of his death to the fort. This failed to please the settlers, who told the Indians they "wished they had not done it, that they should have brought him to them, as they wished to have forbidden him to do the like again." But by then, the friends of the slain man were livid and went to the fort to seek vengeance.[4]

The form that vengeance took revealed much about Lenape responses to Dutch ways of interacting with the natural world. Even though Swanen-dael was a whaling station, established to allow the colonists to harvest the air-breathing creatures from the cold waters of the Atlantic, almost all of the settlers were working in the fields at the time of the attack, toiling to grow the grain that would sustain their own lives. The horses and cows used to work the fields at Swanendael were unlike anything the Natives had seen before in their own land, and the presence of European animals in the settlement only enhanced, in Native eyes, the strangeness of the newcomers. The bovines and equines were entirely alien, but the Lenapes might have seen similarities between the Dutch dog at the fort and their own domestic canines. Yet the beast at the Dutch fort was a great mastiff, bred for size and ferocity, and exotic and terrible in the eyes of the Lenapes. The Indian who related the story of Swanendael's demise to David de Vries, the Dutch ship captain who first discovered its destruction, told him that the mastiff was what they "feared the most," and "had he been loose they would not have dared to approach."[5] But the dog was chained, and the Indians shot arrows at the creature from a wary distance. To the awe of the Indians, it took twenty-five of their arrows to finally bleed the life from it. Although the Lenapes feared the dog above all else, the meeker beasts of the settlement were not exempt from the attack. De Vries, upon surveying the wrecked colony, found lying among the shattered skulls and bones of the settlers the "heads of the horses and cows which they had brought with them." The Indians, in obliterating this foreign outpost from their country, had chosen to destroy all the alien forms of life, placid or fierce, great or small, two-legged or four.[6]

For the Natives of the Delaware Valley, the newcomers had an array of qualities that made them outwardly strange and established their other-ness, including their pale skin; hairy bodies and faces; and strange language, food, clothes, and armaments. But, as illustrated by the occurrence at Swanendael, the ways that Americans and Europeans related to the natural world differed strikingly. To the Dutch, the piece of tin bearing their coat of arms was a tangible symbol of their power, and its destruction was an affront to their status. To the Lenape man who removed it, the tin was unattended in the forest and therefore available to be made into something useful. His avengers, moreover, slew not just the Dutch men they held responsible for his death but also their cows and horses. To the Indians, the animals that the Europeans brought with them, and that were vital to the success of their colonies, were a crucial marker of difference between Native and newcomer.[7]

The whaling station's name, Swanendael, which in Dutch means "the valley of the swans," was far more lyrical than the rudimentary settlement could have possibly deserved.[8] The name stands out in the historical record, however, not for its poetic quality, but as the site of one of the few instances of violence between Americans and Europeans in the Delaware Valley during the seventeenth century.[9] The flash of conflict, sudden and brief, that saw the thirty or so Dutch colonists of Swanendael killed and the settlement wrecked sharply contrasts with the larger history of the Delaware Valley in the era when Native Americans and European newcomers were extensively interacting for the first time. This history seems especially placid in the context of violence and conflict between Americans and Europeans elsewhere in North America. Natives and colonists died at each other's hands in various bloody conflicts up and down the Atlantic seaboard during the seventeenth century. But the history of the Delaware Valley, where the Lenapes encountered successive waves of Swedish, Dutch, and English settlers, seems remarkably tranquil.

Swanendael is an anomaly because of its violent demise, but the history of the tiny whaling station underscores important aspects of the encounter between Indians and Europeans in the region. Some of the patterns that were established there were continued by the colonists of New Sweden, part of the next wave of Europeans to settle the Delaware Valley. Sweden was one of the last European nations to engage in transatlantic colonization. The kingdom's interest in North America began in the 1630s, when marginalized investors in the Dutch West India Company, looking for favorable opportunities for return on their capital, convinced the government of Sweden to establish an American colony. The result was a modest effort at best. The Swedish kingdom, engaged as it was in the Thirty Years' War, had limited resources to expend on such a venture. New Sweden's location on the Delaware was by default; the Delaware Valley was one of the few remaining areas on the Atlantic coast not already settled or controlled by another European power. At its height as an independent colony, New Sweden was populated only by about two hundred settlers. Still, the company and its colonists approached the venture with vigor and high hopes as they sailed on their way to North America.[10] They carried elements of their natural world across the ocean with them, including their cattle, their seeds, and the ideas in their minds. To some extent, they found just what they expected to find; cultural preconditioning allowed them to see the new lands as "over-abundant forests," ready to be tamed and reshaped, and filled with goods and raw materials ready for extraction.[11]

The people that they would encounter called themselves Lenapes, or the "Original People." A scarcity of evidence makes it difficult for historians to ascertain whether the Lenapes existed as a political configuration, or perhaps even as an entity at all, for a significant period of time before European contact, or whether they came into being in the aftermath of the devastation wrought by European diseases. It seems that the Lenapes, as the newcomers encountered them, were a collection of peoples living in scattered, semipermanent settlements throughout the Delaware Valley. Archaeological evidence suggests that they were less extensively engaged in agriculture and more reliant on hunting and gathering for subsistence than were most of their immediate neighbors and that they settled in permanent locations only during the winter months.[12] In any case, the Lenape peoples were unified more by a common language, familial and marriage relations, and trade than by any overarching political structure. The gradual emergence of a more coherent and unified Lenape cultural identity was in many ways the creation of the historical processes following contact with Europeans. During the colonial period, encounters with people as different as the newcomers highlighted similarities and common concerns among Indians that may have otherwise been obscured or unimportant. By the middle of the eighteenth century the Lenapes who survived probably had a more cohesive notion of their common identity than had ever existed in the precontact period.[13]

The natural world of the Lenapes was transformed by contact with the Eastern Hemisphere even before Europeans began to construct settlements in the Delaware Valley. European diseases preceded human contact in much of North America, and to the Americans' world, the changes wrought by plague and pestilence were cataclysmic. Foreign diseases such as smallpox, measles, and influenza swept through Indian populations, often before direct contact with settlers, with devastating effect. Although such maladies tended to strike Europeans during childhood, imparting the survivors with immunity or increased resistance in adulthood, the Indians were what Alfred Crosby has called "virgin soil" for the rampaging microbes; all segments and age groups within the afflicted American populations were sickened at the same time. That several different diseases usually arrived simultaneously, or in successive waves, greatly compounded the force of their destruction.[14] With such a high percentage of the populations sick, the everyday activities that allowed life to go on and held society together virtually ceased. The sick were unable to help the sick, or provide subsistence, or defend themselves from the threats of the outside world. The mortality rate was frightening.[15]

Despite the carnage elsewhere in North America, the consequences of disease for the Indians of the Delaware Valley are not altogether clear. Some archaeological evidence suggests that the decentralized Lenape populations may have been disrupted to a lesser degree than their more densely concentrated neighbors, and Swedish observers in general noted few signs of disease among the Natives. The rare exception, such as Pehr Lindeström, a colonist who published a geographical survey of New Sweden based on his visit in 1650, observed only that the area was once mostly populated by Indians, but that "this nation is much died off and diminished through war and also through diseases."[16] By the mid-seventeenth century, the consequences of depopulation must surely have been significant, especially to those who survived the epidemics. As a result of the political and social turmoil and the crippling heartache of loss that followed the epidemics, it is reasonable to assume that Lenape ways of life were disrupted down to their most fundamental levels.

The ways in which Europeans understood the world and their place in it were changing as well. As a result of contact with the Americas, new foodstuffs, such as maize, peppers, and tomatoes, were becoming staples of subsistence in Europe. Significant plants, like the potato, with its ability to grow in more marginal soils and colder climates, provided the calories and nutrition that contributed to the shift in population and geopolitical power from the Mediterranean to northern Europe in the early modern period.[17] Contact with a new world shook European foundations in other ways as well; new knowledge called into question the authority of biblical and classical sources, and new technologies, such as the printing press, revolutionized the way information was shared and disseminated. Understandings of identity were altered as the Protestant Reformation shattered notions of a unified Christianity and as Europeans learned of encounters with previously unknown peoples and lands.[18]

Despite the jarring impact and the continuing repercussions of the meeting of worlds, important aspects of the ways that Americans and Europeans understood their place in the universe remained firmly grounded in the past. One of the most dramatic concerned the ways that each group conceived of its relations with nonhuman creatures. For Europeans, the world was arranged in an ordered hierarchy, and they knew in no uncertain terms that, except for the angels, they were at the top of what their god had created. The Swedes, like most citizens of Christendom in the early modern period, took seriously God's mandate to "fill the earth and subdue it" and to have dominion over "the fish of the sea, the birds of the air, and the cattle, and over all the wild animals and all the creatures that crawl on the ground," as well as "every seed-bearing plant all over the earth and every tree that has seed bearing fruit on it."[19] The Lenape world, on the other hand, was fully alive with animated power. The beasts and birds, plants and trees, and even the waters and rocks of the land all had powers, personalities, and souls. These spirit beings were not unambiguously subjected by or submissive to humans.[20] Humans and nonhumans instead shared interactive and negotiated relations; rather than expecting submission from all other living things, the Lenapes believed that they shared reciprocal obligations with the forces of life on the earth.

Contrast between hierarchy and negotiations was evident in European and Native conceptions of land ownership and use. Europeans, of course, were familiar with versions of collective ownership and communal labor obligations regarding land. Swanendael itself was a patroonship, a privately held property within the Dutch West India Company that was settled and worked by quasi-manorial tenants. It is unclear how much of New Sweden was collectively held and how much was owned by individual farmers during the colony's independent existence; however, by the time of William Penn's arrival in the Delaware Valley, all of the region's land previously claimed by Euro-Americans was in private hands. Colonists, accustomed to the densely populated conditions of Europe, believed that all land should be owned and put to its best use. The arrangement was hierarchical; the produce of the land belonged to whoever held title, not to those who labored to bring it forth from the earth. Still, this agricultural labor was vital to the success of North American colonial ventures and even more so to those who envisioned colonies as permanent settlements rather than as stations for the extraction of such resources as furs, or wood, or the oil and fat of aquatic mammals. Working the land also ensured its possession. The domination and subjugation of the soil was proof of ownership, and, in European minds, Native wastefulness was justification for dispossession. Indians who lived on the land without farming it (in the European style) put their right to own it in jeopardy. Even at rudimentary places like Swanendael, colonists had to work hard in order to feed themselves; harsh winters were impossible to survive without adequate food stores, and the arrival of supplies from home was rarely on schedule and never absolutely assured.[21]

Although Indian understandings of land ownership depended less on the subjugation of the soil than did those of Swedes, Lenapes did shape the landscape and make extensive use of it. Agriculture was a vital component of subsistence. Fields were cleared with the slash-and-burn method, and the Lenapes planted the "three sisters"—corn, beans, and squash—together in small mounds. What looked sloppy and haphazard to European eyes familiar with ordered rows of single crops was in actuality a deliberate and effective system: the cornstalks served as beanpoles for the grasping vines of the legumes, the low leaves of the pumpkin and squash vines shaded the ground and preserved its moisture, and the bean plants fixed some nitrogen back into the soil, ensuring the continuing fertility of the land. While European observers often downplayed the importance of American agricultural practices in shaping the land, they also often misunderstood notions of ownership. The communal ownership of rights to hunt and farm on land was understood and respected by the Lenapes. But the idea of land as a personal possession or the control of all land rights in the hands of one individual person for perpetuity, as understood by Europeans, was an unfamiliar concept.[22]

The negotiated framework of relationships for Native Americans and the hierarchical framework that existed in the minds of Europeans produced very different approaches to similar issues. The Indians who attacked Swanendael probably viewed the great mastiff as a powerful ally of the settlers, whereas the Dutch colonists viewed the animal as a brute servant. The cows and horses, although they lacked the snarls and fangs of the dog, were still threatening to the Indians because of their strangeness. In Native minds that understood power as a system of negotiated relationships with the nonhuman spirits of the natural world, the alliance between the settlers at Swanendael and these creatures may have hinted that the alien people, despite their unimpressive settlement, possessed extraordinary might. Destroying the settlement's animals along with its human population was a necessary measure to remove the threat of foreign and powerful presence from the land.

Lenape models of reciprocity clashed with Swedish hierarchical domination in other ways as well. Whereas Native American mythology often emphasizes corn and other foodstuffs as divine gifts from powerful and benevolent spirit beings, in Christian mythology the toil of agricultural work is a punishment for the first man's sin. Before the Fall, humans had to expend no effort in enjoying the fruits of the earth, but outside of the garden, the world is filled with thorns and weeds, barren and rocky soil, and stubborn animals that need to be beaten into submission before they serve human needs. The development of what Europeans considered civilization had its foundations in the subjugation of nature, and the theological imperative to conquer the natural world, rarely questioned or examined in the minds of early modern Christians, heavily influenced the attitudes the Swedish settlers took with them to the Delaware Valley.[23]

New Sweden, above all else, was a for-profit venture, and the natural world was seen as wealth in raw form. The colony's founders had high hopes for what might be extracted from "out of the over-abundant forests."[24] Based on the idea that "this land, New Sweden, is situated in a climate with Portugal," the colony's planners expected that its weather would be warm and mild throughout the year, and this expectation colored the entire venture.[25] The colonists were directed to establish such warm-weather industries as salt-making, tobacco-growing, silkworm-cultivating, and wine-making. Unfortunately for the Swedes, transatlantic climates at parallel latitudes are in fact vastly different; winter in the colony was "at times so sharp," said Governor Johan Printz, he had "never felt it more severe in the northern parts of Sweden." Enterprises appropriate for more pleasant climates would not bear rich fruit in New Sweden, let alone provide the cash crop that was critical for turning a speculative colony into a profitable enterprise.[26]

New Sweden found much more success with subsistence agriculture than with the labor-intensive industries of extraction that the colony's planners prescribed, but the ecological implications were nonetheless substantial.[27] European-style agriculture required draft animals; as Governor Printz recognized, "cattle . . . are the principal means for the cultivation of the land."[28] A ship captain who had traveled to the colony suggested that "if Her Royal Majesty would only take ahold with seriousness, the land would soon be fine." The ecological transformation the captain envisioned would require not only animal and human power but "implements . . . which are good, axes and good thick iron spades, good hoes to hoe up the earth with and another kind of broad hoes to hoe the grass with."[29] The resulting harvest would be one of the most important mechanisms of colonization, even if it was extraordinarily frustrating in the early years of the

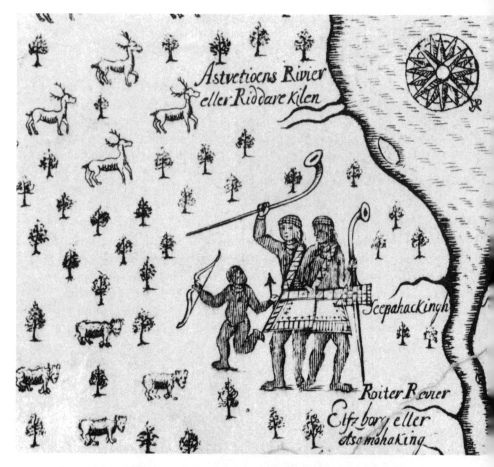

Figure 2 A Swedish view of American nature: fanciful Natives and fanciful animals. Pehr Lindeström map, 1633, detail. From Thomas Campanius Holm, *Kort beskrifning on Provincien Nya Swerige uti America* (Stockholm, 1702). The Library Company of Philadelphia.

colony. Oxen and axes, hoes and plows, were vital to transforming the colony and securing it from bankruptcy, internal collapse, hostile incursion, and Native resistance. The subjugation of the land was more than just a means to these ends. Instead, the transformation of New Sweden from overflowing forest to civilized landscape was itself perhaps the most important end in the minds of the colonizers.

In the same way that skill and toil could create good things from dirt and rain, Printz hoped that the raw materials of New Sweden could be profitably transformed into the armature of civilization by skilled craftsmen. He told his superiors that "we want a good engineer, house-carpenter, mason, brickmaker, potter, cooper, skilful gun- and lock-smiths, and blacksmiths, a chamois-dresser, tanner, tailor, shoemaker, ropemaker, [and] wheelwright"—the people who could take timber, earth, and animal carcasses out of the American forests and shape them into the staples of civilized European life. In pursuit of that vision, Governor Printz took significant steps toward reshaping the physical landscape of the colony with the establishment of a settlement called New Gothenburg on Tinicum Island. There he directed the construction of a mansion that—although made of hewn logs rather than brick and using precious glass sparingly—conformed as closely to the Swedish style as circumstances would allow.[30] He also had a church built and "decorated according to our Swedish fashion, so far as our resources and means would go."[31] Its interior was graced by "an altar of fine quality, elaborate silver drapes brought from Sweden, candlesticks, a cross and other liturgical symbols"; these Lutheran ornaments created sacred space out of the wild and tangled woods of the Delaware Valley.[32] The construction of water and windmills to grind the harvest's produce further gave structure, order, and purpose to the wild currents of New Sweden's streams and creeks and random gusts of wind.

The physical world would be further transformed and subdued with language. The Swedes, fully aware of the power of words, hoped that new names for aspects of the natural world could shelter the colony from threats and preserve it from peril. The proximity of New Netherland to New Sweden made the purity of language an issue of emphasis, and Pehr Brahe, a Swedish chancellor, exhorted Printz to "abolish all expressions from the Dutch which now seem somewhat ingrained." The "Swedish language should be kept, spoken, and written, purely without any mixture of other languages," Brahe insisted. "All rivers and streams as well as herbs and woods [should] be called with old Swedish names."[33] The naming and renaming of rivers, streams, valleys, and settlements would affirm that the Swedes had earned their colony by right of conquest. Such affirmation was all the more necessary because the tiny colony's plans to reshape the world were in many ways more grand than its accomplishments.[34]

The clash between Swedish and Lenape views of nature, with such enormous opportunities for misunderstanding based on unilateral assumptions, might seem like a formula for disastrous conflict. In other colonies, issues of contention, especially over land and resources, led to violence and war during the seventeenth century, as in New England's Pequot War of 1636–37, or Virginia's Powhatan coup of 1622, or New Netherland Governor Willem Kieft's conflict with Natives of the Hudson River region of 1641–45.[35] New Sweden's history was different but not because it had an exceptionally humane approach to its Native inhabitants. Certain circumstances of the colony, especially the relative weakness of both the settlers and Indians and the dispersed population of each group, possibly kept pressure from building to a point that was entirely unbearable for either side. Cooler heads among both Indians and Swedes probably realized that their own people had more to lose by engaging in outright conflict than in maintaining nonviolent, albeit tense and ambivalent, relations with the others. So a bloody, destructive, and hate-inspiring seventeenth-century conflict was avoided in the Delaware Valley. But New Sweden was no peaceable kingdom, and the danger of conflict over differences was real, tangible, and close to the surface in most Lenape-Swedish interactions.

The rift between Lenape and Swedish conceptions of land and ideas about its ownership was critical and immense. But paradoxically, the gap may have been so large and communication between Natives and newcomers so distorted that the misunderstandings never became apparent to either side. The Swedes, certain that they had already purchased title to the land, periodically granted what they considered "new gifts of encouragement" to retain Native friendships; in Lenape minds these were probably required payments to secure continued access to territory.[36] In turn, the Indians, in light of the tenuous foothold and obvious shortcomings of the Swedish settlements, may not have regarded the colonists as permanent invaders and willingly collected what they considered fees for use rights. In any case, no occurrence brought the issue of land ownership into sharp focus.

Not that Swedish officials enjoyed this situation. Indeed, Printz denied any need for the Lenapes at all. "Nothing would be better than to send over here a couple of hundred soldiers," who, he proposed, should stay until they had "broke[n] the necks of all of them in this River." The Swedes could then "take possession of the places (which are most fruitful) that the savages now possess." With such proof that they had "not only bought this river, but also won it with the sword, then no one, whether he be Hollander or Englishman, could pretend in any manner to this place either now or in coming times."[37]

Yet, dreams of wholesale slaughter notwithstanding, New Sweden's precarious status forced it to rest its claims on more pacific relations with the Lenapes. In the minds of administrators of the colony, the most menacing threats came not from Native inhabitants but from competing Europeans. Sweden, late as it was to the game of colonization, with most of its resources channeled into fighting the Thirty Years' War in Europe, was acutely aware of its weak position in North America. Surrounded on the Atlantic Coast by English and Dutch colonies, with a foothold only in a territory that no one else had yet bothered to settle, New Sweden's colonists understood the importance of establishing ownership and control of the land that would appear legitimate to other European powers.[38]

The Indian inhabitants were urgently important in establishing that legitimacy. As Printz explained to the Swedish Regent, Axel Oxenstierna, in 1651, the colony's claims were supported only by "1. by Her Royal Majesty's letters; 2. by copies of the Indian deeds of purchase; 3. by the verbal confessions of the Savages; 4. by three Christian witnesses who at that time immediately offered to prove on their oath that this country lawfully had been bought from the Savages."[39] The legitimacy that the Indians provided for Swedish land purchases in no way guaranteed that their presence in the colony would be sanctioned or even tolerated. But it is likely that the Swedes had more to lose by initiating violence against "their" Indians than by maintaining the mutual ambivalence, however uneasy and tenuous it might have been.

Trade and material exchange were also important to the Swedes as a mechanism for fortifying the position of the colony against its European competitors. Governor Printz was instructed to see to it that the company and its colonists undersold the Dutch and English traders, so that the Indians "may be withdrawn from them, and so much the more turn to" the Swedes.[40] The governor was also to inform the Native inhabitants of the colony that the Swedes were "not come into those parts to do them any wrong or injury, but much more for the purpose of bringing them to hand what they need for their domestic common life, and sell and exchange such things for other things which are found among them and which they themselves have no use for."[41] Yet in trade as well as in land, the relationship was brittle. Printz and other colony administrators complained that the Natives did not make their own wampum, they grew low quality tobacco, and they had access only to inferior beaver skins.[42]

Moreover, Natives and newcomers attached different values not just to abstract ideas of nature or conceptions of landholding also to such tangible objects as tobacco and beaver skins. Natives understood European goods not as completely new things but as objects to be judged within the framework of existing conceptions of value. They used guns in hunting and warfare in the same ways that bows had been. They used new metal tools as they had used implements of bone, wood, or stone. Baubles and trinkets like mirrors or bells, which Europeans congratulated themselves on passing off to Natives in exchange for objects of "real" worth, were valuable to Indians because of the spiritual powers of otherworldliness that they held.[43]

Despite these overarching differences, however, some visible congruences between European newcomers and American Natives invite attention. For example, the majority of settlers in the colony, many of whom were ethnic Finns, had inhabited the forested taiga of northern Europe before coming to the Delaware Valley, and both Indians and settlers might have seen familiar aspects in their practice of woodcraft. The Finns and Lenapes both subsisted on agriculture that was supplemented through hunting and fishing, and although the Indians did not exclusively use firearms, there were similarities in the two groups' methods of hunting, fishing, and tracking. In the colder months, Lenapes dwelt in wigwams that, with their log walls and central hearths, were similar to the colonists' preferred shelters.[44] The canoes that the Indians used were quite like the Swedish punts, and both were important methods of traveling the streams, creeks, and rivers of the Delaware Valley.[45] The sweat lodge, in which water was poured over heated rocks to produce sacred, purging steam, was an important ritual to the Lenapes for healing both body and spirit. The Swedes were so attached to their own steam baths, in which water was poured over hot rocks, that they expended the time and energy to build them in their simple North American settlements.[46] Presumably, both Swedes and the Indians could see the similarities between these cultural customs, but these probably seemed much more like ephemera than signs of cultural convergence. Whatever cultural parallels existed were overwhelmed by starker and more pressing differences, especially the fundamental dissimilarities in Native and colonial thinking about relations with the natural world.

An apocryphal tale recounted by Pehr Lindeström underscores the ambivalence between Swedes and Indians regarding their respective understandings of nature. A young Lenape man while visiting the Tinicum Island home of Johan Printz saw the governor's wife wearing a gold ring and asked her, "Why do you go and drag around such worthless trash on your fingers?" Governor Printz saw an opportunity and responded for his wife, telling the visiting Indian, "If you can produce such trash for me, I will give you all sorts of other good [things] in return, which may be of use to you." The Indian replied that he knew "a mountain full of such trash." Printz demanded a piece of it as proof, promising to give the Indian a trove of Swedish trade goods, including colored "cloth, lead, powder, mirrors, awl-points, and needles." A few days later, the young man indeed returned with a a chunk of ore "as large as a couple of fists, which the said governor tested and which was found to be very good gold." Printz agreed to present the Indian with more goods if he would reveal the location of the mountain of gold. But when the man returned to his people, they killed him "on the spot in the presence of their own sachem or chief, so that this place should not become known to us, thinking that it would tend to their ruin. Thus the road to the mountain remains hidden from us to this present day."[47] The story, however much it fails to let actual voices of the Lenapes reach us, reveals an understanding that land and other natural resources were a critical issue for the Natives as well as the newcomers. That the gold was garbage to the Indians did not matter as much as the perilous lust that Europeans had for it. The Indians in the story murdered their dangerously naïve countryman rather than allow themselves to be ruined as a people by Swedish intrusion onto their land.

In the long term, colonial visions of a land controlled and transformed from "overabundant forests" to an ordered European-style landscape (a landscape maybe free someday of Indians) were entirely incompatible with Native American desires to hold at arm's length the influence and intrusiveness of the newcomers.[48] Nature, already a cause of misunderstandings and a marker of differences between Americans and Europeans, would become even more important as an ideological tool used to underscore the chasm between Indian and colonial cultures, identities, and realities. The Swedish colonist from Pehr Kalm's story, before smashing to death the "red-spotted snake," told the Indian, "Because thou believest in it, I think myself obliged to kill it." The problem between the two men was a growing awareness of difference and incompatibility, and nothing showed that to them more directly, or allowed them to articulate it more clearly, than the way they related to the natural world.

2

❧

COLONIALISM AND THE DISCURSIVE
ANTECEDENTS OF *PENN'S TREATY WITH THE INDIANS*

JAMES O'NEIL SPADY

On an autumn day in 1682, the legend goes, William Penn met leaders of
the Lenapes to settle a unique treaty of peace and amity. According to the
story told and retold during the subsequent centuries, the Native people
quickly lost their initial fear when they met Penn and his unarmed company in the diffuse midmorning light. They supposedly stepped from
under an "elm tree of prodigious size" shading their huts at the edge of
the forest and stood or sat before Penn and his entourage, who were "all
dressed in the plain habit of [their] sect." Gathering beside "each other
under the widely spreading branches" of the tree, several Lenapes examined Penn. In front of him, "spread upon the ground," were "various
articles of merchandise, intended as presents to the Indians," and the
Quaker proprietor "held in his hand a roll of parchment, containing the
confirmation of the treaty of purchase and amity." Benjamin West, who
vividly portrayed the meeting in his 1771 painting, described the event as
representing "savages brought into harmony and peace by justice and benevolence" and "a conquest that was made over native people without
sword or dagger."[1] Penn has exemplified religious and ethnic toleration
ever since.

Although the story of Penn's Treaty enjoyed widespread prestige as historical fact well into the twentieth century, most contemporary historians

suspect that the meeting may never have occurred, at least not as traditionally described. Some historians have come to regard Penn's reputation as
exaggerated, but others still identify Penn's relationship with the Lenapes
as "exemplary," "kind," "benevolent," or "altruistic"—even when they
admit that Penn also sought profit or condescended to the indigenous
people. Historians still praise Penn through quotations of his writings,
through references to his practice of buying, rather than expropriating,
Indian land, and through the contrasting example of James Logan's less
scrupulous real estate deals with Lenape and Susquehannock leaders in the
1730s.[2]

The story of Pennsylvania's benevolent origins is an allegory of colonialism propagated by Penn and later colonists that has obscured the significance of both the severe disruption of Lenape life that Pennsylvania created
and the resistance of some Lenapes to that disruption. Within the wary,
wondering, and studying gaze that Benjamin West gave many of the Lenapes is a hint of the consciousness that challenged Pennsylvania in the
1680s and 1690s, a perspective that was informed by experience with European colonists dating back to the 1620s and 1630s when Holland and Sweden attempted to colonize the Lenapes' homeland.[3] From their experience
with the Dutch and the Swedes, Delaware Valley Native people had come
to expect that colonial expansion would be modest and manageable, and
that often it might fail completely. European immigration remained slight
throughout the period of the absorption of New Sweden into New Netherland in 1655 and the English conquest of 1664. Colonists and Lenapes had
developed a pidgin dialect of the Lenapes' Unami language—the "Delaware Jargon"—and the trade it facilitated fostered personal relationships
between a small group of Dutch and Swedish interpreters and Lenape leaders. Perhaps most important, long before Penn arrived in the valley, these
interactions shaped discursive conventions for diplomatic councils in
which Natives and Europeans covered everyday problems and conflicting
expectations with a rhetoric of a unity, brotherhood, and friendship that,
while keenly felt, was also tactical. Inside and outside of councils, misunderstandings remained frequent, especially when they involved the contrasting gender, leadership, and land-use practices of Lenapes and
colonists.[4]

The Quaker colonization of the Delaware Valley benefited from the personal relationships already established by Swedish and Dutch colonists and
Lenape willingness to allow Europeans to live on the land. But Quakers

Figure 3 Benjamin West, *William Penn's Treaty with the Indians*, 1771. Courtesy of the Pennsylvania Academy of Fine Arts, Philadelphia. Gift of Mrs. Sarah Harrison (The Joseph Harrison, Jr. Collection).

also began a period of determined effort to transform the region both materially and culturally. After Penn's founding of Pennsylvania, compromise was increasingly a Lenape obligation, and brotherhood and friendship increasingly required Lenape subordination. Penn hoped to alter Lenape society fundamentally by bringing thousands of model colonists to live among them. Those colonists placed unprecedented pressure on Lenape gender, leadership, and land-use practices, forcing tough decisions. Some Lenape bands chose to leave the Delaware Valley and others chose to stay and adjust. In either case, Lenapes continued to use the discourse of brotherhood and friendship in councils and to seek affirmations of future justice and security from rapidly growing Pennsylvania, thus contributing their own voices to the archive that would form the myth depicted in Benjamin West's *Penn's Treaty with the Indians*.[5]

European colonization had begun sporadically. In the summer of 1634 a man on the western shore of Delaware Bay observed a ship and its scouting shallop sailing toward the shore. According to Thomas Young, the English captain of the vessel, the man ran along the coastline calling to the shallop's crew. When the boat landed, four other men came out of the woods, but only one was willing to go with the crew to the larger ship waiting in the bay. Young wrote that he "entertained" the unnamed Lenape man "courteously," giving him food and querying him about the bay. Young's interpreter and the Lenapes were probably already communicating through an early version of the Delaware Jargon.[6] The jargon simplified Unami grammar, emphasizing terms useful for trade, such as those dealing with weather, environment, time, trees, fruits, animals, and household goods. Communicating through this imperfect medium, Young gathered that the people of the Delaware Valley were already familiar with European trading and exploration vessels, which periodically visited the area. In fact, Lenape and Mahican men and women had probably traded for European goods as early as 1609. The Dutch had built settlements and forts along the Delaware River in 1623, 1624, and 1632, though all had been destroyed by the Lenapes or abandoned by the colonists.[7]

The jargon worked well for simple trade, but it was poorly suited for more complicated ideas, such as sovereignty, property, and the gender dynamics of social authority. It expressed concepts that were new to the Lenapes through the creation of compound words. One version of the Delaware Jargon created terms for "God the Father," "God the Son," and "God the Holy Ghost" through various combinations of Unami words for "spirit," "father," "son," and "dance." European colonists showed little interest in learning Lenape concepts clearly; thus a word for spirit was often translated as "devil."[8] With complex ideas such as these at stake, misunderstandings were endemic.

The fact that Lenape sachems submitted themselves and the land to the simultaneous and sole sovereign authority of three different and competing colonial powers during the 1630s indicates the extent to which key ideas were lost in translation. When the Lenape spokesmen Mattawiraka, Mittotscheming, Peminaka, and Mahamen met the first Swedish colonists in 1638 and made their marks on a deed transferring most of the Delaware River valley to Sweden, they began a long argument with colonists about the meaning of the councils that produced such documents. Europeans were buying one idea—absolute and inalienable right and sovereignty over the land and people—but the Lenapes appear to have been selling another, the right to use restricted areas for settlement, trade, and agriculture. For Lenapes, the political authority Europeans imputed to the term *sovereignty* was associated primarily with kin groups, not with the land or with a suprafamilial state.[9] And the relational significance of trade for Lenapes— distinct from European thinking about commodity accumulation—could easily be missed or misunderstood, if not ignored. Lenapes desired manufactured goods, but they likely also sought to establish an alliance, not subordinate themselves to a foreign power.[10]

During the early 1640s, these competing principles of control contributed to several crises. In 1648, for example, Mattawiraka and another Lenape named Wassiminetto played the Swedish and Dutch against each other. Upset that the Swedes had settled on the banks of the Schuylkill River on land never intended for their occupation—despite the fact that the 1638 deed Mattawiraka had signed supposedly represented a transfer of the entire valley to them—the headmen approached the Dutch and asked why they did not build on the river as the Swedish had done. Fearing that the Swedes would gain control of the river and block them from the fur trade with the Susquehannocks, the Dutch accepted the Lenape invitation and built a trading station near the Swedish post.[11] The Lenapes planted the flag of the prince of Orange and ordered the Dutch to fire three shots to notify the nearby Swedes of their presence. Dutch representatives took these acts as "a sign of possession" because they wanted to believe that Native people supported their claim. The Lenapes, however, probably used the ceremony to assert their sole authority to determine which limited portions of land their trading partners could occupy. When the Swedes came to protest, the sachems took the opportunity to demand by what right they had settled in this and several other areas in the first place. They expressed wonder that the Swedish colonists attempted to prescribe laws for them and tell them what to do with their own possessions, people, and land.[12]

Between 1648 and 1654, no ships arrived from Sweden at all. The Swedes were not supplied well enough to expand their territorial claims; the Dutch showed no resolve to seize control of the Delaware; and the Lenapes, wanting trade with the colonists in order to facilitate diplomacy with interior tribes, were not inclined to destroy the colonial settlements. A long, slow cross-cultural chess game of deeds, claims, counterclaims, forts, and threats thus ensued among the three parties.[13]

This imperial rivalry soon revealed important distinctions in how Europeans and Lenapes gendered property rights. In 1651, the Dutch met with the sachems Peminaka and Mattawiraka and convinced them to sell a tract of land on the eastern bank of the Schuylkill. The Swedes, in turn, appealed to a "widow" named Notike, along with her son Kiapes, to challenge Peminaka's right to give the land to the Dutch. According to Notike and her kin, Peminaka had been given only the right to hunt on the lands south of the river by Notike's deceased husband. He had no right to sell.[14] Mattawiraka and Peminaka spoke for matrilineal groups centered on women such as Notike. As the principal institution of the Lenape political, social, and economic order, such kin groups gave Notike and other women considerable influence. A Lenape individual derived identity and position within the community from his or her matrilineage. Men inherited the right to be considered for political office through their mother's line, but the actual choice lay with the community's elder women, who were also often responsible for brokering peace with rival communities. Women also produced more than half the community's food as well as surplus corn and tobacco for trade with the colonists and derived much of their influence from the distribution of these goods and the planting grounds that produced them.[15]

The importance of these intercommunity gender dynamics for land transactions with Europeans, however, appears to have been lost on the Swedish and Dutch. The Swedish translation of Notike's position as "widow" separated her from the extended kin group that was the source of her position within her community and placed her instead within a patrilineal and patriarchal model in which women had no property rights beyond those derived from their husbands. How closely Notike and other female and male leaders in the Delaware Valley Lenape communities could follow matrilineal kinship rules in an era of new pressures from an aggressive and patriarchal colonial power is difficult to determine. The colonists clearly showed a predisposition to regard the male sachems as the sole authority with whom they had to negotiate, and the women may therefore have lost some of their customary authority. But even when men traded furs for agricultural implements, they were exchanging the products of male hunting for the tools of female horticultural production. Throughout the seventeenth century, Lenape women must have had a fundamental influence on community decisions, a role elided from most of the documentary record.[16]

When Sweden sent new supplies and a new governor, Johan Rising, in

1654, Lenape leaders—probably all men—quickly proposed a council. If earlier meetings revealed distinct land-use and gender practices, the record of this meeting reveals significant cross-cultural complexities and pitfalls in communication itself. The new governor believed that the Lenapes desired to "come to a pact of friendship and alliance" in which he would be expected "to present them with gifts."[17] In council the governor thanked them for their friendship and expressed a wish for their relationship to remain "friendly," an intention "to treat them well," and a desire to "damage neither their people nor their plantations and possessions." He urged them to make a firm alliance with him and to confirm earlier Swedish land purchases. To all this, the headmen politely answered "Yes." Nachaman, a spokesman from the western bank of the Delaware, praised the Swedes and chastised Lenapes who refused to "see what good friends these are that bring us such gifts." In the past, said Nachaman, Lenapes and Swedes had been as "one body and one heart," and "so should they hereafter be." He promised the Lenapes would maintain a "firmer friendship . . . which he extolled with words, images, gestures and grand airs," at which the Swedes "had to marvel." Nachaman's choice of words seems particularly significant. He glossed a recent history of tension and disagreement with statements of perfect unity and friendship, a tactful and diplomatic misrepresentation of the recent past in the hope of a better future. And importantly, this snippet of council discourse is virtually identical to later statements describing William Penn.[18]

Although the Lenapes invited the Swedes to build a fort and houses near their largest village, which was on the future site of Philadelphia, the apparently smooth proceedings concealed subtle misunderstandings. The sachems crouched on the floor, while the Swedes either stood or sat around a table. In the midst of the discussions, one Lenape spokesman climbed up on the table and sat directly in its center. A Swedish witness described the act as a comical sign of Indian incivility. For Lenapes accustomed in their meetings to sit on an equal plane on the floor, however, the table may have affronted protocol. By sitting on it, the speaker leveled it and turned its flat top into another floor. By not objecting to this gesture, the Swedish seemed to accept the statement. Neither side needed to understand the other to have come away satisfied with its own performance—and convinced of the incivility of the other.[19]

Translations revealed problems too. The interpreter at the 1654 council was a soldier named Gregorius van Dyck who had lived in the colony for

fourteen years and had served in a similar capacity at least since the meetings with Notike in 1651. Toward the end of the meeting van Dyck mis-
translated one Lenape's metaphorical description of an epidemic that had
spread through his community "like fire all around the ship" that seemed
to bring it from Europe. The amused Swedes attributed the statement to
ignorance about the effect of the salt water glistening in the sun as it
sprayed from a vessel, and the governor recommended faith in God to the
Lenapes. "You are crazy, you old fool," the irritated Lenape spokesman
lashed out at the translator. "Before you always used to say that I lied, but
now you lie." Van Dyck, in a condescending effort to correct his blunder,
admitted, "You may indeed be right, I did not believe you to be so intelli-
gent, I am in this matter not so wise."[20] When such simple statements as
an expression of concern about shipborne disease could cause an uproar,
it is not surprising that subtle cultural connotations of deeds and gifts
could lead to much more serious disputes when they simultaneously signified subordination to Swedish authority, in the colonists' minds, and an
alliance of equals, to the Lenapes.

In 1655, the year following the dispute over metaphors for disease, the
Dutch sailed up the Delaware in force and conquered New Sweden. The
population of the colony had been only about four hundred, many of
whom remained under the new regime. During the transition, local access
to European trade goods must have been limited, and Lenapes and Swedes
probably had to obtain them through the Dutch towns of New Amstel on
the lower Delaware and New Amsterdam on the Hudson. After 1664, when
the Dutch lost New Netherland to the English, trade, principally with the
towns now known as New Castle and New York, probably decayed further.
It certainly did not expand, and the colony's total Euro-American population probably did not exceed seven hundred. In the relative absence of the
exchanges and gift-giving that maintained the right of Europeans to live in
the Lenape homeland, attacks on colonists appear to have increased. The
English authorities claimed in 1670 and 1671 that since the conquest, Lenapes and Susquehannocks had killed at least ten colonists and taken supplies from several others.[21]

Despite, or perhaps because of, such troubles, in this period the number
of Swedish and Dutch colonists who knew the Delaware Jargon and individual Lenapes at least as well as did Gregorius van Dyck, multiplied.[22]
Among these were interpreters such as Peter Cock and Peter Rambo. These
men were not soldiers like van Dyck; they were farmers engaged in plant-

ing and in trading directly with local Lenapes for furs and hides. Their understandings and misunderstandings of the Lenapes—from pidgin to perceptions of property—became a formative influence on English Pennsylvanians' initial understanding of and approach to the local Native people. It was probably these men who taught William Penn what he knew of the Delaware Jargon. Among the most important of the early Pennsylvania interpreters was Peter Cock's son Lars. He was born in New Sweden in 1646, probably on the Schuylkill River where his father was one of eight tobacco farmers. By 1675 the younger man had long-standing relationships with Lenapes living at the future site of Philadelphia and was serving New York Governor Edmund Andros as an interpreter. Lars Cock probably translated Penn's early statements to the sachems in 1681, and he interpreted at two initial meetings between William Markham, Penn's representative, and the Lenapes in 1682. The second of these councils probably occurred at his house. An equally important interpreter, trader Israel Helme, became active as early as 1659. English colonial authorities turned to him for advice in 1671 when two Lenape men were accused of killing an English colonist. In 1675 and 1677 the Swedish colonists recommended him as an interpreter for the newly arriving West New Jersey Quakers. And he mediated a 1679 land dispute between New York and the Lenapes.[23]

Although there was sporadic violence, each side appears to have made a decision to pursue nonmilitary strategies. In 1670, Israel Helme, Peter Cock, and Peter Rambo participated in a council at which Susquehannock spokesmen urged the Lenapes not to "kill any more of the Christians." The Lenapes, they cautioned "must know that they are surrounded by Christians." Moreover, "if they went to war, where would they then get powder and ball?" Later, in 1675, Lenapes participated in two councils that reformed their relations with other Native peoples and with the English colonists. As a result of the first meeting between the Lenapes, Susquehannocks, and the Five Nations Iroquois, twenty-six Susquehannock families joined the Lenapes. At the second council, mediated by Helme and other Swedish interpreters, New York Governor Edmund Andros arranged for communication and trade between the sachems and his colony.[24] Attacks on Delaware River colonists ceased.

With the aid of Andros and Swedish and Dutch interpreters, Quakers began moving into the Delaware Valley in the 1670s. Approximately 1,400 colonists arrived in West Jersey between 1677 and 1681, more than double the entire European population of the region during the previous half-century.[25] The demographic dimensions of immigration changed too. The newcomers frequently came as families, not simply as individuals, and the expectations they brought to gender and kinship relations complicated communication with the Lenapes at the same time that their desire for land provoked hostility. "The Indians hate the Quakers on account of their covetousness and deceitfulness," claimed a Dutch traveler. Although "hate" may have been an exaggeration, clearly not all Lenapes were comfortable with Quaker colonization.[26]

The new colonists received ample advice about how to deal with the Lenapes, but, however benevolent in intentions that advice may have been, it was colonial in its implicit assumptions that right order and law were absent among the Native population. Quaker theologian George Fox traveled through West Jersey in 1672 and advised Friends immigrating to that colony that "the eyes of other governments or colonies will be upon you; yea the Indians to see if you order your lives and conversations." Edward Byllynge, credited with formulating many of West Jersey's early laws—and presaging William Penn's policies—advised colonists to negotiate land acquisitions, resolve conflicts with the Indians according to "law and equity," and convict Native people of crimes only after a trial by a jury composed of equal numbers of Europeans and Indians. West Jersey Quaker colonists relied on the Swedes and on Dutch interpreters to communicate these ideas to the Lenapes. Just how such men as Helme and Jacob Falkinburg, a Dutch resident and interpreter, represented the ambitions of the Quakers is unrecorded, but through three deeds Quakers eventually claimed possession of land on the eastern bank of the Delaware extending several miles inland from the falls to the southernmost border of the former New Sweden colony.[27]

West Jersey Quakers matched these exaggerated land claims with similarly exaggerated claims of harmony and unity in their relationship with the Lenapes, but the reality was more complicated. In 1679, colonists became concerned about rumors that the Lenapes were planning to destroy the colony before it became too populous. According to rumor, the Lenapes believed the colonists had brought "them the *Small-Pox,* with the Mach Coat they had" sold them. The colonists and Lenape headmen (with "many more *Indians*") met to discuss the problem. The English recalled what they regarded as careful purchases and complained that because they had been just, kind, and respectful, they knew no reason why the Lenapes should attack them. "Our Young Men may Speak Such Words as we do not like, nor approve of," one Native spokesman responded, "and we cannot help that." But similarly, he continued, "some of your Young Men may speak such Words as you do not like, and you cannot help that." The dispute was then buried under what had become the common discursive practice of Delaware Valley council meetings: "We are your Brothers," the Lenape proclaimed, "and intend to live like brothers with you." He observed "as to the *Small-Pox,*" that there had also been an epidemic in his "*Grandfathers* time" and his "*Fathers* time." The English had not lived in the country then, and just as they had not been responsible for those epidemics, so were they guiltless in the more recent outbreak.[28]

What had begun as a meeting to discuss a conflict over Quaker immigration and disease thus ended with affirmations of brotherhood—without actually understanding the cultural dynamics that produced the conflict. Yet the speaker's concern about rumors and how young men might talk outside the formal council settings where discourses of brotherhood and alliance prevailed revealed how the growing number of colonists increased the frequency of disruptive everyday encounters between colonists and Lenapes. Still, these encounters did not usually produce inflammatory remarks. The 1679 travel narrative of Zeelander Jasper Danckaerts suggests that face-to-face meetings between colonists and Lenapes were common. Danckaerts, possessing little or no knowledge of the Delaware Jargon and receiving only occasional help from interpreters, communicated mostly through the exchange of objects and gestures. He frequently encountered Native people, several of whom seemed to specialize in aiding travelers like him. On one occasion, he recalled, "while we were waiting, and it began to get towards evening, an Indian came on the opposite side of the creek . . . [with] a canoe in which he would carry us over, and we might swim the horses across." On another day, at "about three o'clock in the afternoon a young Indian arrived" at the travelers' lodging and "agreed to act as our guide, for a duffels coat which would cost twenty-four guilder in zeewant [wampum]." On another occasion a Native man appeared to help Danckaert's party cross still another creek: "The Indian, having made himself ready, took both our sacks together and tied them on his back for the purpose of carrying them, as we were very tired."[29]

When reflecting upon such encounters, colonists represented Lenape cultural practices in a way that conformed to European expectations. This was particularly common in discussions of gender. Danckaerts described one Lenape woman as the "wife" of a "king or sackemaker" and as a

"Queen" while emphasizing her domestic—not political—duties. Similarly, Gabriel Thomas, an English colonist, created a dialogue to describe "the manner of Discourse that happens between [the 'Indians'] and the Neighboring Christians . . . when they meet one another in the Woods." The dialogue is an interestingly one-sided exchange by means of question and answer in which an "Indian" man is plied for information about the commodities he owns, his "house," whether he has a "wife," and how many children he has had with her. In his effort to promote a gendered model of exchange he understood—that is, between individual, property-owning men—Thomas ignored the extended kinship relations and the matrilineal practices of the Lenapes.[30]

Representations of gendered Lenape political roles in colonial promotional literature similarly elided other differences. *A True Account of the Dying Words of Ockanikon,* published by West New Jersey and London Quakers in 1682, portrayed its subject as if he were a proto-Christian monarch. According to the pamphlet, when Ockanikon died in West New Jersey at the house of the Dutch interpreter Jacob Falkinburg, the Lenape's nephew, his wife, a shaman, four English women, and a Quaker proprietor of the colony were present along with Falkinburg to witness the process of anointing a new sachem. *A True Account* managed to transform what would have been a matrilineal decision by Ockanikon, his "wife" Matollionequay, his unnamed mother, and other elder women into a male inheritance drama reminiscent of European noble families. Sehoppe and Swampisse—men Ockanikon had previously desired to succeed him—had, the pamphlet explained, insulted the "King" by avoiding his deathbed. Ockanikon's brother's son, Jahcoursoe, thus became the "Intended King" in their place, when Ockanikon urged him to assume an active role in his people's councils.[31]

Whatever may actually have been transpiring in this succession drama, its gendered dimensions were misrepresented to readers of *A True Account* through an emphasis on male terminology to describe Ockanikon's relationships to his potential successors. The nephew Jahcoursoe was indeed the dying man's brother's son—but his more salient claim to inheritance was that he was the grandson of Ockanikon's mother. Nonetheless, it appears that the elderly women of the lineage to which both Ockanikon and Jahcoursoe belonged did not find the nephew an acceptable candidate, and their objections may have been behind Sehoppe's and Swampisse's boycott of the deathbed scene. Two months later, when the Lenapes and William

Penn's representatives negotiated the first agreements for land to settle the Pennsylvania colony, these two men were among the Lenapes who participated. Jahcoursoe, the "Intended King," was not.[32]

A True Account conveyed a portrait of Lenape religious beliefs that was just as distorted—or at least as confused—as that of the role of gender in political succession. After designating Jahcoursoe as his successor and instructing him to live peacefully with the Christians, Ockanikon was asked whether there was *"a great God, who Created all things, and this God giveth Man an understanding of what is Good, and what is Bad, and after this life rewardeth the Good with Blessings, and the Bad according to their Doings."* The question reflected a central tenet of Quakerism: all individuals possess God's inner light and the ability to know his saving power. According to the pamphlet, Ockanikon answered, *"It is very true, it is so, there are two Wayes, a broad Way, and a strait Way; there be two Paths, a broad Path and a strait Path; the worst, and the greatest Number go in the broad Path, the best go in the strait Path."*[33] For Quaker readers, this demonstrated the Lenape man's understanding of true religion and of the validity of Friends' belief in the inner light.

Yet Ockanikon may actually have been ridiculing Quakers from his deathbed. He certainly had been critical of the English before, challenging, for instance, the right of New York Governor Edmund Andros to order surveys of Lenape lands. Moreover, Ockanikon may have been extending the path metaphor used by an unnamed Lenape spokesman (perhaps Ockanikon himself) who declared to the West New Jersey colonists in 1679 that his people were "willing to have a *broad Path* for you and us to walk in, and if an *Indian* is asleep in this *Path*, the *English*-man shall pass him by . . . and if an *English*-man is asleep in this *path*, the *Indian* shall pass him by, and say, *He is an English-man, he is asleep, let him alone, he loves to sleep.*"[34] By stating in a room full of European colonists as he died that "the worst and greatest number" chose the broad path, the dying Lenape may have associated that path with the English and those Lenapes who would live like them.

The broad path had hardly led to a place of blissful slumber for the Lenapes. Even while William Penn's representatives were relying on Swedish and Dutch interpreters to establish his relationship with the Lenapes, the Founder wrote to their leaders and asserted that he was "very Sensible of the unkindness and Injustice that hath been too much exercised toward you." The colonizing peoples of Europe, Penn claimed, had too often

sought "to make great Advantages" of the Indians "rather then be examples of Justice and Goodness unto" them. These injustices had "caused
great Grudgings and Animosities, sometimes to the shedding of blood,"
but Penn hoped that his warm regard would "Winn" them. It is easy,
however, to misconstrue the Founder's sentiments. He wrote his letter "To
the Kings of the Indians" only after he had secured his royal charter, sold
thousands of acres of Lenape land, and dispatched the first boatloads of
colonists to North America. Only later did he purchase the land from the
Lenapes and then, he said, only because he "followed the Bishop of London's councill" in "buying and not taking away the natives land."[35] Moreover, the Lenapes were not as uniformly grudging against the Europeans as
Penn believed. After all, they had so far been successful in limiting colonial
settlements. Their response to Penn was consistent with earlier patterns:
they made strangers into symbolic "brothers" for the purposes of trade
and alliance, attempted to maintain the integrity of their land base, and
connected the arrival of the shiploads of colonists with the diseases that
spread among them. But the sachems could not have anticipated the influx
of immigrants that would arrive after 1682.

Still, as a pacifist, Penn never intended the military conquest of the
Lenapes. Penn reminded readers of his promotional pamphlet, *Some Account of Pennsylvania,* that some ancient colonizers had made colonies
flourish by conquering the minds rather than the bodies of barbarians.
Battling "barbarity" rather than killing people, they had "not only reduc'd
but moraliz'd the Manners of the Nations they subjected." Penn hoped
that the immigrants to Pennsylvania would be the agents of a similar transformation by offering the Lenapes examples of appropriate industry and
civility. Colonies were "begun and nourished by the care of wise and populous Countries; as conceiving them best for the increase of Humane Stock,
and beneficial for Commerce." Ideal colonists, therefore, would be "indus-
trious husbandmen" and day-laborers, "laborious handicraftsmen," "inge-
nious spirits much oppressed for want of a livelihood," younger
disinherited sons, and lastly, men of "universal spirits" who "understand
and delight to promote good Discipline."[36]

Two years later, after he had made his journey to the Delaware Valley,
Penn compared the Lenapes with the ideal colonists he was seeking in
order to demonstrate their capacity for assimilation. His *Letter to the Society of Traders* accentuated the Lenapes' basic virtue but noted several areas
in which they were yet uncivil. Penn considered their language "lofty" but

"wanting in moods and tenses" and vocabulary, an observation that suggests Penn was only familiar with the limited Delaware Jargon of his Swedish and Dutch interpreters. The Lenapes' manners, he alleged, were volatile. Although great orators, they were also "great Concealers" of their thoughts and intentions due to the "Revenge that hath been practised among them." They gained their livelihood with ease. "We sweat and toil to live; their pleasure feeds them, I mean, their Hunting, Fishing and Fowling, and this table is spread every where."[37] As a Quaker, Penn believed Lenapes possessed the access to God's saving grace and eternal truth that made them as much God's creatures as any other person. Though not yet "civilized," the Lenapes, he believed, showed potential to be reformed. They recognized that one great God ruled the world and all things. Like Quakers, they practiced consensus politics whenever considering something of importance. Their personal appearance was very simple and functional. And they had what Penn described as "kings" who ruled the common people. Such Lenape Indians would have seemed strange to Penn's ideal colonists, but in demonstrating the potential to submit to deeds and the proprietary government, they demonstrated the potential to assimilate and presumably vanish into the "good Discipline" of the "Holy Experiment."

Neither Penn nor any of his contemporary Quaker colonists in Pennsylvania made serious missionary efforts among the Lenapes and Susquehannocks, perhaps mainly because they believed that it was "a moral impossibility to accept religious beliefs on other men's directives."[38] Penn did, however, take steps to replace the Native political and economic order, and, although as a pacifist he renounced military force, he fully endorsed the juridical claims of English political culture and expected that English law and custom would ultimately rule. Penn, his deputies, and prominent planters wrote of intentions to have trial by jury using "Six planters and Six natives." But trial by jury was an English institution not necessarily consistent with the kin-based system practiced by the Lenapes. The colonists promised to make amends for offenses of "Word and Deed" but assumed that legitimate disputes would conform to English definitions of authority as recognized by "fellow planters." Similarly, they pledged that the Lenapes would have "liberty to do all things relating to improvement of their Ground, and providing sustenance for the families, that any of the planters enjoy."[39] Yet the only liberties to be enjoyed were those defined by English standards. Such Native rights as that of granting overlapping prerogatives to use the land under the control of different matrilineal families whose leaders—men and women—managed resources for a community of kin would not be recognized.

At first the Pennsylvania colonists were tactful and compromising with the Lenapes, whose spokesmen were cautious but persistent in seeking clarity from the colonists. Although the first deed that Penn's agents negotiated with the help of Lars Cock purported to give the land to Penn's "Heires and Assignes forever," it had to be renegotiated when leaders of other local or kin groups appeared with claims to some of the same land. Several signers of the first deed also signed the second deed, which stipulated more carefully how payment should occur and added various memoranda that attempted to clarify the relationship between colonists and Natives. These urged each side to share intelligence of possible attacks by European and Indian enemies and affirmed a desire for peaceful conflict resolution. They called for freedom of travel, which would protect traders' access to the inland Susquehannocks and Five Nations, on the one hand, and Lenape access to fishing and hunting resources, on the other. And the memoranda called for "a Meeting once every year" to read the stipulations of the agreement—and presumably for the sachems to receive ceremonial gifts from the Quaker colonists.[40]

Penn's recruitment of the colonists he hoped would be examples for the Lenapes to emulate resulted in population increase in Pennsylvania that greatly outpaced the growth in West New Jersey, putting unprecedented pressure on the Lenapes' gendered patterns of land use. An estimated ninety ships carrying 7,200 people arrived in Pennsylvania between 1682 and 1685. By 1700 there were approximately 3,500 colonists along the eastern bank of the Delaware and 20,000 in Pennsylvania. By 1683 game had become so depleted that Lenape men began charging English colonists prices twice as high as what they had formerly charged the Swedish and Dutch. The European influx also resulted in the unceremonious appropriation of fields belonging to Lenape women. Thomas Paschall wrote in 1683 that he knew "a man together with two or three more that have happened upon a piece of Land of some Hundred Acres, that is all cleare, without Trees." Indeed, said Paschall, "the farther a man goes in the Country the more such Land they find."[41]

The competition for resources that resulted from unprecedented immigration, compounded by Penn's claim to absolute proprietorship, caused an early controversy in which the sachem who owned the site of the leg-

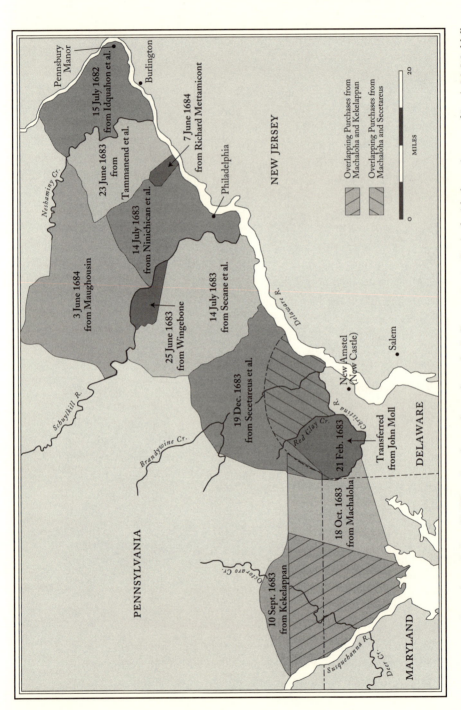

Map 3 Approximate boundaries of William Penn's purchases from the Indians, 1682–84. Revised with the assistance of Louis M. Waddell from Richard S. Dunn and Mary Maples Dunn, eds., *The Papers of William Penn*, vol. 2: 1680–1684 (Philadelphia: University of Pennsylvania Press, 1982), 491.

endary first treaty with the proprietor renounced his "brotherhood" with the English. In 1683, Ninichican had endorsed a deed that claimed to "graunt, Sell and dispose all [his] Right, Title and Interest" to land that included the treaty site, that he had been "in hand paid," and that the receipt had been "acknowledged" by him. Peter Rambo and Swan Swanson, Swedish colonists who had been living nearby for many years and whose families had been trading with local Lenapes since the 1650s, were among the chief interpreters. Later, in September 1683, Penn gave orders to have thousands of acres of this land—including Lenape planting grounds—surveyed. Five thousand acres were to be laid out "so taking in the low Land at Matsonk which the Indians doe plant on." By late 1684, according to a colonist's letter to Penn, Ninichican and "the Indians" were "Mutch displeased at our English settling upon their Land, and seeme to Threaten us, saying that William Penn hath deceived them not paying for what he bought of them." Ninichican was particularly "out of patience" and said that "William Penn shall be his brother no more." The writer hoped that the provincial court would be able to settle the sachems' complaint within two or three weeks, but there is no record of a council to resolve the dispute.[42]

A similar controversy developed after the sachem Tammanend made his mark on a deed in 1683, while Penn was still in the Delaware Valley. Within a year, Tammanend was angry about the expansion of Pennsylvania into what the colonists were calling Bucks County. The sachem insisted that he had not been paid for the territory, drove off some Euro-American colonists, and threatened to use force against colonial surveyors. Agent Thomas Holme wrote to Penn twice about the incidents, but he probably reached an agreement with Tammanend without Penn's input and with the help of local Swedish and Dutch interpreters, who would certainly have advised compromise. When Penn did send instructions in June 1685, he told Holme to be firm with Tammanend. "I gave them many matchcoats, stockings and some Guns in earnest," Penn wrote. "If therefore they are rude and unruly, you must make them keep their word by Just course." Indeed, he continued, "*If the Indians will not punish* [Tammanend], *we will and must,* for they must never see you afraid of executing the Justice they ought to do."[43] Penn wrote these words only a few months before claiming in *A Further Account of Pennsylvania* that rumors of difficulties with the Indians in Pennsylvania were spurious and that "so far are we from ill terms with the Natives, that we have liv'd in a great friendship." The Lenapes, he continued, "offer us no affront, not so much as to one of our Dogs; and if any of them break our laws, they submit to be punished by them: and to this they have tied themselves by an obligation under their own hands."[44]

Penn actively sought to "extinguish" the "Indian encumbrance" on the land through English property law, but the Lenapes apparently expected to receive regular payments for the colonists' continued residence upon the land. In 1684, colonial petitioners complained that Penn had made no regular purchases from the Lenapes. Instead, the sachems had merely accepted gifts and given promises allowing the colonists "to sit down thereon . . . so long as the Proprietarys reciprocal Kindness continue to them in his daily gifts and Presents." This, the colonists insisted, was an unacceptable situation. The petitioners requested that the land be surveyed and that they be required to pay for it only once. In his defense, Penn asserted that onetime fee purchases were what he had always intended and negotiated with the Lenapes.[45] But the sachems clearly only intended to admit Penn to the rights of a sachem—a "brotherhood" of reciprocal obligation and shared authority—not the absolute proprietary rights that Penn and the colonists wanted. They therefore expected Penn and the colonists to give them regular gifts in order to maintain the right to live on the land.

But Penn and the colonists insisted that surveying and expansion continue, and they continued to produce conflict. In the early 1680s, colonists twice complained to the Provincial Council about Indians killing swine. In early summer 1686, the violence escalated when Lenapes living in the vicinity of Philadelphia held a dance near the house of a Zachariah Whitpaine. Whitpaine attended the ceremonies, then went home to bed. Later that night, several Lenapes allegedly killed the entire family of his neighbor, Nicholas Skull, sparing only a young Irish servant; the attackers may have been seeking Israel Taylor, a deputy surveyor active in the area who was staying at Whitpaine's house. When the servant who escaped the slaughter at the Skulls' ran three-quarters of a mile to warn Whitpaine that the Indians were "Coming with Firebrands" to burn down his house, Whitpaine escaped for Philadelphia. Too afraid to flee, Taylor hid in the house all night, but the Lenapes neither burned nor broke into it. In the following weeks the sachems from above the falls held dances and reiterated a threat to kill Israel Taylor if he surveyed any land "before it be bought." With the aid of two Swedish interpreters, Pennsylvania authorities set a date to meet Swampisse and the other sachems.[46] If they had attempted to implement

Penn's instructions to punish the Natives' rudeness and disorderly conduct, they would have met with considerable resistance.

The deed that was supposedly signed on this occasion has not survived, but other conveyances from the mid–1680s sought to force the Lenapes to accept an absolute and permanent transfer of the many overlapping land rights they possessed. One such document conveyed land to "William Penn his Heirs and Assignes for Ever without any mollestation or hinderance from or by Us or . . . any other Indians whatsoever that shall or may Claime any Right Title or Interest." As Penn wrote in his 1690 *Some Proposals for a Second Settlement,* he believed that he was terminating "Indian Pretensions" to the land fairly by "pirchasing their title from them, and so [to] settle with their consent."[47] In 1692, however, Tammanend again challenged Pennsylvania's expansion into the interior. This time he was one of a group of Lenapes who demanded payment for lands then being populated by colonists. Apparently unable to contact Penn, who was in England, in a timely manner, the colonial commissioners gave the sachems what they wanted, but the document that settled this and other episodes included peculiarly strident language for a deed. Tammanend, Swampisse, and others "release[d] and discharg[ed] the said Proprietor his Heirs and Successrs from any farther claims, dues and demands whatever, concerning the said Lands *or any other Tract of Land* claimed by Us *from the beginning of the World to the day and the date hereof.*"[48] The willingness of the tens of thousands of Pennsylvania colonists to compromise with the Lenapes on the terms of land acquisition and use had ended.

Early Pennsylvania had a swift and unmistakable impact on the Lenapes. That English colonists drove off or weakened Native American communities has long been clear. But what has often been obscured is that it was Penn's variety of colonialism that created the disruption. The legend of Penn's Treaty bestows on the Founder and his colony a reputation for benevolence even though they forced the Lenapes to choose either to stay and submit to "good Discipline" or leave in order to preserve a measure of autonomy as a "brother" or "friend" of the colony. To be sure, diseases the colonists brought with them, such as smallpox, forced some decisions to leave; one Lenape claimed that one or even two of them died of disease for every new colonist, and twenty-four shiploads of newcomers arrived between 1682 and 1683. But disease cannot explain the choices of the Native survivors. The pressures placed on the Lenapes' gendered land-use practices must have been an important element in community debates about whether to leave or stay. Besides appropriating fallow agricultural fields that Lenape women had cleared, Pennsylvanians leveled substantial portions of the forest and depleted much of the local game, the hunting of which was a fundamental part of the economic contribution of Lenape men and the education of young warriors.

In the face of these threats, by the first years of the eighteenth century, some Lenapes chose to stay in the Delaware watershed and live in specially designated areas in West Jersey and Pennsylvania; Penn himself had set up one of the reserves on Brandywine Creek. Other Lenapes scattered through Pennsylvania's towns while maintaining altered versions of the older hunting practices, craft skills, and matrilineal kinship ties. Still others began to move well to the west and northwest as early as the mid–1680s. Swampisse, for instance, had relocated with his people some thirty-five miles inland by 1686. While some Lenapes moved, others took a harder line against new land sales. In West Jersey, sachems occasionally refused to sell at all, and both there and in Pennsylvania Lenapes demanded unprecedentedly large payments before permitting new settlements.[49] And some demanded that those payments be in wampum instead of other trade goods, in order to be able to make appropriate diplomatic gifts to the Susquehannocks and Iroquois in whose territories they intended to emigrate.[50]

The narrative of Pennsylvania's founding that portrays as uniquely just this dispossession of the Delawares—the name given to the Lenapes who left their river behind—perpetuates a colonial understanding of the discourse of early treaty councils and the history they produced rather than a Lenape point of view. Even if there was a formal meeting between Penn and the Lenapes in 1682, it probably seemed to the Lenapes, and to the more experienced European interpreters, to be simply the latest meeting with European colonists in order to exchange gifts, promise brotherhood and friendship, and confirm trading alliances. A Lenape narrative of the first two decades of Pennsylvania history would likely express more bitterness, disappointment, and loss than fondness for the Founder Penn. There is no evidence that the Lenapes praised the benevolence or justice of William Penn's policies, at least not until after 1700 and after they became known as Delawares, living in mixed Iroquoian and Algonquian communities.[51]

By contrast, Pennsylvania's version first appeared in Penn's own writing in the middle 1680s. Penn reflected on his recently established relationship with the Lenapes in terms of brotherhood and friendship. This language encouraged the confidence of potential colonists, resonated well with Quaker theology, and echoed council discourse. Penn's own self-approbation at a 1701 council meeting with Iroquois sachems in Philadelphia began the process of turning the council discourse into a historical narrative of unique understanding and benevolence. The "Articles of Agreement" that the meeting produced claimed that "hitherto there hath always been a Good Understanding and Neighborhood between the said William Penn . . . since his first arrival . . . and the severall Nations of Indians." If Tammanend, Ninichican, Swampisse, or any of the unnamed Lenape men and women who supported them in their resistance to Pennsylvania were present, it is not hard to imagine their discomfort. Yet Penn's account echoed the discursive convention of Delaware Valley council meetings. Penn and the Indians pledged "forever hereafter to be as one head and one heart and live in true Friendship and Amity as one people."[52] This last statement would have been as fitting in Lenape agreements with Swedish soldiers or Dutch governors. And eighteenth-century council discourse would continue to feature such statements because for Lenapes, other Algonquians, and Iroquoians, metaphors of unity, brotherhood, and friendship carried important political meaning that was deeply resonant culturally. But such rhetoric should no longer be mistaken for a Lenape historical narrative of early Pennsylvania.

It was not the Lenapes but other Indian communities, some of which had received Lenape refugees, who in councils with colonial authorities promulgated the historical legend of benevolence. After Penn had died, when Pennsylvania's governors met with spokesmen for the Iroquois, Susquehannocks, and Delawares, they regularly described Pennsylvania's history with Indians as especially, if not uniquely, understanding. Pennsylvania governors participated in creating the legend of benevolence by eliminating the sense of a promise about the future, the "hereafter" that Penn had preserved from council discourse.[53] In 1727 and 1728, Governor Patrick Gordon related the myth of Pennsylvania's founding as a story about the past only. Penn, "when he first came into this Province, took all the Indians of it by the hand." He "embraced" them, said Gordon, as "his Friends and Brethren and made a firm League of Friendship with them." He "took all the Indians and the old Inhabitants by the hand and . . . took them to his heart and loved them."[54] A version of this story was well known in eastern Pennsylvania and to Benjamin West, who remembered an old tree customarily regarded by Euro-Pennsylvanians as the site of the legendary meeting. And it was this colonial interpretation of the Lenapes' early history with Pennsylvania that inspired and informed West's painting in 1771, his allegory of colonialism.

3

IMAGINING PEACE IN QUAKER AND
NATIVE AMERICAN DREAM STORIES

CARLA GERONA

Like many other observant early European travelers to America, Swedish
adventurer Pehr Lindeström noted the importance of dreams and visions
in Native American societies. When he sailed into New Sweden in 1654, he
observed, for instance, that Lenapes believed a visit from an animal spirit,
or *paahra*, in a dream foretold a plentiful hunt. The following day the
favored hunter would "be able to shoot as much game and catch as much
fish as ever he want[ed] to." Lindeström doubted neither the veracity of
these hunters' boasts nor the existence of spiritual dreams, but he attributed them to devilish tricks rather than God's grace. In Lindeström's eyes
the "evil one" "undoubtedly" engineered the dreams and the ensuing good
luck.[1]

This example suggests one way that early modern Europeans explained
the spiritual force of Indian dreams: the devil inspired them. But early
Pennsylvania colonists exhibited a much wider array of responses to
dreams than Lindeström. In particular, the English Quakers who followed
in his tracks when they settled in the Delaware Valley believed that God
could speak to anyone in dreams. Like the Lenape and Iroquois Indians
they encountered, Quakers regarded dreams as visionary experiences and
looked to them for spiritual guidance. Because Quakers believed that all
people held latent seeds of truth within themselves, they felt Quakers and

Indians alike could gain access to this inner light and God's truth through their dreams and visions. Unlike Lindeström, Quakers seldom imputed Indian dreams or dreams about Indians to the devil. In fact, they often did just the reverse, recording dreams that highlighted Indian religiosity and capacity for moral goodness. Meanwhile, their own dreams concerning Indians underscored their friendly nature, tending to defuse fear of the supposedly savage and unchristian Natives.[2]

Because both Quakers and the Native Americans they encountered saw dreaming as a significant way to understand spiritual worlds, dreams offered an especially potent means for mutual communication. After all, both believed that anyone could have a spiritual dream. Indeed, such an experience was virtually a requirement for many Indians who were coming of age. Quakers did not require those who joined their fellowship to dream, but many individuals experienced dreams that either initiated or increased their commitment to Quakerism. Both Quakers and Indians deeply wove dreams into institutionalized spiritual practices. Indian ceremonies preserved and reenacted foundational dreams. Quakers, too, relived earlier dreams when they read them in manuscript circulations or printed tracts. Both recognized experts at dream interpretation, whether they termed them ministers or shamans. The specialized field of interpreting, to be sure, was open to many and relied on informal training, but both Indian and Quaker leaders sought to dominate the dissemination of dreams. Indeed, dreams came to play a determinative role in both societies, altering social, political, and even economic practices. The Iroquois, for example, celebrated the dream-guessing feast, in which people had to solve the meaning of a dream and then fulfill its requirements. Quakers did not always implement their decoded dreams, but dreamers implicitly, and in many cases explicitly, hoped that other Quakers would follow the messages contained in their interpretations. In both societies, visionary experiences sought to revitalize the community. Indeed, we have so many recorded accounts of these dreams precisely because they represented attempts to shape the future.[3]

Neither Quakers nor Indians treated their dreams as purely religious messages divorced from other aspects of their worlds. The circulation and exchange of accounts of dreams thus occurred in the midst of an imperial context—a contest over land, goods, and ideas. Above all, Quaker dream stories about Indians conveyed a vision of Euro-Indian relations that sought to disarm Indians. Even if it was just a mirage, Quakers followed William Penn to create a Christian polity in which Indians and Christians might at the very least peacefully coexist as neighbors. And some Quakers sought to usher in a universal Protestant culture that included Native people. Using missionary tactics based on example and persuasion rather than proselytizing and coercion, Quakers increasingly hoped that Indians would recognize Christian truth and voluntarily join both their holy and secular polities.[4]

As time went on Quakers continued to stress similarities between themselves and Indians, not least of all by sharing dream work. Most Indians who told their dreams to Quakers likewise sought to develop good relations with the newcomers, even if they did not always accept Christian ideas. By advancing a vision of a peaceful world and maintaining at least the illusion of harmonious relations with Indians, Quakers interpreted dreams to enhance their myths and elaborate their own distinct form of imperialism. These ideas, first developed during the early period of contact, continued to reverberate throughout the second half of the eighteenth century when peace became even more elusive and more negative ideas about Indians dominated official policy. Quaker accounts of Indian dreams, therefore, not only reflected efforts to keep the peace and assimilate Native Americans, but also revealed political tensions between Quakers and non-Quakers. Friends deployed dreams to distinguish themselves from the violent Puritans of New England; they read their dreams to validate their peaceful experiment in Pennsylvania, and, when peace failed, to justify their efforts to spread a Quaker vision in a world that could not accept it.

As products of the mind, dreams can project fantasy; for both Indians and Quakers, dreams offered a canvas to imagine scenarios that could influence future political and cultural events. But as texts, dreams are also facts. Throughout history people have recorded their dreams, leaving a large yet underanalyzed record concerning the human mind. Psychoanalytic models offer important theoretical paradigms to understand dreams. Yet scholars who rely exclusively on explanations developed during the twentieth century will fail to detect the distinctive historical paradigms earlier people used. No less than did Indians, early American Quakers employed historically specific models of dream interpretation. Cultural historians have shown that in medieval and early modern Europe dreams could increase the social authority of otherwise powerless people; after all, seers were respected for their ability to foretell the future. In addition, Mechal

Sobel's work on "self-fashioning" has provocatively focused on the ways in which the discovery of "self" and "other" in dreams allowed dreamers to confront their "inner aliens" and fashion new more individuated identities during the era of the American Revolution. The coming together of distinctive cultures enabled people to break away from what she terms "we-selves" and write new life stories that analyzed dreams in order to formulate more self-conscious beings. Quakers did write new stories that confronted difference in their dreams, but these narratives often sought to erase the very real distinctions between the two groups.[5]

Recent work on "European consciousness" reinforces the long-standing critique that American historians have privileged European perspectives over Native American ones.[6] Not so in the case of dreams. We actually know more about dreaming among Native Americans than among Euro-Americans. Historians have long recognized that the telling, interpreting, and acting out of dreams formed an integral aspect of Indian religious beliefs. Anthony Wallace's seminal work on Iroquois culture explored the ways in which visionary dreams helped Senecas overcome demoralization and defeat after the American Revolution.[7] Richard White's description of a colonial and postcolonial middle ground in the Great Lakes region included the recognition that "to talk of dreams and to talk of God created a discourse on the supernatural that drew from both cultures." Jane Merritt has shown the ways in which Indian dreams and visions based on a Moravian and Delaware cross-cultural colonial experience defied both Christian and non-Christian categorization and were key to "revitalizing Native American spirituality" and promoting an "Indian Great Awakening" in the 1740s.[8]

Both White and Merritt detail a Euro-American and Indian exchange of stories about dreams, yet their central concern remains the ways in which that exchange ultimately affected Native American communities. Just a smattering of work looks at any of the dreams and visions of colonial Europeans, whether they concern Native Americans or not. By overlooking the import of dreams in Euro-American cultures and highlighting their significance in Native American ones, scholars risk reproducing a binary account of the past that fixes Indians in a sacred (or superstitious) space, while identifying Europeans with supposedly more rational (and secular) cultural trends. By linking dreams solely to Native Americans, historians have relegated a discussion of visionary experiences to the historiographical equivalent of a Native American reservation. To balance the scales we need to explore the ground of European *and* Indian dreams.

Trying to untangle the meaning of accounts of Quakers and Indians who exchanged stories about their dreams presents certain methodological problems. The first consists of defining dreams. Both Quakers and Indians often failed to distinguish between dreams and visions. The written record is peppered with experiences that are labeled a "dream or vision" or a "night dream or vision." If a Quaker recorded a dream or an Indian told of one, it was precisely because it had become something more—a sacred vision. People simply did not make it a point to remember or record what they considered ordinary or insignificant nocturnal experiences. A second problem lies in the clear bias of the sources. Quaker ministers and traders recorded dreams that seemed meaningful to them. Some records of dreams, moreover, originated as oral accounts far removed from their original source. Gone are the many other dreams, both Indian and Quaker, that ministers and traders did not deem important or that did not come to diarists' attention. Also gone are Indians' original interpretations of their dreams, although it is sometimes possible to read against the grain and understand something about them. Yet these source limitations reveal as much as they conceal because the biases illustrate the ways in which dreams circulated among Quakers. Friends developed a corporate process to screen dreams and give them larger significance. When someone (usually a minister) told a dream in meeting, other ministers would also reflect upon the dream and sometimes correct the initial interpretation. Editorial committees had to approve the publication of all Quaker writings, including dreams. Thus, Quakers left a paper trail that enables us to follow their communal shaping of a significant cultural phenomenon.[9]

Even though archives hold a veritable treasure of Quaker dreams on many different topics, scholars are only beginning to explore the centrality of dreams to the formation of early American Quaker culture. Early Pennsylvanians and other Euro-Americans attempted to turn their fantasies into facts in a world that was not only "awash in a sea of faith," but also awash in a sea of dreams. Dreams and their interpretations helped cultivate a powerful, complex, and multifaceted early American spiritual landscape throughout the colonial period and into the nineteenth century. For the Quakers who dominated the province of Pennsylvania and for their coreligionists scattered throughout the other colonies, dreams provided crucial narrative devices to envision and paint a distinctive society that could get along with Indians. Thus far scholarship on Quaker and Indian relations has focused primarily on treaties and trade. An appreciation for the significance and power of sacred dreams in both the Quaker and Indian communities brings us one step closer to understanding the ways in which distinctive religious beliefs helped to shape Penn's visionary experiment of mythic toleration. Indeed, an analysis of dreams uncovers a lost religious world, linked to the world of diplomacy, that reveals much about each group's motives and hopes for the future in a troubled middle ground.[10]

The Quaker attention to Indian visionary experiences began early and was closely connected to a brand of Quaker imperialism that sought to convert non-Christians as it simultaneously competed with other Christians, especially the Calvinists in New England. In 1672 and 1673 George Fox, by then the Friends' most powerful leader, visited the scattered Quakers residing in the American colonies to control wayward members of the sect and perhaps examine the potential of the continent for further immigration. Fox's reliance on Native American hospitality, as well as the Quaker principle that all people could receive God, predisposed him to befriend Indians. He claimed to have delighted his Indian hosts by convening many spiritual meetings as he traveled through their towns. Somewhere on his travels between Virginia and Rhode Island he heard about an Indian vision. According to the story, even before the arrival of Europeans, a prophetic Indian had foreseen that "a white people should come in a great thing of the sea." This Indian urged his countrymen to "receive" the newcomers, "be loveing" toward them and not "hurt or wrong" them at the risk of being "distroyed." But when the English penetrated the coastline, the Indians disregarded his warning and instead fought the foreigners. The Indians thus provoked their own destruction and "never prospered." Europeans noted similar first encounter stories wherever they went, and both Indians and Europeans turned to them to explain new cultural contacts. Europeans recorded these dreams and visions because they justified their invasions with divine authority and confirmed their assumptions of cultural superiority.[11]

Fox was no exception. The vision appealed to both his expansionist and pacifist ideals. He was quick to acknowledge its truth, arguing that it had been fulfilled in various ways. The Indian seer "was a prophet and prophesied truly," for the Europeans, Fox contended, had arrived just as predicted. More important, when the Indians did not behave amicably toward the English, they failed to flourish. One can imagine Fox recounting this narrative to both Indians and Europeans in order to seek harmonious diplomatic relations. The prophecy warned Indians in no uncertain terms to welcome Europeans or be struck down by God. For Euro-American settlers or prospective colonists still living in England, the vision would have assured them that not all Indians were hostile savages, that whites were destined to rule over Indians, and that at least some Native people understood the spiritual repercussions that antagonism toward the English would bring.

By endorsing a prophecy emphasizing pacifism, Fox did not merely provide divine sanction for Quaker settlement in America but also encouraged the Quaker tradition of validating Indian religiosity based on a visionary experience that might enable cross-cultural dialogue to develop on spiritual terms. Few Euro-Americans—and even fewer religious leaders— would have accepted the proposition that an unconverted Indian could prophesy at all. But Quaker George Fox believed that the uninitiated Indian could and did receive a revelation from God.[12]

Fox's version of the vision is of course both a problematic narrative and a questionable interpretation. We do not know who told Fox the dream. An Indian "king" might have unfolded the narrative as he offered the Quaker a shelter for the night, or a seasoned colonist might have related an invented, embellished, or poorly understood anecdote over a cup of home-brewed beer. Even if an Indian told him the vision firsthand, Fox may not have heard an accurate translation or have been handicapped by the limitations of the pidgin in which most Euro-Americans and indigenous people communicated. And even if the words did get through clearly, the storyteller might have been trying to please or trick his listener. Fox's statement that Indians failed to flourish is also problematic. The poverty Fox and his companion John Burnyeat saw among the Algonquians may have had as much to do with seasonal fluctuations in subsistence patterns or redistributions of wealth as with Indian indigence. Yet Fox was already figuring Indians as poor victims who might benefit from European generosity—though at that particular historical moment the reverse might have been more accurate. Modern historians would of course attribute Native American distresses to European germs, guns, and competition for resources, but Fox ascribed them to God's will. The Indians had brought on their own destruction when they ignored the prophecy and acted viciously toward the English. But if they would be peaceful, they too could, according to Fox, enjoy the fruits of being Christian.[13]

Many early Quaker observations about Indians ultimately reflected more about Quakers' bad experiences with Puritans than with the actual Native people Fox and other Quakers encountered. Fox, for one, told a story about an old Indian who might have converted to Quakerism were it not for his fear of the New England authorities who would "hang him and put [hi]m to death and banish [hi]m as they did the quakers." Instead the Native man turned to Puritanism, but said that his people had become worse off when they "left their owne religion." Burnyeat also told a story that vilified the Puritans who drove Quaker Nicholas Upshall into the cold woods for his unorthodox beliefs. Burnyeat contrasted their treatment with an Indian king who saved Upshall and demonstrated true "Christian Practice" by giving him "Land and Kindness." Yet Indians did not always heed Quaker messages of peace, nor did they simply hand over their homes, fields, and hunting grounds. In fact, they often acted violently, and when Indians attacked Europeans, Quakers were quick to blame Indian attacks on God's retribution toward the Calvinists for their earlier cruelty to Friends. Indeed, Quakers neither forgave nor forgot the New Englanders who had hanged four missionaries before 1661.[14]

Because Quakers in Pennsylvania liked to contrast their approach to colonization with the more intolerant actions of New Englanders, mischievous and savage Indians made their appearance in their dreams about New England. Although these dreams did not take place in Pennsylvania's fields or yards, the dream stories nonetheless circulated within the colony, where many Quakers took note of them. In 1702, Thomas Thompson Jr., a Quaker minister from Yorkshire, England, meandered through Salisbury, Massachusetts, where he contemplated "truely" the "states of that country." As Thompson waited for a spiritual opening, he was struck by a vision in which the "word of the Lord" warned him that he would "dung some part of the New England ground with the carcases of mankind if the inhabitants thereof do not speedily Repent and turn to me the Lord . . . greatly bowed in spirit." New England was doomed because the people of Massachusetts had "shed the Blood of [the Lord's] saints" and "made a prey" of Quakers. As punishment, New England would become the victims of "savage Indians."[15]

Thompson's vision and indictment is not an isolated incident. Another divine revelation, thirty years later, struck a similar chord in its condemnation of New England. Quakers titled this dream that circulated up and down the coast the "Swanzey Vision" after the town of Swansea, Massachusetts, which was also the first town Indian King Philip attacked in the 1670s war that bears his name. The dream, like Thompson's vision, warned New England of its sinful state. A voice of God threatened New England with "his Rod" for its crime of "Irreligion and the crying Sins of Pride and Oppression." God would "shake the Earth" with "Wars and Commotions," many would "be slain," and the earth would be "dunged with the Bodies of Men." Like Thompson's vision, the Swanzey Vision attributed this violence to hostile Indians. The "Heathen in North America" would further "slay and carry off [New England's] people, young and old into Captivity." Indian wars above all signified the apocalyptic wrath of God against sinful New England.[16]

The idea that Indian wars represented God's judgment was not a new one, nor was it unique to the Quakers. Massachusetts minister Increase Mather thought that the onset of King Philip's War proved God's displeasure with New England. Quakers, such as Thompson, echoed Puritan assessments and continued to interpret nightmarish visions of savage Indians as a condemnation of New England's errant ways. But Quakers thought Puritans doomed for different reasons.[17] Although Quakers had ended their confrontational invasions of New England by the 1660s, their intellectual crusade against Congregationalists raged on. When a dream or vision pictured hostile savages spawning hellish scenes of destruction, righteous Quakers turned their attention away from themselves and called for reform in New England. The Congregationalists thus supplied an example of corrupt Christianity that, by way of contrast, highlighted Quaker morality. In this sense, Quaker pacifism worked by displacing Indian violence onto New England's conscience, where it already weighed heavy. This triangulation of Puritans, Indians, and Quakers paved the way for and further reinforced Quakers' attempts at creating pacifist alliances with Indians.[18]

Whereas New England symbolized sinfulness, many spiritually oriented Quakers thought William Penn exemplified integrity. As the proprietor of Pennsylvania, Penn fashioned himself as a different kind of ruler who would work hard to establish an atmosphere of peace with the Indians (and prosperity for the Quakers). Penn argued that one God had made all humans; the Founder also learned the Delaware Jargon, offered to buy land from the Indians before settling it, and proposed that a mixed Indian and European jury might adjudicate disputes. His addresses to the Indians appealed to brotherly love and warned them not to shed blood, lest they should make the "great God Angry." Both Quakers and Indians exchanged symbolic wampum during negotiations, and, according to legend, the Delawares presented Penn with a belt that depicted a Quaker and an Indian walking hand in hand to commemorate their friendly relations. In the end, Quaker benevolence—like the mixed juries Penn proposed—proved more rhetoric than reality. But despite this state of affairs, both Quakers and Indians persisted in recalling Penn's generosity to the Indians long after he died. His brief sojourn became a golden age of harmony against which future disruptions could be tested.[19]

Thomas Chalkley, a Quaker minister from Pennsylvania's Nottingham Meeting, recorded an Indian dream in his journal that illustrates the symbolic weight Penn's benevolence continued to carry among both Quakers and Indians following the Founder's return to England. In 1706 Chalkley organized a Quaker religious expedition to visit the Indian village of Conestoga and asked the people who resided there whether they could hold a religious meeting among them. The Indians called a council to ponder the matter, and an elderly Seneca woman argued that a dream she had had suggested it might be "beneficial to their young People." The woman had dreamed that she was in London, which was the "finest Place she ever saw," resembling Philadelphia but surpassing it in size. The woman crossed six streets, and at the seventh she came upon William Penn talking to a crowd. Penn "rejoiced" at seeing her. He also pledged to "come over and preach to" the Indians, which gave her a sense of satisfaction. The woman concluded that Chalkley did not intend to "buy, or sell, or get Gain, but came in Love and Respect" and therefore represented the fulfillment of her dream. In short, Quakers and Conestogas should hold the meeting.[20]

Although women played a diminishing role in diplomatic affairs with Europeans, many continued to participate in political decisions, as when the Seneca dreamer "spoke much in Council." When Chalkley asked his guide why they "suffered" women to speak in their public assemblies, the interpreter informed him that some women were wiser than some men. Indeed, these Senecas had not done anything for many years without asking the advice of the "ancient Grave woman"—also described as an "Empress"—who had narrated her dream. Perhaps unknown to the European men who conducted most official exchanges, dreaming provided Seneca women with a behind-the-scenes tool to continue to influence Euro-Indian relations. After all, only less than forty years earlier a French Jesuit missionary had noted that the Iroquois, and in particular the Senecas, were especially known for their ability to analyze dreams.[21]

The woman almost certainly told her dream to persuade members of her community that an alliance with the Quakers would prove beneficial. Perhaps she genuinely sought to understand the Friends' religion and hoped to gain some of its spiritual power. The woman's evocation of Penn—a commanding symbol of the just Englishman—may have helped her convince the more recalcitrant Senecas of the Quakers' good intent. Mention of Penn might have also reminded Friends of their responsibility to the Indians. Perhaps she hoped the Quakers would present her people gifts. She may even have expected them to send her to England, or at least to Philadelphia, in order to collect the goods. Such long-distance voyages could reap material goods and further enhance her status in her own community. Finally, perhaps the old woman hoped to gain Euro-American favor for the Senecas at the expense of the many other refugee Indian groups that streamed into Pennsylvania's interior. Whatever the elderly woman's motives were—and all of these may have played a role—her dream-based argument supposedly convinced the village to allow Chalkley and the Quakers to proceed with their meeting.

By recounting the dream, Chalkley left Conestoga with a new feather in his cap: he had a story that showcased friendly relations with the Indians. Chalkley's narrative, which was recorded in his published journal, above all highlighted the many similarities between Friends and Indians. Paralleling Quaker practices, Native people paid attention to the spiritual meanings of their dreams. The dream, moreover, satisfied Chalkley that God spoke to the Conestogas and that they were genuinely inclined to consider Quaker religious beliefs. According to Chalkley, they agreed that God gave "Peace and Comfort to the Soul for Well-doing, and sorrow and Trouble for Evil doing," giving a "double Assent" to the idea of a "Light in the Soul." Chalkley also pointed to political parallels. When the Indians gathered in council, for example, they discussed matters "without any Heat or Jarring," just as if they were at a well-conducted Quaker meeting. Although Chalkley thought it was unusual that Indians allowed women a political voice, even this had a corollary in Friends' encouragement of public female preaching.[22]

Chalkley claimed that when the Quakers parted the Indians desired "more such Opportunities." Indian requests notwithstanding, Chalkley and the Quakers do not seem to have returned to Conestoga, even though their home in Nottingham was less than a day's journey away. Indeed, one of the things that stands out about the dream Chalkley recorded is its exceptional nature. Despite the fact that both Quakers and Indians had many dreams, they did not often tell them to each other. Indeed, through the first half of the eighteenth century, most Quakers kept their distance from Indian communities, leaving the exchange of dream stories (and of land) with Indians in the hands of other colonists (including some Friends) who did not share their tolerant religious values.[23]

The non-Quaker interpreter Conrad Weiser thought that dreams were foolish, but as a shrewd diplomat he perceived that they could help him control Indians. This Palatine immigrant, who had spent some of his childhood living with the dream-conscious Iroquois, later served as an agent representing various colonies to the Indians as they sought to make headway into western lands. Weiser, who had also lived at the visionary Seventh Day Baptist religious colony at Ephrata, did not share the Indian, Baptist, or Quaker appreciation for hallowed dreams. In a letter to the German newspaper editor Christopher Sauer, Weiser declared that the Indians "have many silly fancies about spirits, about their dreams, and their sorceries." But the Indian agent nonetheless recognized that dreams could initiate important symbolic and material exchanges in diplomatic relations. Following a conflict in Virginia in 1743 that led to a loss of Indian lives, an afflicted Tuscarora named Saghsidowa told Weiser his dream. In his report, Weiser asked the government to "buy a wooden pipe" in order to "answer Saghsidowas dream." Thus dreams entered into a language of government and diplomacy even amongst skeptical Euro-Americans who did not uphold their sacred value.[24]

The fact that Weiser attempted to satisfy Saghsidowa lends credence to another incident concerning a dream exchange between Weiser and Oneida chief Shickellamy. According to an old tradition, Shickellamy told Weiser a dream in which Weiser gave Shickellamy "a new rifle." Weiser promptly handed over his gun. But a few days later Weiser approached Shickellamy with a dream of his own in which Shickellamy gave him the island of Que on the Susquehanna River. The chief apparently deeded the land but informed Weiser that they should never dream together again.[25] To say that Weiser got the best of Shickellamy in this dream exchange is accurate enough, but it does little justice to the complexity of the interaction. Both Europeans and Indians used dreams to improve their conditions. Regardless of whether the dreams were real or spurious (and we can never know the truth), they could provide an arena to elaborate material demands and hammer out new diplomatic strategies. In this case, the goals of Shickellamy and Weiser were not in total conflict. Weiser wanted property, and Shickellamy had land to sell. Perhaps Shickellamy, who had recently moved to the area, had fewer qualms about alienating a tract of land that was on the periphery of Iroquoia and had most recently belonged to the Delawares. Shickellamy wanted weapons, and Weiser could help him. Not only did Weiser give up his gun, but he also asked the Pennsylvania legislature to supply the Oneida chief with a gunshop and gunsmith so that he could control unruly tributary Indians and provide a buffer zone between the English and French. Thus a dream exchange complemented Weiser's and Shickellamy's negotiations.

The fact that similar dream-swapping stories exist in other places suggests that trade supported by dreams may have provided a more widespread formulaic and ritualized approach to exchanges between Native Americans and Euro-Americans than historians have recognized. Nonetheless, we should not lose sight of the fact that in the end this exchange, like so many others, ultimately benefited the expansion of European colonists at the expense of the Indians. Shickellamy recognized this when he said he would no longer dream with Weiser. And some Europeans, such as Weiser, did not hide their disdain for spiritualizing dreams. Weiser's "enemies" (perhaps Quakers) who handed down this oral tradition probably felt that Weiser had unjustly duped Shickellamy with the dream.[26]

Certainly Weiser, Shickellamy, and Saghsidowa used dreams to help orchestrate fragile truces, but these efforts could not prevent (and may have abetted) further violence in the Susquehanna and Ohio valleys. As tense peace gave way to the brutal bloodshed of the Seven Years' War, a moment of serious crisis and self-reflection gripped the Quaker community. Friends could no longer claim, as they had for almost a hundred years, that peaceful relations with the Indians proved divine favor to them. The fighting and dislocations thus contributed to a feeling of failure in Quaker meetinghouses as many Friends attributed the war to God's anger. Quakers examined their troubled consciences and found that they drank too much, enjoyed worldly pleasures, married outside of meeting, and relied on slave labor. Friends further recognized that they had neglected their fellowship with Indians. Dream interpretations proliferated and gave Friends a window through which to explore themselves, their world, their God. Some dreamers went so far as to reexamine the Quaker relationship to Native

Americans. As they did so, they revisited older pacifist beliefs and promoted a peaceful ideological imperialism that once again looked to symbolic Quaker and Indian dreams.[27]

Ann Whitall had a dream about Indians in the 1740s, but she recorded
it and commented on its significance only during the Seven Years' War.
When Whitall, a devout Quaker from Haddonfield, New Jersey, heard that
Indians had killed some Euro-Americans on the frontier in 1760, the news
reminded her of a twenty-year-old dream that involved "the indiens cilling
of me." The violence had deeply affected Whitall, and the dream made her
wonder whether she and her children were prepared to die. For her, the
war carried an urgent message to reform. Whitall did not understand how
some people could "be so ful of laif and prait [pride?] and lay nothing to
hart." Although her dream did not lead her to advocate changes in provincial Indian policy, she did criticize Quakers for their consumption of tobacco, tea, and calico. To Whitall, the failure in Euro-Indian relations did
not stem from Native American wickedness, but rather symbolized the
larger corruption that infected her society. She especially wished that her
own family would attend religious meetings instead of keeping "evil company" and talking back to her when she reprimanded them. The dream
spoke to issues that she—and most Quaker women—could hope to control: herself and her family.[28]

While Whitall sought to counteract declension in her home, Quaker
leaders involved in ruling the province grew alarmed with the breakdown
of political equilibrium. During the Seven Years' War many Quakers left
the Assembly in protest. In 1756, Quaker merchant Israel Pemberton created the "Friendly Association for Regaining and Preserving Peace with
the Indians by Pacifist Measures" and helped start negotiations with the
disgruntled Delawares. Quakers had, according to one Iroquois spokesman
who felt Quakers had neglected them, finally come back after apparently
being "dead and buried in the bushes." Although the Pennsylvania government sought to ban the meddlesome Quakers from the 1757 Easton proceedings that Pemberton had initiated, Friends flagrantly defied the
prohibition. They attended en masse, observed the proceedings, and advised Delaware leader Teedyuscung to make sure the government did not
commit fraud. One of these self-proclaimed diplomats included the well-
respected Quaker minister John Churchman. His dream symbolized the
possibility for peaceful relations between Euro-Americans and Indians.[29]

Before leaving for Easton, Churchman, who lived west of town, dreamed that he rode toward the east at sunrise. An unusual figure lit up the sky and frightened his horse. But to Churchman the figure resembled an angel: its "motion was as swift as thought," and "it was encompassed with a brightness like a rainbow, with a large loose garment of the same colour down to the feet; it rather seemed to move rather than walk." Churchman calmed his jumpy horse and reined him toward the angelic figure who now "stood still in the midst of many curious stacks of corn" and appeared as "a human form about seven feet high." The angel smiled at Churchman and asked him where he was going. Churchman responded that he was headed toward an elegant building in the distance. The angel seemed to approve of Churchman's course and, vanishing upwards, allowed him to pass through. When he awoke, Churchman reflected that the angel had the "complexion" of an Indian. At the time, Churchman may have understood the dream as a signal to attend the treaty conference, but he did not offer a full interpretation until later.[30]

At Easton, Churchman expressed deep anxiety over the course of the proceedings. A coterie of Pennsylvanians, New Yorkers, and Indians descended on the small town, creating a carnival atmosphere. He and the other Quakers hated the noise and confusion and criticized the heavy drinking (especially by Teedyuscung). They also felt that Pennsylvania Governor William Denny made matters worse by refusing to allow the Delawares their own clerk. At their makeshift religious meetings, Quakers occasionally noted that the gatherings were "satisfactory," but many more were "dark," a result of the "raw careless spirit prevailing over the minds of the people." Peace seemed very distant indeed. The winds shifted when Denny allowed Teedyuscung to hire a clerk, and on the following day, the Delaware finally delivered the kind of conciliatory speech Churchman and the Quakers had longed to hear. Teedyuscung hoped that "we may love like brethren," that "the sun may shine clear upon us, that we, our wives, our young men and children may rejoice in a lasting peace." He sealed his words with the ceremonial presentation of a seventeen-row wampum belt. Now the Quakers knew that the Delawares would cooperate in their attempt to restore peaceful relations. Not surprisingly, the next meeting Churchman attended exuded optimism, and the minister thought the clouds of "distress and suffering" would "somewhat break away."[31]

The positive turn of events at Easton brought Churchman's dream of the angelic Indian back "very fresh." Churchman could now look to it as a signal from God, and he readily disclosed a decisive interpretation of its meaning. The remembrance of the dream resonated with the peaceful overtures the Delawares had "remarkably spoken" and assured Churchman that "the Lord was in [Indians] by his good Spirit." Disputing the argument that Native people were depraved, Churchman stated that because the angel in his dream was Indian "all colours were equal to [the Lord], who gave life and being to all mankind." Moreover, his dream indicated that one did not need to be a professed Christian to be enlightened. Churchman urged Quakers to be "careful to examine deeper than outward appearance" and with a "tender regard to station and education" before forming opinions about other people's righteousness. Only a return to the pacific and universal principles of the founding generation would preserve people from "error in judgement."[32]

Had Teedyuscung kept up his angry front, one suspects that Churchman would have interpreted his dream differently. His analysis of Indian equality depended on a foundation of Indian civility. The large and luminous angelic figure was noble, but he was certainly not savage. To some extent, the figure's association with the rising sun and corn seems to reflect Indian spiritual and religious imagery, but Indians held no monopoly over light imagery and motifs of agricultural abundance. In fact, Europeans who attempted to convert or "civilize" Indians often struggled to convince Native men to give up the hunt and take up agriculture. Churchman's dream therefore pictured a nonthreatening angelic figure who was beautiful and smiling, and, although he had an Indian complexion, he resembled one who had "washed [away] his grease and filth." In both the imagery in Churchman's dream and his experiences at Easton, the Indian only became acceptable when he was cleansed of his war paint. Churchman's dream, then, made the Indians appear peaceful to himself, to the Quaker community, and perhaps to any Native people who might have heard it.[33]

Fear of more wars also inspired another Quaker minister, John Woolman, to visit several Indian towns in 1763. The next year he too had a dream that highlighted the peaceful nature of Indians. In the dream Woolman crossed the woods to bring a message of peace to a warring "chief man" but encountered a few people who labored with guns at their sides. They threatened to kill the Quaker, but when they realized Woolman was unarmed they instead led him to their chief. As they waited in a pleasant garden in front of the chief's home, the guide invited the visitor to dinner, and then the chief appeared with a "friendly countenance." Although

Woolman awoke before he could talk to the man, both his dream and his description of Indians in his journal stress the possibility of amicable relations—that is, if the Euro-Americans would lay their weapons down.[34] Like Churchman's, Woolman's dream sought to recover the pacifist world of the early Penn days.

Thus war led Quakers to become increasingly involved in Native American affairs. In 1758 and again in 1761, Israel Pemberton encouraged coreligionist James Kenny to go to Fort Pitt and run a trading post that would set fair prices and not sell liquor. Kenny, too, saw himself as representing a Quaker legacy of peace. Like William Penn he learned a Native language and prided himself on his fair deals. And like George Fox he self-righteously applauded Quakers for their good Indian relations; Kenny took every opportunity to note that Indians esteemed Friends above other Englishmen. The clerk even claimed that his own discussions with the potentially hostile Shawnees, coupled with the store's fixed prices, had "Stop[ped] about fourty of fifty Wariors just then going against the English." Kenny was also a dreamer. He kept diaries in 1758 and 1759 and again in 1761 to 1762 that detailed many of his own dreams, and he also recorded a few Indian visionary experiences. While it is unclear whether he ever shared any of his own dreams with Indians, there is no question that he engaged in spiritual discussions with his Indian clients and paid close attention to their dreams.[35]

Although Kenny recognized the fragility of the peace, his early dreams exuded optimism. In 1759, shortly after some Ottawa Indians had killed two soldiers and when his assistant had also died, Kenny lay gravely ill. Anxious that his life would soon end, Kenny "beheld in a dream or a vision" a "glorious person" who was marked with a shining star. When he awoke Kenny felt refreshed, believing that the Lord had taken notice of his condition and would watch over him. That same year he dreamed that farmers reaping ripe fields "seemed pleasant." And in April 1762, around the time that his garden began to grow, Kenny dreamed that a large "Yard containing many Stacks of Wheat and many of hay" had been "raised by great Industry on some New Rough Place that [he] thought could never Produce so well as it did." Kenny offered no analysis of these agricultural dreams beyond the affirmation that they were agreeable, but perhaps he hoped that his own literal gardens in the wild would succeed. Yet given the way Quakers interpreted their dreams symbolically, it was just as likely that

Kenny understood the dreams as broader metaphorical signs from God suggesting that the cultivation of Christianity and civility that he sought among the Indians was beginning to work.[36]

Kenny concluded that at least some Indians were warming to Christianity after he "entertained" a sickly "Old Indian" who told him his dream in December 1762. In the elderly man's dream, heaven consisted of a spacious building that hung effortlessly in the air. Here he saw the "Great Creator of all things" who "appeared like a Man" and sat on a "Glorious Seat." The Indian further "imagined" that the Creator looked like the "King of the White People." This god then reprimanded the Indian people for worshipping individual animals as guardian spirits. To illustrate the point, the "Great Creator" opened a door revealing all the different animals and called each one by name. After they responded, the Creator informed the old man that he had already given the animals their names and that the Indians should not give them different ones by adopting them as guardian spirits. Kenny, who thought the practice of giving "Names of many Beasts and Wild Creatures," or worshipping animal spirits, an "Abomination," recorded the incident because "Dreams often come from the Id[ea]s or thoughts that are prevalent in the mind."

The old man's dream, in short, promoted a worldview that sanctioned European cultural, if not political, domination, and it probably represented an accommodationist element amongst the Native Americans in the Ohio Valley. Or perhaps, as a guest in Kenny's home, the old man had embellished the dream to please his host. In any case, instead of conjuring animals in a hunt (as the Delawares did when Lindeström first arrived) this Indian believed (or so Kenny thought) that only a European God could summon animals. At a time when wildlife was becoming increasingly scarce along the Appalachians, Kenny hoped Indians would abandon spiritual beliefs rooted in their older traditions and take up European-style farming. And like most Quakers, Kenny's high esteem of Indian capacity as well as his respect for Indian dreaming ultimately depended on their conversion to Christian practices.[37]

Kenny was much less appreciative of Indian dreams that sought to subvert Christian goals and English conquest. Kenny assiduously kept track of the Delaware prophet Neolin and his crusade against European domination. Based on his visionary experiences, Neolin drew maps showing the way to heaven. In the past, Neolin claimed, the Indians merely walked up a straight line to paradise. But a square over that line now interrupted the

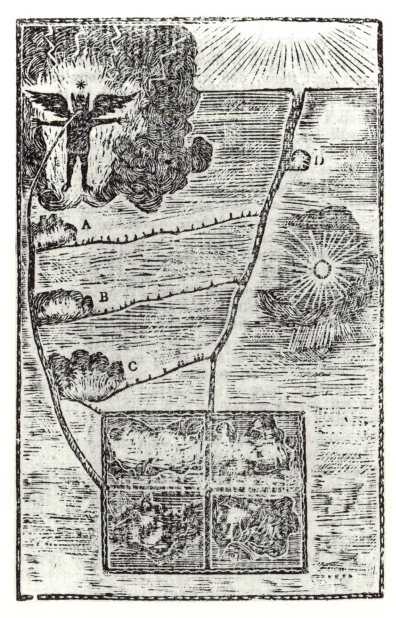

Figure 4 Chart of the Delaware prophet Neolin's teachings, as reproduced from memory by Pennsylvanian John M'Cullough. From Archibald Loudoun, *A Selection of Some of the Most Interesting Narratives of the Outrages Committed by the Indians in Their Wars with the White People* (Carlisle, Pa., 1808–11). The Library Company of Philadelphia.

route, representing the incursion of Europeans. The square had a series of lines jutting out from it, and each one represented sins and vices that Indians had learned from the Europeans. These paths came perilously close to hell and confused Indians trying to take the direct and linear course to a heaven that contained "no White people but all Indians." Neolin urged his followers to quit hunting and avoid all European goods. Kenny recognized the authority that the prophet commanded and dreaded his desire for a "total separation from Us" because it would inevitably lead to bloodshed. Neolin, too, predicted that there would be "Two or Three Good Talks and then War." Unlike the old Indian's dream, no part of the prophet's visions earned Kenny's validation, even though the Quaker might have identified with the cosmographic map and agreed with many of Neolin's criticisms. Instead, Kenny called the Delaware an "imposter" and paid closer attention to the movements of Indians; he even reported an alleged incident of spying to the commanding officer at the fort. Kenny clearly understood the dangerous power that Neolin's prophecy had amongst the Indians: three days after he recorded it Kenny dreamed that a "Mingoe Young Man told me the Mingoes Go to war with the English next Summer."[38]

As the world around him threatened to grow more violent, Kenny's dreams became increasingly terrifying. He soon made it known that he was fed up with frontier living and wanted to return home. In 1763, Kenny had two dreams that featured the devil. The first was particularly obscure. In this dream, Satan looked into Kenny's house but ran away when Kenny stared him down. Kenny felt confident that, if the "Agent" did his part, the devil could be kept away. By "Agent" Kenny almost certainly meant the military officer in control of Indian affairs who could ultimately release him from his post. He did not define who or what Satan symbolized. Did he mean Indian warriors? French warriors? The English rabble that polluted the frontier? His own fear of living in a dangerous place? His apprehension of becoming like the sinful characters on the frontier? Or a more general anxiety over the increasingly negative turn of events? Though evil nearly overtook him in the dream, the dream's final message—like most Quaker visions—was self-righteously uplifting. Kenny ultimately kept the devil at bay.[39]

Although Kenny did not unmask the devil in that dream, he did so in another one in March 1763. Kenny sat with others in a "Strange house" and instantly recognized Satan amongst them. Kenny felt "great abhorance and resentment of Mind" and got up to leave. As he departed, he looked at the devil and "he apper'd to have Christian Frederick Post[']s ficognomy and Dress in all appearance." Kenny thus associated the devil with the Moravian missionary Post who corresponded closely with him and was moreover paid by the Society of Friends. Despite some similarities, the two men, after all, disagreed on many points. Post had remarked that "Indians are Voide of Reason," which contradicted Kenny's view that "in many cases [Indians] will hear to reason and allow it to be right." And just before Kenny had the dream, Post had ministered to drunkards and "musition-ers" in Pittsburgh. Kenny scorned these immoral and irreligious inhabi-tants who drank, caroused, and swindled Indians on the frontier. Their sinfulness made them incapable of instructing Indians in "Sound Princi-ples" and encouraged the Indians to turn to the Catholic French.[40]

Post himself seemed dangerously close to supporting the French when he argued that "papists did not Worship Idols and endeavour'd to Excuse their making such things as if useful." Perhaps most significant, Post mag-nified Kenny's own faults and probably made him feel guilty. Just a few days after Kenny had the dream, Post asked Kenny to accompany him on a missionary voyage, but Kenny refused, saying he was too weak to travel. Although Kenny may not have agreed with all of Post's spiritual principles, the missionary at least had the gumption to bring Christianity directly to the Indians. In contrast, Kenny's own efforts, which centered on the store, had clearly failed to bring either peace or Christianity to the Ohio country. In the end, then, Kenny very much resembled his forefathers who failed to convert Indians. Kenny faulted the French, the Pittsburgh rabble, and Post, and he might have added himself to the list. In this sense, the devil in Kenny's dreams was still a European and not an Indian. Even so, this did not imply much understanding of Indian culture or Indian dreaming. Ken-ny's dream exchanges with Indians—like those of other Quakers before him—helped promote his own view about peace, which was always cou-pled with the idea that Christianity would prevail. This view also required the cooperation of Natives, many of whom were increasingly unwilling to pursue the path of peace. It was only then that Quakers began to fear Indians, and possibly even depict them as devils, in their dreams.[41]

Although Kenny's indictment of Neolin came pretty close, seventeenth-and early eighteenth-century Quakers did not usually accuse Indians of following Satan in their dreams. They instead used dreams to pursue political, diplomatic, and spiritual negotiations that sought the peaceful incorporation of indigenous peoples. Devils, by contrast, represented Euro-American depravity, whether by Puritans, Moravians, or even other Quakers. Only when Delaware, Iroquois, and Quaker cultures renounced peaceful diplomatic solutions—which began to happen during the Seven Years' War and was completed following the Revolution—did Quakers explore the possibility of Indian devils not ready for reform. Only then did it become apparent that the Quaker pacifism that infused their dreams and dream exchanges had failed.

Other Euro-Americans, who for the most part believed in one God and in many cases spoke the English language, disagreed widely about the significance and causes of dreams. By contrast, Quakers and the Indians they encountered—very different groups that shared neither language nor gods—held similar ideas. Both believed in the sacred nature of dreams. Both groups told individual dreams in communal settings to transform their societies. This shared spiritual practice offered a possibility for significant cross-cultural exchange and influenced diplomatic efforts. The fact that Quaker dreams concerning Indians usually conveyed messages of peace and love further heightened prospects for meaningful dialogues. But Indians and Quakers did not totally agree about what their visions ultimately meant. Quakers certainly told dreams for their own purposes, and it is clear that Quakers never sought to understand Lenape or other Indian practices on indigenous terms. In the end, despite the shared spiritual practice, contact with Native Americans and their dreams did not challenge Quakers to defy their Christian worldview. Overall, the primary purpose of the dreams Quakers circulated was to disarm the potentially dangerous Indians peacefully and to advance the Quaker universal expansionist vision. Thus the Quaker legacy of peace did not erase the legacy of conquest. Peace and conquest—like the European and Indian men pictured on wampum belts—walked hand in hand.

4

INDIAN, *MÉTIS*, AND EURO-AMERICAN WOMEN
ON MULTIPLE FRONTIERS

ALISON DUNCAN HIRSCH

No single object better embodies the hopefulness of early relations between Pennsylvanians and Indians than the so-called Great Treaty Wampum Belt. It portrays two men holding hands—one English, one Lenape—to symbolize peace. The chunkier figure wearing a broad-brimmed hat is supposedly William Penn. Whatever the identity of the figures, one thing is clear to the Western eye: they are male. To the English way of thinking, diplomacy was the province of men, and perhaps by the 1680s the Lenapes had learned that Europeans expected to negotiate only with men. But in traditional Indian societies, women were an integral part of the decision-making process, and women continued to attend treaty conferences well into the eighteenth century, in spite of objections by some colonial officials. Perhaps the Native creators of the belt conceived of the figures as generically human, not specifically men. Among the Lenapes, the primary distinctions are between animate and inanimate, human and animal, and the language lacks the gender-specific personal pronouns that English has.[1] So too the wampum belt vocabulary distinguished between humans and animals and symbolic designs, but not between men and women. In the Lenape view, women were incorporated into the belt and the agreement that it represented.

Ever since the treaty belt came into William Penn's hands, it has been

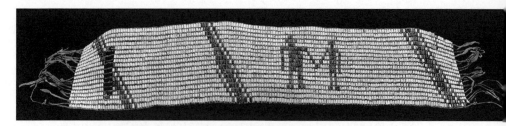

Figure 5 The Great Treaty Wampum Belt, said to represent the agreement between William Penn and the Lenapes at Shackamaxon. Courtesy of the Historical Society of Pennsylvania Collection, Atwater Kent Museum of Philadelphia.

the property of men or male-dominated institutions, and no one has paid any attention to who actually created the artifact.[2] Traditionally, women were responsible for gathering the raw materials and creating the wampum belts used at treaty conferences. This work involved sewing, customarily the work of women in both European and Native American homes. Sometimes the women produced single, individually crafted items; at other times, the work included large quantities of mass-produced goods.[3] Women separated animal sinew to form long threads and carved bone needles for sewing. They gathered shells or traded goods with coastal tribes whose women and children had gathered the shells. Both men and women carved the beads and drilled their holes. Then women planned out the design of purple figures and lines on a white background and began to string the beads, finishing off the ends of each string with decorative knots. Finally, they sewed the strings together. Then the belt went from women's hands into the hands of men. The centuries of silence about women's part in creating the Great Treaty Belt make it an apt metaphor for women's more general historical place on the frontiers between Native Americans and Pennsylvania colonists.[4]

Like their fathers, brothers, husbands, and sons, women lived on multiple frontiers—linguistic, economic, diplomatic, legal, religious, social, and personal—where European, African, and Native women interacted with each other and with men of every ethnicity.[5] Lenape, Oneida, Mohawk, Seneca, Tutelo, and Miami women spoke, traded, and sometimes fought with Swedish, English, French, Scots-Irish, and German women and men. Women interacted cross-culturally on a personal, locally based level far more often than they did in the public arenas of war, diplomacy, and the law. On the social frontier, Native, European, and African women performed everyday activities within a community: sharing hospitality, child-care, gardening, and other work; providing medical care and assisting at each other's childbirths; exchanging information about everything from recipes to gossip.[6] Even the most intimate environment of home and family could become a frontier, not only when strangers came to call or stay overnight, but also on a more permanent basis, through intermarriage, the adoption of captive or orphaned children, and the marriages of children.[7]

Because diplomacy was, in the European world, solely the province of men, Pennsylvania's leaders wondered at the presence of Indian women at treaty conferences and often treated them as irrelevant. As Europeans came in ever-increasing numbers, and Native peoples retreated farther inland, Lenape and Shawnee women came less frequently to these formal meetings. The meetings themselves moved farther from the centers of Euro-American settlement—from Philadelphia, to Lancaster, to Easton, to Fort Pitt—and fewer English and German women came into contact with Native women and men. With the reduction of interactions including women, the danger of interracial violence increased and led to even less cross-cultural contact, creating a vicious cycle that culminated in war. As long as women remained deeply involved at every level of social interaction, there was peace; as women disappeared, or were forced from such interaction, there was war.

Of course, multiple frontiers are simply historians' constructs, categories invented to help make sense of what otherwise would seem a hopelessly messy confusion of past lives.[8] Neither women nor men thought in terms of multiple frontiers; they lived them. In reality, the frontiers all overlapped and intersected. But separating them out for analysis may help us understand women's and men's roles and experiences better. Just as historians have asked, "Did women have a Renaissance?" and questioned whether the American Revolution was merely "an illusion of change" for women, we might ask, "Did women have a middle ground?" And if they did, how did it differ from the "middle ground" of their fathers and brothers, husbands and sons?[9]

In order to find women on the multiple frontiers of colonial Pennsylvania, we need to dig a bit deeper in the archives, as well as at archaeological sites, than historians have done in the past. Bits and scraps of evidence indicate that women were present in all the contact arenas, even if they are largely absent from the official documents and private papers kept by elite males. Historians have all too often taken the silence of the documentary record to mean the absence of women. In order to recover the activities of both Native and European women, we need, as Helen Rountree says, to "go far beyond milking the limited historical resources for all they are worth," although the scattered bits of written evidence on women provide a starting point. But we need to do more than this; we need to "read beyond words," to read the silences in the documents, and to engage in a bit of "controlled speculation."[10] Some of the potential tools for this sort of imaginative (but by no means imaginary) history are ethnographic and historical analogy, genealogy and family reconstitution, and the technologies—such as beadwork and basketry—preserved in Native communities or reconstructed in living history programs. Last but not least, the historian can resort to human talents, such as common sense and empathy, to explore questions of how people might have acted or why they reacted as they did.[11]

As the most visible woman in the written record of interactions between Native people and Pennsylvania colonists, Isabelle Montour serves as a convenient focal point for examining all these frontiers. In summer and fall 1745, Madame Montour—as she was always known in Pennsylvania's records—welcomed a succession of visitors into her home in the central Susquehanna Valley, that great crossroads of the mid-eighteenth century. In early summer, she received interpreter Conrad Weiser and Moravian missionary Joseph Spangenberg, who were on their way home from Onondaga. In September, Moravians Martin and Jeannette Mack came to stay at her house for a month to begin their mission to the local community of Delawares, Tutelos, and Oneidas. Shortly afterward, Isabelle's sister Marguerite and her Mohawk husband passed through with a mule train on their way from the Great Lakes to Philadelphia with packs of furs ready for sale. A few days later, a war party of Iroquois, including one of Isabelle's sons, stayed overnight on their way to fight the Cherokees to the south.[12]

By 1745, Madame Montour was nearly eighty years old and had long since ended her service as an interpreter between colonists and Native peoples. She was then living with her son Andrew and his wife on an island in the Susquehanna, opposite the trading community at Shamokin, at the conflux of major north-south and east-west axes of Pennsylvania's mid-eighteenth century frontier. She had lived all her life at such frontier junctions—in Trois Rivières, Michilimackinac, Detroit, Albany, and Otsatwakin, fifty miles above Shamokin—but her life epitomizes more than just geographic frontiers. As an interpreter and go-between, she had been active on linguistic and diplomatic frontiers, not only between Europeans and Natives but also between the Haudenosaunee and the Great Lakes Indians. She had grown up in the St. Lawrence Valley speaking her mother's Central Algonquin and her father's French, and in the course of her life she had learned a variety of Algonquian and Iroquoian languages, as well as English and some German and Dutch. As the widow of one Oneida warrior and mother to another, she knew military frontiers all too well; she also knew the more pervasive personal violence that sometimes erupted in the absence of full-scale war. As a trader, she bought and sold on economic frontiers. And as a Catholic living on the borderlands between Protestant Anglo-America and traditional Native communities, she lived on multiple religious frontiers.[13]

Underlying these multifaceted frontiers were other, more pervasive arenas for intercultural contact. In the years when she traveled long distances, from the Great Lakes to Albany and back, Montour had enjoyed the hospitality of other women; in her old age, she showed the same hospitality to younger Natives and Europeans. From within her own home, in the various communities where she spent time, she lived on social frontiers. Finally, she embodied the most intimate frontier of all, that within the family itself. The child of a French-Indian marriage, she was part of the early formation of the people called *métis* in New France.[14] After an early marriage to a French voyageur, she married Carondowana, an Oneida war chief. Her siblings married Algonquin, Sokoki, Abenaki, Miami, and French spouses; her children and grandchildren had French, Delaware, Oneida, and Seneca wives and husbands.[15]

Isabelle Montour first entered the public record on the linguistic frontier when she became an official interpreter for New York in 1709, after the murder of her brother, who had led groups of Great Lakes Indians to Albany and interpreted for them. She interpreted for New York Governor Robert Hunter from 1709 until his departure from the colony in 1719, although her name was seldom listed in the minutes. According to one contemporary, Hunter was so suspicious of the official interpreters in Albany that "he had allwise a French woman standing by him who had married one of our Indians to inform him whether the interpreters had done their part truely between him and the Indians." Without her, Hunter said, he would be at a loss, "for I shall never be able to hear the truth but by her means."[16] Montour was one of just a few women who served as official interpreters in the mid-Atlantic region; she may have been the only one to travel as an official go-between, which the records indicate that she did once in 1712, going to Onondaga at the behest of the Albany commissioners.[17]

By 1727, Isabelle Montour was attending meetings between Pennsylvania's Provincial Council and Iroquois or multinational Indian delegations. Although she served as the "interpretress" of record only once, colonial leaders like James Logan and Conrad Weiser consulted with her about events along the Susquehanna, north to Onondaga and west to the Miami country, where she had relatives. A close look at Madame Montour's career reveals that her role may, indeed, have differed from that of male counterparts who served as official interpreters at public treaty conferences. She usually served in a more private capacity, as a personal interpreter for colonial leaders, often at secret meetings with Native representatives. At treaty conferences, her multilingualism enabled her to check the accuracy of other interpreters' work. In between treaties, she gathered information from distant sources through her far-flung family network.

Montour's work behind the scenes of public meetings has parallels in the documented work of women in other instances; it also suggests that there may have been many more undocumented cases of women interpreters. By focusing on the official interpreters taking part in the "clash of empires" saga, historians may have missed evidence that women interpreted in less public forms of cross-cultural interaction.[18]

The English preference clearly was for male interpreters, but when qualified men were unavailable, women took on the work of interpreting at treaty conferences.[19] More often, the records hint, they served as private interpreters for traders, officials, and missionaries. Alice Kirk is the only other female interpreter of record—she interpreted from English into the Delaware language at two 1722 meetings—but she, Isabelle Montour, and other multilingual women interpreted among individuals on more mundane occasions. In 1728, the Provincial Council instructed its male envoys that "it might be advisable that Elizabeth Cornish, who speaks the language, should privately between themselves enter into as close a discourse as possible with Civility [a Conestoga chief] about what news he hears." It was in this private realm of diplomacy, in "close discourse," that women were most valuable in crossing the linguistic frontiers that separated Europeans from Indians in every aspect of life.[20]

Many of Pennsylvania's official interpreters, traders, and go-betweens had multilingual wives or other female relatives who provided essential linguistic expertise. Marriage to multilingual spouses was also an asset to Pennsylvania's traders whose wives, mothers, daughters, and sisters ran the everyday operation of the trading posts that bore their male relatives' names. During the long absences of their go-between husbands, women like Martha Bezaillon and Esther Harris were able to communicate with their Native trading partners along the Susquehanna. Anne Le Tort, the wife and mother of French Huguenot traders and go-betweens, communicated with the Delaware women and men who came to trade, as well as with rival Swedish traders. Later in the century, George Croghan and Thomas McKee had Native wives.[21]

Among missionaries, women often were more multilingual than their husbands. Jeannette Rau was said to be fluent in Mohawk, and Moravians applauded her marriage to Martin Mack in part because her language skills would assist his mission. Other Moravian ministers found spouses who could interpret Algonquian languages for them. Christian Frederick Post married a Wampanoag woman who had been baptized as Rachel; after her death, he married Agnes, a Lenape woman. John Jacob Shebosch married a Mohegan woman in 1746. European second languages were also an asset: when David Bruce and his wife visited the Montours in 1743, her French enabled him to communicate better with the Montour family. Isabelle and her sister Marguerite spoke French, but their husbands and children preferred to speak the native languages of the men, Oneida or Mohawk, and so the Montour women spoke on behalf of their families in encounters with most Europeans.[22]

Euro-American officials and clerks often noted that Indian women attended treaty conferences, usually as an unnamed crowd of "women and children" present at meetings between Natives and Europeans. This pattern remained constant throughout the colonial period. The rhetoric of such meetings was that of brotherhood between Indians and Europeans—"we shall be as friends and brothers," both sides claimed—although the Indian delegation nearly always included women. On one occasion, the Conestoga community made the presence of their women explicit: "An Indian [man] spoke in behalf of the women. We are concluded [included] in the alliances . . . as well as our men; so we ask the governor's protection and desire the governor will kindly accept this present of skins." Governor Keith proclaimed that Pennsylvanians were "ready to protect and defend you . . . as friends and sisters."[23]

In his painting of the Great Treaty, Benjamin West marked the presence of women with a single figure of an Indian mother with her child. The painting, like nearly all the documentary records, does not have any parallel portrait of an English woman, but indirect evidence shows that Euro-American women were present at treaties as well. In 1701, when groups of Delawares, Susquehannocks, and Shawnees visited William Penn at his homes in Philadelphia and Bucks County, Native women were part of the delegation, but only their husbands, fathers, and sons signed the official documents. In July, Penn and his wife, Hannah Callowhill, hosted a party

Figure 6　In the eyes of Euro-Americans, women could appear only on the periphery of diplomatic life. Detail of Benjamin West's *William Penn's Treaty with the Indians,* 1771. Courtesy of the Pennsylvania Academy of Fine Arts, Philadelphia. Gift of Mrs. Sarah Harrison (The Joseph Harrison, Jr. Collection).

of a hundred Delaware Indians from Conestoga at Pennsbury. The Penns were about to return to England after staying in the colony for less than two years, and the Indians were making a farewell visit. The official records note only the group's appearance before the Provincial Council in Philadelphia a few days earlier, but a visiting Quaker minister recorded events at Pennsbury. The Delawares "went out of the house into an open place not far from it, to perform their cantico or worship," John Richardson wrote. After preparing a small fire, the men sat around it in a circle, while the women and children formed an outer circle. They sang "a very melodious hymn, which affected and tendered the hearts of many who were spectators." As they sang, they began to beat on the ground, and then "they rose up and danced a little about the fire, and parted with some shouting like triumph in rejoicing." Two months later, a group of Susquehannocks and Shawnees came to Pennsbury for a similar farewell visit, but in this case no one recorded the presence of the women who surely were there.[24]

Iroquois women and children were in a delegation that met Governor Keith at Conestoga in 1721, but they returned home by canoe up the Susquehanna while the men continued on to Virginia. (Perhaps the men were off to fight the Cherokees, but they did not divulge their purpose to the Pennsylvanians.) On their departure, the Iroquois men thanked the governor for the provisions and his "great care of them and their families."[25] In 1768, Indian agent George Croghan treated with a succession of groups of Native men, women, and children, but he usually recorded numbers for only the adult male participants.[26]

Women on all sides supported treaty conferences and military expeditions through traditional patterns of women's work. At peace conference sites, Delaware and Iroquois women worked with their husbands to erect wigwams for their families to stay in for the duration. Women cooked the meals, mended clothing, and did laundry. On military expeditions, when Indian men traveled without their families, colonial authorities sometimes hired women from local communities to perform these tasks. When delegations came to Pennsbury, Hannah Penn and her servants prepared food and drink for all those in attendance. Upon his arrival at Carlisle in 1758, Christian Frederick Post hired a local woman to cook for the Delaware partners accompanying him westward. Her job was "to dress their victuals, which pleased them well."[27] In the 1760s and 1770s, Pennsylvania women whose husbands or other relatives were stationed at Fort Pitt made shirts and caps by the dozens for trade and baked bread to feed provincial soldiers and their Native allies. Under the threat of conflict, normal domestic economic activity took on diplomatic overtones.[28]

Among Indians, women took part in the decisions made at conferences, as well as the decision to attend a particular treaty in the first place. Time and time again, Indian messengers conveyed their excuses to colonial authorities; "women and children" provided the reason the men could not travel. Shawnees and Cayugas reported that they could not attend a 1722 meeting in Philadelphia because "provisions being very scarce in their towns, they could not leave their families destitute." The other nations had been delayed because "the people of the Five Nations wanted provisions so much, and were so busily employed in looking out for food . . . [and] busy getting victuals as fish out of the rivers and some venison from the woods, but now squashes and pompions [pumpkins] are come they will be able to travel."[29] While men did most of the hunting and women most of the farm work, both were, in fact, family and communal efforts because the usual procedure was for women to process the deer the men killed and for entire families to work together to harvest crops. This communal work pattern was often the reason that Native families chose not to undertake the lengthy journey from the Susquehanna to Philadelphia but asked the governor to come to Conestoga instead, as they did in 1721.[30]

In September 1745, Marguerite Montour and her husband Katarionaka passed through the Susquehanna Valley of central Pennsylvania with a pack of ten horses loaded with deerskins. Marguerite was *métis* and her husband, known to the English as Peter Quebec, was probably Mohawk. They had come from four hundred miles to the west, where they lived most of the year, trading English and French goods for furs and skins from the Miami and other Great Lakes nations. This 1745 trip was probably not unusual; it may well have been an annual event. What was unusual was that Moravian missionaries recorded Marguerite's trip and so left historians with rare documentary evidence of women's involvement in Pennsylvania's eighteenth-century trade.[31]

Pennsylvania's official colonial records give short shrift to Euro-Indian trade as a whole, particularly since much of it was illegal, and they contain few hints of the role of women in it. Older historians who relied on these official records often omitted even those hints of a female presence, obscuring the trail for their successors.[32] Recent historians have done much to recover the Native perspective on the story, but the focus has usually been on Native men and their relationships with European men.[33] Women's names do appear, though infrequently, in the unofficial records of Pennsylvania's trade, in such items as diaries, account books, receipts, and personal correspondence. The few recorded female names represent merely the tip of the iceberg, leaving unmentioned the extent to which women participated, from "harvesting" the animals, to skinning them and dressing the furs and skins, to transporting them for sale. Women were in fact often the silent partners in the trade—silent, that is, in the written historic records that were kept, for the most part, by European men.

The trade required a physical and social space where traders from very different cultures could travel unmolested and meet on common ground to exchange their goods. Trade required peace among nations and among individuals, and peace required communication both on the diplomatic level and on the level of face-to-face personal interaction.[34] It was during personal interaction that women occasionally drew the attention of the record keepers, and usually under particular circumstances: when men were absent, when women had essential skills that no available man had, and when crime or violence made women victims or witnesses.

Trade was a family enterprise among Europeans, Natives, and *métis*. French, English, and German women—wives and daughters of the men registered as "Indian traders" with the Pennsylvania government—were clearly partners in their husbands' and fathers' businesses with Native people. Along the Schuylkill and Susquehanna rivers, Anne Le Tort and Esther Harris ran the trading posts that bore the names of their husbands. Marguerite Montour transported furs as surely as her husband did; she was also the family's interpreter and the family connection to merchants in Philadelphia. Women were in fact not merely participants in trade; they were essential to it. On both sides of the Atlantic, women played a role in creating the goods of the trade, which included many more products than just furs. Deerskins were an important part of the Native contribution to the trade, as were feathers for use in European beds and pillows. Native women in eighteenth-century Pennsylvania, as elsewhere, collected and bundled feathers, trapped small animals, skinned both large and small animals, stretched skins, and dressed furs. They frequently traveled with their husbands to the woods, where together they set up hunting camps. When Weynepeeweyta, a Shawnee, went with her Seneca husband to their usual hunting camp on Monocacy Creek, she was following the traditional pattern of shared labor described by Moravian missionary John Heckewelder:

while her husband hunted, the woman took supplies to the camp and set up "housekeeping." She "takes pains to dry as much meat as she can, that none may be lost; she carefully puts the tallow up, assists in drying the skins, gathers as much wild hemp as possible for the purpose of making strings, carrying-bands, bags, and other necessary articles, collects roots for dyeing." Heckewelder neglected to say that she also prepared food and took care of other daily necessities, not only for her husband but also for other hunters and traders passing through the woods.[35]

"The husband," Heckewelder wrote, "generally leaves the skins and peltry which he has procured by hunting to the care of his wife, who sells or barters them away to the best advantages for such necessaries as are wanted in the family." One Pennsylvania document records the identities of some of these Native women and the sales they made at the Le Tort family's trading post. French Huguenot refugees, Anne and Jacques had come to Pennsylvania in about 1687 with their son James. As the Lenapes and their trade moved westward, the Le Torts moved too, from their first post on the Schuylkill River north of Philadelphia, to the Susquehanna River, near Conestoga, a mixed community of Susquehannock, Conoy, Shawnee, and Delaware Indians. Native women as well as men came to trade, and the Le Torts recorded their transactions, generally identifying the women by their husbands' names. Loosemon's wife bargained for a kettle in exchange for a raccoon skin and the furs of three foxes. Skeetah, the wife of Happecan, received a blanket for two fox furs, and a packet of vermilion dye in exchange for a raccoon. Aspebloagh, a young woman trading in her own right, exchanged a doeskin for a shirt. A Conoy woman traded one fox fur for a looking glass. These women clearly were conducting their own transactions for the products of their own labor—the dressed skins of small animals that they had perhaps trapped themselves—and they traded for goods that they themselves would use. Whereas Lenape and Conestoga men traded for guns, powder, and axes, the women sought cooking pots and fabric and dye for clothing items. Historians have speculated that Indian women pushed men to trade for goods like metal kettles that would lighten their job of food preparation, but the Le Torts' list shows Indian women acting in their own names. Perhaps they were able to bargain directly with the Le Torts because a French woman was an integral part of the business, operating the trading post herself much of the time.[36]

In the one recorded incident where we can hear Anne Le Tort's voice, she appears as a strong woman managing the family business while her husband was away. Competition over trade led to violence between rival European traders, especially if they were of different national origins. The Le Torts' cabin became a focal point for Pennsylvania's trade and a lightning rod for attacks by English and Swedish traders who resented competition and believed that French traders were easy marks because colonial authorities perceived the French and French-allied Indians as the enemy. While Jacques Le Tort was abroad on a visit to England, his wife had given trading goods to the Indians on the promise that furs would be delivered, but rival Peter Yokum, a Swede, tried to persuade the Indians to deliver their furs to him instead in exchange for rum. The Provincial Council summoned Anne to Philadelphia, where Yokum accused her of conspiring with the French and the "French Indians" because she was "tradeing in remote and obscure places where they [the Le Torts] still continue their former way of freedome of commerce with natives." The witnesses against her, Polycarpus Rose and Thomas Jenner, testified that she had become violently angry: "Ryding by the house of Madam LeTort Polycarpus asked her how she did she answered Where have you been hee sayd at Peter Yoakhams she said their was no path for Swades and English rogues there for noe English rogues or Swad shall come on her ground and run in a fury with a horse whip and whipt Polycarpus and called for Lewis to help her a French Canada prisoner taken by our Indians." In her defense, Le Tort said "that the Indians are much indebted to her and little to peter yokum, and that hee came before her hous with rum, and therewith enticed the Indians from her; whereupon shee in her anger, might call him and said Polycarpus Rose names."[37]

European and Euro-American women not only engaged in trade but produced goods for it. On both sides of the Atlantic, they turned American raw materials into finished products, turned skins and furs into clothing and hats, spun and wove cloth to make shirts and blankets for the market. The surviving account books of Pennsylvania Indian agent George Croghan from the 1760s and 1770s offer glimpses into Anglo-American women's activities producing trade goods. Women like Ann Woodhouse, Hannah Swain, and Mary and Ann Girty at Fort Pitt made shirts and caps by the dozens for trade and baked bread to feed Pennsylvania soldiers and their Native allies. Often Croghan and other agents paid the husband, and the account books show only the man's name. But in cases of widows and single women, the payments went directly to those who had done the labor.[38]

On the Native side of the trade, women were essential to transport as well as to production. In May 1723, a New York clerk wrote, "Eighty men besides women and children belonging to several tribes who live upon the borders of Lake Huron and Lake Erie [had] come to Albany to trade." The New Yorkers were following their usual custom of counting only Native men, without giving the number of women and children, because they were interested in the wartime fighting potential of Indian groups, not their overall population. But the Great Lakes Indians traveled in family groups for a very practical reason: women and older children were needed to help paddle and portage the canoes.[39] In March 1725, the Albany clerk noted, Jean Montour and one hired man arrived in three canoes carrying forty bundles of skins. But two men could not have paddled and portaged three laden canoes; women and children must have been their silent companions. In June 1725, Joseph Montour and Jean Fafard came with nine canoes as far as Oneida Falls, where New York traders intercepted them and took their furs. The Albany clerk noted that they had come "in company with nine canoes of Twightwigh [Miami] Indians (among whom they live and are maryd to squas)." Undoubtedly some of the Miami in the nine canoes were these "squaws"—an Algonquian word for women that had not yet acquired its later derogatory connotations—but the clerk failed to note the presence of any women in the party at all.[40]

Where river travel was impossible or difficult, such as traveling west to east in Pennsylvania, horses generally carried the furs to Philadelphia and then European trade goods on the way back. Women were essential to this mode of transport as well. Like Marguerite Montour, other Native women must have helped to lead packs of horses over Pennsylvania's "endless mountains" and across its rivers and streams, which were only partially navigable and at any rate did not traverse the colony from east to west.[41]

Much of women's cross-cultural interaction took place in the familiar, female realm of the home. Native and *métis* women took Euro-American travelers—usually men, but occasionally women also—into their homes. They cooked for their guests, prepared medicines, dressed wounds, and gave or sold them provisions so they could continue their journey. Euro-

American women less often took Indians into their homes, but Quaker and Moravian women and traders' wives sometimes did so, the former out of religious conviction, the latter from practical necessity. These private activities took on political, religious, or economic overtones. On the most personal frontier, Native women had sex (consensual or not) with, and sometimes married, Euro-American or *métis* men.

Penn and other European visitors commented on the generosity of Pennsylvania's Native people. When Marguerite Montour and her husband traveled from Miami country to Philadelphia, they probably spent some nights in Indian villages along the way. Native traditions of hospitality meant that peaceful travelers could reasonably expect to find food and shelter whenever they reached a Native settlement. Along the path in between villages, travelers might find huts or wigwams left by previous inhabitants for shelter or canoes hidden in the brush, left by previous travelers for the use of anyone who needed it. They might even find food, such as the half-deer that Moravian Bishop Spangenberg found along a Susquehanna trail. When Montour family members reached the Susquehanna Valley, they knew they could find a friendly welcome at the home of Marguerite's maternal aunt, Isabelle Montour. These family reunions might have gone completely unnoticed, but in 1745 Pennsylvania's famous "Madame Montour" had other guests as well, Martin and Jeannette Mack, whose journal recorded it.

The demands on Madame Montour's hospitality from summer to fall 1745 were probably unusual in their variety, but many Indian and *métis* women must have hosted colonial leaders, traders, go-betweens, and missionaries, as well as the more traditional guests: traveling relatives, friends, hunters, and warriors. In 1701, William Penn visited Conestoga, where he reportedly stayed in a longhouse. His willingness to lodge in a traditional Indian home made him unusual for a man of his stature, the majority of whom preferred the comforts of even the shabbiest European-style housing, alone or among non-Indian companions. Penn's acceptance of Native hospitality was an act not soon forgotten by his Conestoga "brothers"— and "sisters," the women who cared for him and made him comfortable as an honored guest while he carried on official negotiations with their husbands and other male relatives. Traveling Quaker ministers also found a welcome in Indian villages. In 1706, Thomas Chalkley reported visiting Shawnees and Conestogas at Conestoga, in the company of thirteen or fourteen other Quakers and an interpreter. He met their "queen" or "empress," Canatowa, whose "council to her tribe was, to receive and welcome the missionaries, as they came on a good errand."[42]

In similar circumstances, Count Ludwig von Zinzendorf refused Native hospitality and sat alone, reading, in a small isolated hut. He thereby earned the scorn of Susquehanna's Native women and men and very nearly ruined the Moravian mission to the Indians before it had even begun. Only the considered efforts of later missionaries to stay in the homes of Native and *métis* women made the mission successful in subsequent years. Martin and Anna Mack spent a month at the Montours' island home in 1745 before going to stay with Shickellamy. Madame Montour and her daughter-in-law cared for them and fed them as well as they could at a time of food shortages; in return, the Macks listened to Montour's stories and complaints and, while her son Andrew was away hunting, helped her harvest her cornfield. In 1753, Martin Grube visited Marguerite Montour, by then known as "French Margaret," on the West Branch of the Susquehanna. "She welcomed us to her hut," he recorded in his journal, and "fed us milk and watermelon."[43]

Conrad Weiser and other go-betweens also cemented their relationships with the Indian contacts by staying with the Montours in Otstonwakin, with Shickellamy's family in Shamokin, and with their Onondaga hosts in Haudenausaunee longhouses. Traders slept in Indian villages and hunting camps, although that fact made its way into the historic record only if some sort of problem occurred, since most traders were at best semi-literate and certainly did not keep journals. When the Le Torts had trouble collecting from their native trade partners, they recorded a debt, payable in furs, from a woman they knew only as "our land lady at the Conoy."[44] In 1722, Weynepeeweyta, a Shawnee woman, welcomed English traders John and Edmund Cartlidge to spend the night in the hunting cabin she shared with her Seneca husband; her hospitality only entered the written record because of subsequent dramatic events. The next morning she tried in vain to prevent her husband, Sawantaeny, from getting into a fight with the Cartlidge brothers. When he died as a result of their vicious beating, her status as the relative of a Shawnee chief may have been one factor leading colonial authorities to take the charge of murder more seriously (see chapter 6, below).[45]

Because of the long-standing tradition of hospitality among America's original inhabitants, Europeans who wanted Native trading partners reciprocated, if they were smart. Not all Europeans were. Often fear and cultural prejudice kept them from allowing Indians anywhere near their towns, let alone into their homes, and most never condescended to go into Indian dwellings. Besides the traders and interpreters, Quakers and Moravians were among the few people in English America who both extended hospitality to Native people and accepted Native generosity toward them.[46]

On several occasions, William Penn welcomed groups of Native men, women, and children to his city house in Philadelphia and his country estate at Pennsbury, fifty miles above the city on the Delaware River. In their formal address, the Susquehannock leader Connodagtoh, Shawnee chief Opessah, and other representatives noted how unusual William Penn's behavior was. They thanked him for "giving, us as is well known, his house for our home at all times and freely entertaining us at his own cost and often filling us with many presents of necessary goods for our cloathing, and other accomodations, besides which what he had paid us for our lands, which no governour ever did before him."[47] When William Penn died in 1718, Pennsylvania Indians remembered Hannah Penn's hospitality and sent her a condolence gift of a cloak to wear through the "wilderness of care, or briars, and thorns" she faced as a widow.[48]

As they welcomed guests into their homes, women provided food, clothing, shelter, and medicine across cultural lines. In both European and American cultures, healing was predominantly the province of women, and women were often healers across social and ethnic divides. Madame Montour provided "fever medicine" to Conrad Weiser when he stayed with her on his way to Onondaga, and he recorded, in his Native German, her directions for its preparation for both adults or children. During her stay at Shamokin, Jeannette Mack made visits to Native women who were sick. Providing medical aid was part of her ministry, and she was able to visit Native homes on her own, without an interpreter, because she spoke both Mohawk and Delaware languages.[49]

Hospitality sometimes brought more conflict than understanding, and alcohol abuse by both Euro-Americans and Indians often created problems. As early as 1685, Lenape Indians were complaining about traders getting Indian men drunk and then abusing their wives. The culprits, they said, were Jasper Farmer's servants, who "made the Indians drunk, then lay with their wives, then beat both the men and the wives."[50] A few years after William Penn's visit to Conestoga, Pennsylvania's young deputy governor, John Evans, and his friend, William Penn Jr., did not behave as well toward the colony's original inhabitants as had the Founder. They visited Conestoga, just as Penn Sr. had done, but they exhibited some "lewd" behavior of the "vilest" sort toward "the wives and daughters of the people at Conostogo." Although some Europeans believed that Native women were willing sex partners with any European man, the Pennsylvania proprietor had come to have different ideas and blamed any sexual activity on the young Englishmen involved.[51] By 1706, Shawnee, Susquehannock, and Conoy men had learned to leave their wives at home. Their complaint was that the traders got them drunk and then cheated them of "the fruits of their labor."[52] In 1730, in the midst of a drunken brawl, a Shawnee woman seized a gun from an Iroquois prisoner; the gun went off and hit a "white man," David Robeson, in the leg. At least this was the claim of Lenape leaders, who may have seen the advantage in pinning all the blame on a Shawnee woman and an Iroquois captive. Whether their story was true or not, it bears one similarity to Sawantaeny's murder. In both cases, Native women tried to break up a fight by taking men's weapons away.[53]

Pennsylvania's traders and officials frequently blamed Indian women for the trade in rum, an argument that Indian and *métis* men embraced as a way to absolve themselves of blame. In 1718, Governor Keith told a visiting delegation from Conestoga that he would look into their accusation that traders were illegally bringing rum to their towns. But, he said, Conestoga's leaders bore some responsibility too: "They . . . must endeavour to prevent their women and young people from coming to Philadelphia to purchase and carry up rum from hence, which too many were ready to deliver them privately for their skins."[54] In 1729, the Provincial Council told Delaware, Conestoga, and Conoy leaders that their men "send their women for [rum] to all places where it can be had. . . . If your women would carry none, it would be more easy" to control its sale.[55] By 1754, colonial authorities, however, expressed some doubts about claims that women alone were responsible. They accused Lewis Montour, Andrew's brother, of disturbing the Indians at Aughwick "by bringing strong liquor to them. . . . Lewis sells it very dear to them, and pretends that his Wife, which is an ugly squa, does it."[56] Yet Native men seemed to assume that women would be the ones to travel to buy rum, so perhaps women were the main transporters of alcohol. Sassoonan, the Delaware leader at Shamokin, asked the Provincial Council, in 1731, for traders at Tulpehocken and Paxton to stock rum, "that their women may not have too long a way to fetch it." He did not want rum sold right in Shamokin, but he also did not want the women to have to go all the way to Philadelphia or Lancaster for it.[57]

On the most personal level of all, Europeans and Indians became members of each other's families through adoption or marriage. European and Native children went into the homes of the other group, sometimes willingly as apprentices or "truchements," sometimes unwillingly as captives or slaves. Native women married European men; occasionally European women married Native men. These more personal frontiers are less visible in the written records than the public frontier of diplomacy, but when they do become visible, they show women clearly as active participants in intercultural relations. Like the Susquehanna Valley frontiers outside the home, family frontiers could be much more complex than simply interaction between Indians and Euro-Americans. Living at various times with the French-Algonquin Isabelle Montour were her husband, who was Oneida, their son Andrew and his first wife, who was Lenape, and then his second wife, who was probably Oneida or *métis*, along with their children and Isabelle's niece Catherine, whose father was probably Miami. German, English, and Iroquois visitors regularly added more variety to the already diverse household. Nor was the religious frontier a simple matter of "Christians" divided from Indian "traditionalists." Montour expected Christian religious leaders to baptize her children as eagerly as she remembered Catholic priests baptizing children in New France. She was surprised and hurt when Zinzendorf refused to perform baptisms until a formal mission was established at Shamokin. Religion may have been a contested arena within Montour's own family. Andrew's wife does not seem to have been a Christian. Isabelle was particularly eager to ask the Moravians if there were Delaware Indians at Bethlehem, so perhaps she hoped that they would convert her daughter-in-law and thereby enable her grandchildren to receive baptism there.[58]

Frontier history has become more complex as historians add more layers to the story of contact and interaction along social and cultural borders, in addition to the traditional military and political boundaries. Women are not just another layer to be added to the story but rather a component of each layer, with a presence on military, linguistic, diplomatic, economic, religious, and social frontiers. Recognizing their presence is the first, basic step in researching women's history, "making the invisible visible."[59] As Gerda Lerner has traced it, the initial step for each generation of women's historians has been the resurrection of a few notable women, or "women worthies." The second phase has been "contribution history," the ferreting out of ways that women have "contributed" to the major events of history, as defined by men, through activities like nation building and warfare. The next phase has centered on a series of questions: What have been women's actual experiences? How did they differ from men's experiences? How have women been oppressed and victimized? How have they fought against oppression? This chapter has been an attempt to go behind the silences of the documentary evidence to uncover women's contributions and experiences.[60]

A few "notable" women have been part of the popular historical landscape of the early Pennsylvania frontier since the writing of county and state histories in the nineteenth century and, most visibly, through the commonwealth's historical marker program, which provides a convenient window into the historical memory of women's place on the colonial frontier. One of the earliest markers erected, in 1925, was to "Indian Hannah (1730–1802), the last of the Indians in Chester County"; in keeping with her status as a symbol of a "noble, disappearing race," the marker omits her full name, Hannah Freeman, and her final residence, the county workhouse. Five markers memorialize either Madame Montour or her granddaughter "Queen Esther" Montour; these plaques all identify the women as Indians, ignoring their *métis* identity—a small part of denying what Gary Nash has called "the Hidden History of Mestizo America."[61] One marker identifies Pennsylvania's most famous Euro-American captive of the Indians, Mary Jemison, whose much larger memorial is in New York, where she lived as a Seneca for most of her life. Other women named on markers appear with their husbands or children: Martha Bezaillon, wife of French Indian trader Peter Bezaillon, in Lancaster County; Sarah Shippen Burd, the daughter and wife of traders (Dauphin County); Marie Ferrée, the grandmother of "the first white child in the settlement" of Paradise Township, Lancaster County; and a group of eight Moravian women named with their husbands as part of that sect's Dansbury Mission, destroyed in "the Indian uprising of 1755." Other women are identified only by the husband's names: trader Martin Chartier's "Shawnee wife" and the "Widow Barr," whose Franklin County home provided a refuge from Indian raiders in the 1750s.[62]

The vast majority of wives, daughters, and mothers go unmentioned on the markers memorializing them, just as the trading posts they operated bore only their husbands' names. Anthony Sadowski, John Harris, John Hans Steelman, John Hart, Frank Stevens—none of these men's wives rate any mention, whether they were Native or European, even though most of the women were essential to the business operations. Moravians mentioned women members more frequently than any other group, but, with the exception of the Dansbury Mission marker, all the markers mention only the men: David Zeisberger, John Heckewelder, Christian Frederick Post, John Ettwein. All their wives are invisible. Count Zinzendorf's daughter Benigna accompanied him on his mission and established a school for girls when she herself was only sixteen, but his is the only name on five markers.[63]

The great majority of markers that mention women, though not by name, are memorials to the "massacres" of the Seven Years' War and the Revolution, mostly those committed by Natives on Europeans—the Penn's Creek Massacre; the Lee Massacre; the Leroy Massacre; the Sugarloaf Massacre; the Wyoming Massacre, in which Esther Montour supposedly played a leading role; and the Gnadenhütten Massacre, where traditionalist Natives killed Moravians and Native converts. A few markers commemorate European slaughters of Native women and men, although they rarely use the word "massacre" in this context. Rather, these murders are called the Squaw Campaign and the Paxton Boys' Riots.[64] Looking at the historical landscape of the commonwealth, women's experience on the frontier would seem to have been one of death and destruction, especially for European women. The overemphasis on the few years of war in the 1750s and 1770s skews the entire portrait of the frontier, especially for the image of women's experiences it conveys. In reality, women's cross-cultural experiences were at least as varied as men's.

The final step in Lerner's typology of women's history—once we have uncovered the women of the past, their roles, and their experiences—is to ask how these new insights might transform our general historical knowledge. This essay can only begin to hint at the possibilities. For historians of eighteenth-century Pennsylvania two related questions have loomed large. Why did Delaware, Shawnee, and Mingo warriors attack with such a vengeance in the 1750s after decades of peace? Conversely, why had the peace lasted so long, given the profound hostility that underlay European-Native interaction, hostility evident as early as 1685 in English servants' attacks on Native women? Because women were so often the victims of violence and war, perhaps the answers to these questions lie, at least in part, with them. Peace lasted as long as Native women remained partners, even if silent partners, in the diplomatic process; as long as Native women lived, farmed, and hunted in the Delaware and Susquehanna valleys; as long as the most influential leaders in Pennsylvania's affairs had personal ties, through marriage or adoption, with Native women as well as Native men. When those social connections—relationships in which women were integral—broke down for all but a small minority of traders and missionaries, the possibilities for peace grew dim. The presence of women meant peace; their absence meant war.

II. ❧ FRAGILE STRUCTURES OF COEXISTENCE

5

❧

FEMALE RELATIONSHIPS AND INTERCULTURAL BONDS
IN MORAVIAN INDIAN MISSIONS

AMY C. SCHUTT

Traveling through New England in 1743 on the way to Shekomeko, a Christian Indian village in the vicinity of present-day Pine Plains, New York, the Moravian missionaries Jeannette and Martin Mack depended on the help and guidance of Indians who lived in small settlements in the Hudson and Housatonic river valleys. An "Indian widow" took special pains to help Jeannette through the dangers of a trek during an early February thaw. "Because the deep snows melted," Martin reported, "we proceeded all day in the water," and the Native woman "had to carry my wife across a river." This widow gladly helped Jeannette, whom the Indian saw as her confidante. Leading Jeannette the next day "by the hand," the widow "related to her with many tears what she had done throughout her life" and bemoaned her restless condition.[1]

Eighteenth-century Moravian missionaries, who were German-speaking pietists and recent immigrants to the North American colonies, developed many abiding relationships with Indians. The example of the Indian widow and Jeannette Mack underscores the close connections between Indian and Euro-American Moravian women, who offered physical and emotional support to each other during trying times, including years of dislocation and depopulation among Native peoples. When the widow visited the Moravian mission at Shekomeko, she sought the company of other women.

On her previous visit to the mission, the Macks were not there, but her disappointment in not seeing them was offset by the presence of the missionary Anna Margaretha Büttner, whom the widow "loved inexpressibly." With the missionary Anna Catharina Sensemann also stationed at Shekomeko, the Indian woman "believed now with certainty that she would receive much grace" at the mission.[2]

By the late 1740s, the center of Moravian mission activity among northeastern Indians had shifted from the New York–New England area to the borders of Pennsylvania, where increasing numbers of Native peoples from the Delaware Valley joined the mission. From their headquarters at Bethlehem in the Forks of the Delaware, the area near the conjunction of the Lehigh and Delaware rivers—the territory that, as discussed in chapters 8 and 9, below, had come under Pennsylvania control in the infamous Walking Purchase of 1737—the Moravians sent missionaries farther and farther west throughout the eighteenth century. During these years, they operated missions not only in the Hudson, Housatonic, and Delaware valleys but also eventually along the Susquehanna and in the Allegheny and Muskingum watersheds of the Ohio country. In the process, the Moravians made converts among many Native peoples classified linguistically as Algonquians, although this general label should not mask the ethnic and tribal diversity among them. The Moravians identified many of their first converts as "Mahikander," that is, Mahicans, whose original homelands were in the present-day Albany, New York, area; others they termed "Sopus," that is, Esopus Indians from lands on the west side of the Hudson, farther downriver from the Mahicans; and a few they called "Hoogland" (or Highland) Indians, from east of the Hudson. Another bloc appears as "Wompanosch" in the Moravian records; these were peoples largely from the Housatonic Valley. A large number of early Moravian converts also came from the Forks region near Bethlehem, and the Moravians called these Indians "Delawär." Especially in later years, Moravian missionaries also met peoples they labeled "Mennissing" (that is, Minisinks or Munsees), whose homelands had been on the upper Delaware.[3]

By the time the Moravians encountered the Mahicans and other Hudson Valley peoples in the 1740s, these Indians had already been dispossessed of many of their homelands. During King George's War (1744–48), Euro-American residents of the Hudson region were wary of the presence of Indians among them and of the Moravians' missionary efforts. Rumors abounded that the Moravians were in league with the Indians in a Roman

Catholic plot to support the French during the war. Under pressure from encroaching and increasingly hostile Euro-American neighbors, many of the Mahicans from Shekomeko, along with some Native people from New England, moved to the Delaware Valley, where they lived under the auspices of the Moravians. They first settled near Bethlehem and then, increasingly, gathered with Delawares at a mission called Gnadenhütten on the upper Lehigh. Gnadenhütten grew into a flourishing settlement until November 1755, when other Delawares who were outraged at European expansion attacked the community; most of the missionaries were either shot or burned alive in the house where they had barricaded themselves. For the rest of the Seven Years' War and Pontiac's War, the Moravians struggled to regain a loyal Indian following—a difficult task at a time when Indians and colonists looked on each other with great hostility. After a tenuous peace returned to the borders of Pennsylvania, the Moravians set about rebuilding their seriously damaged operations by establishing the mission of Friedenshütten on the upper Susquehanna and expanding their work to Ohio country sites, including portions of present-day western Pennsylvania and the Muskingum Valley of Ohio.[4]

Throughout years of migrations and struggles, Indian women relied on their relationships with Euro-American missionary women as well as with other Indian women to cope with the drastic changes in their lives. Traditional Native constructions of female identities and roles as well as Moravian constructions of gender powerfully shaped Indian women's responses to Christianity. In many cases, gender identification helped bridge cultural differences and gave Indian and Euro-American women entrée into each other's worlds. These female connections were particularly strong in the 1740s and the 1750s, the first two decades of Moravian mission activity among Native North Americans. Intercultural relationships were tested during wartime and in subsequent decades. Nevertheless, even during the 1760s and 1770s, female relationships would continue to play a major role in Native experiences of Moravian Christianity. More frequently in this later period, however, the task of creating these relationships fell to Indian rather than to Euro-American Moravian women.[5]

Both Indian and Euro-American women living in Moravian communities were constantly confronted with the gender divide. Theirs was a highly segregated world. Although Moravian towns were intensely communal places where men and women called each other "brother" and "sister" and combined efforts in a project to serve Jesus, they were also places where the sexes kept their daily lives and religious practices distinct and often separate. One scholarly view of the evangelical 1740s and 1750s depicts these decades as a time of the "unprecedented appearance of women's voices in the churches"—a fleeting moment when it seemed "there would be 'neither male nor female.'" In one sense, the Moravians reflected this trend, but in another they did not. Indeed, the Moravians touted female spiritual leadership, especially before the 1760s; however, they rooted female ministry in gender difference, not in the erasure of sex-based distinctions. Gender identities were essential to the spiritual practice and theology of Moravian Christianity.[6]

The Moravians contended that people grew in their faith by associating with others among the faithful who were alike in terms of sex, age, and marital status. They believed that women could understand and successfully guide other women because they had comparable experiences. Furthermore, people in the same age range learned much from the example of peers who had similar needs. Finally, Moravians believed that individuals of like marital condition—single, married, or widowed—could help lead each other to Christ. Thus, they organized their communities around these social distinctions. They called their social groupings based on sex and other characteristics "choirs." This choir organization had a major impact on the lives of Moravian women; as one scholar notes, "Women were to preside over the temporal and spiritual lives of each other from birth to death." Women holding the offices of "Eldress (*Ältestin*), Choir Helper (*Chorpflegerin*), Deaconess (*Diakonin*), Choir Labouress (*Chorarbeiterin*), Acolyte (*Acolutha*), and Servant (*Dienerin*)" performed a variety of duties, all of which served a spiritual function, such as preparing other women to take Communion or assisting in the Communion service itself. In addition to these offices, one historian concludes that by 1758 "a total of twenty-seven women were ordained as *Priesterinnen* (female Presbyters or ministers)" by the Moravians, although she acknowledges that the records are vague about their actual roles.[7]

Northeastern Algonquian peoples also constructed distinct though connected worlds for men and women. Delaware and Mahican rituals at first menstruation and in preparation for marriage, for example, highlighted the separateness of female experience. Associating first menstruation with spiritual power, native peoples saw it as an occasion for following carefully prescribed actions. According to the Moravian missionary David Zeisber-

Figure 7 Moravian women—European, Native American, and African—
presented to Christ. Johann Valentin Haidt, *The 24 Single Sisters Choirs,* 1751.
Unitätsarchiv, Herrnhut, Germany.

ger, a young woman entered a period of isolation and fasting at this time, among the Delawares living in a "separate hut . . . with the blanket over her head." An older woman accompanied the girl, keeping her apart from all others, feeding her sparingly, and forbidding her "to do any work." After coming home "looking black, grimy and dishevelled" from "lying about in dust and ashes the whole time," the girl was "washed and dressed in new garments." Among the Mahicans, similarly, a girl menstruating for the first time lived "alone in the woods" and might stay away between fourteen and forty days. Zeisberger described a subsequent two-month period during which the young woman was "required to wear a cap with a long shield, so that she can neither see any one readily, nor be seen," on the completion of which she was free to marry. This practice was apparently quite old. William Penn remarked in the late seventeenth century that before marriage young Indian women of the Delaware Valley donned "something upon their Heads for an Advertisement, but so as their Faces are hardly to be seen."[8]

In addition to such ceremonies that marked female identity, occupational differences and daily responsibilities established boundaries of maleness and femaleness. Men and women pursued distinct though mutually supportive economic activities. Women's traditional duties included planting, cultivating, and harvesting crops. Zeisberger explained that Native women "plant[ed] corn, principally, making of this their bread, which is baked in the ashes, and preparing with it various dishes. Besides, they raise[d] pumpkins of various kinds, potatoes, beans and other vegetables." Moravian John Heckewelder described such communal agricultural work as an opportunity for women to construct relationships: "The tilling of the ground at home . . . is frequently done by female parties, much in the manner of those husking, quilting, and other frolics (as they are called), which are so common in some parts of the United States." Female work was intergenerational; as Zeisberger wrote, the young were "accustomed to work by their mothers, for as the women must pound all the corn in a stamping trough or mortar, they train[ed] their daughters in this and also in such other work . . . as cooking, bread-making, planting, making of carrying-girdles and bags."[9]

Men traditionally pursued their own gender-specific responsibilities, such as hunting and warfare. Although wives handled the drying of animal skins and the preparation of peltries, men had primary responsibility for tracking and shooting game. As experienced hunters, they had the duty of instructing the community's boys in becoming skillful in these endeavors. Often this education was indirect. Youths listened to aged hunters who were "conversing together on those subjects, each, in his turn, relating how he acted, and opportunities for that purpose." Thus, when a boy "killed his first game, such as a deer or a bear," family members praised his having "listened attentively to the aged hunters, for, though young, he has already given a proof that he will become a good hunter himself." Another clearly defined male role was that of the warrior. " 'A warrior's conduct ought to be manly, else he is no man,' " Indians told Heckewelder. A crucial phase of a boy's training was the seeking of a spirit, or manitou, to guide him through life. As part of an initiation ritual, he was put on a strict fast and expected to swallow powerful draughts that induced visions and trances, through which he hoped to receive a guardian spirit who would explain "what he was before he was born and what he will be after his death." Armed with these insights after undergoing physical trials, a youth had passed through an important phase in his training for warfare. Not all boys became warriors, however. Guardian spirits sometimes informed them that they were "not designed for a military life" and "that they are to be physicians, sorcerers, or that their lives are to be devoted to some other civil employment."[10]

By the mid-eighteenth century, boundaries between traditional male and female pursuits were shifting. A significant change occurred in Moravian missions where Indian men were encouraged to participate in agricultural work, previously the woman's domain. At Gnadenhütten, the Moravians usually expected Indian men to represent households when fields were divided among the converts. During a conference in 1747, for example, the missionaries recorded land allotments for six Indian men. And occasionally men did agricultural work for wages. In 1748, for instance, David, who was of mixed Mahican and Wompanosch parentage, used a horse belonging to the Indian Nathanael to plough a field for the Delaware Gottlieb, receiving payment from the Moravians "because Gottlieb" was "very poor."[11]

In spite of the increasing role of men in agricultural production, there were still distinct, though permeable, boundaries between the work of Indian men and of Indian women living in Moravian missions. Women maintained a prominent and even dominant place in the regular tasks of planting, hoeing, and harvesting, and they requested and obtained land when the Moravians assigned lots, particularly if they were living without a husband. At the 1747 conference, the single woman Esther requested one acre for planting, and Sara, whose husband David was absent for an indefinite amount of time, also asked for an acre. Female converts played crucial agricultural roles in the eighteenth century, although some of their tasks, such as haying, were now tied to the European introduction of livestock. Often women worked the fields while men engaged in building projects at the mission. In May 1747, most of the men at Gnadenhütten worked on building a mill dam while "the remaining went with the sisters to hoe corn." The following month, the men began to construct a "milk-house," and "the Sisters went hay-making." In 1767 at the Friedenshütten mission on the Susquehanna, "the Sisters worked diligently in their fields." Women also were still responsible for cooking, preparing foods from corn, meat, vegetables, and wild berries, and gathering hemp to make carrying bags, as they had for generations. They handled these and other traditional tasks while Native men continued to go on frequent hunting trips.[12]

A combination of Moravian attitudes about the importance of sex-segregated activities and the prevalence of gender-defined roles in daily occupations intensified relationships among women in Moravian missions. Although women and men did not worship and work completely apart from each other, women in Moravian missions expected to spend a large amount of time laboring and praying with other women and girls. Besides their shared economic activities, they created strong female bonds through numerous private conversations, through sharing responsibilities of leadership, through mutual assistance in childbirth and in the rearing of children, through specialized Moravian gatherings and groups for women and girls, and through school settings where female teachers and female students interacted with each other.

Conversations between women about spiritual matters were a frequent part of life in Moravian missions. Moravians believed it was essential to examine the state of each individual's heart for evidence of a deep personal connection with Jesus. Female leaders took over much of the responsibility for holding heartfelt conversations with the women of the community. At Gnadenhütten, Jeannette Mack paid innumerable visits to Indian women in their homes, where she conversed with them about their religious beliefs. During such talks, Indian women expressed many of their innermost thoughts and wishes. Absorbing the evangelical spirit of the mission, the Wompanosch Esther revealed to Mack a longing to become a missionary herself and "to go to St. Thomas" with a Moravian contingent working on that Caribbean island. The missionary Anna Margaretha Bechtel, wife first of Gottlob Büttner and then of Johann Georg Jungmann, worked closely with Indian women from 1742 until 1781 with only a few interruptions. Like Jeannette Mack, Anna Büttner/Jungmann listened to female Indians express their deep spiritual needs. The days before Christmas were always a time of spiritual preparation in Moravian missions, and during this period in 1748 Jungmann "visited . . . in the huts and had an opportunity to hold a heart-felt address with several"—probably women because a number of the men were away hunting. At times, Jungmann and Jeannette Mack worked as a team. Together they met with the Wompanosch Sarah, who was the wife of the Moravians' first convert at Shekomeko, pointing out to her "how necessary it was to know one's heart."[13]

Indian women built relationships with both Jeannette Mack and Anna Jungmann as confidantes and expressed sorrow when these and other Moravian women planned to leave mission villages. Martin Mack described the Shekomeko Indians' disapproval of the plan for Jeannette to go to Bethlehem in the later stages of her pregnancy; their opposition was even greater because Anna Jungmann was already away from the mission, affording them no female missionary as a confidante. Martin Mack wrote, "I went to visit our Brethren and Sisters and told them I should soon go to Bethlehem. They askd immediately if my Wife went too, when I told them yes, they askd if we should soon come back again. The Sisters were not well pleased that she should go away too, while Buttner was not yet come home, and *Consequently they should have no Body to whom they could freely speak their Minds*." In 1761, the Indian women at the Wechquetank mission near the Blue Mountains feared the missionary Margaretha Elisabeth Grube might leave them permanently because she seemed near death. Grube had often been ill over the previous few years. While living at Pachgatgoch in Connecticut, she suffered from a cough, fever, fainting spells, and even a hemorrhage. By early 1761, she was forty-five years old and once again extremely ill. After she recovered enough to participate in a Maundy Thursday foot-washing service, the Indian "sisters were especially gladdened" to see Grube "well again." They had "prayed hard to the Savior to let her stay still longer." As "poor children" unable to "succeed without a Sister," they thanked the Savior for her renewed health.[14]

Joining together to face death strengthened bonds between women in Moravian missions. Anxieties about Grube brought Native women together to pray that she might be spared. In other cases when death seemed inevitable, women expected to end life surrounded by those in relationship with them. The death of the Delaware Beata demonstrated how much she valued one last moment of comradeship with Margaretha Grube to ease her passage to the next life. Beata had been baptized in 1746 at Gnadenhütten, where she first lived as a widow and then as the wife of the Wompanosch Zachaeus. Her life had been one of many trials, including seeing ten of her eleven children precede her in death. Because she was extremely ill, the Moravians expected her to die on the evening of March 5, 1762; however, she lived yet one more day. "I know certainly why the Savior did not take me to himself last night," Beata proclaimed from her deathbed. "It was because I still had something left to say to Sister Grube. . . . Now I am completely done, and I have nothing more weighing on my heart. I go now with joy to kiss the wounds of Jesus."[15]

Frequently Indian women ministered to each other through spiritual conversations. Esther, who had been baptized in 1742 at Shekomeko, was one of the most influential women among the Indian converts. Sometimes she knew the feelings of other Indian women in the missions before the missionaries learned of them. Sara "testified to Esther: she was ashamed that she believed that the [Moravian] Brethren did not love her. She feels now, however, otherwise in her heart." When Sara wished to have her newborn child baptized, she approached Esther, saying "if her child could be baptized, she would certainly consider it a great mercy." Esther was also a point of contact for Native women visiting the mission for the first time. One Delaware "widow with three children," who had come to Gnadenhütten from the Susquehanna, approached Esther and complained that "she was very poor" and "had not a bite to eat for herself or for her children." Esther was the conduit for ensuring that the woman received nourishment, possibly using the occasion to converse on spiritual topics.[16]

Some of the closest relationships between Indian and Euro-American women included those individuals, such as Jeannette Mack and the Indian Esther, who shared the oversight of community members. As was true in predominantly Euro-American Moravian communities, women in Native American missions served as spiritual leaders of other women. Esther's and Mack's relationship blossomed as they cooperated in overseeing the women at Gnadenhütten. The Gnadenhütten records demonstrate how each depended on the other as she exercised her authority: "Esther held a fellowship meeting with Mack about her own condition as well as about how things were with the other Sisters in their huts." Mack depended on

Esther to help her understand how Indian women responded to the Moravians, to learn "how things were" in Indian homes. Together they discussed the situation of female members of the community, fulfilling their supervisory role jointly rather than individually. That Esther continued to confide in Mack about her own beliefs demonstrated the depth of their relationship.[17]

Anna Margaretha Mack, Martin's second wife, and another missionary, Johanna Schmick, organized religious events that encouraged bonding between themselves and female Indian leaders, sometimes called *Arbeiterinnen* (laborers) or *Conferenz-Schwestern* (conference sisters). At separate "class" or "band" meetings, the *Conferenz-Schwestern* could pray, sing, and witness to one another. "Toward evening," one spring day in 1754, "Sisters Anna and Johanna had a class meeting with the conference sisters." About a month later they held "a nice band meeting with the conference sisters." With these small-group meetings, the Moravians built unity among female leaders, both Indian and Euro-American.[18]

One important basis for the relationship among Indian and Euro-American women in Moravian missions was their shared experience of motherhood. Women depended on each other to deal with the difficulties of childbirth and to assuage anxieties about their newborns. The Indian mothers Beata and Sarah had called on Jeannette Mack to help them through labor and delivery. Mack acted as confidante and probably midwife for Sarah, whose labor was prolonged. After a Communion service at Gnadenhütten, Sarah returned home and "immediately began to have pains." She quickly called for Jeannette Mack to "remain with her all night as she was certainly about to give birth." While Jeannette tended to her through an agonizing travail, Sarah found comfort in her belief that, for her sins, her "Savior suffered greater pain. . . . And she continued on this topic until the child was born." Mack's duties were less onerous when Beata gave birth to her child because her labor was shorter. After attending a worship service, Beata "sent for Sister Mack" who helped her give birth in about an hour. The missionary Anna Rauch assisted in the delivery of the daughter of the Indians Lydia and Philippus and "blessed the child by means of a heartfelt prayer."[19]

Missionary women were not always present at the births of the children of Indian converts but sometimes instead paid visits soon after delivery. Although the Wompanosch Elisabeth "gave birth in the woods" near Pachgatgoch, Anna Catharina Sensemann came soon after to visit the mother with her newborn daughter. Similarly, immediately following the birth of a daughter to an Indian named Magdalena, the missionary Martha Büninger brought "something to her for her comfort." And Anna Jungmann visited the Delaware Juliana following the birth of a son who, Juliana joyfully announced, had been "baptized with the Savior's blood" and had a "new name," Gottlob.[20]

In a few instances Euro-American women depended on Indian women to help them through childbirth and its related difficulties. At a small Susquehanna mission, Johannes Roth reported that Indians had helped his wife Marie recover after the birth of their first child. Although he did not specify the sex of these helpers, it is likely most were women. In the Ohio country, the Indian Anna Salome "was accounted the best midwife among the Indian Sisters," and she attended the delivery of a son named Christian David to the missionary Anna Maria Sensemann. Because some Moravians considered Euro-American women to be physically weaker than their Indian counterparts, they believed that they needed substantial help during childbirth. Zeisberger expressed admiration at the "very strong bodily constitution" of Indian women. He seemed impressed that some Indian women "go into the woods by themselves and bring their children to the house when they have seen the light of day."[21]

Still, there were limits to how willingly Moravians turned to Indian women to assist in the births of their children. Moravian missionary women sometimes sought out Euro-American midwives in other settlements, even though Indian women were available nearby to help. This was true of Jeannette Mack in 1744 and of the missionaries Schmick in 1753 and Jungmann in 1751 and 1755. Heckewelder also voiced his preference for a Euro-American woman to assist his wife Sarah in delivering their first child. Everything was going well as they awaited the baby, but he "was not without worry and difficulty." Although there were "skilled Indian sisters who could be used in this matter," Heckewelder believed their talents in delivering infants "suit[ed] their own better than to such a weak person as Sarah." Only after finding a Euro-American woman to help his wife could he feel "reassured about the matter."[22]

Despite these obstacles, other circumstances encouraged association and friendship. The Delawares and Mahicans came from matrilineal societies that stressed the bond between women and children. Kinship bonds were strongest in the female line, outweighing the connections between husbands and wives in nuclear family units. In the communities Indians

and Moravian missionaries constructed together, motherhood was similarly highly valued. Moravians described the Trinity as a holy family, consisting of a papa, the little boy Jesus, and a Holy Spirit who offered
"mother-care" and spoke in a "mother-voice." Preparing the converts for
a Communion service, a missionary wrote, "we saw the dear Mother" was
acting upon the hearts of the prospective communicants. Out of a common sense of responsibility for children and shared value in the roles of
mothers, then, Indian and Euro-American women constructed friendships
in Moravian missions.[23]

Indian and Euro-American women participated in baptismal ceremonies for the children of one another, serving as sponsors, or godparents, for
baby girls. As sponsors, these women blessed the recipient of baptism, laying their hands upon the child's head. Because a Euro-American child
might have one or more Indian godparents and an Indian child one or
more Euro-American sponsors, these baptisms signified and strengthened
the bonds between participating Indians and Euro-Americans. In 1758
three Indian women—Esther, Bathsheba, and Rachel—were sponsors for
the newborn girl of the Macks. At the 1763 baptism of the daughter of the
missionaries Joachim and Christina Sensemann, the child was brought into
the church, where her godparents were the Indians Martha, Thamar, and
Johanna. When Johann Ludwig, son of the missionaries Marie and Johannes Roth, was born in 1773, the Mahican Christina shared in sponsoring
the child with Zeisberger and Anna Jungmann and her husband. The sponsors for Beata, the newborn daughter of the Indian couple Lydia and Philippus at Gnadenhütten, included several Euro-American women as well
as the Indian Esther.[24] One of Beata's sponsors was the missionary Anna
Rauch. Mutual concern about Beata forged bonds between Rauch and the
mother Lydia, who clearly saw Anna as a major participant in the rearing
of her child. When Beata was three months old, Lydia announced to Rauch
that "because she had no children, so she shall have this one for her child."
According to the Gnadenhütten records, "Anna was astonishingly glad of
this. Many would not have been so glad if they had been given £1000."
More than likely the Indian woman did not see herself being entirely replaced as Beata's mother but rather saw Rauch as a powerful supplement
to her own mothering. Nonetheless, the episode provides a striking example of the trust between female converts and missionaries.[25]

Sex-segregated religious meetings also offered opportunities for female
relationships to flourish. Baptized Indian women met apart from men,

girls apart from boys, and widows apart from widowers. Typically, women ran the meetings for women and girls. Esther held at least one women's meeting at Shekomeko in New York. Jeannette Mack and Jungmann held widows' worship services at Gnadenhütten, as did Anna Sensemann at Pachgatgoch. In the midst of a deadly smallpox epidemic in 1764, "Sisters Grube and Schmick held several fellowship meetings for the Sisters and the older girls," which had an especially powerful effect on the unbaptized girls. Sometimes these sex-segregated meetings included love feasts, which were simple meals representing the Lord's Supper and the shared meal or *agape* of the early Christians.[26]

A ritual for mothers and mothers-to-be at Gnadenhütten in 1747 brought Indian and Euro-American women together around their common concern for child rearing. "The white sisters today had a love feast with the Indian sisters who have children and with those who are pregnant," the mission diary recorded, noting that the women were moved to tears as they expressed their heartfelt desires to one another. These meetings were a version of the mothers' groups that met at Bethlehem in this same time period. Some of these gatherings were for pregnant women because the Moravians believed that the maternal role began during pregnancy. Expectant mothers, according to Moravian thinking, needed to be cautious because they had already begun to influence their unborn children. Whether in specialized women's meetings or in less formal conversation and whether in Bethlehem or in mission towns, Indian and Euro-American women shared their thoughts and desires, which often centered on their children.[27]

Female relationships in Moravian missions spanned generations, as when teachers worked with students in sex-segregated schools. While informal education occurred in choir and band meetings and through conversations, the Moravians also utilized formal classroom schooling. Probably the most influential teacher was Anna Jungmann, who started a school for Indian girls at Gnadenhütten in September 1747 and taught there, with some interruptions, until the mission's demise in 1755. Jungmann had previous teaching experience among Euro-American children, having worked in the Falkner Swamp school and in the Bethlehem nursery, which housed and educated Moravian children from about age eighteen months. After many years of service, Jungmann was consecrated a deaconess, an office that included the duty of assisting the minister during Communion.[28]

One of Jungmann's prime teaching qualifications was her familiarity with Indian languages. The Moravians took a multilingual approach, and they expected their missionaries to learn Native languages and to use them as part of schoolroom routines. Along with her first husband, Gottlob Büttner, Anna had studied Mahican at Shekomeko. In 1743 she was able to offer her first address in Mahican. By the time she opened the Gnadenhütten school for Indian girls, she had several years' experience in the language. At Gnadenhütten she also began to learn Delaware, and by 1752 it was reported that she could converse in it. As more and more Delaware converts joined the mission in the 1750s, her knowledge of their language became invaluable.[29]

Linguistic ability, combined with Jungmann's concentrated attention on young women and girls, built significant relationships with her students. On a number of occasions the Moravians reported that Indian children were, as one report put it, "always so happy when they are able to go to school." Girls felt free to converse with their teacher, probably because they knew that she could speak in their own language and paid particular attention to female concerns. Jungmann also cared for her pupils outside of class. One fourteen-year-old who may have attended school under Jungmann's tutelage turned to the missionary when she felt the need to express her spiritual longings. The girl "stood at the door of a house and wept many hot tears and asked Sister Jungmann" that the missionaries "remember her and baptize her with the Savior's blood."[30]

Relationships between Indian and Euro-American women were especially strong in the Moravian missions of the 1740s and 1750s. The rich evidence from this period contrasts with material from later decades, suggesting a shift in female relationships. During the 1740s and 1750s, a sizable number of Euro-American women were active in the missions, including Jungmann, Jeannette Mack, Anna Margaretha Mack, Büninger, Rauch, Schmick, Grube, Anna Catharina Sensemann, and Margaretha Hagen. Yet, when the Moravians redirected their mission work to the Susquehanna Valley in 1765, no female missionaries came to the new mission Wyalusing (renamed Friedenshütten) until about a year later when Schmick arrived. She was the sole Euro-American woman at Friedenshütten until the arrival of Jungmann in the latter part of 1769. The next year, Marie Agnes Roth joined her husband at the nearby Schechschequanunk mission. These three female missionaries later moved to Ohio country missions, although Roth returned east in 1773. Sarah Heckewelder, Anna Maria Sensemann, and

Susanna Zeisberger would also go to the Ohio country, but not until the early 1780s. Thus, for much of the period between 1765 and the end of the Revolution, Jungmann and Schmick were the only female Moravian missionaries who spent significant time with the Indians, even though several hundred Indians joined the missions during these years.[31]

The decline in the number of active female missionaries came at a time when the Moravians were restricting women's roles in church and community life.[32] Given the limitations on female leadership and the decline in the number of female missionaries on the frontier, one would expect to see more apathy, as well as resistance, to Moravian Christianity among Indian women after 1765. Interestingly, although it becomes more difficult to trace Indian–Euro-American female relationships, many Indian women still eagerly joined the Moravians. Between 1765 and 1781, just under two hundred female Indians were baptized, including both infants and a substantial number of older girls and women.[33]

Schmick's and Jungmann's long-standing connections with Indian women contributed a great deal to these conversions.[34] Even more important, however, was the work of the female converts themselves, especially those who held mission offices as *Helferinnen* (helpers) or *Arbeiterinnen* (laborers). Indian women maintained the spiritual work they had done in the 1740s and 1750s and became even more important after 1765 as Euro-American women became less available. Church leaders at Bethlehem recognized the need for loyal and active Christian Indian women to carry on mission work when they deemed the revolutionary frontier too dangerous for Euro-American women. In 1778 they sent the following instructions to the Ohio country: "Because the [Indian] Sisters have no [Euro-American] woman to work among them . . . choose faithful and beloved Indian Sisters whom the others accept."[35]

Despite the obvious influence of Moravian terminology, Indian women continued to interpret Christianity for each other, putting it in a familiar language and cultural context for potential and recent converts.[36] The deathbed statement of the convert Sophia demonstrates that they continued to see themselves as spiritual guides to other Indian women long after the 1750s. Sophia had joined the Moravians in 1764 and soon married a Mahican from a prominent Christian Indian family. As she lay dying in Ohio in 1801, she bemoaned her inability to accompany a group planning to leave soon on a mission to the White River in present-day Indiana. "I would willingly have travelled with my husband . . . , but cannot," she said. Sophia spoke proudly of her own past efforts: "I have lived many years in the congregation and have seen how it has gone with us. When our Saviour and our teachers wanted us to move to a new place, in order to make known the gospel to the heathen, I have always found that it was good to go there." Urging other able-bodied Indian women to make the trek, she held up the promise of loving relationships with the women on the White River: "I commission you to go thither in my stead. You are aged and have experience: go and speak to the women there that you may have many sisters."[37]

Sophia's statement underscores how the formation of female relationships—the process of bonding as "sisters" to one another—powerfully shaped Indian women's experience of Christianity and structured an important element of social connections across Pennsylvania's Euro-Indian frontier. At the height of female missionary activity during the 1740s and 1750s, Indian and Euro-American women constructed close ties that ensured loyalty to the Moravians for years to come. As the Moravians became more patriarchal and restrictive toward Euro-American female missionaries, Indian women countered this trend by keeping their work central to the missions, building on their traditional expectations of a matrilineal Indian world with gender-specific roles. They did not assume all the tasks that Euro-American women had performed—none apparently taught school, for example. But their discourses and participation in mission workers' conferences, and their continuing economic contributions, guaranteed a female presence and authority in Moravian missions. Given the turmoil of life along frontiers, relationships between Indians and Euro-Americans were always fragile, requiring careful tending and sustained commitment. Indian and Euro-American women in Moravian missions offer remarkable examples of such commitment. Nevertheless, by the 1760s the Moravians' decreasing reliance on Euro-American women missionaries led to a decline in intercultural female relationships in their missions, contributing to the widening of the social and political gap across frontiers.

6

⚜

THE DEATH OF SAWANTAENY AND THE PROBLEM OF
JUSTICE ON THE FRONTIER

JOHN SMOLENSKI

In early January 1722, near the Pennsylvania-Maryland border, Sawantaeny, a Seneca man who lived in an ethnically mixed Indian settlement
with his Shawnee wife Weynepeeweyta, was killed by the English trader
John Cartlidge. The short version of the story is really quite simple.[1] Sawantaeny died after a drunken argument with Cartlidge that began when
the Seneca accused the trader of failing to deliver all of the rum he was
owed. Sawantaeny may or may not have gone back to his cabin to get his
rifle, but in any case the disagreement quickly became physical. Cartlidge,
thinking his life was endangered, assaulted Sawantaeny, eventually kicking
him to death. With the help of Civility (Tagotolessa), a Conestoga Indian
who had served as a translator and go-between on the Pennsylvania frontier, John and his brother Edmund Cartlidge, also a trader and present at
the assault, arranged a hurried condolence ceremony and burial for Sawantaeny in the hopes that authorities in Philadelphia would not discover what
had transpired.

The Cartlidges' attempts were in vain; word of the Seneca's death
reached Philadelphia, and the Provincial Council of Pennsylvania sent officials James Logan and Colonel John French to the frontier town of Conestoga to investigate in March. Finding substantial evidence that John
Cartlidge was responsible, they decided to try him according to English

law. When French and Logan realized it was impractical "to get such a Number of Christians to undertake that Journey [to Conestoga] as would constitute a legal jury," John and Edmund were hauled to Philadelphia for trial. After releasing the Cartlidges on bail, the Provincial Council sent word to Conestoga to try to recover Sawantaeny's body so that the court could proceed. The spring and summer brought several councils between the provincial government and diplomats representing Delaware, Shawnee, Conestoga, and Iroquois Indians, with each tribe offering its own take on what the Cartlidges' fate should be and how Sawantaeny's death should be resolved. In September, the Iroquois diplomat Tanachaha asked Pennsylvania's Governor William Keith for clemency for John Cartlidge. Against the wishes of some provincial legislators, Keith set Cartlidge free and gave the Iroquois a gift of £110.[2] Relations between Indians and Pennsylvanians along the frontier returned to normal—for the early eighteenth century. Edmund was even able to obtain a license from the legislature to buy and sell Indian lands years later.

This version of the story of Sawantaeny's death raises as many questions as it answers. Why was it so difficult to convene a jury on the frontier? Who would have composed the jury in a case such as this? Why did representatives from different Indian groups ask that Cartlidge be granted clemency? Why was the government of Pennsylvania so divided on granting that request? It also raises questions about the significance Sawantaeny achieved in death. Why did this particular instance of frontier violence come to involve representatives from so many different nations—Conestogas, Shawnees, Delawares as well as Iroquois? Why, to paraphrase historian James Merrell, has Sawantaeny's death proven so difficult to bury?[3]

The answers to these questions lie in the ways that Sawantaeny's death has served as a folktale of justice for those who have examined it.[4] Legal scholar Robert Cover argues that all legal systems, at their root, rely on what he has termed "sacred narratives of jurisprudence" to justify their legitimacy. These narratives, either in the form of written texts or oral histories, grant laws the power of jurisdiction over the communities that circulate them. The weight of a legal system's legitimacy ultimately lies in the power its sacred narratives hold for those within and, even more, for those at the edges of that legal community. Such narratives are invoked not only to instantiate the legal past of the community but also to justify the sovereignty of its legal narratives over another's. These folktales are "jurisgenerative" and "jurispathic" at the same time; the very mythic authority that is capable of bringing a moral and legal community into being is also capable of destroying alternative normative worlds by denying the power or authority of their sacred narratives of justice.[5]

Sawantaeny's death rests at the border between two sets of competing folktales of justice, one historical and the other historiographical. From a historical perspective, the diplomatic councils convened in spring and summer 1722 to discuss how to handle Sawantaeny's death were themselves contests among legal myths and historical accounts. Each side in the negotiations told very different stories of recent events on the frontier, accounts that were contextualized in the legal myths of Pennsylvania's ambassadors on the one hand and of Indian negotiators on the other.[6] Both the Indians living on the Susquehanna and the Iroquois justified their authority on this matter by invoking the idealized history of their friendship with William Penn, the province's founder. At the same time, Governor Keith's position relied on a very different understanding of Penn's history with the Indians, one that cast the proprietor's relationship with the Indians as a benevolent paternalism, not a reciprocal friendship. Settling the jurisdictional questions surrounding Sawantaeny's death meant adjudicating these different narratives.

From a historiographical perspective, interpretation of the Sawantaeny case presents a moral problem as well. Homicides on North American frontiers have often allowed historians to tell their own stories about justice in early American history, looking specifically at whether Native peoples received treatment under the (English) law equal to that received by Euro-Americans.[7] The scholars telling these folktales of justice have attempted, in Alden T. Vaughan's words, mostly to determine whether "the colonists conscientiously applied impartial justice when Indians were the aggrieved party."[8] This project, however, has often uncritically accepted contemporary Euro-American standards of justice as a norm from which to evaluate the past. Moreover, where Indians were accorded different—and, implicitly, unequal and unjust—treatment before the bar, the difference has been attributed solely to Euro-American prejudices, motivations, and choices.[9]

The difficulty with this line of reasoning is that it reduces complex cultural encounters into a narrative of present-day Americans judging "national characters" from their past.[10] This approach, which James Axtell has suggested is common to many moral histories of European-Indian conflict, runs the risks both of casting indigenous peoples as objects rather than

actors in historical narratives and of presuming Euro-American notions of
equal treatment before the law as the normative standard of justice.[11] It
generates folktales of justice that easily solve the jurisdictional problem
between past and present, condemning Euro-American actors in the past
for failing to live up to conceptions of due process and equal treatment
before the law held (roughly) in common between present and past.[12] It
relies on a sense of kinship between modern historians and readers, on
the one hand, and colonial Euro-Americans, on the other—an explicitly
antifiliopietistic stance from which the sins of "our" founding fathers can
be judged. These stories of justice serve a jurisgenerative function, reminding their audience of its collective failures to live up to its ideals in the past,
with an implicit challenge to further its commitments to these ideals in the
present and future. But by ignoring alternative narratives told from a Native perspective, they also serve a jurispathic function, limiting participation in debates over national *nomoi,* past, present, and future, to Euro-
Americans, past, present, and future. These accounts are weakened by their
tendency to "face west" and to see these events from a provincial point of
view, rather than "facing east" to examine them from the Native perspective.[13]

   This chapter attempts to move beyond historical moral critiques that
stress the equal treatment question by exploring the folktales of justice told
by Pennsylvanians and Indians on their eighteenth-century frontier. The
debate over legal authority around the time of the Seneca's death—a debate that intensified after the incident on the Monocacy—created an arena
of conflict for Natives and newcomers alike. Understanding this incident
involves understanding the context in which it occurred; it means looking
at evolving legal boundaries on a shifting frontier and exploring the ways
in which the handling of such episodes changed over time. This intercultural homicide provides one window onto the changing dynamics of law,
authority, and power among and between Native Americans and the immigrants who had settled in Pennsylvania. Situating Sawantaeny's death
within the competing narratives of history, law, and authority, each of the
participants invoked also provides the first step toward a rapprochement
between their folktales of justice in the past and ours in the present.[14]

A more complicated story of Sawantaeny's death might start with conflicts
concerning the provincial government's authority over local Indians dating
as far back as 12 September 1700, when a series of negotiations between

Penn's provincial secretary, James Logan, and the "Susquehanna Indians"—the Conestoga, Lenape, Iroquois, and other peoples living together
along that river—ended in a treaty.[15] Motivated by a desire to protect Native society from the effects of the alcohol trade, the agreement promised
"that no person whatsoever Shall at any time live amongst or trade with
the Said Indians, or bring any Liquors or Goods to Sell or dispose of
amongst them" except those who had received a special license from the
proprietor. Modifying the protections for Indians that William Penn and
other legislators had built into the colony's first legal code, this provision
made the boundaries between Native and colonial society somewhat less
porous than they had been. It made the provincial government responsible
for keeping immoral individuals out of Indian country, using the same
mechanism by which Penn had hoped to keep immoral individuals from
entering Pennsylvania: through passes, seals, and licenses. Moreover, it
bore a remarkable resemblance to the local Quaker Meeting practice of
requiring Friends moving into the region to produce a certificate attesting
to their piety from the meeting they had just left.[16] The "Susquehanna
Indians," a loose grouping with little centralized power, newly formed out
of people from a handful of eastern Indian nations, had turned to the
colonial government to define and defend one aspect of the space between
Indians and colonizers and had accepted European—Quaker, really—
means by which to do so. And in allowing the provincial government control over these issues of space and authority, the Susquehanna Indians had
strengthened their own relationship to the colonial authorities.[17]

This example illustrates the evolving relation between discourse, space,
and the extension of colonial authority in provincial Pennsylvania. Seeking
to expand their authority over the frontier and those peoples who lived on
it, colonial magistrates attempted to make their rules for handling conflict
the law that would govern interactions between provincials and Indians.
Not only did they struggle to define the forms and symbols of displaying
legality (such as licenses, passes, or certificates), they also attempted to
determine where these displays of authority would be seen as legitimate.
Essentially, colonial negotiators endeavored, in halting and often unsuc-
cessful ways, to have diplomatic councils serve the same legitimating functions on the frontier that courtroom proceedings served at home.[18] During
the last decade of the seventeenth and the first decade of the eighteenth
centuries, formal meetings between Indian negotiators and the provincial
government most often took place in Philadelphia during meetings of the

Provincial Council and, at other times, at Conestoga. During this formative time in colonial diplomatic relations, Indians came to the colonials more than the colonials came to them.[19] Thus, diplomatic discourse at treaty councils functioned, spatially at least, similarly to discourse in provincial courts. These councils provided, for Natives and colonials, sites for the reporting, discussion, and adjudication of words and events that took place elsewhere, a central space for making private words and deeds public and recirculating them to new audiences on the peripheries.[20]

At the same time, the means by which treaty councils were constituted as a central cultural, political, and discursive space were quite different from the means by which magistrates and citizens produced and negotiated legitimacy in Pennsylvania courtrooms. Sessions of county courts opened with an invocation of the Crown's and Penn's authority, legitimating colonial magistrates through their relation to these centers of political authority. Indian authority at the outset of diplomatic encounters was constituted not simply through performative speech but also through the offering of gifts and a display of material signs of legitimacy, specifically wampum.[21] In a 1705 council at Conestoga, for example, the Indians on the Susquehanna greeted James Logan and his party and "though they were very poor, presented us with some skins."[22] Governor John Evans was likewise given gifts of skins, pipes, and tobacco during a trip along the Susquehanna to quell fears of war between the Susquehanna Indians and the Iroquois nations.[23] Colonial diplomats were slow to realize the importance of gift-giving in establishing their own legitimacy to Indian negotiators, a fact that irked Pennsylvania's Native peoples and did little to foster harmonious relations. Although by 1709 Governor Charles Gookin was cognizant enough of this custom during a council with "Mingo," or Ohio country Iroquois Indians, to remind the Assembly of "the immediate necessity . . . for a supply to make them a reasonable present," provincial officials honored this custom more often in the breach than in the observance.[24]

Perhaps the most critical gift exchanged at these diplomatic councils was wampum. Indian negotiators used the sacred shell beads to establish their authority to provincial diplomats. The wampum was not a means to build a social relationship through which negotiation could occur—the rationale for gift exchange—but a sign of discursive and political authority.[25] Provincial clerks noted this practice from almost the beginning of diplomatic exchanges; the first Lenape to meet the royal governor Benja-

Figure 8. Pennsylvania provincial secretary James Logan, portrait by Thomas Sully (after Gustavus Hesselius), 1831. The Library Company of Philadelphia.

min Fletcher in 1693 opened peace negotiations by "la[ying] a belt of Wampum at his Excellency's feet."[26] The Lenape sachem who came to Philadelphia a year later did likewise, depositing a belt of wampum before Fletcher so that he might address the governor "in the name of the rest of the delaware Indians."[27] This practice was common to other eastern Indians as well. In February 1708, for example, the Conestoga interpreter Indian Harry opened a council that he had initiated at Philadelphia by "laying upon the board Six loose strings of white Wampum for his Credentials," so that his message to the Provincial Council might be trusted.[28] Eight months earlier, a Nanticoke negotiator along the Susquehanna had similarly showed Evans belts of wampum as evidence both of his people's peaceful relations with Maryland, Pennsylvania, and the Iroquois and of his own authority to negotiate a peace with the province.[29]

Wampum served not only as a sign of an Indian negotiator's authority to deliver a message, but also as the message itself. At the 1709 council in Philadelphia, a Mingo speaker rose before assembled diplomats and magistrates, "laid on the Board a Belt of Wampum, as a Token to Confirm what he had to speak," and then relayed information about tensions between Maryland Indians and the Iroquois nations.[30] Nine representatives from the Tuscaroras, Conestogas, Senecas, and Shawnees similarly "spoke on" eight belts of wampum sent both to break off hostilities on the Pennsylvania frontier and to solicit Governor Gookin's help in negotiating a more stable peace.[31] Nor were Indians the only diplomats who granted wampum such authoritative power; provincial officials increasingly grasped its meaning as well. In sending the Conestoga Kneeghnyaskoate as a messenger to the Onondagas in 1705, Evans made sure that the emissary carried "a small Parcell of wampum for his Credential" to empower him to inquire in Evans's name about rumored strife between the Onondaga Indians and the Susquehanna Indians.[32] In the same way, the presence of a wampum belt sent by the Iroquois to New Castle by way of Indian Harry was enough to convince Gookin that rumors of Iroquois aggression on the frontier were credible.[33]

At treaty conferences, such tactile signifiers of cultural authority as wampum were more than simply mechanisms by which discussion could proceed. They were often the subject of the discussion itself. A May 1700 petition written on the Brandywine and delivered to Penn expressed the Susquehanna Indians' dismay that three frontier traders had "produced a paper with a large seale and pretended it was a warrant from the Governor" in an attempt to claim some Indians among them as their servants. The Indians' sense of the problems such a counterfeit symbol of authority posed underscored the importance that Natives and Euro-Americans alike placed on such symbols as wampum, warrants, passes, and licenses.[34] Provincials and Indians discussed frontier traders' licenses and certificates on several other occasions. Evans, for instance, reassured the Susquehanna Indians who arrived at Philadelphia in June 1706 that the government had "made a Law to prevent any injuries to them from the Christians, and . . . had also enacted in that Law, that no person should trade with them, but such as should first have a License from the Governor under his hand and Seal."[35] The question of traders without licenses or with fraudulent licenses was also the main topic of discussion at the February 1708 conference between Indian Harry and the Pennsylvanians.[36] And perhaps most preposterously, Gookin, at a 1710 meeting, suggested that those Indians desiring to migrate eastward should be required to produce licenses before moving just as traders traveling to Indian country or Quakers moving to another Meeting were supposed to bear certificates of good behavior: "We acquainted them . . . that if they intend to settle and live amiably here, they need not Doubt the protection of this Government in such things as were honest and good, but that to Confirm the sincerity of their past Carriage toward the English, and to raise in us a good opinion of them, it would be necessary to procure a Certificate from the government they leave, to this, of their Good behaviour, and then they might be assured of a favorable reception."[37]

This discussion suggests the authority that negotiators on both sides afforded material markers of authority in constructing neutral cultural spaces such as treaty councils and in controlling movement across the boundaries between Euro-American and Indian societies. The treaty council relied on mutually recognizable material signs to legitimate its proceedings to those present and to those to whom news of the event would circulate. Employing political rituals that were truly indigenous to none of the participants involved, the treaty council was an attempt to craft a political site that was, culturally speaking at least, peripheral to both Natives and newcomers. Moreover, the same material signs that allowed authoritative entrée to diplomatic discussions—trade goods, wampum, licenses, seals, passes—also gave entrée to Indian country for traders and later even for other Indians. The fact that the display of such symbols of authority operated as frames for the negotiations revealed that Indian diplomats and provincial officials agreed on their importance; the fact that such signs sometimes proved bones of contention revealed that each side occasionally disagreed with the ways in which the other employed them. Controversies arose not necessarily over the need for material signs of power in mediating the boundary between Pennsylvania and Indian country, but rather over whose signs—the Indians' or the Euro-Pennsylvanians'—would be most authoritative.

At root, conflict over signifiers of authority reflected deeper questions between provincials and Indians over speech, space, and sovereignty. Magistrates in Pennsylvania were interested not simply in forcing Natives to accept passes, seals, and licenses as uniquely authoritative signs, but also in forcing them to accept the larger political, social, and conceptual edifice that went along with them. If Indians were to be protected, it would have to be under Pennsylvania's laws, not their own. Before his journey back to England in 1701, Penn reiterated his desire—expressed earlier during the colony's founding—to punish harshly those colonizers who harmed Indians. To do so, "the Governor Desire[d] that when ever any Transgressed the said Law, and Came, Contrary amongst them, to agreement they would forthwith take Care to give information thereof to the Government, that the offenders might be duly prosecuted."[38] Penn thus elucidated an ambiguous aspect of the Great Treaty signed six months earlier, which had promised swift justice against any Christians who harmed an Indian but had not specified which brand of justice would be applied.[39] Five years later, Evans likewise emphasized to local Indians that applying Anglo-American law on the frontier would "prevent any injuries to them from the Christians." He also added that if colonials did harm Indians, the government would lay "greater Punishments on those that should Committ them, than if they were done to the English themselves."[40]

The hopes of Penn and Evans for equal justice were based on English standards. Perhaps not surprisingly, therefore, the region's indigenous peoples showed little interest in the "protective" power of Anglo-American law. One month later, at a council at Conestoga, Gookin's proposal for certificates was met by a strong claim by Natives for the authority to mete out justice in their own way. The Onondaga spokesman Connessoa, through the interpreter Indian Harry, offered among his demands necessary to keep peace in the region "that (notwithstanding our hearty desyres of a peace) yett if any Man affronts You, be not daunted, but revenge Your Selfs."[41] What various Indian negotiators repeatedly asked for was not legal but political and military protection. Although they accepted, and in some ways even encouraged, the encroachment of Pennsylvania's authority farther west on the frontier, they wanted it on their terms. Aware of the Iroquois' increasing attempts to extend their political dominance southward and the violence that this push had caused, Indian groups along the Susquehanna repeatedly sent messengers to enlist the provincial government's aid against the Iroquois Confederacy.[42] Thus, Indians and colonials could no more agree on how the provincial government's authority could best be used on the frontier than they had been able to agree on whose signs and symbols of authority should take precedence in diplomatic rituals.

Although Pennsylvania's rulers were convinced they could extend their authority westward through the same mechanisms they used to regulate public conduct in the provincial core, this belief rested on a false analogy equating provincial courtrooms and treaty councils. In point of fact, the differences between these two institutions far outweighed the similarities. The difficulties of managing the multiple discursive streams that moved into and through county courtrooms were significant; the difficulties of managing the frontier rumors, whispers, and hearsay that found their way into treaty councils were far greater. Despite enjoinders from different groups "that, no creditt be given to false reports," rumors of war were still a continual problem.[43] Tellingly, although Susquehanna, Iroquois, and Conestoga Indians agreed with the provincial council that such dangerous discourse was a problem, they disagreed with the councilors' proposed solution; the Indians wanted to decide for themselves whether or not to credit frontier rumors, while the provincial council insisted that all rumors be reported to Philadelphia.[44] Given the Indians' disdain for this proposal, the councilors' hope—thoroughly unrealistic as it might have been—of managing the flow of discourse throughout the Native countryside was even more likely to fail than their hope of stamping out all disorderly speech at home.

Of course, the difficulty of managing unruly discourse over such a large space and such a diverse population was not the only reason that Pennsylvania's Provincial Council failed to impose its vision of cultural order on diplomatic treaty councils and the territory they covered. The most basic problem was that of sanction: quite simply, on the frontier the council had no effective control over the behavior of Indians and little over that of their own settlers. Although provincial governors slowly learned to use gifts of guns, matchcoats, and stockings as carrots to encourage Indian

participation in their endeavors, they had no effective sticks. Despite Gookin's absurd mandate that frontier Indians carry certificates, provincial
magistrates had no means of punishing Natives that were as effective as
peace bonds or physical punishment, to name two of the ways in which
the colonial courts disciplined Pennsylvania's citizens. Through these sanctions provincial magistrates attempted to craft "good men" from "good
laws," and it was the lack of such sanctions that limited their authority on
the colonial periphery. Unless the provincial government could find ways
to bring Indians into the same system of punishment it used to sanction
its own citizens, provincial claims of jurisdiction over the frontier were
inherently problematic.

On 14 March 1722, James Logan and Colonel John French, representing the
proprietary government, held a council at Conestoga with leaders from
the Conestoga and Delaware Indians to discuss Sawantaeny's death. The
provincial records noted that "divers English and Indians" were also present.[45] Logan, addressing the Indians as his "Friends and Brethren," opened
the meeting by invoking the memory of William Penn and the "firm
League of Friendship and Brotherhood" the Founder had established with
Pennsylvania's Native peoples. "Agree[ing] that both you and his People
should be as one Flesh and Blood," Penn and the Indians' predecessors
had covenanted that neither side should suffer injury to the other. Having
heard, then, "that one of our Brethren had lost his Life by some Act of
Violence, alledged to be done by some of our People," Logan had called
the council "by the full Powers with which we are invested to inquire how
the matter came to pass, that Justice may be done" in the Sawantaeny
affair. He concluded his address with a final call to friendship, noting, "We
shall suffer no Injury to be done to any of you without punishing the
offenders according to our Laws."[46]

Through translators, including Civility, Logan interviewed witnesses to
the incident at Monocacy. Despite conflicting reports, some elements of
the case quickly became clear. The Cartlidges, assisted by two servants,
William Wilkins and Jonathan Swindel, were on the frontier hoping to
trade rum for furs. Their wares were in demand, and all agreed that Sawantaeny had received quite a bit of rum and had been drinking through the
night before his run-in with John Cartlidge. That morning "the Sinnekae
said he must have more Rum, for that he had not received all he had
bought." After Cartlidge refused him, the Indian went back to his cabin to

retrieve his gun.[47] When he emerged, Edmund Cartlidge and Wilkins managed to grab Sawantaeny's weapon, and after "stripping off his clothes," John Cartlidge assaulted him. Following repeated blows, Sawantaeny managed to crawl back to his cabin, where he died the next day.[48]

By 17 March, Logan and French had heard enough to send John and Edmund Cartlidge to Philadelphia in sheriff's custody "for suspicion of Killing the Indian mentioned in their report."[49] The decision had been made to try the Cartlidges in the provincial capital, not on the frontier. This choice was not perfect, for it meant that the jury would be unable to see a key piece of evidence—the body of the dead man. As the two Pennsylvania commissioners noted, Sawantaeny's corpse had been buried in the woods "three days thence" from Conestoga, making it "impracticable" for the commissioners to convince a provincial jury to travel west and see the body.[50] The Cartlidges arrived in Philadelphia on 22 March and were granted bail two days later.

The jurisdictional problems posed by cases like Sawantaeny's were hardly new. Legal boundaries had been one of the first issues William Penn had addressed at Pennsylvania's founding when he passed laws regulating the conduct of sailors and other travelers to the colony. Penn also called for the creation of "mixed" juries in criminal cases involving colonists and Indians, with "six on each side" to settle the matter.[51] There is no evidence, however, that such a jury was ever called between the passage of laws allowing for it in 1683 and Logan's and French's trip to Conestoga in 1722. Moreover, although colonials frequently discussed Indians in provincial courts—some colonists were tried for violating laws regulating Indian affairs—Indians themselves rarely ever appeared before the bar. And while there had been instances of interracial homicide on the Pennsylvania frontier before, Sawantaeny's death was the first time the Provincial Council had concerned itself with a homicide in which an Indian was the victim.[52] Thus, Logan and French had little precedent to guide them in deciding the Cartlidges' fate. There is no direct evidence that either was aware of the province's early statute calling for mixed-jury trials, but in any case it would have been difficult—if not impossible—to apply.[53] Penn's statute stated that when an Indian had been wronged, the provincial government was required to contact "the king to whom such Indian belonged" so that he could summon an appropriate group of Indian peers to be empanelled in the jury. Given Sawantaeny's ambiguous ethnic and political affiliations, Logan and French would have had a difficult time determining his "king."

As a Seneca living on the Pennsylvania frontier—outside of Seneca and Iroquois country—with a Shawnee wife and amidst bands of Delaware, Shawnee, and Conestoga Indians, under whose jurisdiction was Sawantaeny living? To whom did he belong?[54]

Faced with the prospect of entering legally uncharted territory, the two councilors instead fell back upon a familiar legal system: their own. But their decision to apply English law to settle the murder of an Indian may have resulted less from their legal reasoning than from their interpretation of changing political relations on the frontier. Sawantaeny's death occurred during a period when the rhetoric of Pennsylvania's diplomats toward their Indian counterparts was changing. Although Pennsylvanians continued to mention the peace and harmony that had existed between them and the Indians, they also increasingly stressed the importance of using European methods of conflict resolution to maintain that amity. The Provincial Council had warned the Conestoga Indians in 1715 that they should "be very careful on their parts that no difference should arise between any of their and our people, or if there should that they would acquaint us with it immediately, that we might duly inquire into it, and Justice should be done them if they were in any way wronged."[55] William Keith gave a similar warning to Conestoga diplomats two years later.[56]

Within this context, then, Sawantaeny's death may have presented Logan and French—and by extension, Pennsylvania's government—with a test case, an opportunity to increase the authority of the colonial legal system over the province's Indians by ensuring that justice would be determined according to European rules. Provincial magistrates may have disagreed sharply over matters of policy and power; the Sawantaeny case came in the middle of a major power struggle between Logan and Governor Keith that dominated Pennsylvania politics throughout the decade.[57] Yet neither Logan nor Keith questioned the appropriateness of applying English laws to settle the Sawantaeny affair. Thus, despite a stated desire that "Justice may be done," the Sawantaeny case may have been another instance in which English colonists invoked law as a cover for their political ends.[58] Colonial officials who had never before shown any interest in providing Pennsylvania's Indians equal treatment before the law became interested in doing so when it provided a means of expanding provincial sovereignty further west, particularly when that sovereignty could be extended over unruly Euro-Americans as well.

*   *   *

A second—and perhaps more likely—possibility is that examining the colonists' intentions is the wrong approach. Perhaps the absence of Indians in colonial courts represented Native—and not Anglo-American—preferences. After the Cartlidges were released on bail at the end of March 1722, Pennsylvania government officials continued to negotiate with the province's Indian neighbors to determine the traders' fate. Governor William Keith, in a council at Civility's cabin in Conestoga in early April 1722, reiterated his government's commitment to equal justice. Addressing the "Chiefs of the Mingoes, the Shawanois, and the Ganaway," Keith reminded them "that if any one hurts an Indian He will be tryed and punished in the same manner as if he had done it to an English Man."[59] He then asserted that he thought he had "acted herein like a true Friend and Brother," adding that he expected the Indians to "look upon me even as a child would respect and obey the Words of a tender father." Keith noted that he anticipated the Cartlidges would be tried "as soon as . . . any . . . Proof can be had that the Indian is dead or was actually killed by them."[60]

Keith's response met a mixed reception from Civility, who noted that the local Indians were "ready to receive his Words, and . . . willing and content to follow his Advice: For they know the Governour to be Absolute Rule[r], and it becomes them to submit." Yet the memory of William Penn, Civility argued, was revered because he would not do as other Europeans did, "by Calling them Children or Brothers only: For often Parents would be apt to whip their Children too severely; and Brothers sometimes differ." Penn also had said that "the Indians should be esteemed by him and his People as the same Flesh and Blood with the Christians, and the same as if one Man's Body was to be divided into two parts." In an oblique reference to the role of alcohol in Sawantaeny's death, Civility concluded by reminding Keith that Penn himself had hoped to prohibit the sale of rum to Indians. The Indians "could live contentedly and also grow Rich," he noted, "if it was not for the Quantitys of Rum that is suffered to come amongst them contrary to what William Penn had promised them." The Conestoga diplomat punctuated his invocation of Penn's memory by "Holding a Parchment in his Hand which they received from William Penn."[61] In the end, Keith agreed to check the amount of rum that reached the Indians, but the question of the Cartlidges' fate—and the reach of English law on the frontier—had not been settled.

After this April meeting at Conestoga, negotiation regarding the Cartlidges continued. In May, messengers from the Iroquois Confederacy and the Conestoga Indians arrived in Philadelphia to discuss Sawantaeny's death and the provincial government's response.[62] Keith reminded the Iroquois, as he had previously reminded Civility and the other communities on the Susquehanna, that the Cartlidges must be tried "by the Laws of our Great King," which treated cases such as this one differently than did Native justice. Once he had finished trying the Cartlidges according to English law, he continued, he would be happy to meet with more Indian delegates. Whereas Indian custom called for those who killed another to make monetary or material reparations to the family of the deceased, "the Laws of our Great King" could not be "alter[ed] or disobey[ed] . . . in the least point" and could not allow such a form of justice; instead, a jury would have to determine if John Cartlidge acted in the heat of passion or in cold blood. If the latter, he would be executed. The governor was telling both the Iroquois and the Indians of the Susquehanna not to get involved in the prosecution of Sawantaeny's alleged killers.[63]

Keith continued to meet with representatives of the Iroquois nations throughout the summer, reiterating his desire to punish the Cartlidges "according to our Laws, in the same manner as if they had killed an Englishman."[64] The Iroquois, however, steadfastly urged that John Cartlidge be released. In August their messenger Satcheechoe told Keith that the Iroquois "desired John Cartlidge might be released out of Prison, and the injury done to [their] Kinsman be forgot."[65] During a September council at Albany, Tanachaha, another Iroquois representative, told Keith that "we think it hard the persons who killed our friend and Brother should suffer, and we do in the name of all of the five Nations forgive the offence, and desire You will likewise forgive it, and that the men who did it may be released from Prison and set at Liberty, to go wither they please."[66] Tanachaha used Sawantaeny's status as a Seneca—a fellow brother in the Iroquois League—to press his claim. In deference to this request, Keith told the Iroquois that, upon his return to Philadelphia, the Cartlidges would be set free. The next day, the Iroquois surrendered to Pennsylvania all claims to the lands around Conestoga where Sawantaeny was killed; Tanachaha's profession of authority over his fellow Iroquois had been transformed overnight into a declaration of Iroquois sovereignty over the entire region and the Indians who lived in it. Following this, the governor and the Indians exchanged gifts, thereby cementing Pennsylvania's position as a treaty partner within the Iroquois Covenant Chain.[67] The Sawantaeny incident was, for all intents and purposes, over.

Retelling the end of *l'affaire Sawantaeny* does not, however, answer one of the central questions raised at the beginning of the chapter: why did both the Iroquois nations and the Indians on the Susquehanna work for the Cartlidges' release? Iroquois motives were different from those of the Conestoga, Delaware, and Shawnee Indians on whose behalf Civility negotiated, but they seem relatively straightforward, and the Six Nations appear to have gotten what they wanted. Although Keith refused to call his £110 gift at the Albany conference a "condolence payment" to atone for Sawantaeny's death, it appears to have functioned as such in everything except in name. Moreover, Keith's decision to grant the Iroquois' request for clemency after he had previously denied similar requests from the Indians on the Susquehanna effectively recognized the Iroquois as the dominant Indian power in the region.[68] Both Indian groups had claimed Sawantaeny as a "brother," but Keith's selective gift-giving and treaty making legitimated only the Iroquois claim. The Iroquois used the Seneca's death as an occasion to display their affection toward Keith, seizing the opportunity to strengthen their diplomatic ties to the province and weaken those between Pennsylvania and the Indians on the Susquehanna.

Although this may summarize the Iroquois' motives, it does not explain why Civility would have worked for the Cartlidges' release on behalf of the other Indian groups along the Susquehanna. A hint can be seen in Civility's statement to Governor Keith in May 1722. Recalling the Founder's words about Europeans and Indians being of "one Blood," Civility challenged Keith's attempt to play the "Father" to his Native "Children," with all of the inequality that these terms implied. This objection to familial language suggests that he rejected the terms on which Pennsylvania had hoped to incorporate the indigenous people around Conestoga into a colonial political and legal system in which justice meant European justice. Civility's invocation of Penn also served as a reminder that the colonists had not lived up to all of their agreements to live in harmony with the Indians. Embedded within Civility's acquiescence to the governor's "Absolute Rule," then, was a critique of the ways in which that rule had been enforced. By retelling the story of Penn's treaty with the Indians, Civility challenged the legal narrative within which Keith contextualized European-Indian relations, framing them instead within the local history—the local knowledge—of Pennsylvania's frontier.[69] This narrative of friendship and alliance, not metaphors of bodily or familial interconnection, provided the dominant linguistic frame for Civility's claims.[70]

Civility's response to Keith's speech was hardly unique in these respects.

Sawantaeny's death occurred during a period in which colonial-Indian negotiations were marked by subtle semantic conflicts over terms of address. While European negotiators often referred to Indians as "Brothers" or, less often, "Children," Indians stressed, as Civility did, that Indians and Europeans were of "one Blood" but in "two parts."[71] Pennsylvanian-Indian negotiations were also marked by conflicts over interpreting recent diplomatic history. During the decade before Sawantaeny's death, Indian negotiators invoked Penn's promises to Conestoga and Delaware Indians in order to critique what they viewed as illegal and unethical encroachments by settlers and traders on Native lands. In 1715, for example, Sassoonan, speaking for the Delawares, informed Governor Gookin during a meeting at Philadelphia that his people had come "to renew the former bond of friendship that William Penn had, at his first coming," made with them, implying that Penn's successors had not filled the Founder's shoes. Three months later Sotyriote, speaking for the Conestogas, also used Penn's example to chastise Gookin mildly.[72] These negotiators' claims to a special relationship with "Miquon"—the Delaware name for Penn—were pointed challenges not only to Pennsylvania's government but also to those Iroquois diplomats who invoked their old relationship with "Onas," as the Founder was known to the Iroquois.[73] They may also have represented some jockeying for position between the Delawares and Conestogas as each group tried to make itself the premier group among those Indian nations along the Susquehanna. By grounding the negotiations within mythohistoric narratives of peace, such Indian diplomats as Civility, Sassoonan, and Sotyriote were able to shift the discussions away from Euro-American frames of justice and legitimacy into a moral context more familiar to Delaware Valley Indians.[74]

The motives for this frame switch, and its implications for Civility's requests for clemency for John Cartlidge, can perhaps be gleaned from an Indian council in May 1723, some months after Sawantaeny's death. Upon being told by Keith—who surely thought he was smoothing over rocky relations with this comment—that English "Laws make no distinction between our people and yours," Civility, speaking on behalf of the Indians on the Susquehanna, dissented. He told Keith that "The Indians well approve of all the Governor Had said except where he told them that the English Law made no difference between the English and the Indians, for they should not like, upon an Indians committing a fault, that he should be imprisoned as they had seen some Englishmen were."[75]

This statement—which, granted, was made more than a year after Sawantaeny was killed and eight months after Indian requests for clemency led to the release of his killer—suggests that perhaps the stance of these Indians was motivated by a desire to remain independent of European laws, a desire to retain their sovereignty and their ability to determine justice in their own manner. That these aims coincided with Iroquois attempts to the same end suggests that Civility's pains to manage Sawantaeny's death himself, on his own terms, were likewise attempts to remain independent of Iroquois influence. Civility's attempt to bury Sawantaeny immediately, without involving the Iroquois or Keith, implies that the primary goal of the Indians at Conestoga was some form of autonomy from outside control, even as the Delaware, Conestoga, and Shawnee maneuvered amongst each other for status and influence.[76] Equal justice under English law—and an implicit acceptance of its sovereignty over them—was the last thing that Civility, Sassoonan, and others living around Conestoga wanted. If the Iroquois nations' success in claiming authority over the Susquehanna River valley and over the Indians who lived there prevented the settlement of Sawantaeny's death from becoming a complete triumph, the temporary check on English legal authority that the settlement represented was a partial victory for the assorted nations at Conestoga.[77]

The resolution of Sawantaeny's death did not settle many of the problems underlying the difficult negotiations of 1722 and 1723. A series of unrelated homicides in 1728 brought thorny jurisdictional problems to a head. In early May 1728, Walter and John Winter, two brothers living on Skippack Creek on the Pennsylvania frontier, received a report—incorrect, as it turned out—that Indians had killed two nearby colonials. Having recently heard rumors of an impending invasion led by foreign or "Spanish Indians," the Winters decided to take matters into their own hands. Electing to "defend" themselves against attack, they grabbed their rifles and went immediately to a nearby cabin where a Delaware man, Tacocolie, lived with his family. There they opened fire, killing Tacocolie, his wife Quilee, and their son while wounding their two daughters.[78]

    Governor Gordon's response was immediate and stern: he moved speedily to apprehend the Winter brothers for murder. He then convened a council at Conestoga to meet with Conestoga, Shawnee, Delaware, and Conoy diplomats to allay their fears and told them he was "grieved . . . exceedingly" by the news of the Winters' actions. He assured the Indian diplomats that the murderers were captured "and are now in Irons in a

Dungeon to be tried by the Laws of the Great King of all the English, as if they had Killed so many of his Subjects." Gordon also noted that provincial officials had found the bodies of the Winters' victims, "who by my order were laid in a Grave and covered with Shirts and Strowds."[79] The Winters' fate stood in marked contrast to the Cartlidges' six years earlier; they were hanged that July in Philadelphia. Their corpses were a sign, to Indians and provincials alike, of Gordon's punitive legal potency.

But the governor's concerns went beyond the death of Tacocolie and the punishment of his murderers. He also used this council as an occasion to bring up another killing. "About eight months agoe," Gordon announced that he had "received an account that an English man was Killed by some Indians, at the House of John Burt, in Snake Town" and that he "expect[ed] the Indians will doe us Justice by apprehending the Murtherers that they may be punished."[80] Having framed his punishment of the Winters for Tacocolie's death as evidence of his good intentions toward the Indians, the governor used the homicide at Snake Town to suggest that Pennsylvania's Indians were obligated to reciprocate, in the name of friendship, harmony, and justice, by helping him punish Indian murderers under Anglo-Pennsylvanian laws. In doing so, Gordon had not only claimed provincial jurisprudence as the appropriate standard for "equal" justice; he had also claimed "Onas"—Pennsylvania's government—as the only sovereign capable of ensuring that appropriate and equal punishment was meted out to Indian and colonist alike. And although he accepted the Indians' collective refusal to pursue the accused on the grounds that the murder at Snake Town had been committed by an Indian "of another Nation," he did not relent from his initial position that equal punishment meant Anglo punishment.

Gordon's position became even clearer later that year when he received a report that Timothy Higgins, servant to a trader living near the forks of the Susquehanna, was hanged by Shawnee warriors.[81] Calling a council at Philadelphia with Delaware, Iroquois, and "Brandywine" Indians, Gordon reminded his assembled guests of the speed with which he had executed Walter and John Winter and urged them to take care that any Indian harming a Euro-American "be punished for it, that we may have the same Justice as if a Christian had done the wrong."[82] Accordingly, he hoped that these Indian leaders might locate the murderer from Snake Town as well as the Shawnees who had killed Higgins. Nor was this October 1728 treaty council Gordon's last mention of the Winters' execution. The governor reminded Indian diplomats of his actions at treaty conferences in 1731 and 1735 and again called for equal punishment of violent offenders, colonial and Natives alike, by provincial authorities.[83]

Gordon used this invocation of the execution—couched within a longer discussion of Penn's ancient friendship with the Indians—as a way to obligate provincial Indians to uphold Anglo-Pennsylvanian law in much the same way that Native diplomats such as Civility, Sassoonan, and Tanachaha used narratives of their people's friendship with Penn to urge the provincial government to live up to what they saw as its rightful obligations. In any case, Gordon was relentless in insisting that British laws should prevail on the frontier. In 1732, he raised this issue again, finally getting Iroquois diplomats to agree to stop harboring fugitive slaves owned by Pennsylvanians.[84] In two separate meetings in August 1733, he convinced Conoy and Delaware diplomats that if the rumors of Conoy attacks against colonizers on the frontier were accurate, these tribes would help deliver the murderers to the provincial government for punishment according to colonial laws.[85] Gordon's successors continued the theme; at a major treaty conference with the Six Nations in 1736, Logan and Thomas Penn reached an agreement with the Iroquois that an Indian thought to have murdered a provincial on the frontier would be turned over to colonial magistrates to be hanged.[86]

That same 1736 conference, however, also indicated what was at stake in these negotiations over frontier legal authority. The question was not simply how far westward the provincial government's authority spread; it was also who had authority westward of whatever boundary line would be established. Debates over individual acts of frontier violence took place in the midst of ongoing political negotiations about space and authority. Since the early 1720s, the Iroquois had repeatedly asserted their authority over the mixed population of Conestogas, Delawares, and Shawnees living in the Susquehanna Valley. At the same time, provincial officials were playing a political sovereignty version of what Francis Jennings called "the deed game," the means by which Anglo-American negotiators recognized individual Indians as tribal leaders for the purpose of purchasing land from them, regardless of whether or not these supposed sachems wielded any actual authority within Native communities. This shoehorning of indigenous practices of land usage and tenure into an Anglo-American legal idiom was essential to the spread of colonial property and sovereignty westward.[87]

Provincial officials in Pennsylvania likewise shoehorned perceived disorder on the colonial frontier. Worried about the cost and difficulty of maintaining harmonious political and economic ties with several independent Indian groups, Gordon and his successors embarked on a plan of recognizing the Iroquois' tenuous—the Conestoga, Delaware, and Shawnee might have said fictitious—claims to sovereignty over the Susquehanna River valley. By ratifying these assertions of jurisdiction, provincial negotiators helped transform frontier spaces into Iroquois territory.[88] The process had started with the resolution of Sawantaeny's death when Keith's £110 gift to settle the matter had gone to the Iroquois and not to the Susquehanna Indians, recognizing Iroquois sovereignty over them as he accepted their cession of land to him. Similarly, Gordon had asked the Conestogas in 1728 to become sureties for the Shawnees moving into the region, holding the Conestoga Indians—themselves seen as subordinate to the Iroquois—responsible for the Shawnees' actions.[89] In 1732, Gordon sweetened his demands that the Iroquois stop harboring fugitive slaves with an acknowledgment that the Iroquois were sovereign over Shawnee residents in the Susquehanna region.[90]

Gordon was resolute in his efforts to the very end. In 1735, at the governor's last Indian conference before his death, the Conestoga diplomat Civility invoked the 1700 and 1701 treaties with Penn as a sign of the Susquehanna Indians' political independence from the Iroquois; he even argued that the Shawnees—who had not yet migrated to Pennsylvania in 1701—were covered by the treaty and therefore independent of the Six Nations as well.[91] Gordon not only rejected Civility's claims to political independence outright, he denied the Susquehanna Indians any autonomy at all. He insisted that from that moment on, if the Susquehanna Indians wanted to stay in Pennsylvania's good graces, they were obliged to treat as enemies all other Indians "without some sufficient Credential from this Government to show that they come as Friends." Gordon had, in effect, denied the Conestogas and Shawnees the right to determine who their allies and who their enemies were.[92] The Penns' formal declaration in 1736 that the Iroquois were the sole sovereigns, by right of conquest, of the entire Susquehanna Valley and of all the Indians residing in it, then, was a culmination, the final act in a long attempt by Pennsylvania's provincial government to deny the sovereignty of those local Indian groups—the Conestogas, Delawares, and Shawnees—who asserted their independence and to recognize the sovereignty of the Indian confederacy as a way to enable the expansion of colonial settlements.

Telling folktales of justice about Sawantaeny's death is a difficult task indeed. This can be, in Cover's terms, a jurisgenerative project; retelling this story can provide an opportunity for reimagining the implications of the colonial American past and help frame new conceptions of law, justice, and authority. In his essay on the ethics of practicing early American history, Michael Meranze has eloquently called for a thorough rethinking of the ways historians write about struggle, conflict, and oppression in the American past. While appreciative of the intentions behind social historians' efforts to demonstrate how the poor, enslaved, or disenfranchised survived in the face of difficult odds, he notes that undoing the historical mythology behind American nationalism involves more than celebrating resistance to oppression. This process demands an exploration of historical paths not taken. Instead of symbolically appropriating the struggles of the oppressed, "we must mark . . . the gap between our present and its lost alternatives."[93] The history of homicides on the Pennsylvania frontier, illustrating as it does the slow erosion of the Delaware Indians' autonomy, evokes the gap between a modern mid-Atlantic whose Indian history has been effaced and an earlier era when the Conestogas and Iroquois were able to prevent the extension of colonial sovereignty westward. Meranze further suggests that historians examine internal contradictions within American society, "mark[ing] the point in which the dominant is not what it thinks it is—and vehemently seeks to control that gap." He argues that analyzing "the inner contradictions of our dominant values" would reveal how "our institutions and our selves are constructed to deny the gap between what we are and what we think we are."[94] Meranze's approach neatly accords with historians' criticism of the unequal justice meted out by colonial magistrates; it forces "us" to come to terms with the colonial inequalities embedded in "our" legal historical past.

But this kind of morality tale about the colonial past, its message implicit in historical accounts of homicide and explicit in Meranze's analysis, is dangerously jurispathic in another sense. In challenging "us" to confront the broken promises "our" ancestors made, this narrative tactic assumes that critical agency will be executed solely within a Euro-American, Enlightenment framework. Meranze's assertion that historians might develop an ethical solidarity with past victims of oppression without explicitly identifying with the historical subjects of their work belies his emphatic use of the first-person plural when urging his readers to action. Despite their intentions, historians hoping to find legal equality on the early American frontier risk replicating the hegemonic tactic favored by such provincial governors as Keith and Gordon. By casting the Indians as victims of a hypocritical White double-dealing, they take Native incorporation into colonial—and contemporary—narratives of justice and authority for granted, ignoring the fact that such negotiators as Civility and Tanachaha participated in colonial legal narratives selectively and at times with great reluctance.[95] Forcing "us" to face up to the ways in which "our" treasured national institutions denied alternate possibilities in this manner silences the very alternate folktales of justice—those in which Indians resisted incorporation into the master narrative of American colonization—that Meranze would have us pay attention to.

Modern folktales of justice about Sawantaeny's death, then, become difficult to tell precisely because the fate of the Cartlidges was the subject of so many competing folktales in 1722. Sawantaeny's ambiguous identity had made his death both a powerful symbol and a political opportunity for those involved in its aftermath. Logan, Keith, Civility, Sassoonan, Sotyriote, and Tanachaha all told different tales of peace and justice that served their ends in different ways. The governor and the councilor expressed their desire, after the fact, to afford Sawantaeny equality under their law. They claimed him, in effect, as a Pennsylvania citizen to tell stories about their sovereignty over Pennsylvania and all of its inhabitants, Euro-American and Indian. The Indian diplomats, on the other hand, claimed Sawantaeny as a kinsman in stories about their own authority and influence over the region and its peoples.

Although telling folktales of Sawantaeny's death and its aftermath involves, on some level, the creation of histories jurispathic to cultures of the past, historians must balance their desire for moral judgment with a sensitivity to the multiple moral narratives embedded within their stories. Far from leading contemporary historians and readers down a slippery slope to "moral relativism" (often inveighed against but infrequently defined), such a sensitivity may increase their appreciation and respect for local moral and legal worlds and may caution them against presuming a single normative world as a universal standard of justice.[96] Put simply, "we" must be careful how we claim Sawantaeny's story, and for what purposes. This exercise in reconstructing folktales of justice about frontier killings from various Native American perspectives—with its suggestion that the nonpunishment of John Cartlidge may have represented justice and the Winters' hanging injustice to those Indians involved—represents a first step toward such a moral history of legal boundaries on the colonial frontier.

One perspective, of course, is missing from this history: Sawantaeny's. What kind of folktale of justice might Sawantaeny have told about his own death? As a Seneca who hunted and lived with his Shawnee wife amongst a mixed group of Delaware, Conestoga, and Shawnee Indians, what might he have thought? Would he have applauded the Iroquois' claim for legal authority over the Susquehanna and its Indians? Would he have supported Civility's attempts to keep the Iroquois and the Europeans out of legal affairs on the Pennsylvania frontier? Or would he have desired to see the Cartlidges swing on the gallows, as Keith had allegedly intended? Without understanding more fully how Sawantaeny's own stories of his life would have resolved his multiple identities, it is impossible to know how he would have understood these difficult issues.[97] Representatives from the Conestoga, Delaware, and Iroquois nations all claimed Sawantaeny as a kinsman in their efforts to legitimate their authority over Conestoga, subsuming him within their folktales of justice. No such attempt to claim Sawantaeny as a kinsman will be made here; making him into an ancestral national character—affirming his posthumous place in an American national heritage—runs at least as many risks of jurispathic interpretation as any of the works cited above.[98] Rather than speak for him in a language he would not understand, I will let him rest in peace and let that story remain untold.

7

JUSTICE, RETRIBUTION, AND THE CASE OF JOHN TOBY

LOUIS M. WADDELL

"Oh Lord, Mammy, the Indian most killed me," lamented eight-year-old Ann Hunter amidst her tears after she ran into her parents' home in the frontier community of Paxton on the night of 14 February 1751. She told her parents, Robert and Elizabeth Hunter, of being painfully sexually assaulted, while she was out gathering syrup trays, by a Nanticoke known only by his anglicized name, John Toby.[1] Like the murder of Sawantaeny, this alleged sexual assault raised complicated issues not only of diplomatic relations between Native Americans and Euro-American colonists but also, and more importantly, of the sovereignty of the law on the eighteenth-century Pennsylvania frontier. The fragile structures of coexistence that kept violence at bay sometimes required that definitions of justice be stretched in ways that became almost unrecognizable to either side. This chapter explores the legal, political, and social history of an alleged sexual assault and contrasts it with interracial homicide and crimes against property. No attempt is made to critically examine the foundations of the legal system adopted from England.

As was noted in Chapter 6, jurisdictional questions were often raised around the particularly tricky issue of homicide. Alden T. Vaughan has commented that from the beginning of English North American colonization, those Native American communities that entered into treaties with colonies, either through friendship or because they had been conquered, agreed to surrender to the colonial courts any members who might kill colonists or damage colonials' property. The converse, however, was not true; colonists who killed Native Americans or damaged their property faced colonial, not Native, justice.[2]

The Native American custom requiring a young male to show he had killed an enemy in order to qualify as a warrior was so strong that Indian communities were under pressure to condone male-on-male murders or at least to limit retribution to compensating a victim's family by giving them valuable items. Furthermore, Northeastern Woodland peoples were acutely aware that their numbers were steadily declining in the face of increasing swarms of Euro-American settlers. Thus, Native American leaders were usually unwilling to expose their people to the possibility of capital punishment at the hands of Pennsylvania courts. Disagreement about the status of peace and war was also a contributing factor. Native American leaders had no particular reason to heed the rhetoric of diplomats in Philadelphia, New York, London, or Paris. They must have viewed many of the killings of Euro-American settlers as part of an ongoing war on the frontier, even when neither provincial nor imperial authorities recognized a formal state of conflict. One of the excuses offered on behalf of the Paxton Boys when they massacred twenty helpless Conestoga Indians in December 1763 was that a state of war existed, although the government clearly did not classify the Conestogas as an enemy nation.[3]

But rape was a far different matter. Euro-American and Native American societies agreed in basic principle that violent sex acts should be discouraged. Historian James Axtell has made a strong argument that the traditional accounts of Native Americans violating Euro-American women are fictitious, and he stops just short of concluding that rape under these circumstances never occurred in the colonial period. Axtell posits that a Native American taboo against incest evolved into general intolerance of any form of sexual molestation of captives who might become adopted kin. He believes that many of the lurid atrocity narratives about Indian behavior expounded by colonial authors have distorted history and contends that captive Euro-American women were not forced to marry Indian males. Furthermore, rape should never have occurred when Indians raided settler communities because warriors believed their spirit-being allies would desert them if they sexually abused the enemy's women. Axtell also found evidence that Native American males simply did not find Euro-American women attractive.[4] Not all of Axtell's arguments apply directly to John Toby and Ann Hunter, but the legendary assumptions of wanton Indian male lust are false.

For Conrad Weiser, acting in his capacity as a magistrate of Lancaster County, the Indians' attitude toward rape must have presented ambiguities. Although Weiser had recently refused Governor James Hamilton's commission to attend an Indian conference in Albany, the brilliant Pennsylvania German negotiator was still keen to prevent warfare on the frontier, and so he acted in a prompt yet diplomatic manner in response to the Hunters' complaint that Toby had raped their daughter.[5] John Harris, leader of the Paxton community, had written Weiser on behalf of the Hunters. Because Harris's message reached Weiser as he was riding to Cumberland County on other business, the magistrate was able to reach Harris's house the evening following the alleged rape. Swollen waters on Paxton Creek, however, kept him from going to the Hunters' home until the following morning. Harris accompanied him there and, to assure fair treatment for both the injured family and the accused, he brought two others along. One was Mrs. James Armstrong, wife of the magistrate who, in 1744, had launched the legal process following the murder of his relative, the trader John "Jack" Armstrong, by the Delaware Mushemeelin. Mrs. Armstrong could be expected to sympathize with the Hunters and to understand little girls. Weiser also brought John King, a Nanticoke leader who lived with a small group of people of that nation in cabins close by the Paxton settlement. King told Weiser that the Nanticokes would surrender Toby to the provincial system of justice only if they received an order directly from Governor James Hamilton. But he also pointed out that the Nanticokes regarded sexual attacks as especially heinous criminal behavior.

At the Hunters' cabin, Weiser took depositions from two women who had examined Ann immediately after the attack: Ann's mother and a "stranger" who had been in the house at the time, Elizabeth Bethy. Both swore that Ann's genitals had been swollen. The mother testified that the attack had drawn blood. Elizabeth Bethy refused to confirm this statement, although she suspected that Mrs. Hunter had wiped the blood away. Bethy's deposition did imply, however, that Toby had appeared to be drunk because he had been staggering and he was soaking wet from having fallen into the creek. Both Toby's intoxication and Ann's bleeding might have been used in court to judge the severity of Toby's actions.[6]

But in all this we have no explanation why the Indian was in the Hunters' home in the first place on the evening of the fourteenth. A Valentine's Day celebration seems very unlikely in this eighteenth-century Scots-Irish setting. He might have been invited in just to dry off. It is not clear whether Toby was drunk when he entered the home, or whether it was liquor the Hunters gave him that went to his head, but the very absence of comment on that point is a hint that the Hunters' bottle was involved. They would have had every reason not to voluntarily admit they had served liquor to Toby, for it would have made them appear partly responsible for his conduct. Liquor, hospitably offered by settlers to Native Americans had, on other occasions, led to violence that Pennsylvania officials had sometimes blamed as much on the Euro-American suppliers as on the Indian perpetrators.[7]

When Toby had first entered the home, Elizabeth Hunter had sent Ann out to collect some tin vessels placed beneath sugar maple trees to gather sap because she was worried that the Indian might steal them. Where was the man of the house during all this? Robert Hunter was not specifically mentioned in the section of Weiser's deposition describing Toby's initial visit to the home, before the Indian exited to pursue the child, although later Hunter said he tried vainly to chase Toby down after Ann had returned and told how she had been violated. The question of Hunter's whereabouts is important. His apparent absence suggests that the women of the family trusted Toby enough to allow him to dry himself at the fireplace, yet at the same time they said they feared he would pilfer the sugaring equipment outside. Both attitudes show how the Euro-American population in such ethnically mixed surroundings viewed its Indian neighbors.

At the Hunters' home, Weiser questioned Ann directly for details. She said that Toby had left the house after she did, found her, embraced her, and told her he "must lie with her." In the rough original or first copy of his narration, Weiser had written that Toby had "throwed or layed" Ann down, but someone—presumably Weiser himself—crossed out "layed," and Weiser did not include that word in a neater copy he made of the report later on. Ann said Toby lifted her clothes and "hurted" her, at which point she began to cry. Responding to her tears he let her go, and she ran "as much as she could" toward home. But the Nanticoke pursued her, falling down at one point on some rocks that cut a bleeding wound in his forehead. When he seized her a second time, he again threw her down and said he wanted to "play" with her. Hearing her mother call from the cabin for Ann to come home, Toby released her and ran away. Weiser, questioning the child closely, noted that she did not know if the attacker had caused her pain with, as Weiser wrote it, his "fingers or . . ."—followed by what survives only as one or two heavily crossed out words. In this context, the deleted expression must have referred to John Toby's penis.[8]

Weiser's next move was to reinforce his own authority by inviting another magistrate to join him, but no one was immediately available. He then tried to reach the local Nanticoke community to ask them to a conference to decide what to do, but he soon learned that the other Nanticokes had fled fearing reprisals from the Hunter affair. Weiser decided instead to perform his duties more subtly, and he convinced John King to cooperate in placing Toby in a relaxed situation before criminal accusations were leveled at him. As an intermediary, Weiser chose Henry Rennox whose dwelling was immediately adjacent to the Nanticoke cabins. Three days after the act of violence, Rennox invited King and Toby to enjoy a Sunday's hospitality, including dinner, at his home. With King's approval, Weiser set up a plot to entice Toby into an intimidating situation. In addition to Weiser and King, the dinner party included several other Euro-American settlers from the Paxton community, although it is not clear who or how many they were. Both Indians surrendered their guns as they entered the building, King, of course, intending to make Toby feel that he was not being singled out. The fact that Toby apparently accepted the invitation at face value is another clue to the kinds of fraternization that often bridged the gap between frontier Euro-Americans and Indians, even as the number of violent encounters was increasing.

The Sunday invitation to dine must have seemed like normal Paxton behavior to Toby or else he would not have attended. As other guests were arriving, Weiser and King conferred privately outside the building, but Toby soon came out and joined them. Perhaps they thought Toby had heard "Hunter" uttered in their conversation, and for that reason they gave him the excuse that they had been talking about hunting. Then, the three went back in to join the group, and everyone drank some wine. One of the settlers cajoled Toby into loaning him his knife in order to cut some tobacco. The warrior reluctantly obliged but was now growing suspicious and noticeably excited. When Weiser invited him to sit by the fire, he balked. The guest who was cutting tobacco told Toby he would return the knife as soon as Toby sat down, and, with Weiser's also insisting that he be seated, the Nanticoke complied. When Weiser made the accusation of rape, Toby replied that he had been so drunk on the fourteenth he could not remember what had occurred. In response, Weiser announced that as a magistrate of Lancaster County he had no choice but to send Toby to jail in Lancaster. Three settlers took the prisoner there, without encountering physical resistance from Toby or verbal objections from King. That evening, Weiser wrote a statement to the entire Nanticoke community living along the Susquehanna and sent it with some wampum, using John King as his courier. He told them that the imprisonment was to last until Governor Hamilton could consider the case, and he described the crime as "Ravaging a girl of about eight years of age . . . (or at least abus[ing] or wound[ing] her so that her life was despaired of) which crime by English Law is death to any man."[9]

From Heidelberg, Lancaster County, on 20 February, Weiser wrote Governor Hamilton a revealing letter that altered the entire story:

> In my last Journey to Cumberland I was Stopt at Paxton in Lancaster County, because of a Complaint made to me (as to a Magistrate) against one John Toby a Nonticook Indian for ravaging or attempted to ravage a girl of about Eight years of age. The narrative of my proceedings are hereby sent also a Copy of a letter I send to the Nonticook Indians at Wayomoik and thereabout with a string of Wampum. I have been under great Concern about the affair. I had sent for Mr Forster the next Magistrate but the Roads being so bad he could not come till most night after I had committed the Indian. I omitted in my narrative that after the Indian was committed Mrs. Armstrong the wife of Mr. James Armstrong Came to John Harris at my request, to her and to the mother of the child and to Elisabeth Bethy I gave it in charge upon their oath to Examine the child, and to make report unto me in what condition the Child was in, and whether or no they thought that the Indian had the Carnal Knowledge of the Childs body. They made joint report that the Child was like to do well, and that they were assured the Indian had not the Carnal knowledge of the Childs Body. Whether in this case or in the rest of my proceedings I did right or wrong I humbly submit to your Honours Judgment being well assured that I acted to the best of my Knowledge. I must also inform your Honour that Robert Hunter the father of

the Child would not be bound to prosecute the Said Indians for his Crime, pleading he was a very poor man and could not afford to go to Courts, and in truth he is a very poor man, in my opinion he seamed rather inclined to do himself Justice in taking revenge on the Indian.[10]

Definitions of carnal knowledge and explanations of its importance have differed over the centuries, but Weiser and the three examiners probably meant that penetration had not occurred. At most, then, Toby could be charged with a form of sexual assault falling short of the legal definition of rape.

Although rape was a capital offense, there is good reason to believe that it often went unpunished in colonial Pennsylvania. In England rape had carried a death penalty since 1575, and this continued until the Victorian criminal code reforms. David Hackett Fischer contrasts the strict enforcement of penalties against rape in New England with the way the crime was largely ignored in colonial Virginia. A Virginia historian, Hugh F. Rankin, hypothesizes that rape within the Euro-American population of the Old Dominion was so common that the courts ignored it, but when African Americans or Native Americans were suspected of violating Euro-American women, the law was enforced.[11]

The Pennsylvania rape statute of 1700, which was written to cover all males except African Americans who might "commit a rape, or ravish a Maiden or Woman," did not include a death sentence. Perpetrators instead received thirty-one lashes, seven years of hard labor, and forfeiture of their estate; second offenders were castrated. Disallowed by the Queen in Council in 1706, the statute was promptly reenacted verbatim by the Assembly, with the exception of the castration provision. This measure prevailed until the enactment in 1718 of Governor William Keith's comprehensive reform of Pennsylvania's criminal code, which replaced the standards established under William Penn with law then current in England. Thereafter, "rape," without reference to "ravishment," was joined with three other felonies—buggery, sodomy, and robbery by highway assault—which were made punishable according to whatever statutes were current in Great Britain for those crimes. This meant capital punishment.[12]

Still, the history of colonial Pennsylvania records only a single execution for rape in the period from 1681 to the Declaration of Independence.[13] In May 1772, Patrick Kennedy of Thornbury Township, Chester County, was hanged for his part in a gang rape of Jane Walker the previous November. Kennedy's three companions were also found guilty but were pardoned by Governor John Penn on recommendations from the trial court judges. The testimony provided by three of the defendants and the victim had differed widely, but all agreed that Walker had been subjected to physical violence in some form. Kennedy appeared to have taken the lead by tying Walker's leg to a tree and beating her with a stick; she contended that he had raped her twice himself, as well as preparing her for the others to violate her body and encouraging them to do so. Nonetheless, the four written statements of testimony, compiled within a span of a single day, were so contradictory that the jury's reasons for preferring Walker's story over the others, and the sentencing judges' reasons for recommending mercy for all but Kennedy, are not readily apparent.[14]

The late-Saturday-night drunken traipsing through dark farm fields of this quintet—Walker and four unmarried male laborers—was in sharp contrast with the Toby-Hunter affair. The Indian could easily have crushed the little girl's bones, yet he used his strength only to embrace her and throw her to the ground. The Jane Walker affair, however, involved five adults adventurously roaming around in search of good times, until a moment came when they fell out over how good times should be accomplished. Although Jane's interpretation of the evening's events had been enough to convince the court, her reputation was probably tarnished by implications in her assailants' depositions. They suggested that she had been enticing the four males to the cabin of a "free Negro named Cuff" for the purpose of prostitution after all five had been thrown out of a respectable tavern by the lady of the house. Walker they described as being so drunk she could no longer stand up, and one of the accused rapists said she was spreading the pox.[15]

That the alleged perpetrator in the Ann Hunter case was an Indian also distinguishes it from the Walker episode. As Weiser's letter of 20 February reveals, Ann's reexamination by Elizabeth Bethy, Mrs. Armstrong, and Elizabeth Hunter not only eliminated the carnal knowledge factor but also determined that the child had not been permanently injured. And there was a growing tradition in Pennsylvania of acquitting Indians who had committed violent acts under the influence of alcohol when the victims had suffered no lasting physical harm. Such leniency had been exercised by the Provincial Council president, James Logan, in March 1738, when he condoned the release from custody of a Conestoga Indian who had stabbed two Euro-American men outside Samuel Bethel's tavern on Lancaster's center square. Two Native American men had entered the tavern one evening asking for liquor, one conspicuously displaying a large, dangerous knife. This led the attendant, Bethel's wife, to clear out the customers and lock the door to prevent trouble. Lingering outside, the two Indians broke a window to attempt to reenter. Two Euro-American patrons came out to quiet them, and a struggle ensued. One of the Euro-American men was stabbed so seriously that for some time his survival was in doubt. When he finally recovered, however, the court in Lancaster released the Native American assailant. Logan wrote to the Conestogas to explain that Pennsylvania would not prosecute because the victim had recovered, although the culprit was obligated to personally pay the injured man's medical expenses. Such mercy was not extended to Euro-American criminals in comparable situations, Logan assured them, although he did not mention what factors in the Native Americans' background made this appropriate. He made it clear, however, that because Anglo-American law rested on individual responsibility it could not condone payments made by the tribe, friends, or family of a guilty Indian on his behalf nor, when physical punishment was involved, accept a surrogate to endure the suffering in place of the guilty party.[16]

A further expression of leniency occurred when a Mahican from Esopus in New York named Awannameak assaulted Henry Webb, a settler in the Minisinks' lands, in May 1740. The causes underlying Awannameak's action were not recorded, but even Native American spokesmen did not defend his conduct. At first it had been questionable whether Webb would live. A week after the attack, Governor George Thomas sent Nicholas Scull with a letter to the Mahican headman at Esopus, Menakikickon, demanding the surrender of Awannameak. The governor argued that just as all "officers and people" were expected to run down any colonist who fled after committing a crime, so "we expect when any of your people commit a crime your people shall . . . find them and cause them to be kept in Prison till they can be prosecuted and punished, but if the Offence be not Murther or some such grievous crime, a lesser punishment is inflicted on their Bodies, or sometimes they are fined in a sum of money to make Satisfaction for their crimes." Thomas wanted the Indian to pay "Satisfaction" to Webb, who was now certain to live, as well as the charges for his "Cure and Nursing and Keeping." The governor added that if Awannameak could not pay, his friends could pay for him and the warrior could then later repay them by his "diligence in hunting." Scull carried the letter to Menakikickon in Esopus but was rebuffed by apparently frivolous excuses: Menakikickon claimed to be too sick to search for Awannameak and was also too busy because he had to supervise the women who were planting the village's corn.

By August, Webb could walk but was said to have lost his jawbone, his capacity to speak, and his ability to earn a living. In September, the Assembly—apparently despairing of collecting reparations from Menakikickon—gave Webb £10 cash and paid his physician £13. At another Philadelphia conference, in July 1742, Governor Thomas renewed discussion of the case with the Onondaga spokesman Canesatego, who insisted that Awannameak had been sufficiently verbally punished by his nation's superiors and would not be surrendered to Pennsylvania authorities because Webb had recovered his health. He said, "The Indians know no punishment but death. They have no such thing as Pecuniary Mulcts; if a man be guilty of a crime he is either put to death or the fault is overlooked." Canesatego was also able to place Thomas on the defensive by saying that the Indians gave credence to rumors that Pennsylvania had deceived them by announcing that two men who had killed Indians, the Winter brothers, had been hanged in July 1728, when in fact they had been secretly released and sent away to another colony. There the matter stood, a precedent for releasing violent Indian offenders when their victims had recovered and for not imposing fines or ordering compensation for the victims.[17]

The assault on Ann Hunter had taken place within a society in which officials not only sometimes excused acts of violence committed under the influence of alcohol but also remembered the confusion of 1744 surrounding the Jack Armstrong murders. In remote Jack's Narrows in the Juniata Valley, a Delaware named Mushemeelin had taken revenge on Armstrong for seizing his horse to settle a debt. Although Mushemeelin had apparently overpowered Armstrong and hacked his body to pieces, many irregularities cluttered the path of English justice. For one thing, because the only living witnesses to the killings were the suspects themselves—Mushemeelin and his two assistants—Pennsylvania decided to accept the pronouncement of Shickellamy, the Iroquois diplomatic resident among the Shamokin Delawares, that Mushemeelin alone had murdered Armstrong and the two companions, and had lied when he said he had been acting in self-defense. Shickellamy had accepted the story told by Mushemeelin's two assistants—that Mushemeelin did all the killing—over the accused's own statements. Also unusual was the provincial government's seeming inability to hold firm to its announced policies when opposition arose. Pennsylvania had initially demanded that Mushemeelin's assistants be surrendered to them as trial suspects, but the demand was withdrawn when both the Delaware chief Olumpies and Shickellamy asserted that they believed the two were innocent. The Indians eventually allowed the assistants to be examined, but only as witnesses with strict assurances that they would not be indicted or physically confined. Another irregularity was Governor Thomas's acceptance of a gift from the Delawares of a bundle of pelts which he gave to the murder victims' relatives, although he had made a statement, just as James Logan had, that the Native American tradition of allowing a murderer's family or tribe to pay compensation to the victims' relatives, and in some situations even substitute another person to be executed in place of the murderer, was unacceptable under English law with its emphasis on individual responsibility.[18]

In October 1744, the Assembly passed a speedy trial law that protected Indians accused of capital felonies occurring on the frontiers of the province by moving the trials from the nearest rural county seat to Philadelphia. The removal of such trials from frontier courts decreased opportunities for local Euro-American juries to vent their prejudices against Indians. The same statute also halted lengthy preindictment confinements of Indian suspects, which many Native people regarded as punishment in itself. In order to provide the legal authority for trying Mushemeelin in Philadelphia, the statute was, curiously, written to apply to pending as well as future trials, in defiance of the customary legal stricture against retroactive legislation. Accordingly, Governor Thomas moved Mushemeelin's imprisonment and trial from Lancaster to Philadelphia, but he did it not so much to assure a fair trial as to avoid embarrassing his government by having a trial and probable execution take place in Lancaster, for all to see, at the very time a treaty was being negotiated between Pennsylvania, Maryland, and Virginia and the Iroquois Confederacy. This was the Treaty of Lancaster, held in June and July 1744, which was, as the next chapter explains, an event of vital importance to the three governments. Mushemeelin was hanged in Philadelphia on 14 November.[19]

Comparing these irregular methods of 1744 with the administration of the Ann Hunter case, it appears that, up to the point of Toby's arrest, the criminal justice process had improved in the intervening seven years. On the other hand, Mushemeelin's trial was at least based on the circumstances of the crime, not on political issues separating an Indian nation from the provincial government. No court of law ever heard the Ann Hunter case because Toby's fate became a negotiable item in the bargaining process between the Nanticokes and Pennsylvania's government.

Toby remained in the Lancaster jail until some time in the summer of 1751, when Governor Hamilton released him. By then, the possibility of Ann being permanently injured had evaporated, and the Pennsylvania custom of forgiving violent acts committed by intoxicated Indians after their victims fully recovered might have been Toby's salvation. But discussions between the governor and the Nanticokes determined his fate instead. These occurred at a conference in August 1751, in Philadelphia, a session of the Provincial Council attended by five Nanticoke representatives with Weiser also in attendance. The Nanticokes' spokesman thanked Pennsylvania for releasing Toby, whom he described as having been jailed for "abusing a White girl," and begged the Council to remove any lingering ill will between the two communities. Although there had been no court proceedings, Hamilton classified Toby as guilty, referring to "the crime your brother whom we put in Lancaster Jayl was guilty of." The Euro-American community's anger would be dispelled, Hamilton promised, but only because the Nanticokes had interceded for Toby and Toby himself had promised to mend his ways.[20]

At this conference the Nanticokes put a larger issue on the table. They asserted that at the time they had begun to leave Maryland in 1742, Pennsylvania had assigned them a location at the mouth of tributaries of the upper Susquehanna River, where they were authorized to live among the Delawares. The area they occupied turned out to be the mouth of the Juniata River, but the claim that they had done so at provincial direction flies in the face of other accounts of the removal that say it was authorized only by the Onondaga council of the Six Nations, not by the Pennsylvania government. The Nanticoke spokesman proceeded sheepishly to admit that on its own initiative the tribe had recently left the Juniata and moved to the Wyoming Valley, and he asked Hamilton to condone the new location and pledge to protect their presence there. Hamilton refused, saying only that Pennsylvania had no objection to a Wyoming residency provided "all the other Indians now there approve of it." Surprisingly, the legitimacy of the small Nanticoke community adjacent to Paxton, where Toby, King, and a handful of others had lived until February, was not discussed at all.[21]

It is difficult to understand why the Nanticoke representatives had tied Toby's case and the move to Wyoming together; it is as if they were offering thanks for one concession—Toby's freedom—and then asking for another one. If they meant to suggest that future incidents of violence between their people and the settlers would be prevented once they had a protected home in far-off Wyoming, they did not express the point clearly, at least as their speeches were recorded in the treaty minutes. Perhaps the Nanticokes wanted Pennsylvania to counterbalance the authority the Six Nations Iroquois council held over them. Indeed, an incident that took place during the Nanticoke delegation's trip home suggests that their purported Iroquois overlords did not approve of what had been said to Governor Hamilton. As the delegates passed through Germantown, the Nanticokes assaulted and nearly killed "an Albany Indian" who accompanied them. Perhaps this companion was an Onondaga who was attacked for disputing the Nanticokes' pretensions to holding their lands from Pennsylvania rather than the Six Nations.[22]

Be that as it may, by the 1760s Toby had risen to a middle level of leadership within his community. He was apparently not haunted by the Ann Hunter affair, and there is no reason to believe it had discredited him among the Nanticokes. Yet it is difficult to be certain, for we have only two glimpses of Toby's later life, and each is very impersonal. In September 1766, Toby and five other leaders from the Nanticoke, Conoy, and Mohican community at Otsiningo (or Chenango), conferred with Governor John Penn in Philadelphia. Otsiningo was a multiethnic population center in Iroquois territory on the site of today's Binghamton, New York, and the Nanticokes, having moved from Wyoming, were now largely concentrated there. The delegation complained that a Pennsylvanian, licensed trader John Anderson, had robbed them of "ore" from a mine they owned in the Wyoming Valley. Penn answered that he would try to prevent a reoccurrence, but he cautioned that the valley was too far away from Philadelphia to be carefully policed by his province. At the end of the conference the governor offered some token diplomatic gifts and was asked to add two riding horses, one for Toby and one for a Conoy headman named Last Knight. These were provided so that the two could make the trip home in comfort, but it obviously represented recognition and respectability for Toby.[23]

Toby's final appearance in the historical record was at a condolence conference at Shamokin, in August 1769, called to express sympathy for the murder several weeks earlier of Young Seneca George, whose father of the same name was a leader of the community at Otsiningo. As recounted by James H. Merrell, during the final conference session, the question of punishment of the presumed murderer, a young Pennsylvania German farm worker named Peter Reid, was discussed, and the elder Seneca George learned that Reid was the "sister's son" of the now deceased Conrad Weiser. One of Weiser's sons explained that, in spite of this kinship connection, the family had no objection to Reid being punished if found guilty. Yet, on hearing of Reid's kinship to the elder Weiser, a friend he had so much admired, the old Seneca became highly emotional and swore that he forgave Reid as well as all other frontiersmen who had mistreated Indians in the past. He then eloquently appealed to both Indians and colonials to bury their old quarrels.[24]

On the same day, Turbutt Francis, acting in a threefold capacity as commander of Fort Augusta, a civil magistrate, and the provincial spokesman appointed to attend the condolence conference, wrote to James Burd, also a magistrate, in Lancaster. He asked Burd to help John Toby recover a chestnut horse that the Indian claimed had been stolen from him by Thomas French of Lancaster. Toby named three Euro-American men who he was confident would confirm that they had seen French in possession of the horse.[25] Unfortunately, there is no record of what became of Toby's complaint, but the incident is important. Toby could not have forgotten the humiliation of 1751, when his life was spared as token compensation to the Nanticokes by the provincial government at the same time it was rejecting that nation's plea for a guarantee of the land where they resided. Perhaps, too, Toby lamented the useless killings of the Conestogas and Young Seneca George. He had learned to play the Euro-Americans' game; unlike Mushemeelin he would not resort to violence when his horse was stolen but would use the English justice process instead. If Old Seneca George had such veneration for a dead Euro-American man that he could forgive his own son's murderer, why should Toby not capitalize on the matter and balance out the Indians' surrendering of retribution for the murder by having Thomas French branded as a horse thief and by using Pennsylvania's authorities to recover his horse for him?[26]

No records remain to trace Ann Hunter and her family. Perhaps, like John Toby and Mushemeelin, the Hunters regarded an Indian's incarceration of several months' duration as adequate punishment. But it is more likely that as poor frontier settlers, the Hunters did not have any way to take revenge. Nor did the procedures followed in administering the case stand as legal precedents because the decision made at the diplomatic level supplanted the judicial process. As a case study, then, the Ann Hunter affair is important in showing that both Native people and Euro-Americans were in general agreement on what constituted criminal behavior, that departures from established procedures were made to prevent a single criminal act from precipitating general warfare, and that individuals' interests were subordinated to the diplomatic compromises necessary to preserve the peace.

8

THE DIPLOMATIC CAREER OF CANASATEGO

WILLIAM A. STARNA

Looming over the legal and diplomatic struggles of mid-eighteenth-century Euro-Pennsylvanians and Native Americans was the phantom—and occasionally the reality—of Iroquois power. As Pennsylvania officials surveyed what appeared to be chaotic communities of Delawares, Shawnees, and other displaced Native peoples in the Susquehanna and Ohio countries, they sought order in the fiction of Iroquois suzerainty over the multitudes—and feared bloodshed should Iroquois traveling the "warriors' path" southward turn against the province. Meanwhile, both Indians and Euro-Americans on the frontiers could find their aims thwarted, and perhaps even their homes sold out from under them, through deals made over their heads by the proprietors' government and headmen who invoked the name of the Grand Council of the Iroquois League. In these tangled affairs, no name loomed larger during the 1740s than that of the Onondaga headman Canasatego.

He "was a tall, well-made man; had a very full chest, and brawny limbs," said Marylander Witham Marshe, who saw him in action at the Treaty of Lancaster in 1744. "He had a manly countenance, mixed with a good-natured smile," and at "about 60 years of age" remained "very active, strong, and had a surprising liveliness in his speech."[1] Historians, however, have not always been as flattering in their assessments as was

Marshe. In the eyes of some, Canasatego was little more than a purveyor of "braggart falsehoods," a "rum-guzzling windjammer," a "burly, bibulous chief," and a "blowhard."[2] Yet in recent years a revisionist view has emerged, transforming Canasatego into a moralizer in political theory, earnestly lecturing colonial officials on "Iroquois concepts of unity" and delivering up admonitions that "would echo throughout the colonies for over a generation," to be used "not only as a rallying cry against French colonialism but also against British tyranny." The "process of assimilating Iroquois ideas of unity" into the national psyche, and eventually into the Constitution itself, the revisionists say, began with Canasatego.[3] Somewhere in the middle of all this might lie the truth.[4]

Canasatego first appears in the historical record in 1742; his subsequently documented career lasted but eight years. An early translation of his name is "upsetting a house placed in good order," but modern linguistics finds the term unrecognizable.[5] He did not carry any of the known fourteen Onondaga hereditary sachem titles, and so it is unlikely that Canasatego held office as a league chief.[6] Instead, he was probably a speaker, possessing impressive verbal skills and mastery of diplomatic rituals, shrewdness, and personal ambition—qualities that together propelled him into the political arena and made him one of the "chief men" at Onondaga.[7] Little more can be added except to conclude, with ethnohistorian William N. Fenton, that he "dominated politics just then at Onondaga."[8]

Nothing is known of Canasatego's early years. At the peak of his influence, he lived in the village of Sagogsaanagechtheyky, which in 1743 consisted of some forty bark-covered houses scattered along a two- to three-mile stretch of Onondaga Creek in what is now central New York.[9] His "very large and roomy, and well built" home was a short distance from the council house, the center of Onondaga politics.[10] With him resided his wife, a son and daughter, and also a Catawba boy, most likely a war captive.[11] Outside the family dwelling was "a large pole . . . with an English flag on it," a signal of Canasatego's political affection.[12] Zila Woolien (also Zila Woolie, Zillawoolie), a brother, lived in the nearby village of Tiatachtout.[13] A nephew, whose name is not recorded, was killed by colonists just before Canasatego appeared at a 1749 council in Philadelphia.[14]

In the decades before Canasatego came to the notice of Euro-Pennsylvanians, peace had come to the Iroquois only in exchange for European dominance. Changing village life, an economic downturn, and "a diplomacy

increasingly oriented merely toward preserving maneuvering room between powerful surrounding colonies told the tale."[15] Moreover, epidemics
continued their devastation. A "contagion," smallpox, ravaged their villages in 1716–17 and again in 1731–32, this time having spread from colonial
populations in and around Manhattan and New Jersey.[16] In the fall and
winter of 1746–47, Onondaga, where much of Iroquois political business
was conducted, fell victim.[17] Along with disease and its inescapable disruptions of village life came its baneful companion, famine. On his first journey to Onondaga in 1737, Conrad Weiser, the interpreter and Indian agent
for Pennsylvania, spoke with Indians living in the upper reaches of the
Susquehanna Valley who were "so short of provisions now, while twelve
years ago they had a greater supply than all the other Indians; and now
their children looked like dead persons, and suffered much from hunger."[18] Indians appeared in "such numbers" at a treaty conference at Philadelphia in 1742 that Pennsylvanians could only assume that they were
trying "to escape the famine that was sweeping the Indian country."[19]
There Canasatego himself reported that the Senecas had "not come down
. . . on Account of a famine that raged in their Country, which had reduced
them to such Want that a father had been obliged to kill two of his Children to preserve his own and the rest of his family's Lives."[20] Conditions
were apparently little better eight years later. After visiting the Senecas
in summer 1750, the Moravians John Cammerhoff and David Zeisberger
returned to a Cayuga village which they had passed through earlier. They
unexpectedly discovered that "the corn had given out, and [the Cayugas]
had been compelled to procure much from Onondago, carrying it on their
backs, a very troublesome mode of transportation."[21]

Although Cammerhoff and Zeisberger ate well at Onondaga, where
there appeared to be no shortage of food, they did have to confront the
ruin of alcohol abuse.[22] After a night of heavy drinking, it took all of Canasatego's influence to bring the village council together to discuss the Moravians' several petitions.[23] It had been much worse in the Seneca town of
Ganataqueh, where Cammerhoff and Zeisberger witnessed a "drinking
bout" that left everyone in "a state of intoxication."[24] At Zonesschio, another Seneca village, the Moravians walked into the middle of a drunken
brawl, a harrowing scene filled with "shouting and quarreling" among the
Indians, who "all looked mad with drink." "On our way," reported Cammerhoff, "we were everywhere surrounded by drunken savages . . . some
of whose faces wore an expression more dreadful than anything we had

ever seen, showing that they had been in this frightful state of intoxication for some days."[25] The situation there deteriorated, and the Moravians were forced to seek a cramped refuge in the loft of one of the houses, "under a shingle roof, on which the sun shone, intensely hot."[26] Two days later, after another miserable night, they managed to slip out of the village while "the drunken savages were in their huts, not a creature to be seen. Even the dogs, numbering nearly 100 in the whole village, were all quiet, wonderful to relate, and not a sound was heard."[27] Poverty was a constant companion to these grim scenes; the Indians' frequent pleas for help signaled their real privation and lent an awful reality to their distress.[28]

The "illusion of power" that the Iroquois, shrewdly and cynically abetted by the English and French, had fostered for decades began to vaporize in the 1730s and 1740s.[29] The Iroquois design to link the Ohio Indians, many of whom were the transplanted Iroquois referred to as Mingos, to the central fire at Onondaga, never succeeded.[30] In 1730 more than one thousand Foxes, Iroquois allies in the west, were trapped by a force of French and Algonquians while fleeing to Seneca villages, with several hundred killed and the rest taken prisoner.[31] In the meantime, the French had pressed farther into Iroquoia with the building of a fort at Crown Point on Lake Champlain, while the English, for their part, began buying up Mohawk land.[32]

Thus the Iroquois found themselves under military and political assault from the north, west, and east, while simultaneously facing unrelenting clashes with such southern Indian foes as the Catawbas. The hardships caused by famine, disease, and drink further complicated matters, all of which encouraged an exodus of people who resettled in the Ohio country.[33] In their weakened condition, those Iroquois who remained in their homelands—excepting the Mohawks—sought to protect their collective flanks by allying themselves with Pennsylvania.[34]

That province was ready for a marriage of convenience. In 1736, Shickellamy, the noted Oneida headman who served ostensibly as the Iroquois' overseer of the Shawnees in Pennsylvania, and Hetaquantegechty, a Seneca, led a large number of canoes filled with more than one hundred Iroquois people and their headmen down the Susquehanna River.[35] The delegation, which significantly included no Mohawks, came to continue business started as early as 1732 when James Logan, the peripatetic Pennsylvania official and de facto superintendent of Indian affairs, along with Weiser and Shickellamy, had launched a new provincial Indian policy that would "strengthen the hands of the Six Nations, and enable them to be the better answerable for their Tributaries."[36] Reduced to its essentials, this policy guaranteed that the Iroquois "would police Pennsylvania's woods in return for Pennsylvania's recognition of their sole right to do so."[37]

After the treaty council, Weiser accompanied the Indians to Shamokin, where, operating under Logan's instructions, he arranged for the Iroquois to release their claim to lands in the lower Susquehanna Valley, lands to which they actually had no legitimate title. Beyond the presents given to the Indians, what Francis Jennings called the "big bribe," was that the Iroquois received official and exclusive recognition as the lone bargaining agent for Indian lands in Pennsylvania. Not incidentally, they would also exercise supremacy over all of the other Indians there. Knowing that their hand had been strengthened, the Iroquois then petitioned the Pennsylvania authorities to notify Maryland and Virginia that they fully expected compensation, as they put it, "for our Land now in their occupation."[38]

Of equal interest with the consummation of the strategic alliance between the Iroquois and Pennsylvania is the new direction these developments signaled in the internal politics of the Iroquois. Virtually none of the headmen who appeared at the 1736 council, or afterwards at Shamokin, were at all familiar to Weiser or any of the other Pennsylvania officials.[39] Instead, they represented a faction—independent of, and possibly in opposition to, the existing consensus among the Iroquois—that sought a counterbalance to the predominance of New France and New York in the Iroquois' economic and diplomatic life.[40]

Though Canasatego was not on the list of participants at the 1736 meeting, it is likely that he was in attendance.[41] He was certainly present when an Iroquois delegation returned to Philadelphia in July 1742 to receive the remainder of their compensation for releasing the Susquehanna lands.[42] Identified on this occasion for the first time as the Onondagas' speaker,[43] he opened the conference with an account of how some of their "Young men" had, without authority, sold "two Plantations on the River Cohongoronta" to "Some white People." Skillfully employing the story as an allegory, he reminded Governor George Thomas that the Iroquois had not forgotten the 1736 agreement obligating them "to sell none of the Land that falls within the Province of Pennsylvania to any but our brother Onas, and that to sell Lands to any other is an high Breach of the League of friendship."[44]

The phrase "within the Province of Pennsylvania" was significant in light of the fact that the 1736 agreement had preceded Pennsylvania's infamous Walking Purchase. In the early 1730s, two of the three Penn brothers—John and Thomas—produced what they claimed to be an old deed as authority to appropriate the lands of the Lehigh Valley Delawares, which had been purchased in 1700 by their father William. The terms of that sale set forth the tract's northward extent as the distance a man could walk in a day and a half, following the course of the river. The walk, however, was never completed; at a point along the way, a dispute had arisen about whether the river should be crossed at the Indian settlement at Tohiccon, breaking off the whole affair. Three decades later, the Penns demanded that the interrupted walk of 1700 again be undertaken. Pressed by the Penn brothers, and also by several of the Iroquois nations, the Delaware leadership reluctantly withdrew its opposition and signed a purported deed in August 1737. Less than one month later the second walk took place. Hired runners struck out on a path that had previously been cleared (and thoroughly reconnoitered) at a pace that left their Indian witnesses struggling to keep up, covering a distance of some sixty miles in the time allotted. Moreover, the runners did not follow the winding course of the river, as the original agreement had stipulated, but instead walked a straight path and then drew a right-angle line, parallel to the river, from the most distant point. From there it was a four-day trek back to the river. Through this trickery, the Penns were able to lay claim to all of the territory between the Delaware and Lehigh rivers, lands that many of the Delawares would refuse to abandon.[45]

In 1742, then, Canasatego and the Iroquois were in a position to do far more than merely collect what had been pledged on the eve of the Walking Purchase in 1736, for Pennsylvania needed them to deal with the recalcitrant Delawares. After Governor Thomas had presented the goods promised in 1736—45 guns; 500 pounds of powder; 600 pounds of lead; 100 blankets; 100 shirts, shoes, stockings; iron tools; tobacco and tobacco pipes; and 25 gallons of rum—Canasatego was confident he could extract more. "It is true we have the full Quantity according to Agreement, but if the Proprietor had been here himself, we think in regard to our Numbers and poverty, he would have made an Addition to them," he announced. "We therefore desire, if you have the Keys of the Proprietor's Chest, you will open it and take out a little more for us." The Iroquois fully understood, Canasatego said, that their "Lands are now become more Valuable; the white People think we don't know their Value, but we are sensible that the

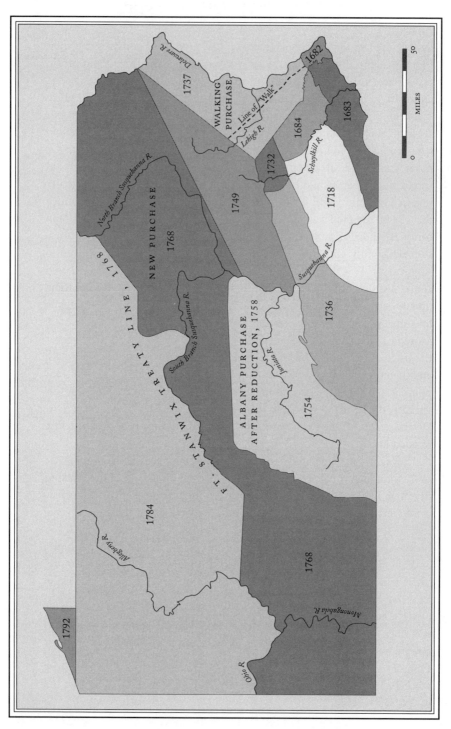

Map 4 Six Nations Iroquois land cessions to Pennsylvania, 1736–92. Claims of other Native nations excluded; revised from Paul A. W.

Land is Everlasting, and the few Goods we receive for it are soon Worn out and Gone."[46] Calling attention to the fact that Euro-Americans had settled in territory north of the area released in 1736 for which the Iroquois had "never received any Consideration," he demanded additional payment. The governor gave the appearance of raising a number of objections but in the end delivered goods to the tune of at least £300.[47]

Governor Thomas may not have anticipated Canasatego's importunity, but he had decided before the meeting to test the resolve of his new-found friends and the new policy of inflating Iroquois hegemony over the varied Indian communities with which Pennsylvania had to deal. Taking his turn before the council, Thomas raised the issue of the Delawares and a "disturbance about the Lands the Proprietor purchased from them" that they had provoked with "insolence . . . [and] utmost Rudeness and ill Manners."[48] "As you on all Occasions apply to Us to remove all White people that are settled on Lands before they are purchased from You, and we do our Endeavours to turn such People Off," he continued, "We now expect from You that you will cause these Indians to remove from the Lands in the forks of Delaware, and not give any further Disturbance to the Persons who are now in Possession."[49] Outmaneuvered by the governor and bound by the new Iroquois-Pennsylvanian alliance, Canasatego was trapped. Thomas had responded favorably, if perhaps with feigned reticence, to Canasatego's request for more presents. As a consequence, Canasatego found himself burdened with an obligation. But more important, the Iroquois were compelled to exact obedience of their tributaries over whom they had been assigned authority by the 1732 and 1736 agreements.

Two full days went by before Canasatego rose in council to reply to the governor's challenge. And when he did, he pulled out all the stops. Agreeing with the governor that the Delawares had "been a very unruly People, and . . . altogether in the wrong in their Dealings," he turned to the Delawares and their headman Nutimus, who had been a party to both the original Walking Purchase of 1700 and that of 1737.[50] "Let this Belt of Wampum serve to Chastize You," Canasatego thundered. "You ought to be taken by the Hair of the Head and shak'd severely till you recover your Senses and become Sober; you don't know what Ground you stand on, nor what you are doing. . . . We conquer'd You, we made Women of you, you know you are Women, and can no more sell Land than Women. . . . This Land that you Claim is gone through Your Guts. You have been furnished with Cloaths and Meat and Drink . . . and now You want it again like Children you are. . . . This String of Wampum serves to forbid You . . . for ever medling in Land Affairs."[51] Canasatego ordered the Delawares to move to either Wyoming, on the Susquehanna's north branch, or to Shamokin. "We don't give you the liberty to think about it," he concluded. "Take the Advice of a Wise Man and remove immediately."[52]

Despite the force of his rhetoric, a closer examination reveals that Canasatego, without a blink, had entirely submitted to the governor. He had no choice and could save face only by holding forth in what Jennings called unfettered "rodomontade."[53] Canasatego's take-charge stance, however, bolstered the Iroquois' pretense of hegemony over its their "tributaries" and kept the Delawares within the fold and away from the French. It also gave the Iroquois desperately needed maneuvering room between the competing French and English colonial powers who, as almost everyone knew, were about to enter into a war.[54] Canasatego's other intention, however, was to secure the good graces of the Pennsylvania governor. By doing so, he hoped to keep the "road" between the Iroquois he represented and the Pennsylvanians "clear and free" of "obstructions" and "incumbrances."[55] It was on this path, after all, that he wanted European goods to continue to flow, goods that would be a hedge against the difficult times his people were enduring. It was also on this road that Iroquois warriors could travel unimpeded against their erstwhile enemies, the Catawbas.

In summer 1743, Weiser, accompanied by John Bartram, the botanist, and Louis Evans, a mapmaker, traveled north from Pennsylvania to resolve a serious matter with the Iroquois.[56] The previous winter a party of mostly Onondaga warriors on their way to raid the Catawbas had been attacked by Virginians. Several were slain, and the Iroquois vowed revenge. Aware of the danger to its exposed frontier settlements, Virginia immediately sought to defuse the situation, asking Pennsylvania to have Weiser act as a mediator. Not wanting to be drawn into a wider conflict that might involve the fractious and unpredictable Shawnees, Pennsylvania obliged, and so did Weiser.[57]

Upon reaching Onondaga, the Pennsylvanians were escorted to their quarters. "After we had eat some dry'd Eels boild in Hominy, and some Matts had been spread for Us to lye upon, Canassatego and Caheshcarowanoto, of the Chiefs, with several more, came to see Us and receiv'd Us very kindly," Weiser reported. The visitors and their hosts "smoak'd a Pipe of Philadelphia Tobacco together, and had some further discourse on things of no Consequence."[58] There is no record of any interaction between Canasatego and Weiser following the 1742 treaty, but enough trust had grown between them to embolden Weiser to invite the Onondaga to meet him "in the Bushes to have a private Discourse" on those consequential things they could not discuss publicly. "We met a little way distant from the Town," Weiser recalled. "I brought with me my Instructions and the Wampum I had, and told him that as he was our Particular friend and well acquainted both with Indians and white People's Affairs and Customs, I would tell him all my Business, and beg his Advice how to speak to everything when the Council should be met. He assured me of his good will and Affection to the Governor of Pensilvania and all his People, and that he would do for me what lay in his power."[59] Canasatego took this message to the Onondaga headmen who later in the day summoned Weiser to meet with them. Tocanuntie ("otherwise call'd the black Prince of Onondago")[60] gave Weiser the advice he sought and also mentioned that the Pennsylvanian had "done very well and prudent to inform the Onondagoes . . . before the rest of the Counsellors." Because most of the members of the raiding party killed by the Catawbas had been Onondagas, that nation would "altogether be left . . . by the Council of the United Nations to answer."[61]

Armed with this advice, Weiser, representing Virginia, asked Canasatego to speak for him "in Open Council." When the meeting opened, the dead Onondagas were condoled (among them was Shickellamy's cousin), and £100 sterling in goods provided by Virginia's lieutenant governor, William Gooch, were distributed to the mourning families and the "Publick Council."[62] Then "the Chain of friendship" between the Iroquois and Virginia was mended and assurances made so that both the colony's "back Inhabitants" and any Iroquois warriors passing by them on their way to the Catawbas would be of "good behavior." Lastly, the alliance between the Iroquois and Pennsylvania was reaffirmed.[63]

When that alliance was next confirmed, in the treaty at Lancaster in 1744, additional evidence emerged on how Canasatego maintained his position as an Onondaga headman and speaker for the Iroquois. The council brought together the Iroquois—again with no Mohawk participation—and government officials from Pennsylvania, Maryland, and Virginia. Its purpose was to resolve the land claims the Iroquois had made against the Chesapeake provinces in the treaty of 1736 and to inform the Iroquois of the start of what British colonists would call King George's War.[64] Pennsylvania's Governor Thomas had instructed the commissioners of Virginia and Maryland about the significance of this meeting. The Iroquois, positioned on "a Frontier" with some of the colonies, would be, "If Friends, . . . Capable of Defending their Settlements; If Enemies, of making Cruel Ravages upon them; If Neuters, they may deny the French a Passage through their Country, and give us timely Notice of their Designs. These are but some of the Motives for cultivating a good Understanding with them."[65]

Maryland had called the conference; therefore, Iroquois protocol dictated that its commissioner speak first. He began by disputing the Iroquois territorial claim, arguing that there was "little reason to complain of any Injury from Maryland." If by making such a claim the Iroquois "designed to Terrify" Marylanders, they should think again, for the provincials, who were "numerous, courageous, and have arms ready in their Hands, will not suffer themselves to be hurt in their Lives and Estates" that they had possessed "above One hundred Years." Nevertheless, he was there to listen to whatever grounds there were for the claim, and if any had merit, to "make them some reasonable Compensation for it."[66]

The next day, Canasatego replied with a lengthy history lesson, combined with a bit of knucklerapping:

> When you mentioned the affair of the Land Yesterday, you went back to old Times, and told us you had been in posession of the Province of Maryland above One hundred Years; but what is one hundred years in comparison to the length of Time since our Claim began?—Since we came out of this Ground? For we must tell you that long before One hundred years Our ancestors came out of this very Ground, and their Children have remained here ever since. You came out of the Ground in a Country that lyes beyond Seas, there you may have a just Claim, but here you must allow Us to be your elder Brethren, and the Lands to belong to us long before you know anything of them.[67]

As Jennings wryly observed, Canasatego's monologue was "the only known occasion upon which the Iroquois claimed ancestors in Maryland."[68] Nonetheless, it firmly set the tone for the conference, for all appearances placing the colonies in the awkward position of having to pay substantial sums for a claim they knew was bogus. "Altho' we cannot admit your

Right," Maryland complained, it nevertheless put up £300 in Pennsylvania currency, partially in goods. Pennsylvania added another £300. Virginia was especially brusque as it laid out £200 in goods and another £300 in gold: "As we have already sayd enough to you on the Subject of the Title to the Lands you Claim from Virginia, we have no occasion to say any thing more to you on that head, but come directly to the Point. We have open'd the Chests, and the Goods are now here before you."[69]

The Old Dominion, however, would have the last laugh. Canasatego, for all of his skills at discourse and negotiation, apparently did not fully grasp the significance of the conference much beyond its gifts and gold and the renewed recognition of the Iroquois' ostensible hegemony over Pennsylvania's Indians. Blinded by his perceived victory, he seems not to have examined, or understood, the record of what he had agreed to. He and the other Iroquois headmen believed that they had ceded only the Shenandoah Valley to Virginia. Yet the deed's language far more expansively "renounce[d] and disclaim[ed] not only all the right of the said six nations, but also recognize[d] the right and title of our sovereign the King of Great Britain to all the lands within the said colony [of Virginia] as it is now or hereafter may be peopled and bounded by his said Majesty . . . his heirs and successors." According to Virginia's royal charter, those lands within its boundaries extended all the way to the Pacific. By the following April, the Williamsburg government had granted petitions for some 300,000 acres of western real estate.[70]

In June 1745, Canasatego, with several other headmen, again welcomed Weiser and his party to Onondaga. Weiser had instructions from the governor of Pennsylvania, acting on a request from Virginia's Gooch, to arrange a peace between the Iroquois and the Catawbas. His visit was timed perfectly as the Onondagas, along with delegations of other Iroquois, were preparing to travel to Canada at the invitation of the French governor.[71] Meeting in council, representatives of the Iroquois, again with no Mohawks participating, deferred any decision to attend a treaty with the Catawbas until the diplomats returned from Canada. They also assured Weiser that they knew "the French Governor . . . will try to gain upon us, but it will be in vain for him, as we have already agreed what to say to him and will not go from it."[72] Still, Weiser reminded the Iroquois of promises they had made at Lancaster at least to maintain neutrality in the imperial war.[73]

Canasatego did not accompany his fellow Onondaga headmen to Canada. According to Weiser, he had "staid at home to meet the Governour of New-York in Albany (as they said) some time this Fall."[74] Canasatego, however, was at Onondaga to greet the Moravian bishop Augustus Spangenberg upon his return from Oswego, from whence the Iroquois delegates had departed for Montreal.[75] There is no reason to doubt Weiser's assessment of why the Onondaga headman did not go to Oswego and then to Canada. Canasatego's strongly pro-English sentiments might also have influenced him to stay put. Whatever the case, he acted as the chief speaker at the upcoming Albany conference, conveying in detail to the assembled Indians and colonial officials what had gone on in Montreal.[76]

The October 1745 meeting in Albany brought together an array of government officials from New York, Massachusetts, Connecticut, and Pennsylvania, and a contingent of more than 460 Iroquois, among them between 40 and 50 headmen, this time including Mohawks, but no Senecas. A number of Mahicans also participated.[77] The council was called ostensibly to determine the source of a rumor, circulated the previous winter, that the citizens of Albany were about to attack the Mohawks.[78] For the Iroquois, the meeting could not have come at a more inopportune time: they were in the midst of debating the peace overtures of the Catawbas; they were facing problems with the Shawnees in the west, who were slipping from their political grasp and sidling up to the French; and they needed to consider the report of their deputies recently returned from Canada.[79] Nevertheless, the council proceeded. "I saw Canassatego and the rest of my old friends today," Weiser, who attended the Albany conference in his capacity as interpreter for the Pennsylvania commissioners, reported on his arrival.[80] At the council, Canasatego and the Mohawk headman Hendrick were the Iroquois speakers. Governor George Clinton of New York, who had called the gathering, set an agenda that went beyond squelching the "rumor," the significance of which was fast diminishing. First, Clinton wanted a full report from the Iroquois on their wartime dealings with the French governor. Second, suspecting that overtures had been made by the French, he wanted to impress the Iroquois with "the power of the united English colonies."[81]

Canasatego obliged the governor, furnishing him with a detailed account of what had happened in Montreal. He repeated the Iroquois' pledge to remain neutral "unless the French should come through our Settlements to hurt our Brethren the English, which we would not permit."[82] Earlier, when pressed by Clinton to take up the hatchet against the French in King George's War, Canasatego had promised only to keep it "in our Bosom," out of sight of both the French and the Iroquois' Indian allies. Although the Iroquois refused to commit themselves, Canasatego and several other Onondaga headmen were deeply concerned about New York's and New England's insistence that they enter the fray.[83] And they wondered why Pennsylvania had not been present at the council session to hear Clinton's request to take up the hatchet. Weiser recorded what the Onondaga headmen had confided to him in a private meeting about how "the Warr between the French and English had formerly Eat up all their People that had too rashly engaged in it without any Cause, and that the White People daily increasing saved themselves and the Indians decreased." In the future, the Indians vowed, they would "be more careful before they destroy'd one another again."[84]

Canasatego and other Onondaga headmen saw through the pretext of any "union" that was said to prevail among the British colonies. They also recognized the very real military, political, and economic dangers this lack of unity posed to their people. Fearing the abilities of the French to draw the neutral Iroquois to their support, New York, Connecticut, and Massachusetts sought unsuccessfully to commit them to a declaration for the English. Pennsylvania was against any engagement of the Indians whatever.[85] As he had at Lancaster, Canasatego urged the English to put aside their differences and formulate a single policy in their dealings with the French and, as important, with the Iroquois: "You our Brethren should be all united in your Councils, and let this Belt of Wampum serve to bind you all together; and if any thing of Importance is to be communicated to us by any of you, this is the place where it should be done."[86] Canasatego knew full well what the outcome for his people would be if the English were not of "Good Agreement" or unable to keep the French at bay.[87] He did not mention the ever-widening divisions in Iroquois communities and what they might portend, that the risks for the Iroquois would only increase if factionalism continued. He seems to have remained much less prescient about the future of the Confederacy than he was of English-French relations.

Canasatego attended his last recorded treaty conference in August 1749, one year after King George's War ended. Pennsylvania hoped to purchase additional Iroquois lands west of the Susquehanna, where, as subsequent chapters in this volume will show, unauthorized settlement by Euro-American squatters was becoming a major irritant to Native peoples and the proprietary government alike. Weiser had urged proprietary officials to refrain from using open force against the squatters until after the treaty, "when all proper means ought to be used to make a purchase from [the Iroquois] . . . for some part of that land between the Kititany or Endless mountains and alleghiny Hill," including "all the Lands on the Waters of Juniata."[88] The plan was for the arriving Iroquois delegations to rendezvous north of Philadelphia and to proceed from there. But the Senecas, traveling alone, went on ahead. They met with the governor in the city and were given a message to take to the Iroquois council at Onondaga, "to know if they wou'd sell any and what Lands to the Proprietors."[89]

More than a month later, leading "a mob of 279 hungry Indians"—among them Tutelos, Nanticokes, and Delawares, as well as Iroquois—Canasatego appeared at Weiser's farm in Tulpehocken, expecting to treat again with the Pennsylvanians. Weiser was in a panic over how he would feed and shelter so many people, and he let Canasatego know of his displeasure from the start. Instead of greeting his old friend with a handshake, he stood silently for several long minutes, publicly displaying his anger.[90] He told the headman that he and his people had no business in Philadelphia other than to get drunk. Furthermore, they could anticipate no presents from the proprietors and could not expect to be fed—food cost money.[91] Unchastened by Weiser's diatribe, Canasatego waited until the next day to respond. He chided his friend, reminding him that colonists had always been invited to "take Share with us be it no thing or Some thing and we have allways done So." Iroquois expected the same kind of hospitality "when we went to philadelphia and never have been reprimanded for it after this manner." If they were no longer welcome in the Pennsylvania capital, "perhaps it is because you got all our lands that you wanted from us and you dont like to See us any more and Consequently our fate is the Same as our Cousins the delawares and Mohickans."[92] Still, Canasatego offered Weiser an escape from this reproach, asking whether his message of the previous day was his own or on the instructions of "our Brethren in philadelphia." Recognizing that his loss of temper had insulted Canasatego and could cause irreparable damage to any further negotiations for land, Weiser responded that he had only meant to offer advice. If the Iroquois took it, "well and good," and "If not it was well and good again as to what belong to me."[93]

Figure 9   Conrad Weiser Homestead, Womelsdorf, Pennsylvania. Pennsylvania Historical and Museum Commission, Harrisburg.

Weiser escorted the delegation to Philadelphia. During the proceedings there, Canasatego expressed his dismay at the number of Euro-American squatters who had taken up lands on the Susquehanna's eastern bank beyond the Blue Mountain. On their way to Philadelphia, they had seen "papers which were Interpreted to us to be Orders for these People to Remove," yet "Notwithstanding your Engagements," he complained to Governor James Hamilton, "many People have settled on the East side of Sasquehanna, and though you may have done your Endeavours to remove them, yet we see these have been without Effect."[94] In response, Hamilton tried to shift responsibility for the encroachments to Indian residents of the Susquehanna and Juniata valleys who sometimes cut individual deals with squatters, allowing them to remain (as discussed in Chapter 10, below). "We shall not find it difficult effectually to remove all these Intruders if some of your Indians do not give them Countenance," Hamilton asserted, but "if we turn the People off you must not defend them nor invite them there again." In what Provincial Secretary Richard Peters called "an Expedient to quiet them," the governor tried to purchase the entire

Juniata River valley from the Iroquois. Canasatego, however, agreed to sell only a small parcel of land on the east side of the Susquehanna; in a process becoming painfully familiar on the proprietors' maps, this somehow became a huge swath of territory between the Susquehanna and Delaware rivers between the borders of the Walking Purchase and the Wyoming Valley.[95]

Thus at Philadelphia in 1749, Canasatego again managed to parlay a limited sale of lands to which the Iroquois held only tenuous claim into material advantage for his people. What is equally significant, however, is the Onondaga's recognition of just how badly the Iroquois had fared while trying to maneuver between the two competing European powers. In his opening speech, he had metaphorically brightened the "Chain of Friendship" between the Iroquois and Pennsylvania, declaring that "notwithstanding all that has happen'd, we are not chang'd in our Regards for you but continue to be the same still to the People of this Province as ever."[96] He then reminded the Pennsylvanians that the Iroquois were "a frontier Country between your Enemy and You, so that we have been your Guard, and things have been manag'd so well as to keep the War from your Doors, and tho' we have been expos'd to many Calamities and Blood has been shed among us, yet we did not trouble you with any account of our hardship during all this War, nor has any thing that has happen'd lessen'd our Affection for you, which we assure you of by this Belt, and desire the same return of Affection from You."[97] It would be easy to conclude that Canasatego's speech was preparatory to one more attempt to shake down Pennsylvania. After all, King George's War had not involved the Iroquois to any great degree. Yet after many years of only limited Iroquois success in dealing with the English and French, he must have come to the realization of just how dangerous the Iroquois' position as a "frontier Country" was.

But Canasatego's own position was even more dangerous; within a year he would be assassinated. The last non-Indians to report seeing him alive were Cammerhoff and Zeisberger during their visit to Onondaga in June 1750. On their arrival, they were escorted to the council house where they saw "a goodly assembly of important people sitting around their fire, Ganassateco in the midst of them. . . . He knew at once who we were, called us by name, and seemed very much pleased to see us. He began to laugh for joy, in his peculiar manner, and one felt and saw that we were welcome guests."[98] After a brief meeting, Canasatego and his visitors returned to his

house. "He came to our fire, and appeared so pleased to be able to enter-
tain us, that he scarcely knew how to express his joy," the Moravians recalled, imagining themselves to be "at a great court, where all the affairs of
state are concentrated." Canasatego was engaging, asking about old
friends, the news from Philadelphia, and how the journey had gone. "He
told us that he had much to do, and many matters to arrange."[99] Two days
later, a Sunday, the Moravians arose and were treated to "a bountiful
meal" during which "Ganassateco's manner was very kind and cheerful."
Later in the morning he showed them a Catawba's scalp, "skillfully painted
and tied to a stick. . . . It was the subject of a long discourse." Shortly
thereafter, Zeisberger suggested to Canasatego that he and Cammerhoff
meet with him privately, "so that we might give him a clear idea of our
wishes, and that he might then propose them to the Council for us, as we
were not perfectly familiar with their language and customs."[100]

On 6 September 1750, Weiser and Daniel Claus, the protégé of Sir William Johnson, arrived at Onondaga to find "the Indians in great Mourning
and Grief on account of their Head Sachem Canaghsadigo being dead a
few days before by Poison which was suspected to have been conveyed into
his Victuals by some french Emissaries that then resided at Onandaga Lake
under the Disguise of Traders."[101] In the day journal he kept while at
Onondaga, Weiser was somewhat more circumspect. "Since this CH
[Cammerhoff] was in the Sinniken [Seneca] Country and told the Indians
there that he had bought land from Canasago at onontago and paid him
with silver truk. This last article I dont belief but it is Currantly reported
at onontago and by private Intelligence I had it was the occassion of Canasategos death."[102]

Canasatego's successor was Tohaswuchdioony, "a proffessed Roman
Catholick, and altogether devoted to the French."[103] He offered Weiser his
own version of what had happened "in the bushes" between the Moravians
and Canasatego. The old man, he said, had been bribed "with large presents" to sell land to the Moravians. Questioned later by some of the Iroquois headmen in Canasatego's absence, Cammerhoff admitted giving
gifts, adding, however, that they were "for Canasatego to divide among the
Indians as he pleased."[104] After the headmen admonished him "for not
diliver[ing] this things in open Counsel," Cammerhoff went on to warn
the Indians "not to let the white people settle to much of their land which
would make the Indians poor and ruin the trade."[105]

Cammerhoff told a different story. He and Zeisberger had gone to

Onondaga and solicited Canasatego's assistance for three reasons: to request permission from the Iroquois council to send two of their brethren to Onondaga to learn the Indians' language; to send a blacksmith to the Nanticokes and Shawnees; and to visit the Seneca villages.[106] There is no reference in his journal to any attempt to purchase land. On the contrary, he announced to Canasatego, among other things, that the Moravians "were no traders, and did not come to them [the Iroquois] from love of gain, or desire to seize or buy their lands."[107] Cammerhoff wrote that he did give Canasatego gifts, but "in the presence of two other headmen, Kagokaga and Gashekoa, [and] told him that these were presents sent by our Brethren to the Council in Onondaga. . . . He asked us whether they were intended for all, and when we replied, 'For all the chiefs,' he accepted them."[108] At no point did Cammerhoff say that he was questioned by the headmen. Indeed, he frequently commented on how well he and Zeisberger were treated throughout their stay in the Onondaga village.

Tohaswuchdioony may have been aware that Weiser and Cammerhoff had not always seen eye-to-eye, or had decided to plant his own seeds of doubt for the purpose of making his story more believable.[109] Whatever the case, he told Weiser that Cammerhoff was questioned about why Weiser himself had not come with the Moravians' petition. According to Tohaswuchdioony, the answer was that Weiser "is of another sort of people and no more in favour and after our people that will learn to speak your language Come back he will have nothing more to do with Indians affairs."[110] All indications are, however, that Canasatego may have been assassinated, not for taking a bribe to sell land, but because he was an obstacle to the designs of the pro-French faction at Onondaga.[111] Tohaswuchdioony provides the key. Weiser reported that he "was told by Tahashronchdioony the Chief, that all the Belts of Wampum belonging to the Publick from the several English Governors that remained unanswered at the Death of Canassatego, and found in his Possession, were by his orders burned [buried] with him. This the said Chief said to make Canassatogo a Thief after his death; some imagine that his Widow and Family stole them."[112] As Jennings observed, "this yarn is simply not credible." When the Onondagas buried the wampum, they "ended the obligations implied by the belts without having to come back to the colonials in a hostile posture. A new start would have to be made," even though not all of Canasatego's policies would be abandoned.[113]

As a senior member of the old guard, Canasatego was politically vulnerable and increasingly isolated. Several of his allies in the pursuit of the Pennsylvania strategy were dead, including Shickellamy and also his fellow Onondaga headmen, Caxhayion, Solkiwanachty, and Toganiha.[114] Canasatego's failure to obtain anything of substance at Philadelphia in 1749—politically or materially—may have contributed to the success of the French-leaning Indians at Onondaga. At a council held there on 14 September 1750, Conrad Weiser stood by as "the speaker gave a string of Wampum of nine rows, and gave another of the same seiz, with a Belt of Wampum to Coffer the grave of Canasatego."[115]

That Canasatego's recorded career as a headman was but a brief eight years may be an artifact of the surviving documents. Others certainly left a much longer trail in Euro-American archives. Yet his brief efflorescence may actually reflect the battering that Native leaders and their people had to endure during what was, to say the least, a troublesome and often desperate era. Upholding that smoke-and-mirrors phantasm, the "Iroquois mystique," became a burden that no one could continue to shoulder. To try and walk the increasingly thin diplomatic line between competing and often hostile European sovereigns, while at the same time dealing with Indian foes, was no easy task. And in the face of disease and famine, that timeworn axiom, "if you feed, you lead," must have loomed large in the minds of many Native headmen and their followers. Canasatego was one of several Iroquois leaders who sought to meet these challenges; others would continue on this path through to the dark days of the Revolution, less than three decades away. The extent to which he succeeded is remarkable. But as events unfolded around him, Canasatego may have wished that he had been born at another time.

III.   ⸱   TOWARD A WHITE PENNSYLVANIA

9

DELAWARES AND PENNSYLVANIANS AFTER
THE WALKING PURCHASE

STEVEN C. HARPER

The Walking Purchase of 1737 and the council of 1742 in which Canasatego declared the Delawares "women" led to the dispossession of the Delawares and their replacement on the landscape by Euro-American settlers. From the outset, Delawares considered the Walking Purchase wildly unjust and complained of Euro-American encroachment. They responded in varied ways: attempting to remain on lands at the Forks of the Delaware or migrating westward; moving in and out of Christian communities and Christian identities; protesting and seeking accommodation with provincial officials—until 1755 when all such efforts collapsed in the bloodbath of the Seven Years' War. But at least since the early 1740s, many Delawares recognized that their people and the residents of Penn's province were fast becoming "No more Brothers and Friends but much more like Open Enemies."[1]

As Francis Jennings showed, the fact that no very great disturbance occurred in the wake of the Walking Purchase is not evidence that Delawares failed to recognize it as a grave injustice.[2] Delawares complained about the Walking Purchase and all the colonial settlement that preceded and followed it, but they were ignored, then silenced. The idea that Delawares were content with the Walking Purchase until officious Quakers coaxed them to complain originated in the official Pennsylvania reports designed to cover the impropriety. Informed but less partisan investigators locate blame with the Pennsylvania proprietors and their agents.[3] Indeed, Delawares began complaining as soon as the walkers crossed Tohickon Creek and had not stopped when the Moravian missionary John Heckewelder heard them late in the eighteenth century.[4] Teedyuscung, perhaps Nutimus's nephew and his choice to succeed as sachem, continued to complain eloquently in the generation after the purchase. A source sympathetic to the proprietors noted that "about the year 1756, or rather long before, the Indians under Tediuscung made loud complaints against the proprietaries of Pennsylvania for defrauding them of their lands."[5]

The complaints, in fact, began several years before the infamous walk, in a period when Euro-American settlers were already streaming into the Forks uninvited; as a Delaware recounted, "people came fast . . . , so that in a short time it was full of Settlement and the Indians were oblig'd to remove farther back."[6] Traders and settlers made significant inroads into the upper Delaware Valley in the late 1720s and early 1730s. Among the first was Pennsylvania chief justice William Allen, who received a grant from the Penn family for some ten thousand upper Delaware Valley acres. A French Huguenot, Nicholas Dupui, bought part of Allen's acreage on 10 September 1733.[7] That year, land warrants were issued to Edward Marshall (who would be the sole finisher of the brisk walk of 1737) and his brothers above Tohickon Creek.[8] Scots-Irish settlers encroached on lands at the Forks of the Delaware and Lehigh rivers by 1735.[9] Mainly Presbyterians, these early settlers infiltrated the Forks before the purchase, as did at least one other Euro-American, trader John Mathers.[10] On the eve of the walk, Daniel Broadhead received a warrant for six hundred acres from Thomas Penn. All of these individuals had every interest in seeing the purchase through to completion in hopes their warrants would be confirmed with legal patents. Allen in particular became giddy at the profits to be made.[11]

As the Land Office began issuing patents to justify Allen's optimism, Delawares were no longer able to simply disregard the fraud of 1737. In January 1740 they filed a formal complaint about encroaching settlers with Pennsylvania chief justice and upper Bucks County resident Jeremiah Langhorne. "If this practice must hold why then we are No more Brothers and Friends but much more like Open Enemies," the Delawares said.[12] Governor George Thomas issued a condescending response, feigning astonishment at Delaware demands to be paid for lands within the bounds of

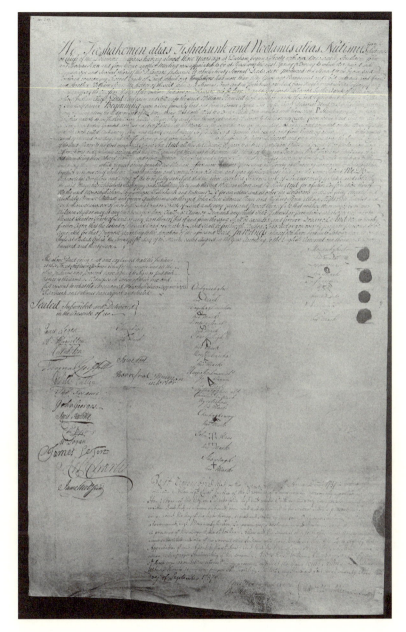

Figure 10   Deed of Nutimus, Teeshakommen, et al. . . . to John, Thomas, and Richard Penn, 25 August 1737: The "Walking Purchase." Pennsylvania State Archives, Harrisburg.

the purchase and urging Nutimus to "consider well what you do." Thomas assured the Delaware that should conflict occur, the English enjoyed numerical superiority and intimated that the Iroquois Confederacy would come to the province's aid.[13]

Meanwhile, on the Lehigh River, John and Thomas Penn were making plans to build the town of Easton and impose a series of manors and baronies on the Forks landscape, making it look much like their mother country. Ever since their visit to the confluence of the Lehigh and Delaware rivers in late 1734 or early 1735, the Penns had coveted the place and envisioned a commercial center there.[14] Their idea of accommodating the Delawares to these schemes was to designate an Indian manor up the Lehigh beyond lands already surveyed for paying customers.[15]

In the early 1740s, increasingly intrusive settlement rapidly transformed the entire landscape of the Forks. One notable venture involved the English itinerant evangelist George Whitefield, whose contacts with Moravian bishop Peter Boehler in Savannah, Georgia, led to plans for "a Negro school in Pennsylvania where he [Whitefield] proposed to take up land and settle a town."[16] Between 30 April and 4 May 1740, Whitefield finalized arrangements to purchase five thousand acres from Allen for £2,200. Allen realized a 440 percent profit on his five-year investment.[17] Whitefield named the tract Nazareth and hired Moravians under the direction of Bishop Boehler to build the proposed school. Doctrinal differences between Whitefield and the Moravians apparently brought the cooperative venture to an abrupt end, but the Moravians were determined to stay in the area and establish settlements from which to operate their ambitious educational, industrial, and proselyting ventures. As seen in chapter 5, these would prove vital to maintaining communication across a deepening frontier divide. Nathaniel Irish interested Boehler and then his replacement, Bishop David Nitschman, in a five-hundred-acre Allen tract astride a creek and bordered on the south by the Lehigh River in the heart of present-day Bethlehem. From a stock of nearly a dozen pioneers, supplemented by the immigration of "sea congregations," the Moravian settlement grew and thrived. Within a few years Moravians extended their settlements between Bethlehem and Nazareth and the surrounding Forks land. They built mills and cultivated farms under the direction of the far-sighted Bishop Augustus Gottlieb Spangenberg. Count Nikolaus Ludwig von Zinzendorf, patron of the United Brethren in Saxony, came to Pennsylvania from 1741 to 1743 and oversaw Moravian settlement and proselytizing. Moravian tradition recalls the 1740s as a time of love feasts, abundant harvests, and "Indians who were friendly, and came to the farms on brief visits. They even helped in the harvesting and gave good service." But sometimes "lurking in the vicinity" were what some Moravians called "wild Indians."[18]

These, presumably, were the source of what the late eighteenth-century missionary John Heckewelder recalled as vehement protests "against the white people for settling in this part of the country, which had not yet been legally purchased of them, but, as they said, had been obtained by fraud." Pennsylvania officials gave no heed and urged the Moravians to do likewise.[19] But Moravians desired to convert Indians, not overtly displace them. They determined, in William Penn fashion, to compensate the Delawares for lands already purchased from Allen. Zinzendorf, said Heckewelder, "paid them out of his private purse the whole of the demand which they made in the height of their ill temper, and moreover gave them permission to abide on the land, at their village, where they had a fine large peach orchard, as long as they should think proper."[20] Teedyuscung's brother, Captain John, whose village occupied part of what is now Nazareth, received compensation from the Moravians for his houses, orchard, and grains and was permitted the freedom to enjoy the fruit of his labors.[21] Delawares, then, loudly complained against Euro-American settlers who threatened their rights to the land but experienced mutually agreeable relationships with Moravians and others as long as they were compensated or able to remain on the land. Moravians understood that the key to maintaining peace with the Delawares was to negotiate with them; to this they were always agreeable. "Unfortunately," as historian Jane Merritt observes, "not all men were Moravians."[22]

Nor did all Delawares respond to the Walking Purchase and its diplomatic aftershocks in the same way. Following Canasatego's 1742 demand that they leave the Forks, many Native American residents relocated to the Susquehanna Valley, where the Presbyterian missionary David Brainerd tried to minister to them in 1744. They were anxious, he reported, because "the white people had abused them and taken their land from them."[23] When he traveled to the Forks to try to convert the few remaining Delawares there, he found them resentful as well and worried that they would reject his message because of the abuse they endured at the hands of Euro-American settlers. "The number of Indians in this place is but small," Brainerd wrote. "Most of those that formerly belonged here, are dispersed, and removed to places farther back in the country. There are not more than ten houses hereabouts, that continue to be inhabited; and some of these are several miles distant from others."[24]

One of the few who both remained and listened to Brainerd was Tunda Tatamy. In 1733, at the same time Euro-Americans were beginning to scramble for lands in the region, Tatamy applied for "a piece of land of about 300 Acres on the Forks of Delaware." Receiver General James Steel sent word to Bucks County deputy surveyor John Chapman to make a formal survey "with caution and by Consent of the Indians."[25] Tatamy acquired this acreage as "consideration of services he had rendered as interpreter and messenger to the Indians."[26] Tatamy received a patent for his farm on 28 April 1738, a patent converted to fee simple status four years later, shortly after Canasatego's speech demanding that the Delawares vacate the Forks.[27] Tatamy did not approve of the proprietor's schemes, but his prior service as the Penns' guide and interpreter no doubt explains his favored treatment. The Penns' grant to Tatamy upheld Canasatego's demand that Delawares generally vacate the Forks while rewarding the prominent Delaware for his service.

The curious note from Steel to Chapman, that Tatamy's survey should be conducted with consent of the Indians, leads one to wonder how Tatamy's adoption of English property ways shaped his identity during this tumultuous period. Did he in some way consider himself estranged from "the Indians" around him? Moreover, one wonders what connections beyond coincidence with his property acquisition informed Tatamy's conversion to Christianity. During the extended process of acquiring his farm, which lay in the heart of the Forks land encompassed by the walk, Tatamy, his Delaware wife, daughter, and two sons became Presbyterians. On 26 July 1742—a mere two weeks after Canasatego's "women" speech—Count Zinzendorf visited "Tatamy's reserve" and found him "farming in a small way on a grant of 300 acres given him by the Proprietaries' agents." Tatamy welcomed Zinzendorf and his entourage and entertained them with "an account of the mode of sacrifice practiced by his heathen brethren." The missionaries capitalized on the chance to speak of "the great sacrifice of the Lamb of God, made for the remission of sins." How their teaching resonated with Tatamy cannot be known. Zinzendorf noted only vaguely that Tatamy "professed Christianity."[28] After Canasatego ordered them to depart, Tatamy, Captain John, and other Delawares petitioned the Pennsylvania governor for permission to remain at the Forks, arguing that they intended to live the settled life of other Christians, harmoniously with settlers and in "enjoyment of the same Religion and Laws with them."[29] Provincial Secretary Richard Peters, an ordained Anglican minister, doubted the sincerity of "those rascals, the Delaware Fork Indians," had them catechized, and determined that they only "pretend[ed] to be converted to the Calvinistical scheme of religion." So much the worse then, thought Peters, that on their petition they "had the impudence to subscribe themselves, 'Your Honour's brethren in the Lord Jesus.'"[30]

When Brainerd again visited the Forks in 1744 and enlisted Tatamy as his interpreter, the missionary perceived little spiritual progress in him. "He was," said Brainerd, "well fitted for his Work in regard of his Acquaintance with the Indian and English Language, as well as with the Manners of both Nations. And in regard of his desire that the Indians should conform to the Customs and Manners of the English, and especially their manner of living; But he seem's to have little or no Impression of Religion upon his Mind, and in that Respect was very unfit for his Work."[31] Brainerd wanted it noted on earth and in heaven that he "labour'd under great disadvantages in addressing the Indians, for want of his [Tatamy's] having an experimental, as well as more doctrinal Acquaintance with divine Truths."[32] To the missionary, Tatamy "appeared very desirous that the Indians should renounce their Heathenish Notions and Practices, and conform to the Customs of the Christian World" but lacked "concern about his own Soul."[33] Of Delawares less receptive to his ministrations, Brainerd wrote in frustration, "the manner of their living is likewise a great disadvantage to the design of their being Christianized. They are almost continually roving from place to place."[34]

Nonetheless, Brainerd's persistence, coupled with the threat of removal, convinced perhaps a dozen Delawares including Captain John and ultimately even Tatamy and his family to embrace Christianity with sufficient fervor to meet the missionary's standards. Unsurprisingly, Brainerd's account of Tatamy's conversion is generically Calvinist. During late July 1744, while Brainerd preached and the knowledgeable but spiritually slumbering Delaware interpreted, Tatamy "was somewhat awaken'd to a concern for his Soul; so that the next Day he discours'd freely . . . about his spiritual concerns, and gave . . . [Brainerd] an Opportunity to use further Endeavours to fasten the Impressions of his perishing State upon his Mind." Still "these impressions seem'd quickly to decline, and he remain'd in a great Measure careless and secure, until some time late in the Fall of the Year."

For several weeks Tatamy languished. "At this Season divine Truth took hold of him, and made deep Impressions upon his Mind. He was brought under great Concern for his Soul, and his Exercise was not now transient and unsteady, but constant and abiding, so that his Mind was burden'd from Day to Day' and 'twas his great Enquiry, *What he should do to be saved*."[35]

According to Brainerd, Tatamy lost considerable sleep and was "under a great Pressure of Mind . . . while he was striving for Mercy." He envisioned what "seem'd to be an impassible Mountain before him. He was pressing towards Heaven as he thought, but his Way was hedg'd up with Thorns that he could not stir an Inch further. He look'd this Way and that Way, but could find no Way at all." Tatamy labored persistently but in vain for deliverance. He could not "help himself thro' this insupportable Difficulty" until he finally "gave over striving, and felt that it was a gone Case with him, as to his own Power, and that all his Attempts were, and forever would be vain and fruitless." Brainerd struggled to discern whether Tatamy's "own *Imagination*" or "divine *Illumination*" was at work, and only pronounced himself "satisfi'd" when Tatamy became "divorc'd from a Dependence upon his own Righteousness, and good Deeds." Subsequently, Brainerd found Tatamy "as if he was now awaked out of Sleep." Convicted of his sin and misery, the convert sensed the "impossibility of helping himself by any Thing he could do," and only then found a powerful assurance of hope. After this conversion experience, Brainerd saw in Tatamy's "publick Performances" external evidence of a changed nature. Now Tatamy preached with "admirable Fervency, and scarce knew when to leave off." This change was so "*abiding*" that Tatamy was no longer tempted, though "much expos'd to *strong Drink* . . . moving free as Water; and yet has never . . . discover'd any hankering Desire after it." In all this, Brainerd concluded, Tatamy manifested "considerable Experience of spiritual Exercise, and discourses *feelingly* of the Conflicts and Consolations of a *real* Christian." He appeared "like another Man to his Neighbors."[36]

A baptismal ceremony on 21 July 1745 sealed the changing cultural identities of Tatamy and his wife, whose name is unknown. Tunda Tatamy became Moses Tatamy. Similarly, Joseph Peepys, Thomas Store, Isaac Still, John Pumpshire, and Stephen Calvin exchanged traditional names for appellations of apostles, prophets, or reformers. These were the same Delawares who stayed in the Forks or New Jersey and adapted to English property ways. Many Pennsylvanians were not as critical of these Delaware conversions as was Richard Peters when he labeled them "rascals." Those who were more sympathetic saw the Delawares maturing from the stock category of "savage" to that of "civilized Indian." If these Pennsylvanians never quite considered Tatamy one of them, at least the propertied Presbyterian Delaware was on his way to becoming "one of our Indian Friends."[37] By the 1750s, Tatamy, who thought of his property as "my place in the forks,"[38] had learned to write, as had his son William. His daughter Jemima also enjoyed "the advantage of some schooling."[39] By "improving" and acquiring recognizably English rights to property, and finally by fully embracing Presbyterianism, Tatamy identified himself in loose terms as a peer of fellow Presbyterian and property holder William Allen. If the remaining socioeconomic gulf mocked such tenuous parity, Tatamy's cultural adaptations gained him a degree of acceptance in eighteenth-century Pennsylvania society that most Delawares never achieved. His ability to speak English, his willingness to adopt European-style farming, and his conversion to Presbyterianism empowered him to continue living at the Forks. He continued to serve Pennsylvania as a negotiator and translator. During the long controversy over the Walking Purchase, he furnished clear statements of Delaware history and evidence against the proprietors.[40]

Tatamy's accommodations left a mixed legacy to his family. His son William was shot by a colonist near Bethlehem in July 1757 and lingered a month before dying. Tunda himself apparently died in 1762. His daughter Jemima received an education financed by Quakers, but little else is recorded about her. In 1769 the Pennsylvania Assembly granted the request of Tunda's son Nicholas for two hundred acres in perpetuity because of "the Services of his father, an Interpreter, and faithful friend to this Province."[41] At that time, he was, like his father before him, described as "Tatamy, an Indian." The 1790 and 1800 federal censuses, however, categorize Nicholas's descendants as White. This racial reclassification suggests that it was only possible for Delawares to maintain possession of land at the cost of surrendering their Delaware identity.[42]

Still, this was perhaps a preferable fate to that of Delawares who made different choices. Brainerd's account lamented the "paganism" of the Susquehanna Delawares and their Native American neighbors. Nonetheless, many of these people were attracted to the Moravians, including Teedyuscung, who remained on the fringes of the purchase for several years. As mentioned in the previous chapter, the Iroquois deeded to Pennsylvania the land lying north of the Walking Purchase in 1749. Simultaneously, Teedyuscung and many other Delawares living in kinship groups at Meniolagomekah received baptism at the nearby Moravian mission of Gnadenhütten, at present-day Lehighton on the western edge of the Walking Purchase. The Moravians also attracted Teedyuscung's brother Weshichagechive because their Native followers "were very happy and contented in their Hearts, and that they liv'd no longer like other Indians, doing bad Things."[43] He requested baptism and was christened Nicodemus in June 1749.

Other members of Weshichagechive's kinship group followed, including Teedyuscung. The Moravian missionaries sought signs of true religious conversion in Teedyuscung but found him "unstable" and of a "wavering disposition." Still, Teedyuscung was apparently deeply moved by the doctrine of redemption through Christ and became "convicted of sin." After passing a probationary period, on 12 March 1750 "he was baptized in the little turreted chapel on the Mahoning" by a Moravian bishop who described him as "the chief among sinners."[44]

For reasons that remain obscure, Teedyuscung left the Moravians and accepted an Iroquois invitation to move north to Wyoming in spring 1754. Displaced and highly dissatisfied, he and other Delawares brooded over "the Injuries they had receiv'd from the English in being cheated of the Fork Lands and obliged to retire farther back over the Mountains[.] This so enraged them that they resolved no longer to bear the Injuries." Braddock's 9 July 1755 defeat by the French and allied Indians gave these Delawares "a favourable Opportunity of taking Revenge" for the injustices of the Walking Purchase.[45] According to a nineteenth-century Moravian historian, Delawares determined that "wherever the white man was settled within this disputed territory" they would attack by surprise and without mercy, taking scalps, burning homes, outbuildings, and crops.[46]

In October 1755, Delawares and Shawnees descended on the settlements of Euro-Americans within the bounds of the Walking Purchase. Easton, Bethlehem, Nazareth, and the hinterland became a hotbed of fear and activity. Farther west, Delaware warriors descended on settlers at Penn's Creek below Shamokin, killing above a dozen and carrying off nearly that many more. A few weeks later Euro-Americans at Great Cove on the Susquehanna met similar fates at the hands of allied Indians under the Delaware Shingas. By early November, raiders struck from the Tulpehocken Valley to the Minisink and over the Delaware River into New Jersey. Later that month, they attacked the Moravian settlement on the east side of the Mahoning River adjacent to Gnadenhütten and slew or captured several men, women, and children. Then, on Christmas eve, warriors burned Gnadenhütten itself.[47] Early the next year, Teedyuscung—whom Richard Peters described as "near 50 Years Old, a lusty, rawboned Man, haughty and very desirous of respect and Command" and able to "drink three quarts or a Gallon of Rum a day without being drunk"—returned to the Forks with a vengeance to lead additional attacks in Northampton County. According to Peters, "He was the Man that persuaded the Delawares to go over to the French and then to Attack the Frontiers."[48] Teedyuscung's Delawares and their Shawnee allies claimed more than one hundred lives.[49] The retribution took an especially high toll on Edward Marshall, the walker of 1737. Although he confessed that the Delawares had been defrauded, Marshall had no affection for them and they none for him. When violence broke out he took his family to New Jersey and remained there until spring 1756. Shortly thereafter, Delawares descended on his home near Jacobus Creek, shot his daughter Catherine, and kidnapped his pregnant wife, whose scalped remains were later discovered in the Poconos. Having not found Edward at home, Delawares returned in August and killed his son Peter but again missed their main target.[50]

The Delaware raiders also threatened their kinsmen who remained loyal to the Moravians, supposedly warning that their ears would be opened with a hot iron if they refused to hear the call to war.[51] A 29 November 1755 letter dictated by fourteen Indians, including five Delawares, among whom was a Moravian named Augustus, pleaded with Governor Robert Hunter Morris to protect them from both Teedyuscung's forces and Euro-Americans bent on counter-retaliation. They specifically cited conversion and recognition of English property ways as justification. "We have hitherto been poor heathen," they protested, but "the [Moravian] Brethren have told us words from Jesus Christ our God and Lord, who became a man for us and purchased salvation for us with his blood" and "permitted us to live upon their land." For Morris, this acknowledgment of the efficacy of Christianity and legitimacy of Moravian land rights under Pennsylvania law earned these Native Americans the protection of the colony. "As you have made it your own choice to become members of our civil society, and subjects of the same Government, and determine to share the same fate with us," the governor replied, "I shall make it my care to extend the same protection to you as to the other subjects of his Majesty."[52]

But most Euro-Pennsylvanians were in no mood to offer much protection to any Indians. On 16 December 1755, Edward Shippen wrote to Chief Justice Allen, foremost holder of Forks real estate, about a "courageous, resolute" frontiersman who was curious to "know whether any handsome premiums is offered for scalps, because if there is he is sure his force will soon be augmented."[53] A few weeks later Richard Peters wrote to Thomas Penn to assure him that no matter how much he spent to defend the colony, "little good will be done without giving handsome rewards for scalps," despite problems that might arise from indiscriminate attacks on Delawares "who are or may be inclined to be our friends."[54] Several companies of frontiersmen, Peters reported, had already "voluntarily offered themselves" to take advantage of the offer of cash for scalps.[55]

The "rudeness, lawlessness, and ignorance of the back inhabitants . . . will bring a general Indian war over us," Conrad Weiser complained to Thomas Penn. "They curse and dam[n] the Indians and call them murdering dogs into their faces without discrimination, when on the other hand these poor Indians that are still our friends do not know where to go for safety; in the woods they are in danger of being killed, or their young men joining our enemy. Among us they are in danger of being killed by the mob."[56] Delawares were indeed caught in an awful dilemma. They could have no sense of security as an independent body between the Iroquois, the Pennsylvanians, and the French. From the Wyoming Valley in November 1755 the Delawares Weiser had in mind sent word to Governor Morris emphasizing their dependence on and loyalty to the English and begging for information and assurance. "We are as children here," the message read, "till we receive words. We believe that we are in great Danger For we hear the Hatchets fly about our Ears and we Know not what will befall us, and therefore We are afraid."[57]

In Philadelphia on 14 April 1756, Governor Morris declared war on the Delawares over the opposition of a Quaker-dominated Assembly. Sir William Johnson, King George's superintendent for Indian affairs in the northern department, was just then planning how he could conciliate Delawares through Iroquois diplomatic channels. He fumed that "these hostile Measures which Mr. Morris has Entered into . . . [were] Throwing all our Schemes into Confusion" and giving the French an advantage. "What will the Delaware and Shawonese think of Such Opposition and Contradiction in our Conduct?"[58] A variant of Johnson's question occurred to Thomas Penn, who wondered about a rather different French advantage. Reflecting that scalp bounties would lead to "private murder" of men, women, and children, Penn expressed his concern that "in some of the French pieces lately published we are reproached with it as a cruel and unchristian-like practice."[59]

The tumultuous social and cultural transformations and adaptations that rocked the Upper Delaware River Valley in the wake of the Walking Purchase defied all attempts at categorization. In the eyes of most Pennsylvanians, neither Christian names nor solemn rituals could guarantee Delawares' rights to lands in or outside the bounds of the Walking Purchase. In Delaware minds, survey documents that began describing their land as "vacant" could not alienate ancient claims. Nor could imposed fences, gardens, and manors transform the landscape without disastrous consequences. Delawares responded to their dispossession in a variety of ways. They complained and resisted, capitulated and converted. They ultimately gave much more than ground. Tatamy and a few other Delawares forged new identities acceptable to European colonists, though the process proved neither seamless nor painless. Other Delawares mediated a middle way by adapting Moravian ideas and forms. Still others, like Teedyuscung, sought payment in kind for the toll of colonization. Alas, having forsaken an idealistic commitment to peace for more pragmatic means of possession, most Pennsylvanians were only too eager to return that violent payment with interest.

10

❦

SQUATTERS, INDIANS, PROPRIETARY GOVERNMENT, AND LAND IN THE SUSQUEHANNA VALLEY

DAVID L. PRESTON

On 1 November 1755, early in the Seven Years' War, approximately ninety Delawares, Mingoes, and Shawnees attacked the Euro-American settlements in the Great Cove Valley in south-central Pennsylvania. Squatters began moving into the valley as early as the 1730s, but the provincial government did not purchase the Great Cove lands from the Six Nations until the Albany Congress of 1754, in a fraudulent arrangement that the Indian attackers refused to recognize. Columns of smoke rising from the valley, bloating corpses of settlers and livestock, and refugees fleeing eastward were visible signs of the warriors' successful offensive. So, too, was the capture of several Euro-Americans the Indians considered to be squatters on their lands, including Charles Stuart, his wife, and their two small children.[1] A short distance from the scene of their capture, the war party halted, and some English-speaking Indians informed Charles Stuart in excruciating detail of the execution that awaited him.[2] But Stuart lived to see another day, largely because the Delaware leader Shingas reminded his comrades that the squatter had "lived on the Frontiers and that their People had Frequently Call[ed] at [his] House in their Passing and Repassing between Aughwick and Fort Cumberland and had Always been supplied with Proviss[ions] and what they wanted Both for themselves and Creatures without Ever Chargeing them anything for it."[3]

Stuart's experience reveals far more than the familiar story of encroaching settlers, frontier violence, and grueling captivities. It vividly illustrates that the Seven Years' War in Pennsylvania was a war between neighbors. Throughout the ridge and valley country of the Appalachians, squatters had frequently encountered Indians at their homesteads. The Stuarts, for example, settled in the Great Cove sometime in the late 1740s, probably after King George's War (1744–48). Their homestead was near the Tuscarora Indian path, and, as Shingas remembered, they had extended hospitality to untold numbers of Indian travelers over the years. Such apparently amicable encounters raise the question of how ordinary people on the frontier—Euro-American and Indian farmers, hunters, and their families—shaped their worlds at a local level.[4] How did the Delawares, Shawnees, Iroquois, and other Natives—many of whom were relatively "new Settlers" themselves—interact with neighboring Euro-American families?[5] How, and by whom, in such a complex matrix of interactions, were Indians actually dispossessed of their lands?

A close analysis of the face-to-face meetings among ordinary people reveals an important aspect of the colonial encounter that has largely escaped historians' attention: how colonial and Indian frontier inhabitants intensely negotiated with each other over boundaries, land use, and possession both before and during the upheaval of the Seven Years' War. In spite of their conflicts and misunderstandings, they coexisted, communicated, and crafted mutually beneficial relationships in such routine encounters as small-scale trading of corn, alcohol, tobacco, and wild game. Some squatters acknowledged Indians' occupancy and approached them for permission to remain on the land or tried to purchase it from them without the authorization of proprietary leaders. Natives also enlisted European farmers as tenants in an adaptive response to colonial expansion in Pennsylvania, New York, and South Carolina. In the Mohawk Valley, for example, one group of German farmers rented land from the Canajoharie Mohawks for nearly two decades. Under such arrangements, Euro-American farmers typically paid Indians yearly fees in return for planting rights. Some farmers hoped that these extralegal actions (along with their improvements) would bolster their claims when the government actually purchased the lands. Settlers cleverly exploited their local relationships with Indians to resist the proprietors' attempts to eject them. For many frontier Euro-Americans, then, negotiations and trading relationships with the Indians were means to landed ends—part of the lifelong process of achieving competency, asserting masculine patriarchal ideals, and building prosperous farms.[6]

Thus the struggle for lands in eighteenth-century Pennsylvania was at least a triangular contest among proprietary officials, squatters, and Indians. But often the contest had as many as nine dimensions as Pennsylvania, Maryland, Virginia, the Six Nations, Susquehanna Indians, Ohio Indians, squatters, land speculators, and British officials in Whitehall all battled for control of the same valuable patches of ground. Imperial officials, proprietary agents, and speculators alike fretted over the unofficial relationships that squatters and Indians were forging, for these ties threatened their interests. Squatters did not pay for land, they did not pay quitrents, and they blurred visions of orderly settlement. Colonial officials regarded unlicensed settlers as "mutinous spirits" who would "cut and mangle the best parts of the Country and make it impossible for the Proprietors to appropriate . . . good lands for their own use." In 1749, Thomas Penn envisioned a dark future in which "we shall have the Country intirely over run with people, who will neither pay us our due nor submit to the Laws of the Country."[7] Informal or unofficial negotiations between ordinary Euro-Americans and Indians also threatened the government's claims to exclusive jurisdiction over diplomatic negotiations with Indians. The need to extinguish Indian title made it essential that the Pennsylvania proprietors try to maintain rigid control over Indian diplomacy and the purchase of land by treaties. From William Penn to John Penn, proprietors and other officials issued stern warnings against private individuals buying land or otherwise "intermeddling" or "tampering" with Indians.[8] Colonial magistrates occasionally prosecuted squatters for trespass, burned their cabins, and ejected them, but such means could not resolve the problem. Squatters' confrontations with colonial authorities are a useful reminder that Pennsylvania's frontier diplomats were aggressively negotiating their own economic interests, vision of orderly expansion, and definition of property.[9]

The relationships among proprietors, squatters, and Native Americans reveal the permeable nature of the eighteenth-century frontiers and yield insights into larger processes that would transform those frontiers into juridically and racially defined colonial borders after the Seven Years' War.[10] They shed light on the interplay of local events with imperial developments, on the entire spectrum of cultural contact (from routine encounters between ordinary people on the frontier to official diplomacy between colonial and Native leaders), and on the complicated, often indirect, processes by which proprietors and ordinary settlers eventually displaced Native peoples.

Conflict on the eighteenth-century Pennsylvania frontier belies the colony's reputation as "the best poor man's country in the world," a place where Euro-Americans could easily attain landed independence and enjoy religious toleration. To be sure, Pennsylvania's alliance with the Six Nations sustained an exceptional period of peaceful relations from the 1680s to the 1750s. Pennsylvania, however, advanced the most expansive settlement frontier in all of British North America, and it could not forever hide from the consequences of its displacement of the Shawnees, Delawares, and multiethnic Susquehanna Indians. By the 1750s, Euro-American settlements had pushed relentlessly into the area southeast of the Blue (or Kittatinny) Mountain, an imposing, nearly unbroken ridge running diagonally across Pennsylvania from southwest to northeast.[11]

Even as the territory occupied by Euro-Pennsylvanians expanded, an eighteenth-century "feudal revival" in North America was fast eclipsing the province's reputation as "the best poor man's country." Between 1730 and 1745, proprietors from New York to Pennsylvania to South Carolina began to revive old land claims that had not yielded wealth in the seventeenth century. In keeping with this trend, William Penn's indebted sons asserted their proprietary rights to restore their shaky finances, initiating an aggressive policy of raising land prices and quitrents, collecting quitrents in arrears, and ejecting trespassers. They also colluded with Canasatego and other spokesmen for the Six Nations Iroquois to purchase frontier lands that were actually settled by Shawnees, Delawares, and Susquehanna Indians.[12] Not coincidentally, the Pennsylvania government, negotiating with the Six Nations, bought the disputed lands out from under resident Euro-American and Indian settlers in 1749, 1754, and 1768.[13]

Squatters' decisions to ignore proprietary claims and treaties with the Iroquois were prompted in part by the Penns' aggressive land policies and socioeconomic conditions in the colony. One squatter remarked that the Scotch-Irish had been "so much oppressed and harassed by under Landlords in our own Country" that they came to America "with the chief and principal view of being, in this foreign world, freed from such oppression." Settlers also objected to land speculators' practice of buying land cheap and selling it dear. One colonial farmer believed that "the removing of them from the unpurchased Lands, was a Contrivance of the Gentlemen and Merchants of Philadelphia, that they might take Rights for their Improvements when a Purchase was made." In a period when economic inequality (in terms of land ownership and proportionate wealth) in Pennsylvania was growing, settlers bristled at tenancy, rising land prices, and rampant land speculation, which drove freeholds further out of reach.[14]

By the late 1740s, then, unsettled lands (especially in older settlements) were becoming scarce and too expensive for poor immigrants disembarking at Philadelphia. Proprietors, meanwhile, saw their wealth dwindling away as discontented families either migrated down the Great Valley into Maryland, Virginia, and the Carolinas or ventured into Indian country to establish homesteads. The settlers' desire for competency and landed independence was the most important motivation in their decisions to plant themselves on Indians' territory. Squatters' deeply held beliefs in the value of their labor and improvements to the land sustained their hopes of eventually possessing legal title to their properties. Indeed, when unlicensed settlers had an opportunity to apply to the proprietors for land on good terms after the government's 1754 and 1768 purchases, they would do so. In the eighteenth century there were no overt acts of collective squatter resistance against the proprietors over land policy. Like their accommodations with the Natives, squatters' defiance was limited and practical.[15]

Squatter families began moving north up the Susquehanna Valley and west along the Juniata Valley in the 1730s. Many poorer Ulster emigrants in search of land moved directly to the frontiers after disembarking at Philadelphia. The life of Simon Girty, Sr.—whose family appears on a list of squatters compiled by Provincial Secretary Richard Peters in 1750— illustrates one of many Euro-American paths to the frontiers and personal relations with Natives. Girty immigrated from Ireland to Pennsylvania in 1735. He quickly entered into the fur trade and developed contacts with Delawares in the Ohio country; he undoubtedly became familiar with the geography of the central Appalachians through the course of his westward journeys. After his marriage to an English woman named Mary Newton in the late 1730s, Girty established a homestead in the Path Valley, present-day Franklin County. He continued his fur-trading activities without official license until Peters and Cumberland County magistrates expelled him and his family and burned their cabin to the ground in 1750. Like Girty, many squatters were unlicensed Indian traders or had informal connections to the Indians. Such individuals may have occupied frontier land under the pretense of trading, or Natives may have given them permission to establish posts at convenient locations. Trader George Croghan believed that the Juniata Valley squatters were "a Set of White Men that make their living by trading with the Indians." Many settlers—or "litle Traders" as the Provincial Council called them—"without any Authority from the Government take a few trifling Goods and go into the Woods to sell them." It is likely that some squatters saw a brief stint as a trader as a means to acquire land.[16]

A "frontier exchange economy" prevailed in the decades before the Seven Years' War. As recent historians have argued, Euro-American and Indian settlers' economic goals and social organization were similar, at least temporarily. The newcomers had taken extraordinary risks in moving families, possessions, and livestock over steep mountains. Once ensconced in the mountain valleys, the inhabitants must have been exceptionally cognizant of their isolation and vulnerability. There were no forts to flee to, no military forces to mobilize quickly, no roads to facilitate trade with more settled parts. Poorer frontier families typically lived in temporary log cabins in small, isolated clearings. They subsisted, in Indian fashion, through hunting and agriculture and depended on Indian largesse. Peaceable dealings with their Native neighbors were a necessity on a frontier that was still an Indian world and one increasingly threatened by French imperial power.[17]

Native peoples in turn faced a potent combination of zealous proprietors, ecological changes, and rapid expansion of colonial settlements, all of which dramatically heightened tensions in the region. Many Susquehanna and Delaware Valley Indians had found little evidence of benevolence in the Penn family's actions. The colony's strong alliance with the Six Nations was partly designed to bring the Delawares, Shawnees, and Susquehanna Indians (and their lands) under Iroquoia's preponderant power. The proprietors presumed that "the Five Nations have an absolute Authority over all our Indians" and negotiated with the Iroquois for Delaware, Shawnee, and Susquehanna Indians' lands. Incidents like the Walking Purchase of 1737, the loss of key hunting and agricultural grounds, ecological changes, unprincipled Euro-American traders, and settlement expansion prompted many Delawares and Shawnees living in eastern Pennsylvania to migrate to the Juniata Valley, the Ohio Valley, and Iroquoia after the 1720s. Yet, as the previous chapter shows, Indians did not simply retire westward when

Figure 11. Pennsylvania provincial secretary Richard Peters vigorously asserted proprietary claims against those he considered squatters. Portrait by John Wollaston (attrib.), c. 1758. Courtesy of the Pennsylvania Academy of Fine Arts, Philadelphia. Gift of Mrs. Maria L. M. Peters.

colonial settlements appeared in their valleys. Some Delawares, Shawnees, and Conestogas remained east of the Appalachians intending "to live and dye where they are now settled." Other Indian peoples weakened by warfare and disease—Tuscaroras, Nanticokes, Tutelos, and Conoys—migrated northward and settled in the Susquehanna and Juniata valleys.[18]

Thus Euro-Americans moving onto frontier lands did not enter a vacant wilderness. Multiethnic Indian towns and farms still lined the Juniata and Susquehanna valleys; Native hunters sought game in the same bottomlands that squatters were using. On the Juniata, the Shawnee leader Kishacoquillas presided over twenty families at the town of Ohesson well into the 1740s; further upstream was the Delaware town of Assunepachta, which contained twelve families. A group of Tuscarora settlers continued to live in the Tuscarora or Path Valley until the 1760s and maintained ties with their kin living in Iroquoia and in the Carolinas. In his 1747 journey through the Conococheague Valley in Pennsylvania and Maryland, the Rev. Michael Schlatter noted that "in this neighborhood there are still many Indians, who are well disposed and very obliging, and are not disinclined toward Christians." Although Schlatter may have misrepresented Indian attitudes, he rightly noted that Natives and newcomers shared the same valley.[19]

Euro-Americans apparently had no qualms about living near Indian towns or amidst the numerous individual Native American families who remained in the area, and some Indians were willing to accommodate limited numbers of newcomers. In the late 1740s, Arthur Buchanan and three Scots-Irish families approached the Shawnees at Ohesson and received permission to settle on the Juniata; Buchanan evidently developed close ties with the Shawnee leader Kishacoquillas. In 1755 George Armstrong applied for 300 acres of land along Tuscarora Creek that was "opposite to the settlement of the Indians called Lakens." Turbut Francis described his tract as lying "about 3 miles below the place where an Indian lived whose name was Connosque." Even if Francis had no personal dealings with Connosque, it is significant that Indian peoples and Indian landmarks figured so prominently in his mental landscape. He added that the creek running through his tract was "almost opposite to the place that John Thompson a Delaware Indian formerly lived."[20]

Perhaps Thompson was among those Native Americans who were dissatisfied over colonists' encroachments and removed to the Ohio country. Others were relocating closer to Iroquoia. A Nanticoke band that had once lived at the mouth of the Juniata River, for example, had established a new settlement in the Wyoming Valley by 1750. Tuscaroras settled among the Iroquois "brought forward the subject of the history of their land on the Juniata" to three Moravian missionaries in 1752. They told the Moravians that they were "deeply grieved to see white people living on their lands. They wished to have them removed." The Tuscaroras' desire to avoid "dissension in their land" explains why they chose relocation over confrontation. But many Native families could not forget the familiar faces of farmer-hunters who had displaced them. When Indian warriors attacked Pennsylvania's settlements in 1755–58, they frequently targeted the very settlers who had earlier invaded their lands. As Teedyuscung concluded, "the Land is the Cause of our Differences; that is, our being unhappily turned out of the land is the cause."[21]

The Brandywine Delawares, living near Philadelphia, illustrate the larger processes of displacement accompanying European settlement; the Delawares faced ecological changes similar to those that had sparked open warfare between Algonquians and English in the seventeenth-century Chesapeake and New England. Hannah Freeman, a Delaware woman who remained in the area, testified that "the country becoming more settled[,] the Indians were not allowed to Plant Corn any longer"—probably because of unpenned livestock and an inability to relocate seasonally to new lands—and so "her father went to Shamokin and never returned." In a 1729 letter to Lieutenant Governor Patrick Gordon, the Lenape sachem Checochinican complained that "the Land has been unjustly Sold [to the proprietors], whereby we are redused to great wants and hardships." He described his people as "greatly disquieted" and complained that "new settlers would not even allow them to cut down trees for their cabins." Whereas Euro-Americans saw the trees and livestock as their property, Natives did not give up the right to bark trees for shelter and treated the colonists' roaming livestock as, at best, fair game and, at worst, a source of "dissension" in their land. Colonists' unpenned livestock trampled Indian cornfields and, running free in the woods, competed with deer for food. Declining numbers of deer and other game also remained a thorny issue between Euro-American and Indian settlers.[22]

Nevertheless, colonial and Native inhabitants were capable of communicating effectively and creating mutually beneficial relationships with one another. Indians and Euro-Americans lived beside each other in a world of great ambivalence: friendship, harmony, trust, understanding, and amity coexisted with antagonism, suspicion, fear, misunderstanding, and enmity. Squatters often bartered, worked, socialized, and hunted with Indians at their homesteads. The frontier inhabitants could readily and clearly communicate, perhaps through the Delaware Jargon or through English-speaking Indian intermediaries. Meetings must have been an almost daily occurrence for settlers and traders who often lived along well-worn Indian paths. Perhaps Native and colonial travelers found lodging and food at their respective cabins. Rural artisans, such as blacksmiths, repaired weapons or mended hatchets and pots for the Indians. A settler named Richard Thomas believed that he had entertained and provisioned "the king of the five nations" and other Iroquois; they took up "their Lodging near to his house, whear they Resided about fore days and nights" in July 1727. A Delaware sachem "in want of provisions received ten bushels of meal from a miller on Tulpehocken Creek" in 1730. The missionary David Brainerd complained of Indians who "upon Christmas days" in the 1740s went "to drink and revel among some of the white people." When the Seven Years' War began in 1755, John Bartram captured the sense of betrayal that many settlers felt in light of such past hospitality: Indians destroying "all before them with fire ball and tomahawk" in 1755 had once been "allmost dayly familiars at thair houses eat drank cursed and swore together were even intimate play mates."[23]

Underlying peaceful interactions was a current of disagreement. Euro-American and Indian settlers were competing over such crucial resources as hunting grounds, springs, and alluvial soils for agriculture. As previous chapters demonstrate, different cultural beliefs about alcohol use, land use, property, and reciprocity in social interactions made Euro-Indian encounters prone to break down into fights, brawls, and, more infrequently, murders. Moreover, some squatters were openly hostile to "friendly" Indians. James Patterson, who began trespassing in the Juniata Valley in the early 1750s, carved out loopholes in his log cabin in case of attack. His Native neighbors frequently visited his homestead "on the friendly mission of bartering furs and venison for rum and tobacco." But Patterson—"Big Shot" according to legend—used these visits to gain much-needed food supplies and to intimidate the Indians. He allegedly fired at a target posted on a nearby tree whenever Natives visited so that they could see what might happen to his human targets.[24]

Unofficial meetings between Euro-Americans and Indians, whether peaceful or violent, remained a potent issue for many British colonial governments. As squatters began moving up the Susquehanna and Juniata valleys, they established farms astride major Indian trade routes and north-south war paths that Iroquois parties used to attack their Catawba and Cherokee enemies in the Carolinas. Colonial officials in Pennsylvania, Virginia, and the Carolinas feared that the intruders would provoke these war parties to open conflict. During the winter of 1742–43, the nightmare almost came true when a group of Virginia squatters inflicted eight casualties on an Iroquois war party. Only the deft diplomacy of Conrad Weiser, Shikellamy, and Canasatego staved off war between Virginia and Pennsylvania and the Six Nations, but their efforts could not quiet fears that such incidents would happen again.[25]

Squatter encounters with Indian war parties also provided occasions for misunderstanding over the meanings of reciprocity and property. Villages in the Susquehanna Valley had long been centers of hospitality for travelers and especially for Iroquois warriors who camped near the colonists' homesteads and requested (or demanded) food and supplies. Well into the 1760s, Iroquois passing through expected supplies from Euro-American and Indian settlers alike. Often alcohol took the place of less troublesome fare. During his journey to Onondaga in 1737, for example, the provincial interpreter Conrad Weiser encountered a destitute and ragged Iroquois warrior north of Shamokin, a major Indian town in the upper Susquehanna Valley. The warrior's condition resulted in part from a raid against southern Indians that had gone awry and in part because he "had squandered a part of his property drinking with the Irish" at a backcountry tavern or homestead. An Iroquois imbibing with the Irish is only one indication that squatters frequently socialized with members of war parties. In 1749, George Croghan reported that an Iroquois warrior was killed while drinking with his comrades on the way home to Onondaga. The four Iroquois men stopped at a "Stillhouse" or tavern along Aughwick Creek and one of them died from knife wounds during a scuffle. Croghan promised to "Secure all the white Men that was att the plese till I find outt the Truth of the affair." He believed that such meetings occurred frequently enough to justify a stiff fine on "all Stillers and Tavern keepers . . . for Making the Indians Drunk, and Espesely warriers."[26]

Squatters routinely used such encounters to engage in unauthorized negotiations for rights to live on Indian land. Shikellamy complained of a German squatter named Frederick Star who moved to the Juniata Valley in the early 1740s and claimed "a Right to the Land meerly because he gave

a little Victuals to our Warriours, who stand very often in need of it."
Shikellamy desired that Pennsylvania officials would "take the Dutchman
by the Arm and . . . throw him over the big Mountains within your Borders." Similarly, in July 1742, a Six Nations delegation at Philadelphia complained of squatters along the Conococheague Creek who brazenly
approached some Iroquois warriors "while they were hunting." According
to the Iroquois speaker, the squatters "made some proposals about the
Purchasing of Land from them," and the Iroquois warriors tentatively
agreed to "receive five Duffield Strowds for two Plantations on the River
Cohongoranta [Potomac]." The warriors, of course, had no authority to
give away land and probably thought that the strouds were gifts, not down
payments.[27]

Shikellamy's protest was only one in a decades-long series of Indian
complaints about trespassing in the Susquehanna and Juniata valleys. The
Susquehanna Indians, as Weiser once reported, were "very uneasy about
the white peoples Setling beyond the Endless mountains on Joniady [Juni-
ata], on Shermans Creek and Else where." In 1749, they reported that
"above 30 familys are setled upon [their] land this spring, and dayly more
goes to setle thereon; some have setled all most to the heads of Joniady
River along the path that leads to Ohio." As Weiser's phrasing indicates,
the Indians' conceptions of frontiers or borders usually involved mountains. They viewed the long ridgeline of the Blue Mountain as a natural
divide between their settlements and Euro-American settlements. Ogash-
tash, a Seneca sachem, once argued that "our Boundaries are so well
known, and so remarkably distinguish'd by a range of high Mountains."
The Iroquois also saw the Susquehanna Valley as an important border zone
between Iroquoia and Pennsylvania. As the major north-south war paths
ran through that zone, Iroquois diplomats and warriors saw firsthand the
constant seepage of settlers into the fertile river valleys.[28]

Pennsylvania officials usually replied to Indian complaints with official
proclamations warning trespassers to remove and forbidding them to purchase lands from Indians. But proclamations alone could not effectively
stem the rising tide of squatters, and the government finally took direct
action in response to Indian complaints. The proprietors' first major attempt to remove squatters by force occurred in August 1748 in the Path
Valley. Set between sharp and rugged mountain ridge lines, such pockets
of alluvial soils attracted both Indian and Euro-American settlers. During
Weiser's journey to the Ohio country to conduct treaty negotiations with

the Wyandots in that year, the proprietors ordered him to expel squatters who had taken up residence along the Allegheny path, the main trade route between the Ohio country and the Susquehanna River. In what might appear at first glance a strange twist of events, Indians and squatters combined to resist the evictions. About fifty miles west of George Croghan's trading post on Aughwick Creek, Weiser and a few local magistrates encountered the Oneida sachem Scaroyady (Monacatootha) with a group of Indians who were probably Ohio country Mingo Iroquois. The squatters had somehow received advanced warning of Weiser's mission and appealed to the Indians for help, lest they "be turned off by the Government." The Indians did not insist that all of the Euro-Americans be unconditionally removed. Instead, they "desired that at least two familys, to wit, Abraham Shlechl and another, might stay, that they, the said Indians, had given them liberty, and that they thought it was in their power to give liberty to" whomever they preferred. Scaroyady made it clear to Weiser that "if any of the people now living there was turned off, no other Body should setle there, they [the Indians] being informed that as soon as the people were turned off others would be put on the land" who would presumably be more favored by the government.[29]

Scaroyady's comment reveals that some Natives were willing to accommodate trustworthy Euro-American settlers who had demonstrated good will and hospitality. His insistence that "no other Body should setle there" reflected the Indians' unwillingness to negotiate with the Pennsylvania government for lands that would be permanently alienated and settled with outsiders unknown to them. Scaroyady and his party clearly had established friendly relations with a few squatter families and may have genuinely sympathized with their plight. Weiser reported that "the people used [the Indians] well on their coming by, and Informed them of the design" for their eviction. The squatters, like Indian settlers, mostly desired small plots of land for farming, whereas the proprietors negotiated for hundreds of thousands of acres. Moreover, Scaroyady must have perceived the squatters' disaffection from the provincial government and perhaps hoped to forge informal alliances with them to forestall a more wholesale and irreversible invasion of his people's territory.[30]

But why would Scaroyady and his companions allow certain families to stay given the Susquehanna Indians' previous complaints? Why did the Oneida sachem believe that he had the authority to decide on the matter? Weiser himself was at a loss to explain it.[31] Scaroyady was probably granting these people some kind of usufruct rights to Native lands for farming or hunting. Native peoples in the eighteenth century, including Mohawks and Oneidas in Scaroyady's Iroquoian homeland, frequently invited displaced or indigent neighbors to live among them; they also bestowed usufruct rights upon favored individuals in instances of "associative adoption," a reflection of the strong hospitality ethic that bound Native societies together.[32] Such complicated and overlapping rights were a major source of controversy between the proprietary government and the Indians over whom it hoped to extend its legal sovereignty.

The changing political and military balance of power in the Ohio country may also have influenced Scaroyady's decision. Keenly aware of English and French designs on the Ohio country, he perhaps hoped to retain trustworthy settlers as sources of information on colonists' intentions. When the disgruntled Shawnees and Delawares migrated to the Ohio country in the 1720s, they cultivated close ties to the French. Both Pennsylvania and the Six Nations fretted over their inability to control the independently minded Ohio Indians. By the end of King George's War in 1748, however, some western Indian nations, such as the Wyandots and Miamis, were breaking ties with the French, whose expansionism they feared, and entering into alliances with Pennsylvania; hence the warm reception Conrad Weiser received when he traveled to Logstown in 1748. On that occasion, Scaroyady urged Weiser to delay any action on illegal settlement until after the Logstown meeting, at which point the Six Nations would arbitrate the affair. Indians in the Juniata Valley were probably resentful of Iroquois decisions regarding their homes, but as client peoples, they were expected to defer to Iroquois leadership.[33]

As discussed in chapter 8, the problem of illegal settlement was much on the minds of both Pennsylvanians and the Iroquois delegation, which was represented by Canasatego at the Philadelphia treaty of 1749. On that occasion, Governor James Hamilton attempted to shift responsibility for the squatters' encroachments to the shoulders of the Indians who had "give[n] them Countenance" and seized the opportunity to propose a land purchase to diffuse the crisis. He and other proprietary officials hoped that the swath of territory between the Susquehanna and Delaware rivers, transferred to Pennsylvania by the 1749 treaty, would lure unlicensed settlers away from the troubled Juniata Valley. Hamilton accordingly assured the Indians that squatters would yield to his proclamations to remove, "especially as they may be provided with Land on the East side of Sasquehanna within the new Purchase."[34] Thus squatting increasingly became the ideological pretext for colonial land purchases in the eighteenth century. Controlling the frontier and its inhabitants was an important corollary of colonial Indian policy. Members of the provincial elite espoused general views of social evolution in which frontier people living without law were degenerating into a state of savagery. They argued that lawless and violent settlers would inevitably spark a war with the Indians. Peters greatly feared that "the lower sort of People who are exceeding Loose and ungovernable from the mildness of the Constitution and pacifick principles of the Friends wou'd go over in spite of all measures and probably quarrel with the Indians." He worried that "the People over the Hills are combin'd against the Government, are putting in new Cropps and bid us Defiance." Believing that "it would be impossible to preserve the Peace of the Province," Peters urged the Penns to resolve the Indians' grievances over colonial encroachments. But the provincial secretary's resolution did not include respect for Indian sovereignty. Pennsylvania officials believed that squatters had to be contained and peace preserved by purchasing disputed lands from the Six Nations by whatever means necessary. In 1749, Peters suggestively informed the sons of William Penn that "all mouths were full of the necessity of an Indian purchase" as the only way to forestall a frontier war.[35]

In fact, proprietary officials were even willing to fabricate a diplomatic crisis, anticipating that Natives would try to resolve it with a treaty culminating in a land purchase. Even as war loomed in 1754, Weiser suggested to the proprietors that "our people Should be let loose to Set upon any part of the Indian lands upon giveing [security] for their Complying with the Proprietary terms after [purchase;] the Indians would Come in and demand Consideration and what Can they Say, the people of pensilvania are their [brethren] according to the treatys subsisting." The only problem with Weiser's plan was that the squatters had never been on the proprietors' leash.[36]

To contain the threat posed by land negotiations between squatters and Indians, the proprietors worked to completely dispossess both groups. Like southern planters who saw the Appalachians as a possible haven for runaway slaves, proprietors considered the possibility that endemic squatting might result in a total loss of control over frontier lands. Weiser and other colonial officials feared that illegal settlement, if not "nipt in the bud," might lead to a lasting accommodation between Indian and Euro-American settlers. According to Peters, Weiser apprehended "a worse Effect, that is that . . . [squatters] will become tributary to the Indians and pay them yearly sums for their Lycense to be there." Settlers paying tribute to Indians would be a complete disaster for the Penns, who were deeply in debt at the time and dependent on income derived from land sales and quitrents; as Thomas Penn once observed, "the regulation of our Quit Rents is of the utmost consequence." And in 1749, Weiser claimed to know "positively" that squatters "are got into this way [paying tribute] on the East side of Sasquehanna' beyond the Hills and receive acknowledgements and are easy about those Lands." Weiser envisioned that Pennsylvania's rulers would "not only have all the abandon'd People of the Province to deal with but the Indians too and that they will mutually support each other and do a vast deal of Mischief." Peters agreed that "this consideration has alarm'd me more than any other."[37]

Colonial officials were never able to discover which Indians had granted rights to colonial farmers—an indication of just how peripheral the officials could appear in local negotiations and how elusive and personal such arrangements could be. Thomas Penn believed that the culprits were Delawares at Shamokin and that they should be "severely reprimanded." Peters speculated that the Indians had given tracts of land to trader Thomas McKee, who had married a Shamokin woman, but he reported as certain that Shikellamy, Shamokin Indians, Delawares, and Nanticokes had all "levyd large Contributions" from neighboring colonial farmers. Years later, an indebted Andrew Montour, emulating what seemed to be a customary practice, also tried to attract Euro-American tenants. Some Indians living around Shamokin, aware of the value Euro-Americans placed on their lands, accepted white settlers as tenants as a way of making them dependent upon Native landlords. Eighteenth-century land records confirm that such relationships existed. One squatter named William Smith, who settled below Shamokin in the 1740s, claimed that his improvement was made "with the consent of the Indians." The relationships that some settlers and Indians were forging on the frontier clearly represented a threat to both the colony's land policy and the social order as the authorities saw it.[38]

In May 1750, Pennsylvania took forceful action to circumvent any challenges to their authority. Acting on the complaints Canasatego had made in 1749, Governor Hamilton sent Peters and Weiser west of the Susquehanna to eject squatters "on the Lands beyond Kittochtinny [Blue] Mountains, not purchased of the Indians." Peters, Weiser, and eight Cumberland County magistrates assembled at George Croghan's trading post at Aughwick. Five Shamokin Indians also accompanied them as observers.[39] Peters conducted the 1750 expedition as a quasi-military operation to suppress a "set of Scoundrels." Thomas Penn later commended the "Hussar Spirit" that Peters had displayed, which was "nothing less than which will do with these People." For the latter half of May 1750, the magistrates scoured the mountain valleys of the Juniata watershed, ejecting squatters, arresting a few of them, and burning log cabins. Although Peters's report listed neither the total numbers of people living in each household nor squatters in the areas the expedition left untouched, the number of households he counted still astounded officials: five stood along the Juniata, eleven along Sherman's Creek, eighteen along the Path Valley (including one occupied by "Abraham Slach," probably the "Abraham Schlechl" whom Scaroyady defended two years earlier), four along Aughwick Creek, and twenty-three in the Great Cove.[40]

Most of the trespassers "had nothing to say for themselves but craved Mercy." They readily confessed to Peters that they had "no Right or Authority" to settle there. The provincial secretary magnanimously informed the evictees that "they might go directly on any Part of the two Millions of Acres lately purchased of the Indians" in 1749 and offered large families the chance to live rent-free on his manors until they could support themselves. Magistrates entered the trespassers into recognizance for £100 and into bonds to the proprietors for £500. Then, after "great deliberation" the authorities decided to burn the empty log cabins: "Mr. Weiser also giving it as his firm Opinion, that if all the Cabbins were left standing, the [Shamokin] Indians would conceive such a contemptible Opinion of the Government, that they would come themselves in the Winter, murder the People, and set their Houses on Fire." After removing their personal belongings, the indebted squatters painfully watched their labor and improvements go up in smoke.[41]

Although historians often stereotype squatters as outlaws prone to violence, the vast majority acquiesced to the magistrates and acknowledged that they were intruding on Indian lands. Although some squatters who lived near the border—perhaps hoping to play off Maryland and Pennsylvania—petitioned Maryland officials for warrants for their lands, nothing ever came of their proposal.[42] Apparently only one violent incident marred the expedition. On 24 May, Peters, Weiser, and the magistrates approached

Andrew Lycon's log cabin located along the Juniata. A band of unidentified Indians had "fixed their Tent on [Lycon's] Plantation" the night before—another indication of the frequent social interactions between Natives and squatters. Lycon resisted the authorities and "presented a loaded Gun to the Magistrates and the Sheriff, said, he would shoot the first Man that dared to come nigher." This outburst gave the Indians "great Offence," and members of Shikellamy's family who were present insisted that the authorities burn Lycon's cabin, "or they would burn it themselves." Lycon was "disarmed, convicted, and committed to the Custody of the Sheriff" and "carried to Gaol." Such actions effectively extended the province's legal system into the interior: although the unpurchased lands remained outside of Pennsylvania's jurisdiction, squatters were bound to appear before Cumberland County courts.[43]

Peters's official report on the sixty-one squatter households he counted—incomplete as it is—provides a revealing glimpse of frontier families and their lifelong quests for land and security. Contrary to historians' image of transient and rootless wanderers, most of these squatters persisted on the frontier, despite proprietary expeditions and later Indian wars. Of the sixty-one households ejected in 1750, at least forty-three remained in the area in the 1750s and the 1760s. In theory, proprietors cringed at the idea of allowing squatters to claim land rights based upon their "illegal" improvements. But in the end, most returned to their claims and gained some tenuous hold on land—if they were not killed in the Seven Years' War or, as was Charles Stuart, in Pontiac's War. Very few of these inhabitants ever succeeded in gaining letters patent, but many filed applications to have their lands surveyed (which conveyed a modicum of legal title) and even issued caveats against one other. Others evidently secured lands elsewhere. Peters, for example, gave verbal guarantees to many settlers that they would have preemption rights when the government purchased the lands west of the Susquehanna so long as they agreed to proprietary terms. Among those who took advantage of the offer was William White, who warranted 100 acres of land in territory purchased from the Six Nations (but not from its Indian occupants) at the Albany Treaty of 1754. In 1782, White's widow Mary still occupied their original tract in what became Cumberland County; she owned an additional 280 acres of land and a few livestock. In such ways colonial legal titles replaced informal arrangements between Indians and Euro-Americans.[44]

The results of squatters' lifelong quests for land and commitment to property rights suggest that their friendly relations with Indians may have been short-term accommodations in order to master the "wilderness" and the Indians. One dispossessed settler named Peter Falconer, in Peters's words, believed that otherwise "it woud be impossible that Peace coud have Subsisted long" between Indians and settlers.[45] Still, the squatters' relationship with the proprietors, land speculators, interpreters, and colonial agents doubling as Indian diplomats who were determined to use treaties to extract land concessions was just as ambivalent. Proprietors' land purchases in 1749 and 1754 and again in 1768 preempted both Native and colonial inhabitants' claims. At Albany in 1754, for example, the Pennsylvania delegation, primarily Peters and Weiser, orchestrated a deceitful land deal with the Iroquois for a vast area west of the Susquehanna River extending clear to the Ohio country. Proprietor Thomas Penn ordered that the Juniata Valley be settled "as fast as possible" with colonists who could pay for land and quitrents. The Albany Purchase may have alienated both the Six Nations and the Ohio Indians more than settlers' encroachments. When the Seven Years' War began, Indian war parties from the Ohio country specifically targeted settlements in the disputed Albany Purchase, including the Great Cove Valley where Charles Stuart lived. A Delaware war party also targeted Andrew Lycon's homestead in 1756—another indication that Natives did not forget their dispossessors. Lycon was mortally wounded in combat after he and his neighbors killed a few of the warriors: "one of the Indians killed was Tom Hickman, and Tom Hayes, all Delawares, and well known in [those] Parts."[46]

Although the proprietors failed to evict the squatters, their efforts to do so fulfilled vital legal and diplomatic functions that paid off in the short term with much more clarity than the murky resolutions of jurisdictional controversies over individual murders and rapes discussed in previous chapters. First, the provincial government asserted jurisdiction over frontier lands whose boundaries were disputed with Maryland, Virginia, and Connecticut.[47] Second, Pennsylvania employed its strong ties to the Six Nations to graft Iroquois claims and influence onto Delawares', Shawnees', or Susquehanna Indians' territories. The colony's land purchases from the Six Nations extinguished Indian title, ended squatter occupancy, and secured the areas from other colonial competitors, epitomizing what Dorothy Jones has termed "colonialism by treaty" or the exploitation of intercultural diplomacy to acquire land. Third, provincial expeditions against squatters extended the province's legal system into the interior.

Fourth, removing illegal settlers cleared the way for surveyors, land speculators, and legal settlers who could purchase land and pay quitrents. The
dispossession of Native peoples created repetitive crises for Indian and proprietary negotiators and helped to ensure a level of intercultural warfare
that dwarfed the sporadic violence that had plagued the tense relations
between the squatters and Indians who had previously shared the land.[48]

Illegal settlement became an imperial crisis in the 1760s when such British officials as Thomas Gage and William Johnson struggled to secure the
new empire that Britain had won from the French. The crisis became so
serious that by 1768 the Pennsylvania Assembly enacted the death penalty
for individuals convicted of settling on Indians' lands. Despite such draco-
nian measures, colonists from Virginia, Maryland, and Pennsylvania
breached the Appalachian barrier and settled on the Ohio Indians' lands
in the Monongahela Valley, particularly along Redstone Creek. From an
imperial perspective, uncontainable illegal settlement and chronic racial
violence in the trans-Appalachian west jeopardized the entire edifice of
empire in North America. After nearly a decade of warfare, many settlers
who went west despised Indians and demanded revenge. The worst nightmare of British officials was the possibility that settlers' encroachments and
their frequent murders of Indians would lead the colonies into a war with
a powerful pan-Indian confederacy. As subsequent chapters show, imperial
officials, ordinary colonists, and Native peoples struggled to establish firm
legal and racial boundaries throughout the 1760s. Both the Proclamation
Line of 1763 and the Paxton massacre symbolized how Pennsylvania's permeable eighteenth-century frontiers were becoming rigid racially defined
borders.

Yet even as Pennsylvania became the "dark and bloody ground" of the late
eighteenth century, older patterns persisted. In 1765, as the violence of the
Seven Years' War and Pontiac's War had barely begun to subside, a group
of squatters planted corn alongside an Indian named Mohawk Peter, his
Euro-American wife, and their family. And in 1768, Native Americans
again resisted a proprietary expedition to eject trespassers, fearing that the
squatters' removal portended a British attack on the Indians.[49] These were
fleeting vestiges of a formerly common world of everyday relationships
between ordinary people on the frontier. Native dispossession was not simply a function of greater numbers of Euro-American farmers invading an
Indian neighborhood. Euro-American and Indian settlers coexisted in river

valleys, negotiating land use, possession, and boundaries, and they formed temporary alliances based on hospitable social and economic relationships. Euro-American farmers occasionally lived as Indians' tenants without provincial legal title to the land. Perceiving those relationships as a threat to their interests, the proprietors aggressively asserted colonial jurisdiction over the disputed areas. Their egregious land purchases from the Six Nations resulted in dispossession of the resident Natives and some Euro-American squatters and fueled Indians' desires for retribution. The triangular contest involving squatters, Indians, and proprietors reveals how complex, ambivalent, and contingent stories of life on eighteenth-century American frontiers could be.

11

⁂

VIOLENCE, RACE, AND THE PAXTON BOYS

KRISTA CAMENZIND

On the morning of 14 December 1763 approximately fifty armed Euro-American men burned down Conestoga Town in Lancaster County and killed six of the Indians living there. Thirteen days later, between fifty and one hundred "Paxton Boys," as they were called, galloped into the town of Lancaster.[1] There they killed the remaining fourteen Conestoga Indians who had taken refuge in the town's workhouse in the hopes that local officials would protect them from further attack. The slayings were carried out in a brutal fashion. An eyewitness account by William Henry described the Lancaster workhouse yard as a chaotic, bloody, "horrid sight." In the yard Henry observed Will Sock, a man the Paxton Boys insisted was a spy, lying on the ground; "across him and [a] squaw lay two children, of about the age of three years, whose heads were split with the tomahawk, and their scalps taken off." Toward the middle of the yard Henry noticed another man had been shot in the chest; "his legs were chopped with the toma-hawk, his hands cut off, and finally a rifle ball discharged in his mouth." Henry concluded that "In this manner lay the whole of them, men, women and children spread about the prison yard; shot, scalped, hacked and cut to pieces."[2]

The brutality of the massacres shocked colonial leaders in Philadelphia. Benjamin Franklin denounced the murders as an "atrocious Fact, in Defiance of the Government, of all Laws human and divine, and to the eternal Disgrace of their Country and Colour." He castigated the men who perpetrated the violence as "CHRISTIAN WHITE SAVAGES."[3] The indignation of Philadelphians quickly turned to alarm when news arrived that the Paxton Boys planned to march to the city and "remove" 140 Moravian Indians housed on Province Island in the Delaware River. Provincial leaders interpreted the Paxton Boys' proposed march as a direct threat to the peace of the city and to the authority of the government. Governor John Penn requested that the Assembly grant him "full powers to repel those bold Invaders of Law and Justice, and support the Honor and Dignity of the Government."[4] In the minds of the colony's leaders, the Paxton Boys threatened to bring the violence and disorder associated with the frontier to their orderly city.

The marchers never reached Philadelphia. Instead, the 250 frontiersmen stopped in Germantown, where, on 7 February 1764, they met with a delegation of Philadelphia's leading men. When the marchers realized that the residents of the city had armed themselves against their arrival, they agreed to return to their homes, leaving two spokesmen to present their case to the provincial government.[5] A week later, these men, Matthew Smith and James Gibson, presented to the governor and the Assembly a *Declaration* and a *Remonstrance* that sought to justify the actions of the Paxton Boys as legitimate acts against Indians who were "falsly pretended Friends." The *Declaration* and *Remonstrance* also protested the presents regularly granted to Indians, the insufficient number of troops protecting the frontier, and the inequitable allotment of representatives in the Assembly, while insisting upon the institution of scalp bounties and a return of all captives taken by the Indians during the Seven Years' War and the ongoing conflict known as Pontiac's War.[6] Neither branch of government responded to these entreaties, and a disgruntled Smith and Gibson soon left the city.

The Paxton Boys' massacre and march represent a crucial turning point in the history of Pennsylvania. For the first time in the province's history, a group of colonists engaged in an extralegal, large-scale, and organized act of racial violence. Historians have offered a variety of explanations for the Paxton Boys' significance. Some scholars have ignored the racial component of the massacres and argued that the Paxton Boys were early frontier democrats who acted to reform representation in the Assembly.[7] Other historians have successfully refuted the contention that the Paxton Boys were nascent democrats, arguing instead that they were foes of democracy

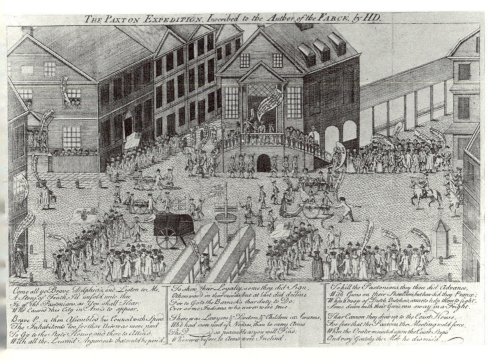

Figure 12 Contemporary satire of Philadelphians' efforts to mobilize against the Paxton Boys' march on the capital. Henry Dawkins, *The Paxton Expedition*, 1763. American Philosophical Society, Philadelphia.

who turned to violence and force when the government failed to meet their expectations.[8] Similarly, some scholars maintain that the events of 1763 reflected the general disorder and lawlessness of the colonial frontier.[9] More recently, historians have emphasized the role race played in the massacres. Historian Alden Vaughan, for example, has memorably stated, "the Paxton Boys' principal legacy was 'open season' on the Indian, friend or foe."[10]

Although the Paxton Boys did inaugurate a new era of racial violence, historians do not yet understand how frontier settlers made the transition from peaceful coexistence with Native Americans to bloody racial violence. As previous chapters indicate, William Penn's "holy experiment" and the long peace it generated had been tenuous and hard won, but it had held for seven decades. Euro-American frontiersmen did not simply pick up their guns and hatchets in December 1763 in a spontaneous fit of rage;

rather, their behavior evolved from symbolic to actual violence against Indians over the preceding nine years. The creation of a racial enemy entailed an evolution in thinking, and it served a specific, gendered purpose for frontier Pennsylvanians. By creating a racial enemy, Euro-American frontiersmen were able to legitimate an act of cowardice—killing unarmed men, women, and children—as an act of male valor.

Exploring the transformation in behavior and the evolution in thinking that took place on the Pennsylvania frontier in the mid-eighteenth century not only illuminates an important moment in the province's experience, it also deepens historians' understanding of a central theme in American history. The Paxton Boys' massacre of the Conestogas was part of a larger pattern of Euro-American violence against Native Americans that had characterized British North America almost from the moment of settlement.[11] Pennsylvania's peaceful relations with its Native neighbors made it exceptional among the major colonies until the mid-eighteenth century. The Paxton Boys' massacre marked the culmination of a process that began with the Seven Years' War and that moved Pennsylvania into the mainstream of British North America's racial history. Indeed, the brutality of the Paxton Boys and their subsequent march to Philadelphia were integral in the development of the image of the American frontier as a place where White men expressed their manhood through acts of violence against Native Americans.

The key to explaining the Paxton Boys' behavior lies in examining the experiences of Euro-American frontier settlers during the Seven Years' War, a conflict that began in 1754 when a company of Virginia militiamen under the command of George Washington clashed with French and Indian warriors in what would become western Pennsylvania.[12] The ramifications of this watershed conflict were felt throughout the province, but nowhere more acutely than on the northern and western edges of Euro-American settlement. On Pennsylvania's war-torn frontier, Delaware Indians attacked and burned Euro-American farms, capturing and killing hundreds of settlers.[13] Thousands more Euro-American frontier families fled their farms in panic, abandoning hundreds of thousands of acres of land that had represented the expansive potential of Pennsylvania's agriculture. The dislocation, fear, and turmoil sparked by the war created a fertile environment in which the racial hatred and regional distrust that had been latent for seven decades could gestate and ultimately explode. In 1758, Major General John Forbes ended the war in Pennsylvania when he seized the French Fort Duquesne at the forks of the Ohio River, renamed it Fort Pitt, and expelled the French from western Pennsylvania. After three years of war, the Pennsylvania frontier returned to peace and Euro-American settlers again took up their relentless pursuit of prosperity. Five years later, in a conflict called Pontiac's War, a series of Native American assaults on British forts from Fort Detroit to Fort Pitt ushered in a return to war on the Pennsylvania frontier. In the winter following this renewal of hostilities, the Paxton Boys sought a bloody revenge against the Conestogas.

The violence of the war proved transformative for Euro-American frontiersmen. When Delaware Indians attacked farms and families they destabilized Euro-American households and patriarchal identities. The gendered crisis induced by the war prompted Euro-American settlers to hate their Native American attackers and to begin to group all Indians, even friendly neighbors, into the category of racial enemy. The apparent failure of the colony's supreme patriarchs—the government in Philadelphia—to effectively protect the frontier convinced frontiersmen that the residents of Philadelphia required instruction in their new racial philosophy. Provincial leaders did not seem to understand that Euro-Americans in British colonies owed their loyalty and support first and foremost to one another. Further, the experience of witnessing Native attacks and their aftermath instructed Euro-American frontiersmen in the use of violence—a lesson they would put into practice when they murdered the Conestogas and threatened the Moravian Indians in Philadelphia. During the war, gender, race, and violence became inextricably intertwined. The conjunction of these forces produced the Paxton Boys.

The Seven Years' War shattered life along the Pennsylvania frontier and forced everyone living there to adapt to a volatile new environment. The French and Indian offensive that displaced Euro-Americans from their homes ironically led to the consolidation of previously isolated farming families. Whereas before 1755 Euro-American settlers resided on isolated farms separated by a mile or more—and, as the previous chapter shows, often interspersed with Native American villages and homesteads—once the raids commenced, families congregated together for mutual protection and support. Once gathered, frightened Euro-Americans engaged in a variety of collective acts, from petitioning the government in Philadelphia for protection, to fortifying their houses and building forts, to harassing Indians and government representatives, to riding around the countryside in

mobs. In the heated context of war, the collectivity of Euro-American settlers' response provided a venue for the maturation of previously existing
tensions on the frontier.

Euro-American frontier settlers projected their anxiety outward in two
directions: toward Native Americans and toward provincial officials. As
the previous chapter demonstrates, some Euro-Americans and Indians in
the early eighteenth century forged personal relationships and loose alliances against the legalistic incursions of the Penn proprietors. The Seven
Years' War strained and often severed those bonds, and friends became
enemies. Simultaneously, Euro-American settlers grew to distrust colonial
officials, who claimed the authority to control the pace of frontier expansion and who had sponsored immigrant settlement as a "cordone of defense" but who refused to aid the Euro-American inhabitants of the region
just when they needed it the most.[14] Faced with the apparent betrayals of
Native friends and provincial administrators, Euro-American frontiersmen
lashed out at any Indian who crossed their path, as well as at any representative of the government who failed to accede to their demands immediately.

The war posed an obvious threat to Euro-American settlers' survival,
but it also caused frontiersmen to fear for their status as men. The French
and Indian campaigns directly threatened the two pillars of their identity
as adult men and as patriarchs: their land and their families. The quest for
land—the underpinning of a man's economic independence or what Daniel Vickers calls "competency"—drove men onto the frontier in the first
place.[15] Once they had laid claim to a plot of land, men relied on the labor
of their wives, children, and perhaps indentured servants and (rarely)
slaves to build houses and barns, to raise livestock, and to cultivate crops.
When Indian raiding parties swept through a neighborhood, they systematically assaulted the "improvements" of farming families. Raiders burned
buildings and crops; they slaughtered or seized cattle; they killed some
men, women, and children; they took others captive; and they forced the
remaining population to flee. In addition to destroying Euro-American
men's basis for economic survival, the violence and terror of the war undermined their ability to perform their patriarchal duty of protecting their
wives and children. Not only were women and children killed, they were
carried away to an unknown fate. That another man, especially a Native
American man, could control the labor of one's family and presumably
gain sexual access to his wife must have terrified frontier patriarchs. In

short, French and Indian raiders assaulted the material and emotional foundations of Euro-American men's patriarchal identity and sense of manhood.[16]

The interplay between distrust of a distant government, anger toward Native Americans, and an imperiled patriarchy was apparent from the earliest days of the war. A November 1755 "meeting" of angry Euro-American settlers that confronted provincial interpreter and county magistrate Conrad Weiser at Tulpehocken Creek provides a vivid illustration of the panic that coursed through the frontier when Indian warriors threatened, or were thought to threaten, an area. The episode began when a frantic messenger burst into a meeting between Weiser and some visiting Indians, informing them that a group of men was collecting at Tulpehocken in response to a recent raid. The messenger also warned that the Indians should not be sent that way without an escort as "the People ware so enraged against all the Indians, and would kill them without Distinction." Weiser decided to go to Tulpehocken to assume command of the men gathering there. For their protection, he brought the Indians at his house along with him.[17]

When Weiser's party arrived at Tulpehocken it was greeted by four or five hundred men who lined the road shouting noisily "why must we be killed by the Indians and we not kill them!" After Weiser passed off his Native charges to a six-man escort, he turned his attention to holding a "sort of Counsel of Warr" among the officers who had been selected by the freedmen of the county. When a plan to raise and pay a guard was presented to the gathered mob, they "cried out that so much for an Indian Scalp they would have, (be they Friends or Enemies)." After Weiser informed them he had no power to institute a scalp bounty, he reported, "they begun, some to Curse the Governor; some the assembly; called me a Traitor to the Country who held with the Indians."[18]

In one short emotional outburst this collection of men summed up the growing outrage on the frontier: the leaders of the colony—the governor, assembly members, and local magistrates—appeared to favor the Indians above their own settlers. As Weiser struggled to pacify the mob and explain the limitations of his and the government's power, his friends warned him that some among the group intended to shoot him. He was spared this fate when news arrived that Indian warriors were attacking a nearby farm. Although the report proved to be false, the crowd dispersed as people rode or ran off "without any Order or Regulation." A dejected Weiser returned home where, he vowed, he would defend his farm and family as long as he could in troubled times. He concluded from his experience in Tulpehocken that "there [was] no Doing with the People without a law or Regulation by the Governor and Assembly."[19]

The incident at Tulpehocken laid out the roles that the various inhabitants of Pennsylvania frontiers would play for the remainder of the war. Men like Weiser, local officeholders with connections to Philadelphia, worked to institute some sort of order among Euro-Americans. Common male settlers, on the other hand, motivated by patriarchal duty, the desire for self-preservation, and a healthy measure of panic, called for assistance from the government and grew dangerously disgruntled when their requests went unanswered. Meanwhile, Indians neutral in the war or allied with the British moved among the settlers at increasing peril in the face of mobs who lumped all Native people together as the enemy. Until General Forbes captured Fort Duquesne in 1758, Euro-American suspicions continued to fester in response to repeated small, but deadly, Native incursions. It is important to note, however, that organized racial violence was still eight years away. In fall 1755 Euro-American frontiersmen were only beginning to learn the lessons of violence and racial hatred the war would teach them.

Overwhelmed by the real or potential violence of the war, Euro-American settlers sought to protect their dependents and their land by appealing to a higher authority. In so doing, they recognized the hierarchical nature of patriarchy in British North America. They were small patriarchs who farmed modest plots of land in a region distant from the center of economic and political power. Thus, they wrote petitions to the patriarchal head of the colony—the governor—asking for ammunition, forts, guns, and soldiers.[20] The failure of the governor and the Assembly to respond to these entreaties and to provide an acceptable level of protection ignited regional animosities and fostered a sense of alienation among frontier settlers that would prompt them to take their message to Philadelphia in person in February 1764.

Through dozens of petitions, Euro-American settlers appealed to the political patriarchs of the colony. Petitioners bowed to convention when they repeatedly began their missives with the phrases "Humble petition" or "Humble Suplication," but further appeals to benevolent paternal authority in the body of many petitions suggests that their conception of how a good patriarch should behave ran much deeper than such ritual language. Petitioners sought to elicit the sympathy of the government by focusing on the "naked and Defenceless" state of their "Bleeding Country" and how its inhabitants were "Exposed to the Inhuman Cruelty of Barbarous Savages" and "the Ravages of our Restless, Barbarous, and Merciless Enemy." They maintained that it was the governor's duty as the patriarch of the colony to protect them. "Your Honour's compassion as to a kind and careful Father of whose tender concern for us we are well assured," they concluded, was their "Only door of Hope (Next to the Divine Goodness)."[21]

For their part, provincial leaders embraced their beneficent patriarchal role. "I shall upon all Occasions be studious to protect the People committed to my charge," Governor Robert Morris assured the Assembly upon his arrival in the colony in 1754.[22] Morris and his compatriots understood that the power of a patriarch, whether a governor or a father, entailed the duty to protect dependents. As Paul Gilje puts it, "the eighteenth-century world was hierarchical; the upper levels of society, in good paternalistic fashion, held that they were the stewards of the community."[23] By composing petitions to the government of Pennsylvania, frontier patriarchs fulfilled part of their patriarchal duty to enlist assistance from a higher power in a time of emergency. By ignoring the pleas of the petitioners, patriarchs in Philadelphia failed to live up to the petitioners' ideal—and their own rhetoric.

Petitioners stressed their desperate condition as a way of appealing to the paternal sympathy of the government, but they did not fully relinquish their power when they wrote. Buried within supplicating entreaties was the threat that, if the government did not protect them, Euro-American settlers would abandon the frontier, and the heart of the province would be left open to the enemy. Inhabitants of York County forcefully summed up the situation when they wrote "that[,] as the County of Cumberland [to the west] is mostly evacuated, and part of this become the Frontier, the Enemy may easily enter and take Possession of Provisions sufficient to supply many thousand Men, and be thereby enabled to carry their Hostilities even to the Metropolis."[24] Warnings that the frontier could recede to Philadelphia recurred often in the petitions and letters of Euro-American settlers. Petitioners in Lancaster County reported "Hanover [township] is upon the point of flying and we cannot tarry if they fly, and our flight will open a way into the heart of the Province."[25] Implicit in such images was the specter that, if Philadelphians did not support frontier defense, the violence and disorder associated with the region would soon visit the city.

Even though authorities in distant Philadelphia appeared to turn a deaf ear to cries for assistance, patriarchs engulfed by war continued to struggle to meet the needs of their dependents. In particular, local officials in frontier towns had to deal with the refugee crisis sparked by wartime attacks. Euro-American frontierfolk clogged backwoods paths as they sped toward the safety of established towns. Many of the refugees were in desperate condition. "It's a very Sorrowful specticle," Adam Hoops insisted, "to see those that Escaped with their lives [have] not a Mouthful to Eat, or Bed to lie on, or Clothes to Cover their Nakedness, or keep them warm, but all they had consumed in Ashes."[26] Hundreds crammed into towns like Bethlehem, Carlisle, Easton, Lancaster, and Reading in hopes of protection. In January 1756, the refugee population at Bethlehem, Friedensthal, and Nazareth peaked with an additional 556 people crowding into those Moravian communities.[27] The arrival of so many impoverished refugees placed enormous burdens on "the Charity of the other Inhabitants."[28]

Recurrent references to families, and especially to women and children, in descriptions of the refugees demonstrated how Euro-American settlers understood the world in familial terms. In November 1755 James Burd declared Shippensburg "full of People, they being all moving in with their Famillys[,] 5 or 6 Famillys in a house."[29] John Potter made clear that men in positions of responsibility had obligations to an extended Euro-American frontier family when he described his role as sheriff of Great Cove in patriarchal terms. "Last night," he reported in 1755, "I had a Family of upwards of an hundred of Women and Children who fled for Succor."[30]

Men who chose to stay on or near their farms despite the danger were preoccupied with the patriarchal task of sheltering their dependents. When Delaware warriors appeared (or were reported to appear) in a given neighborhood, Euro-Americans often "concluded it best for the Neighbors to collect themselves together, as many as They could, in some one House." After Indians began attacking homesteads in Lower Smithfield Township in Northampton County, for example, nine families gathered at Philip Bozart's dwelling, while "a great Number" of others convened at the farms of two other neighbors.[31] These houses were frequently fortified in some manner and stood as makeshift forts, the main purpose of which was to protect women and children.[32] Thus, even after they heard gun shots at a nearby house, the people at Bozart's house "were afraid to venture to go and see what had happened that Day, as they had many Woman [sic] and Children to take Care of, who if they had left might have fallen an easy Prey to the Enemy."[33]

In addition to these makeshift strongholds, Euro-American settlers began constructing new forts, which they envisioned as places where women and children could be lodged for safety. The leading men of Cumberland County resolved to build five strongholds and "that all the Women and Children be deposited in the large forts."[34] Similarly, James Burd declared that Fort Morris at Shippensburg, "in which we intend to throw all the Women and Children," was being constructed with "great Vigour."[35] The forts erected by the provincial government also served as sanctuaries for displaced family members. Jacob Morgan at Fort Lebanon requested that Governor William Denny increase the number of men under his command in part because "upward of 60 Women and Children" had fled to his fort for protection.[36]

With their families safely sequestered in forts of one kind or another, Euro-American frontiersmen were free to try to confront their enemy. They did so in many cases by forming into mobs, like that at Tulpehocken, and patrolling their neighborhoods in search of raiding parties.[37] Such ad hoc groups produced a good deal of bravado but provided little direct threat to their foes. In the end, they were more successful at scaring off raiders with their noisy approach and at burying corpses than at engaging the enemy in combat. When approximately three hundred men formed a company under Conrad Weiser, for example, they grandly and unanimously agreed "to die together and engage the Enemy whereever they Should meet with them—never to enquire the number, but fight them, and so obstruct their marching further into the Inhabited parts . . . and so save the Lives of our Wives and Children." Yet despite their brave declaration, group members disbanded quickly and returned to their farms in a disorderly fashion without making their neighborhood notably safer.[38]

Instead of confronting Indian warriors directly in the early days of the war, many men engaged in a type of symbolic warfare. In late October 1755 around one hundred men collected in Berks County to "oppose the Indians." William Parsons instructed them to march to a gap in the mountains near Swatara Creek, to build a "Breast work of Trees, and to stay there two or three Days." Parsons was dismayed when "they went no farther than to the Top of the Mountain, and there those that had amunition, spent most of it in shooting up into the Air, and then returned back again, firing all the way, to the great Terror of all the Inhabitants thereabout." Other groups of men engaged in the same type of panicked and apparently counterproductive behavior throughout the county.[39]

The almost palpable sense of fear coursing through the frontier during the Seven Years' War made the collective and symbolic nature of crowds especially meaningful. Gathering in large numbers reinforced camaraderie among Euro-Americans in a given neighborhood. More important, to assemble with the express purpose of "opposing the Indians" allowed them to feel a moment of mastery in an out-of-control situation. Even the apparently wasteful act of firing guns wildly into the woods had meaning. In so doing, Euro-American frontiersmen engaged in a metonymic style of warfare wherein one action—firing guns—stood in for the act of waging wholesale war against the Indians. This was more than a metaphoric substitution when something external stands in as a substitute for the original object. Metonymic substitution makes an attribute or a part of an object stand for the whole; thus the relation between object and metonym is more intimate than between object and metaphor. As a result, the meaning, and the emotions, associated with the original object adhere much more potently to a metonym than they do to a metaphor. Because firing guns was an integral part of making war, the act of shooting into the woods provided frontiersmen with the cathartic reward of making war to project themselves, their dependents, and their land. Firing guns in the woods did not simply *represent* making war—in the settlers' worldview, it *was* making war.[40]

The Euro-American tendency to blend fears of the Native Americans and trepidation about the woods amplified the metonymic nature of frontier crowd activity. James Merrell has noted that, despite all the emphasis on the fertility and richness of Pennsylvania in promotional writing, the inhabitants of "Penn's Woods" still divided the colony into "the Woods" and "the Inhabited Part of the Country." The former was constructed as a place of darkness and danger, while the latter was a place of safety and productivity. As Merrell puts it, "wilderness is a state of mind, not a state of nature. . . . That is why transplanted Europeans living in *Penn's Woods,* the (steadily expanding) domain under English control, could talk fearfully of *the Woods,* the Indian countries lying beyond the limits of colonial settlement." "Penn's Woods" was civilized by its latinate translation into "Pennsylvania," but the frightening and unknown "woods," "wilderness," and "bushes" were equated with the "skulking" and "lurking" Indians who lived there.[41] When Euro-Americans rode into the woods, they entered what they understood to be the dangerous domain of the Indians. When they fired their guns they effectively made war on the Indians, even if no actual Indians were present. The reward of gathering to shoot weapons at random was psychic rather than military or literal.

The men from Berks County may not have killed any Native people that fall night in 1755, but they did take the first step toward adopting real, large-scale violence against all Indians. In direct contradiction to the Quaker tenet of pacifism that had guided the province for seventy-five years—and in violation of the customs, described in chapter 10, that they had forged with their Native neighbors—they took up their guns and fired them in anger. Further, the combination of metonymic violence and the concentration of excited people encouraged Euro-Americans to act out their suspicions and aggressions in a manner unprecedented in frontier Pennsylvania. In eighteenth-century British North America, crowds provided their participants with a sense of solidarity that legitimated their actions and their viewpoints. Additionally, participation in crowd activity could strengthen an individual's adherence to the message or sentiment of the community.[42] During the Seven Years' War large gatherings of men provided a venue for Euro-American settlers to express their hostility toward their Native neighbors while simultaneously strengthening their sense of racial solidarity among themselves and their perception of racial difference from Indians.

A variety of circumstances contributed to growing prejudice and prompted settlers to behave aggressively toward any Indians they met. The most important was the violence inflicted by Delaware raiders, but settlers' inability—or unwillingness—to determine which Indians engaged in violence and which eschewed it amplified their anxiety. The Delawares, an already loose conglomeration of people, split into eastern and western factions before the war. Most of those in the Ohio country prosecuted the war in earnest, while those in the east took up arms, remained neutral, or promoted peace depending on local or individual circumstances.[43] As the war progressed, embattled Euro-American settlers saw little reason to distinguish the various loyalties and political positions of the Indians in Pennsylvania and the Ohio country. Indeed, many were convinced that members of the various communities of Christian Indians, who publicly professed pacifism and loyalty to the British, were really spies or supporters of those who pursued war against Pennsylvania. Suspicion of Christian

Indians hardened during Pontiac's War. In 1764 the Paxton Boys expressed such hostility when they asserted in their *Remonstrance* that there were "strong grounds, at least to suspect their Friendship, as it is known that they carried on a Correspondence with [our] Enemies" and that there was "undeniable Proof, that, the *Moravian Indians* were in confederacy with our open Enemies." That their evidence—three dead Indians carrying "Blankets, Ammunition and Provisions"—was hardly conclusive failed to deter the Paxton Boys from believing that all Indians were suspect and in league with, if not the same as, their wartime enemies.[44]

Ironically, because diplomatic initiatives brought the people who had waged war against the British into the settled areas of Euro-Pennsylvania, the peace negotiations necessary to end the war compounded confusion over the difference between allied and enemy Indians. Between 1756 and 1758 representatives of the eastern Delawares, the western Delawares, and the Six Nations met with Pennsylvania's governors and Quaker leaders in a series of conferences at Easton.[45] Although the conferences slowly steered the colony back to the shores of peace, the presence of these Indian delegations added to the turmoil created by the hundreds of displaced Euro-American settlers who poured into Easton and surrounding towns for protection. "We are not sure whether they are Friends or Enemies," Justice of the Peace Timothy Horsfield complained.[46] But some observers of the treaty negotiations drew more definitive conclusions. Townspeople grew alarmed when they recognized "that the Shirts which the Indian Women had on were made of Dutch Table Cloaths, which, it is supposed they took from the People they murdered on our Frontiers."[47] The linens may have been purchased legitimately, but it seemed as though the Indians who had come to make peace were mocking the settlers by wearing the spoils of their raids.

In this bewildering situation many Euro-American settlers focused on the perceived differences between themselves and all Native Americans. In Northampton County, where displaced Euro-American settlers, Moravian Indians, colonial officials, and Indians attending conferences collided throughout the mid–1750s, the calls for racial clarity were especially loud. From the opening days of the war, local residents focused their anger on Christian Indians who inundated the towns of Easton and Bethlehem. They issued repeated verbal threats against the peaceful Christian Indians in the towns and in nearby communities. "There is such a Rage in the neighborhood against the said poor Creatures," Moravian leader Augustus

Gottlieb Spangenberg explained, "that I fear they will mob us and them together."[48] Similarly, Weiser reported that "The cry of the common People, of which the Town [Bethlehem] was full, was very great against the Indians, and the poor People did not know what to do or what to say, finding all the People so enraged and using such language."[49] Like the men who fired their guns in the woods, settlers who verbally harassed peaceful Indians engaged in metonymic substitution. In this case, they assumed that any individual or group of Indians could stand in for all Native Americans.

Weiser and his fellow justices of the peace and magistrates in frontier counties, along with Moravian missionaries and Quaker members of the Friendly Association for Regaining and Preserving Peace with the Indians, worked to protect and support friendly Indians during the war. While frontier officials arrested disorderly settlers and escorted parties of Native Americans through the province, the Euro-Moravians at Bethlehem provided displaced and frightened Christian Indians with shelter and sustenance.[50] The most influential group concerned with the interests of Native Americans was the Friendly Association. Because of their commitment to pacifism, pious Quakers did not feel they could continue to play an active part in a government engaged in war; consequently, ten Friends resigned their seats in the Assembly in 1756.[51] As an alternative to formal political service, leading Quakers formed the Friendly Association as a vehicle through which they worked to restore peace to the province. The philanthropic organization provided thousands of pounds sterling worth of presents for the Indians attending the peace conferences and also paid for messengers to spread the news of the peace initiative to far-flung peoples. The Friendly Association proved instrumental in helping the Indians in the Ohio country and the Pennsylvania government reach a peace accord in fall 1758. For their efforts, the Quakers earned the undying animosity of Euro-American frontier settlers. Indeed, the Paxton Boys listed Quaker leaders among their enemies when they marched to Philadelphia.[52]

Working against the efforts of Friendly Association and other groups and individuals sympathetic to the Indians was the metonymic logic of Euro-American frontier settlers. As the war progressed, the behavior apparent in the opening days of the war moved toward its logical extreme—racial violence. Although there wasn't a linear progression from settlers careening through the woods firing their guns to threatening and harassing small groups of friendly Indians, both actions were ways in which Euro-American men went about defending their dependents and their patriarchal rights. The metonymic logic inherent in those acts was more sinister than simple symbolic substitution. Where metaphoric or symbolic substitution entailed attacking a representation of the true object of hostility, metonymic acts involved attacking an actual part of the hated object. Further, metonymic violence against a few Indians presumed the existence of a unified and essential Native identity. Both facets of the logic were necessary for racism: a monolithic racial identity and the willingness to attack any Indian as a metonym for the race. Thus, the racism apparent in the actions of the Paxton Boys in 1763–64 was an extension of the actions of earlier Euro-American frontier crowds.[53]

Striking out against a racialized enemy became a means of reasserting authority at a time when the violence and dislocation of the war destabilized patriarchal identities: settlers could justify an attack on any Indian as the necessary action of men defending their families and ways of life. The logic of a racialized enemy meant that an action that might otherwise be seen as an act of male cowardice—murdering a community of defenseless Native Americans, for instance—became an act of masculine valor. Racialization was also a way for Euro-American frontier settlers to assert their supposed superiority over the Indians. Finally, it enabled Euro-American settlers to demand support from provincial and imperial officials. If Native Americans formed a naturally coherent group, then all White people constituted a similarly cohesive unit. The conclusion of such logic was that White patriarchs in Philadelphia owed their loyalty and support first and foremost to their fellow White patriarchs on the frontier and not to the Indians who also resided there.

Euro-American settlers needed to assert racial unity because of the gaping regional divide between themselves and provincial leaders in Philadelphia. The overlap between regional and racial issues in settlers' minds was apparent as early as the incident at Tulpehocken in 1755. In many ways Weiser was an obvious target for settlers upset with the disruption of the war because he embodied what settlers interpreted as the divided loyalty of the provincial government. On one hand, he held political office, had been elected to command the men organized to defend the country, and exerted himself to bring order and peace to the frontier. All of these factors reflected the respected position he held in the colony. On the other hand, his work as the colony's primary Indian interpreter meant he had close relations with various Native leaders and groups and often represented their interests in public. Euro-American settlers wondered if Weiser was dedicated to the defense of the colony or if he was loyal to the Native Americans with whom he treated and negotiated. The same question could be asked of a colonial government that made ineffective efforts at defense while simultaneously struggling to maintain, reaffirm, and extend relations with the Indians, as evidenced by the repeated conferences at Easton.

Contradictory attitudes toward Native Americans arose because provincial and British imperial leaders recognized differences among Native Americans who fought with the French, those who allied themselves with the British, and those who remained neutral. Unlike many frontier settlers, imperial officials understood that Native Americans had a role to play in the British Empire. Indians were valuable allies whose familiarity with the territory made them ideal scouts and warriors. Drawing on transatlantic Whig ideas, British officials admired the "heroic" Indian warriors as far better defenders of the empire than the ineffective and "corrupted" colonials.[54] And, of course, any Indian allied with the British, or who declared neutrality, was one less warrior fighting for the French. For these reasons, colonial officials took active steps to protect peaceful Indians in Pennsylvania, in opposition to both the frontier understanding of patriarchal duty and the growing metonymic logic that led to racism.

Provincial leaders attempted to protect Christian Indians out of patriarchal regard for the men and women who had converted to Christianity and who lived among Euro-Americans on the frontier. Some of these groups had decades-long relations with Pennsylvania. The Conestogas, for example, had been allied with Pennsylvania since the beginning of the eighteenth century.[55] Accordingly, in 1756, Governor Morris ordered John Ross "to take the [Conestoga] Indians now in Town into Your Charge, and Care and Conduct them to the Manor of Conestogo." Morris explicitly instructed Ross to guard the safety of the Indians as they traveled because "the minds of the Inhabitants are not a little disturbed at the Murders committed by the Enemy Indians, and the People living on the Road . . . may not be well disposed towards them." Once at Conestoga, Ross was to build shelters for the Indians and see to their basic comfort. In addition to providing Ross with £50 to see to the Conestogas' immediate needs, Morris also made arrangements for their long-term maintenance.[56]

When the Paxton Boys killed this same group of people seven years later, they expressed not only their hatred of the Indians, but also their displeasure with an official policy designed to support a Native community. The willingness of provincial leaders to subsidize a group of Indians and their concurrent unwillingness to comply with Euro-American settlers' demands for protection heightened regional tensions within the province. Frontier inhabitants felt as though their petitions were going unheeded and that Philadelphia leaders had abandoned them to a "merciless Enemy." From Paxton Township in 1755, an exasperated Reverend John Elder protested that, "Tho we are careful to transmit them [reports of attacks] to Philadelphia and remonstrate and Petition time after time, yet [it is] to no purpose."[57] Two years later he put his point more succinctly: "It's well known that Representations from the back Inhabitants have but little weight with the Gentlemen in power, they looking on us either as uncapable of forming just notions of things, or as biassed by Selfish Views."[58] Here Elder pinpointed a central lesson of the war: provincial officials comfortably ensconced in cosmopolitan Philadelphia looked down upon frontier settlers and adopted an agenda that did not prioritize frontier defense.

Tensions between the frontier and Philadelphia subsided when peace returned to Pennsylvania in late 1758 and the need for direct support dissipated. The interlude of peace and regional harmony, however, proved to be uneasy and short-lived. Soon after General Forbes's success at Fort Duquesne, Euro-Americans moved to reclaim the lands from which Indians had evicted them. When he traveled through Cumberland County, the westernmost extreme of provincial settlement, the Reverend Thomas Barton found "the People are returning everywhere to the places they had abandoned and within the last 18 months the number of Houses and Inhabitants in Carlisle are doubled."[59] In 1763, just eleven years after it had been laid out, the town of Reading in Berks County boasted 1,300 residents. As Anglican minister Alexander Murray exclaimed, "the Country for Miles round" was "thick peopled."[60]

The rapid expansion of Euro-American settlement, however, only served to reinforce the concerns over land that had prompted Native Americans to wage war in 1755. Indeed, several ominous incidents between 1760 and the outbreak of Pontiac's War in 1763 exposed the animosity that simmered while Euro-Americans resumed their farming enterprise. In February 1760, Governor James Hamilton issued a reward for the capture and conviction of the people responsible for the Christmastime murder of a Native family near Carlisle. The bodies of a man and a boy had been found scalped, but a woman and another child were still missing. Hamilton rushed to reassure the Indians in the area "that the Perpetrators of this horrid Crime, when discovered and convicted, shall suffer Death the same manner as if they had killed an Englishman."[61] His assurances were in vain; the murderers were never caught.

In spite of the governor's efforts to reassure the Indians and to foster peace on the frontier, the settlers continued to display hostility toward the Indians they encountered. In fall 1762, when Captain Patterson discovered evidence of forty to fifty Indian warriors in Lancaster County, he led his men into battle against them. Four of Patterson's men died in the engagement, and eight Indians were killed.[62] This incident came months before the beginning of Pontiac's War and likely involved Indians going on a hunt or traveling through the province. Most ominously, in July 1763, Thomas McKee, a magistrate in Paxton Township, complained that he had "a good deal of Difficulty By the Inhabitants" who openly threatened to shoot Indians and collect their scalps for the bounty. McKee feared that the men would take out revenge for their sufferings "[per]haps on Some Innocent [Indian] familly."[63] Five months later, the racial animosity in Pennsylvania that had matured during the Seven Years' War reached its climax when the Paxton Boys attacked the Conestogas.

In the end, the legacy of the Paxton Boys was not simply "'open season' on the Indian." The Paxton Boys bequeathed the legacy of a frontier associated with the violent defense of White patriarchy against a racialized Native American enemy. In a tangible sense, the Paxton Boys emerged from the particular gendered, regional, and racial environment of the Euro-American frontier during the Seven Years' War. To be sure, racial animosity was not universal after the Paxton Boys retreated from Philadelphia. Some Euro-American frontier farmers continued to form friendly and cooperative relationships with their Native neighbors, and leaders within the Native and Euro-American communities persisted in advocating a peaceful coexistence in the province. Nonetheless, when the Paxton Boys crossed the line from metonymic to real violence, they signaled a new era in Pennsylvania's history. William Penn's vision of peace and tolerance was abandoned by many in favor of the violent removal of all Indians from Penn's Woods.

Just eleven short years before the American Revolution, the Paxton Boys marched to the city where the Declaration of Independence would be signed, not on behalf of democracy, but in the name of racial solidarity. One of the hallmarks of the new nation would be its relentless expansion westward to the Pacific. Fueling this expansion was the racial and gendered construction of the frontier expressed by the Paxton Boys. During the nineteenth century, figures as diverse as Davey Crockett and Francis Parkman built upon the experience of people like the Paxton Boys to construct a popular image of the frontier and the trans-Mississippi west as a place where White men expressed their manhood through violence against nature and against Native Americans. In his almanacs and his autobiography, Crockett created a caricature of himself and of the frontier that appealed to the popular reading masses. In the more scholarly context of a Boston Brahmin's journey west, Parkman's *The Oregon Trail* replicated the popular image of the frontier as a place where White men could find their masculine identities in opposition to Native Americans and to nature.[64] The roots of these and other nineteenth-century constructions of the frontier lay in eighteenth-century experience. The march toward the Paxton Boys during the Seven Years' War was one starting point for the progress of Manifest Destiny across the continent.

12

"REAL" INDIANS, "WHITE" INDIANS, AND THE CONTEST FOR THE WYOMING VALLEY

PAUL MOYER

In October 1755, eight years before the massacre of the Conestogas, forty-nine men from the Paxton district of Pennsylvania rode into an ambush along the east bank of the Susquehanna River. The party, led by merchant and fur trader John Harris, was returning home after visiting settlements along Penn's Creek that had been recently devastated by Indian raiders. More than half a dozen Paxton men were shot dead or drowned in the river trying to escape. Their assailants were probably Delawares.[1] About fifty miles north and as many years later, the Pennsylvania frontier was the scene of another deadly ambush. In July 1804, Edward Gobin, a surveyor employed by Pennsylvania land speculators, was "shot through the body with a rifle bullet" and killed while working near the Tioga River. A proclamation issued by Pennsylvania Governor Thomas McKean offered a reward for the capture of Gobin's murderers, described as "a company consisting of about eighteen persons, dressed like Indians."[2] Gobin was one of many surveyors and land agents who became victims of White settlers who fought government authorities and powerful speculators for possession of frontier land in postindependence America. The pseudo-Indian insurgents responsible for Gobin's death were what many people referred to as "Wild Yankees," settlers holding deeds issued by Connecticut-based

land companies who resisted Pennsylvania's attempts to impose its authority over them.

The juxtaposition of these two episodes raises important questions.
How, in the fifty years between 1750 and 1800, did the Pennsylvania frontier
go from being a place where Indians and Euro-Americans intermingled to
a place where the only "Indians" to be found were disguised and disgruntled White settlers? And why did those disgruntled Whites dress as Indians?
The fact that such behavior was not confined to Pennsylvania but was
repeated on the frontiers of Maine, Vermont, and elsewhere makes the
question even more pertinent.[3] Such manipulation of ethnic identities suggests a deeper question: how did the experience and memory of Indian-
White conflict shape the contests over land and authority that plagued the
American frontier into the nineteenth century?

Many factors contributed to the transformation of the Pennsylvania
frontier. Disease, war, the expansion of Euro-American settlements, and
the impacts of Indian-European trade devastated Native communities and
undermined their autonomy.[4] But jurisdictional disputes between colonies
and colonists also contributed to the process. As previous chapters have
demonstrated, the expulsion of Indians was directly connected to the rise
of conflicts over property and power, not only between Native Americans
and colonists, but also among White settlers, land speculators, and government officials. The replacement of "real" Indians by "White" Indians was
one consequence of intercolonial land disputes and of numerous face-to-
face conflicts waged by ordinary people over frontier land. Another was a
culture of violence that was profoundly shaped by White settlers' contact
with Indians and their experience of bitter, racially charged frontier wars.

The story of the Wyoming Valley, a narrow strip of land along the north
branch of the Susquehanna River, highlights how late eighteenth-century
land disputes were both products and catalysts of Indian dispossession.[5]
The contest there, which emerged in the 1750s and was not completely
resolved until the early 1800s, was multidimensional, involving various
groups of Indians, Pennsylvania and Connecticut, and the settlers and land
speculators who entered the Wyoming region under their auspices. A distinct culture of violence emerged among the valley's White settlers—a culture of violence in which the legacy of conflict and contact with Indians
is undeniable. Indeed, one of the most important links between Indian-
European competition over land and later battles over jurisdiction and soil
rights that emerged during and after the Revolution was the violence that

White frontier settlers deployed, first against Indian adversaries and later against the land speculators, government officials, and settlers who threatened their soil rights.

The Wyoming dispute grew out of problems endemic to British America: conflicting colonial borders and overlapping land grants. Imperial officials, who often possessed little knowledge of the American landscape they parceled out, issued vague or inaccurate patents that either interfered with earlier grants or encroached on competing claims. In addition, Indians, with their decentralized political systems, their own jurisdictional controversies, and their distinctive cultural definitions of property rights and ideas about "nature," commonly resold the same piece of land to different purchasers—or rather, various Native leaders granted permission for various Euro-Americans to use a single plot of land for varied purposes.[6] As a result, colonies that assumed these grants ceded absolute possession frequently became embroiled in territorial disputes. Pennsylvania and Connecticut were no exceptions. In 1662 Connecticut obtained a charter from Charles II that awarded that colony a massive tract running from Pennsylvania's eastern border west to the "South Sea," a domain 120 miles wide by several thousand miles long (see Map 2). Although no one seemed to notice at the time, the royal grant that established Pennsylvania in 1681 conveyed to the colony's proprietor, William Penn, territory well within Connecticut's 1662 charter bounds. Penn's gift brought forth no immediate howls of protest from Connecticut; indeed, the New England colony let its extensive western claim lay dormant for almost a century. Only when Connecticut began to experience a land shortage in the 1750s did its inhabitants begin to reassert their charter bounds. The New Englanders, having only recently settled a decades-long border dispute with New York, decided not to challenge the territorial integrity of their western neighbor but focused instead on land west of the Delaware River claimed by Pennsylvania.[7]

Three Connecticut-based land companies—the Susquehannah and the First and Second Delaware companies—played leading roles in what would become the Wyoming dispute. The origins of these companies lay in the failed efforts of Connecticut residents to obtain permission from their colony to settle western lands. In May 1750, the inhabitants of Simsbury sent a petition to the Connecticut General Assembly requesting a town grant west of the Hudson River in order to relieve overcrowding in their community. Although the legislature rejected the petition, other towns joined

Simsbury in calling on Connecticut to assert its latent charter claims. Between 1750 and 1753, the Assembly received a total of twelve such petitions. One, submitted by the inhabitants of several eastern towns in March 1753, contained the first mention of the Wyoming region. The Connecticut Assembly rejected all of these entreaties for fear of upsetting the recently negotiated boundary settlement with New York and because most legislators believed that any claim based on the 1662 charter would not withstand close legal scrutiny. In response, the petitioners shelved their plans to obtain modest town grants from the legislature and set out upon the more ambitious scheme of establishing a colony west of the Delaware River.[8]

The Susquehannah Company was born from this effort to create a new Connecticut in the west. The company's structure evoked the town-founding traditions of Puritan New England; it was not a legally chartered corporation but a self-created entity whose existence depended upon the consensus of its members. Unlike early New England towns, however, the Susquehannah Company did not obtain land through the colonial assembly. Instead, it rested its claims upon the direct purchase of Indian lands. Moreover, the company added a commercial ethic to the communal approach of seventeenth-century town corporations; its shares could be sold or traded for a profit.[9] Interest in the venture soon spread throughout New England, and the company, which started out with three hundred members in summer 1753, had expanded its ranks to eight hundred shareholders by 1754.[10]

The creation of the Susquehannah Company placed Connecticut, Pennsylvania, and the region's Indians on a collision course. At the company's first meeting on 18 July 1753, shareholders agreed to send a committee of seven men to the Susquehanna Valley to find a site suitable for settlement, purchase the land from the local Indians, and survey it into towns and lots. This "Journeying Committee" departed in October, explored the region, surveyed several town sites, and made its way back to Connecticut.[11] In November, Pennsylvania's provincial secretary, Richard Peters, reported to the proprietors the "disagreeable News" that people from Connecticut had been to Wyoming and had "made great disturbance among the People" with the news that they would return in the spring "with a Thousand Men and settle those lands."[12]

Pennsylvania's proprietors were not the only ones disturbed. The Iroquois of the Six Nations claimed possession of the Wyoming Valley and, according to Pennsylvania Governor James Hamilton, were "highly offended" at the prospect of this land being "overrun with White People." The few Nanticoke Indians who inhabited the valley must have also been discomfited by the arrival of the Susquehannah Company's emissaries. In addition, the news angered Delaware Indians from the Moravian settlement of Gnadenhütten. Hoping to forestall Euro-American intrusions and encouraged by the Six Nations, about seventy Delawares led by Teedyuscung occupied the Wyoming Valley early in 1754.[13]

Later that year, the Susquehannah Company and Pennsylvania's proprietors both made aggressive moves to secure possession of the Wyoming Valley—moves that placed Indians and Indian soil rights at the center of the conflict. Indeed, as Peters later observed, the dispute was not only "between Subject and Subject but between Indian and Englishman."[14] The Albany Congress of 1754, which provided a backdrop for Pennsylvania's and Connecticut's continuing struggle over the Wyoming Valley, drew Indians deeper into the conflict.[15] The New Englanders purchased millions of acres of land in the upper Susquehanna and Delaware valleys from Iroquois Indians attending the conference without asking the permission of provincial or imperial officials.[16]

To make matters worse, rumors spread that the Indians who ratified the agreement only did so after being plied with generous amounts of alcohol. For their part, the Iroquois who signed the agreement did so without consulting the council of the Six Nations. Adding to the confusion, in an effort to check the New Englanders, Pennsylvania's delegation to the Albany Congress also obtained a deed from the Six Nations—a deed that covered much of the same land purchased by the Susquehannah Company (see Map 4). Now, not only conflicting colonial charters divided Pennsylvania and Connecticut, but also competing Indian purchases. Moreover, the Albany Congress drove a wedge between the Six Nations and the Delaware Indians who actually occupied the Wyoming Valley.[17]

The Albany Congress marked a turning point, not only for the colonies and colonists involved in the Wyoming dispute, but also for the Indians who inhabited or claimed land between the Delaware and Susquehanna rivers. The Congress itself saw the Six Nations relinquish control of the Wyoming region. More important, the conference spurred both Connecticut and Pennsylvania to redirect their energies toward recruiting settlers to occupy their claims. The Connecticut land companies, believing that actual occupation was the best way to secure territory, were determined to settle the valley. The outbreak of the Seven Years' War, however, delayed their plans for five years. This imperial conflict was linked, at least locally, to the Wyoming dispute. The moves made by Pennsylvania, Connecticut, and the Six Nations at Albany outraged the Indians of the upper Susquehanna and Delaware river valleys, who used the onset of hostilities between the French and the English as an opportunity to even the score.[18]

The advent of permanent Euro-American settlement transformed the Wyoming dispute from a conflict primarily involving legal jockeying between colonial governments, land companies, and Indians to a struggle in which ordinary colonists would play an increasingly dominant role. After the Treaty of Easton in 1758, the Delawares abandoned the war, allowing the New Englanders to believe things were safe for them to forge ahead with their plans for settlement.[19] By summer 1760 word reached Philadelphia that Connecticut settlers operating under the auspices of the Delaware Company had formed a settlement along the Delaware River at a place called Cushietunk. In September, Teedyuscung visited Governor James Hamilton in Philadelphia to complain of the New Englanders' arrival and to warn him that, if they did not leave, the Delawares would "turn them off." The timing of the Connecticut settlers' arrival was particularly bad for Pennsylvania's proprietary government. Not only was the province's territorial integrity being challenged, but many feared that the intrusion would lead to another costly Indian war. The prospect of Indian-White violence became even more immediate in August 1761 when the Six Nations denied the validity of the Susquehannah and Delaware company purchases.[20] Tensions further increased when the Susquehannah Company decided to send a large party of settlers to the Wyoming Valley in May 1762.[21] Once more Teedyuscung led Indian resistance to the company's plans. Upon returning from an August treaty conference in Lancaster, where he had again protested the arrival of the New Englanders, Teedyuscung encountered more than a hundred recently ensconced Susquehannah Company settlers. He and his Indian companions traded angry words with the New Englanders and managed to scare them off with threats of violence. But the Delaware leader knew that he had only won a temporary reprieve.[22]

More than any other event, Teedyuscung's murder in April 1763 encapsulates the role of the Wyoming dispute in the dispossession of the region's Indian inhabitants. Teedyuscung burned to death while asleep in his house. His death was no accident; twenty neighboring dwellings also burst into flame, destroying the Indian village at Wyoming. There is little doubt about who was behind these acts of arson. Less than two weeks after the fire, a dozen Connecticut families took possession of the settlement, and within a month more than 150 New Englanders were planting crops and building cabins.[23] Teedyuscung's assassination did not guarantee New Englanders an easy occupation of their western claims, however, for both Indians and imperial authorities set up new obstacles to White settlement. Fearing that the arrival of large numbers of colonists along the Susquehanna would provoke a war with the Six Nations, the Privy Council issued orders in June 1763 that forbade further settlement in the Wyoming region.[24] Yet the orders arrived in North America too late to halt either the settlers or the conflict. Four months later, during Pontiac's War, Teedyuscung's son, Captain Bull, led a Delaware war party that slaughtered or took captive the New Englanders who remained in the Susquehannah Company settlement.[25]

The failure of the Privy Council to avoid bloodshed between Indians and Euro-Americans in the Susquehanna Valley reflected a much larger process. Territorial and jurisdictional conflicts like the Wyoming dispute made it almost impossible for provincial or imperial authorities to regulate frontier expansion or protect Indian soil rights. Connecticut settlers were determined that no one, Indians or Pennsylvanians, would keep them from occupying their claim. Likewise, Pennsylvania officials, realizing that Indians could no longer serve a useful role in the Wyoming dispute, turned to other methods to maintain their hold on the valley.

The Fort Stanwix Treaty of 1768, which established a "line of property" between Indians and Whites, became the focus of both Pennsylvania's proprietors and Connecticut's land companies. Pennsylvania saw Fort Stanwix as an opportunity to take control of the territory between the Susquehanna and Delaware rivers. As with the Albany Congress of 1754, the Six Nations played a prominent role in the province's efforts to acquire land in the Susquehanna Valley. Pennsylvania's proprietors supported the fiction that the Six Nations held sovereignty, by right of supposed conquests made in the seventeenth century, over Indian lands in Pennsylvania and the Ohio country and avoided the stubborn refusal of Delawares, Shawnees, and other Indian groups to sell their lands by dealing directly with their Iroquois "overlords." For their part, the Six Nations were happy to oblige. First, such dealings helped to reinforce their image as the premier Indian power brokers of the north. Second, by controlling the process of land cessions, the Iroquois traded away other Indians' territory while keeping their homeland largely intact. Finally, the Iroquois stood to benefit from the considerable gifts of trade goods that came along with treaty negotiations. Indeed, at the conclusion of the Treaty of Fort Stanwix, the Six Nations received gifts worth £10,000.[26]

Thus Pennsylvania acquired additional territory—the "New Purchase"—between the west and north branches of the Susquehanna River from the Six Nations. Governor John Penn leased one-hundred-acre tracts in the Wyoming Valley to Amos Ogden, an Indian trader from New Jersey; John Jennings, a leading Northampton County official; and Charles Stewart, a wealthy New Jersey speculator, for a term of seven years. Penn authorized these men to issue leases to settlers who promised to support Pennsylvania against the inroads of Connecticut claimants. Meanwhile, the Susquehannah and Delaware companies interpreted the Fort Stanwix Treaty (which placed the boundaries of Euro-American settlement west of the Susquehanna River) as a cancellation of imperial orders forbidding the settlement of the Wyoming region and as a go-ahead for their expansionist plans.[27] Thus, after 1768, the Wyoming dispute, formerly a multidimensional contest between Indians and colonists, became a struggle primarily between Euro-Americans.

The Wyoming dispute, like other frontier contests over property and power, contributed to a culture of violence among colonists—a culture of violence first deployed against Indians and later turned against other Euro-Americans. From the start, violence between Indians and colonists and violence among Euro-American land claimants was intertwined. In the Wyoming region, the bloody confrontations that occurred between Indians and colonists during the Seven Years' War, Pontiac's War, and the U.S. War for Independence schooled White settlers in terror tactics they later used against White adversaries. In short, Indians may have been forced from the Wyoming Valley, but the legacy of Indian-White conflict lived on.

The person who best exemplifies the connections between Indian-European conflict and White-on-White disputes over land and authority is Pennsylvania's notorious Indian killer and frontier outlaw Lazarus Stewart. Stewart was born in 1734 in Hanover, a settlement in what was then Lancaster County, Pennsylvania. His family, along with thousands of Scots-Irish, had immigrated to the frontier in the late 1720s. Stewart possessed a well-earned reputation for violence; by the time he was thirty-seven, Pennsylvania had issued warrants against him for murder, assault, riot, arson, and treason. On one occasion he beat a constable with an axe handle and threatened another man that he would "cut him to Pieces, and make a Breakfast of his Heart."[28] But Stewart was far more than a violent outlaw: he was also a father, a man respected by his neighbors, and a local military leader who gained his first taste of war leading a company of provincials during Braddock's ill-fated expedition in 1755. In the years that followed, he served as a captain of a ranger company.[29]

Stewart's service during Pontiac's War set the stage for his entry into the Wyoming dispute. In fall 1763, Pennsylvania ordered one hundred men under Captain Asher Clayton, including a company under Stewart's command, to proceed to the Wyoming Valley, remove the Connecticut settlers there, and destroy their crops in order to deny them to Indian forces. When Clayton's troops arrived at Wyoming, they found that the New Englanders' settlement had already been destroyed by Captain Bull's Delaware warriors. One victim, a woman, had reportedly been "roasted"; the rest "had Awls thrust into their Eyes, and Spears, arrows, Pitchforks, etc. sticking in their Bodies." Instead of removing the New Englanders, the Pennsylvanians ended up burying them.[30]

Soon after his visit to Wyoming, Stewart played a leading role in the Paxton Boys' massacre of the Conestogas, crystallizing an enduring pattern of anti-Indian violence and lawlessness.[31] In 1765 Cumberland County inhabitants, fearing that government-sponsored traders intended to sell firearms to Indians, attacked and plundered pack trains laden with trade goods. Later, the rioters, who became known as "Black Boys" because of the soot they smeared on their faces, resisted British troops and colonial authorities who attempted to restore order.[32] In another incident in January 1768, two frontiersmen, Frederick Stump and John Ironcutter, murdered ten Indians. Again, people defied provincial authority; when Cumberland County officials arrested Stump and his accomplice, a mob descended upon the county jail and set them free.[33]

As seen in the previous chapter, woven throughout these outbreaks of racialized violence was a criticism of Pennsylvania's government for its failure to fulfill its patriarchal duties of protection and for its inability to equitably distribute, or effectively rule, frontier lands.[34] On 27 March 1769, Stewart and sixty-three frontier inhabitants added their voices to this rising tide of dissent when they sent a petition to the Pennsylvania Assembly expressing their dissatisfaction with the colony's land policies. In particular, the petitioners asserted that favoritism had denied them access to lands in Pennsylvania's "New Purchase." Even though land office regulations limited claimants to three-hundred-acre grants, government insiders had managed to engross thousands of acres. Worse still, the land office allowed well-connected gentlemen to file their claims before ordinary settlers had an opportunity to do so, thus enabling them to secure the best lands.[35]

Concern among Pennsylvania's western inhabitants for effective local government and equitable land policies set the stage for an alliance between Stewart's Paxton Boys and the Susquehannah Company. It also set into motion the process by which they redirected the violence once aimed at Indians toward fellow Euro-Americans. Stewart believed that the company could provide them with an opportunity to obtain land and escape Pennsylvania's rule. He and other leading men from Hanover, Paxton, and Donegal townships in Lancaster County began negotiations with the company late in 1769. The frontiersmen offered to rid the Wyoming Valley of Pennsylvania claimants in return for a land grant, and the company eagerly accepted the deal.[36] In February 1770, Stewart and his followers journeyed to the valley to join the New Englanders who had settled there in defiance of Pennsylvania's provincial government. In March, John Penn informed his brother Thomas that more than fifty "lawless villains" had marched from Lancaster County and "plundered and destroyed" the homes of proprietary tenants at Wyoming.[37]

The intervention of the Paxton Boys intensified an ongoing struggle for control of the Wyoming Valley between Yankees (settlers holding Connecticut deeds) and Pennamites (those who occupied the land under Pennsylvania's auspices). The fight commenced when a contingent of forty Yankee settlers arrived in February 1769. Another two hundred New Englanders reinforced them in the spring.[38] These Connecticut claimants ran headlong into Pennsylvania authorities and Pennamite settlers who had taken up land in the valley. The two sides exchanged shots and on two occasions Pennsylvania officials arrested Yankee settlers, including their leader Major John Durkee. The Connecticut claimants were briefly forced from the valley in November when Sheriff John Jennings arrived with a force of more than two hundred armed men supported by a cannon. This event was not the end but rather the beginning of a frontier war. Between 1769 and 1771, Pennamites and Yankees engaged in a seesaw conflict during which the Wyoming Valley changed hands five times.[39]

The struggle spawned increasing levels of brutality. Baltzer Stager, one of Stewart's followers, became the first victim of this violence when a Pennamite bullet took his life on 28 March 1770. Connecticut claimants also committed their share of hostile acts. John McDonner, for example, recalled how he and twenty-eight companions painted themselves like Indians and "abused and Robbed" Amos Ogden and those who leased land from him. Zebulon Butler, a leading Connecticut settler, kept a memorandum book in which he recorded similar assaults on Pennamites. On 23 February 1770, he noted that "the Boys went and Laid [John] Solomon's House level with the Earth." Five days later, Yankees "Leveled [Charles] Stewarts House to the Ground."[40] The Pennamites retaliated in September 1770 when a party of 150 men under Amos Ogden captured the entire valley and plundered its Yankee settlers. By spring 1771, when reinforcements from Connecticut allowed the Yankees to reconquer the valley, a number of colonists had been killed and wounded in gun battles, and several hundred more had been stripped of their property and possessions.[41]

Lazarus Stewart contributed to this rising tide of bloodshed and plunder. In January 1771, he and his followers dispossessed several Pennamite inhabitants and took possession of a Pennamite fort. In response, Northampton County Sheriff Peter Kachlein raised a posse—which included Deputy Sheriff Nathan Ogden, Amos Ogden's brother—and surrounded Stewart and his men. After days of waiting, Ogden and several others approached the fort and tried to talk its occupants into surrendering. Stewart ended these negotiations when he placed his rifle through a loophole and shot Nathan Ogden dead. Others in the fort then opened fire and wounded three other Pennsylvanians. As in the past, Lazarus Stewart and his men escaped justice. The night after the killing they slipped out of the fort and fled. This sort of cold-blooded killing, which had become increasingly common between Indians and Whites after the Seven Years' War, came to characterize the struggle between Pennamites and Yankees. Wyoming's White settlers not only took to dressing like Indians when they robbed and assaulted one another, but they also began to engage in a brand of violence they had learned in their struggle against Native Americans.[42] The culture of violence, forged in the fires of Indian-White conflict and frontier land disputes, survived into the American Revolution and beyond.

Indeed, the Revolution in the Wyoming Valley saw an intensification of violence as Pennamites and Yankees rekindled old animosities by wrapping them in issues of revolutionary allegiance. In the valley, the term "Tory" became roughly synonymous with Pennamite and "Whig" with Yankee.

The origins of this development lay in the fact that in 1774 Connecticut formally annexed the Wyoming region and dubbed the new territory Westmoreland County. The Continental Congress, wishing to reduce intercolonial friction and present a united front against Britain (and much more impressed with Connecticut's revolutionary zeal than with Pennsylvania's), temporarily ratified the New Englanders' jurisdiction. In light of this, it is easy to understand why Yankee settlers sided with Whig forces. With Yankees assuming the title of Patriots, many Pennamites became Tories, not because they necessarily had any greater love for King George than did Connecticut claimants, but because Yankee-controlled revolutionary committees persecuted Pennsylvania claimants and alienated them from the American cause.[43] Thus the stage was set for the continuation of bloodshed in the Wyoming Valley. In December 1775, William Plunket, a Northumberland County magistrate, led more than five hundred Pennsylvanians in an effort to eject Yankee settlers from their lands. Four hundred Connecticut claimants commanded by Zebulon Butler intercepted this "band of Tories" along the banks of the Susquehanna River. In the battle that ensued, Yankees killed or wounded half a dozen of Plunket's men.[44]

The extreme violence that marked the revolutionary period in the Wyoming Valley was not only a product of enduring animosities between Pennsylvania and Connecticut claimants, but of renewed conflict between Indians and Whites. In 1778, seven hundred Indians and Euro-American Loyalists under the command of John Butler descended upon the valley and killed more than two hundred Connecticut claimants (including Lazarus Stewart) at the battle of Wyoming. This engagement was just as much a continuation of the Wyoming dispute as an episode in the war for U.S. independence. Among the Indians who served under Butler—most of whom were Senecas and Cayugas—were a number of Delawares who must have looked upon the campaign as an opportunity to take revenge on the New Englanders who had invaded their territory. Likewise, many of the Euro-American Loyalists who accompanied Butler were old Pennamites who had been forced from their farms by Yankees. Among these was Frederick Vanderlip, a dispossessed Pennsylvania claimant who returned as a member of Butler's Rangers, a Loyalist military unit.[45]

The Indians, Whigs, and Tories who inhabited the upper Susquehanna Valley during the Revolution fought without mercy. Combatants and noncombatants alike became victims. North of Wyoming, Indians and Loyalists killed more than forty women and children when they destroyed the settlement of Cherry Valley in New York. Whigs responded in kind. The four thousand Continental Army soldiers who invaded Iroquois territory under the command of General John Sullivan in 1779 did not discriminate between combatants and noncombatants. Tioguanda, an Onondaga chief, recounted that Sullivan's men killed women and children when they raided his village. The crops, livestock, houses, and tools of Wyoming inhabitants also became military targets. Both British and American commanders waged brutal campaigns in which sources of sustenance that could not be taken from the enemy were destroyed. Indians and Euro-American Loyalists devastated the Pennsylvania frontier during a large-scale expedition in 1778 and in more than thirty raids between 1780 and 1782.[46] Settlements in the Wyoming Valley bore the brunt of these attacks. In 1777, Connecticut rated Westmoreland County's taxable estates at £20,322 and counted 515 taxable inhabitants. Two years after the disastrous battle of Wyoming, officials valued county assets at a mere £2,353 and only about a hundred taxables remained.[47]

In the same way that the Seven Years' War and Pontiac's War had schooled men like Lazarus Stewart in the ways of violence, the War for Independence initiated the next generation. The experiences of a single Connecticut claimant, John Franklin, illustrate this process. Franklin, whose father had purchased a Susquehannah Company share in 1754, arrived in the Wyoming Valley in winter 1774. Once there he established a farm on his father's claim, raised a family, and held a variety of town and county offices. After serving in the Westmoreland County militia, he volunteered to accompany Sullivan's 1779 expedition against the Six Nations. A year later, Franklin became captain of a company of Wyoming men raised by the state of Connecticut. By the end of the war, he had emerged as one of the valley's leading Yankee settlers and was fully prepared to put his military experience to use.[48]

Late in 1782 the Wyoming dispute entered a new and more violent phase when the Confederation government attempted to adjudicate the dispute between Pennsylvania and Connecticut. A special court convened at Trenton, New Jersey, decided to award jurisdiction over the disputed territory to Pennsylvania.[49] But the "Trenton Decree" only reignited the conflict, for the competing land claims of Yankee and Pennamite settlers remained unresolved. The Wyoming Valley again became the scene of violent competition over land and authority as Pennamites reentered the region to press their claims and Yankees lined up to resist them. Armed conflict erupted in fall 1783 and raged through the following year.[50]

John Franklin was at the center of Yankee resistance. Drawing on his experience during the War for Independence, he helped to orchestrate a campaign of terror against invading Pennamites and Pennsylvania authorities. Racially charged conflict between Indians and Whites during the Revolution colored Franklin's attitudes and actions and those of his fellow Yankees. During the war, many frontier settlers had come to associate Tories with Indians and to view them as being just as "savage," "uncivilized," and undeserving of mercy as their Native allies. As Gregory Knouff reminds us, frontier Patriots saw Tories "not only to be traitors to their country but also traitors to their race." By extension, Wyoming's Yankee settlers, who considered their Pennamite opponents little more than thinly disguised Tories, found it easy to apply the same brutal treatment to them as they had to their Loyalist and Indian adversaries. Thus in 1787, when Franklin issued an order for Yankee settlers to muster "Completely Armed and equipped" in order to stop the "Pennsylvania Loyalists" from forming a militia, he tapped deep veins of revolutionary rage.[51]

As a result, conflict between Pennamites and Yankees after independence was more brutal and bloody than the confrontations between Pennsylvania and Connecticut claimants in the 1760s and 1770s. Whereas a few White settlers were killed and wounded before the Revolution, dozens of Pennamites and Yankees became casualties in the fighting that took place in the valley between 1783 and 1785. In July 1784, for example, opposing armed patrols exchanged shots after they stumbled into one another. Two Pennsylvania claimants, Henry Brink and Wilhelmus Van Gordon, were wounded and two Connecticut claimants, Elisha Garret and Chester Paine, killed.[52] Four days later, Yankee settler Benjamin Blanchard received a gunshot wound in the thigh. The following day, a rifle shot killed another Connecticut man. Later that month Pennamites shot John Franklin through the wrist and killed Nathan Stevens.[53] In August, Yankees killed one Pennsylvania militiamen and wounded three others in a skirmish that came to be known as the battle of Locust Hill.[54] Late in September, Yankees shot and killed Lieutenants Andrew Henderson and Samuel Reed during a raid on Wilkes-Barre's garrison of Pennsylvania state troops.[55] In October, half a dozen Pennamites and Pennsylvania militiamen became casualties during an intense gun battle with Connecticut claimants near Abraham's

Creek.[56] In another practice highly reminiscent of revolutionary-era frontier warfare, Yankees and Pennamites plundered each other's farms, leaving families stripped of provisions, tools, livestock, and other essentials. In one instance, Henry Brink testified that Yankees "armed with Rifles and Pistolls" seized 350 bushels of corn and two of his cows. Once the Yankees had taken what they wanted, they ordered Brink to "quit the Country" and threatened that if he did not go "they would drive him before the Muzzle of their guns."[57]

The violence that marked the Wyoming dispute was shaped by decades of conflict between Indians and Whites; however, the similarities between Pennamite-Yankee violence and violence between Indians and colonists go only so deep. First, conflict between Pennamites and Yankees never gained the racial component of struggles between Whites and Indians. Connecticut and Pennsylvania claimants may have come from different regional backgrounds, but they did not perceive each other as different races. More important, Wyoming's White inhabitants never dehumanized each other as they did Indians. Pennamites and Yankees may have attacked and even killed each other, but they did not engage in the scalpings and mutilations that marked violence between Indians and Whites. Even Lazarus Stewart, who contributed to his reputation as a violent man when he killed Nathan Ogden, did not repeat the sort of butchery that made his attacks on the Indians at Conestoga and Lancaster so infamous. Moreover, Pennamites and Yankees may have assaulted, dispossessed, and terrified women and children but they did not indiscriminately slaughter them.[58]

The culture of violence that emerged along the Pennsylvania frontier was not just defined by its level of brutality and bloodshed but also by a symbolism steeped in decades of racialized conflict that endured well beyond the Revolution. Indeed, the feature of the Wyoming dispute that best highlights the connections between Indian-White conflict and the rise of agrarian unrest along the postindependence frontier is the fact that frontier insurgents often disguised themselves as Indians. When "Wild Yankees" assaulted, threatened, and intimidated Pennsylvania land claimants, surveyors, or government officials, they donned an "Indian" guise, which usually meant that they blacked their faces, draped blankets over their bodies, and wrapped handkerchiefs around their heads. "Indian" assaults increased in frequency after the War for Independence. For instance, more than a dozen Wild Yankees dressed as Indians kidnapped Timothy Pickering—a leading Pennsylvania official in the Wyoming Valley who would later become a prominent figure in national politics—in the summer of 1788 and kept him a prisoner in the woods for several weeks. Likewise, in 1792, a band of Indian-disguised Yankee insurgents fired upon and later raided the camp of a group of Pennsylvania surveyors along Tunkhannock Creek. And in 1801 a large number of Yankee "Indians" tarred and feathered Thomas Smiley, a settler in the employ of a group of Pennsylvania land speculators.[59]

The use of disguise and Indian imagery by Wild Yankees was deeply rooted in European traditions of popular protest as well as the more immediate legacy of the American Revolution. Mummery, street theater, mocking rhymes—all common features of European festivals—offered common people a way to critique their social superiors, temporarily undermine bonds of deference, and defy government authority. Like European rioters, frontier insurgents blacked their faces and donned elaborate disguises to hide their identities from the authorities and, in the role-reversing tradition of European mummery, to transform themselves from farmers into agrarian rebels.[60] Of course, White frontier inhabitants did not have to look back to their European roots to formulate protest; the American Revolution, an event fixed in the memory of many settlers, furnished rebels with a wealth of ideas and precedents. In particular, the Boston Tea Party did much to connect Indian imagery with the struggle for independence in the minds of Euro-American colonists.[61]

Beyond age-old traditions of popular protest and the memory of the American Revolution, contact between Indians and Whites had a significant impact on the character of resistance along the postindependence frontier. Pennsylvania's Wild Yankees used Indian imagery not only to hide their identities, but to strike fear in their enemies. Wyoming settlers who had once lived under the threat of Native American attacks usurped the image of the Indian to forge an effective terror tactic. Land agents and surveyors who ventured to the frontier feared that people who looked like Indians might be as savage as Indians. As it turned out, their fears were not groundless. In Pennsylvania, Wild Yankees murdered Edward Gobin; in New York and Maine, other agrarian insurgents dressed as Indians killed a sheriff's deputy and a surveyor's assistant.[62]

Under the leadership of John Franklin, Pennsylvania's Indian-clad Wild Yankees maintained their resistance to the state of Pennsylvania into the nineteenth century. Only in the 1810s did a combination of government compromises and a more rigorous enforcement of the law undermine Yankee insurgency. For their part, Connecticut claimants increasingly turned their backs on violent resistance as the process of farm building and frontier development made the prospect of accommodation with Pennsylvania more attractive and the purchase of state titles economically feasible. This pattern of reconciliation was repeated across the frontier until America's White Indians had themselves disappeared.[63]

The Wyoming dispute shows us that frontier land disputes pitting colony against colony and colonist against colonist were often intimately connected with relations between Indians and Whites. In addition, events in the Wyoming region demonstrate how such jurisdictional struggles contributed to the dispossession of Native Americans. The victims of violence in the Wyoming Valley were not only White settlers but also Indians like Teedyuscung. Moreover, the dispute between Pennsylvania and Connecticut forced both colonies to attempt to secure their claims, first by purchasing the land from Indians supposed to be its owners and, second, by occupying their claims with Euro-American settlers. Both strategies undermined Indian soil rights and disrupted Native communities.

The story of the Wyoming dispute also reveals something else. Even though Indians largely disappeared from the upper Susquehanna River valley after the Revolution, their impact on frontier life continued in the form of a distinct culture of Euro-American violence and protest. Pennsylvania's Wild Yankees and other White settlers who fought for land and autonomy in postindependence America did so armed with a legacy of racialized violence rooted in decades of struggle against Indian foes. Frontier insurgents, hoping to use the image of the savage Indian to their advantage, appropriated Indian guises as they fought government officials and land speculators. On a deeper level, frontier settlers who faced dispossession at the hands of the rich and powerful took on the identity of Indians they themselves had helped to dispossess as an expression of their deep alienation from a society that seemed to deny them the opportunity and independence that they so valued.[64]

13

WHITENESS AND WARFARE ON A
REVOLUTIONARY FRONTIER

GREGORY T. KNOUFF

At first glance, the narratives that Pennsylvania frontier veterans of the U.S. War for Independence told in their nineteenth-century pension depositions appear as myriad unrelated stories. Ostensibly, the deponents described disparate groups of European and Native Americans struggling for control of the trans-Allegheny west. One significant commonality, however, is apparent. The war and its memory were crucibles for the formation of popular racial ideology and the construction of a White male nation. Former Pennsylvania soldiers consistently disregarded their own intrusions onto independent Indians' and rival Euro-Americans' lands and carefully created descriptions of a war in which they had reactively defended their communities. Veterans described homes threatened by an undifferentiated "Indian" enemy and went out of their way to style themselves "Whites" in contrast to "the Indians." Biologically oriented notions of "Whiteness" formed in the late colonial and revolutionary periods created definitions of U.S. citizenship and fostered wartime unity among diverse groups of Euro-Americans. They also implicated Indians as "non-White" yet allowed revolutionaries to adapt aspects of Indian culture, especially methods of warfare, without imperiling their sense of superiority. For these Euro-Pennsylvanians, otherness and American national identity were not defined by cultural difference but according to perceptions of skin color.[1]

Veterans' understandings of the Revolution and national identity helped solidify the early republic's equation of White manhood with citizenship. With property ownership requirements for suffrage beginning to decline during the Revolution and largely vanishing by the 1820s and 1830s (the era when pension depositions were given), Americans came to place a greater emphasis on gender and race than on class in defining the body politic. Historians have already noted how, in the Revolution's aftermath, racism was increasingly deployed as a formal ideology to deny rights to African Americans, both slave and free. Pennsylvania veterans' retrospective tales recorded in the depositions reveal a parallel process whereby Indians, no matter how culturally assimilated, were imagined as excluded from rights in the republic by virtue of their lack of Whiteness. The concept of the White male nation, then, was rooted in the nation's revolutionary genesis, and the late eighteenth-century frontier was one of the most vital among multiple sites where racial identity was historically constructed.[2]

Perhaps the most obvious recurring theme in the veterans' narratives was their description of the war as a defensive struggle against an undifferentiated Indian foe. This strategy was designed to Other all natives as a single group and to emphasize their culpability as the initial aggressors. Northumberland County militia ranger Peter Keister, for example, explained that the war on the Pennsylvania frontier "was an arduous service marked by individual murders and burnings [by] the Indians of our men." He "recollect[ed]" that "Michael Lamb, John Ebby, John Clinesmith[?], and Jacob Beekle were killed by the Indians." He also recalled that "John Stomilch[?] and his wife were murdered on their farm," having been "tomahawked and scalped." Similarly, Bedford County militiaman George Wertz reported that he had "volunteered his services for the defense of his fellow citizens" and went "scouting through the county and spying after the Indians and marching [to] any place threatened with danger, at any time and on all occasions." Angus McCoy, who served in the Washington County militia in summer 1781, recounted how he "volunteered to guard the then frontiers on Chartiers Creek" in response to "the Indians [who were] being very troublesome." James Thompson of Northumberland County simply stated that "in the spring of 1778, we were called out to guard the frontiers against the incursions of the Indians."[3]

In addition to suggesting that all Indians were the same and enemies of the United States, the reactive way these stories were framed by veterans served a number of other functions. Perhaps most obvious, it rationalized conquest both during and after the war. Rather than simply describing their motivations in terms of a desire for access to Indian lands, soldiers argued that they were forced to fight to defend their communities. Nowhere do they suggest that Indians in the region might have been acting to defend themselves, even though the veterans well knew that powerful independent Indian groups in the region had made their interests patently clear. In April 1777, for example, western Pennsylvanians received word of "a message from the Chiefs of the Mohawks, Onandagoes, Cayugas, Senecas, Tuscaroras, Missaragoes, and Chippawas, to the Virginians and Pennsylvanians now at Venyngo," informing them that they had "unjustly settled upon their lands on the Ohio and Susquehannah" and must "quit them immediately or abide by the consequences . . . and not make any excuse."[4] The Native coalition against the revolutionaries grew as ever more Indians became convinced that their aggressive neighbors threatened them. By summer 1777, Shawnees began to raid settlements on the frontier they contested with both Pennsylvania and Virginia in response to the murder of their neutralist leader, Cornstalk, by militiamen from the Old Dominion. Around the same time, large numbers of Iroquois supported British operations in New York. By 1778, revolutionaries on the frontier faced "the Senecas, Cayugas, Mingoes and Wiandots in general, [and] a majority of the Onondagas." Significant numbers of Mohawks, Miamis, Shawnees, Potawatomis, and Ottawas, among others, also took up arms. The growing size of the antirevolutionary coalition may well have led Pennsylvanians to overestimate the numbers that were united against them and played into the construction of an undifferentiated image of a singular "Indian" enemy. Yet in reality many groups, such as the Delawares, remained split in their allegiances, and significant numbers of Oneidas and Tuscaroras allied with the revolutionaries.[5]

Although veterans rarely discussed it in their narratives, the acquisition of Native American lands was clearly a major war aim of local Euro-Americans, despite the half-hearted efforts of some Continental officers to restrain them. The wartime behavior of the soldiers spoke for itself. In 1779, the Continental commander of the Western Department, Colonel Daniel Brodhead, lamented that "some persons, yet unknown are committing trespasses on the Indian lands near Wheeling." Meantime, officers chastised men of the Eighth Pennsylvania Regiment who "presumed to mark trees in the woods with initial letters and their names at large, thereby giv[ing] great uneasiness to our good friends and allies, the Delaware nation," which rightly perceived the soldiers' determination to claim tracts of their real estate. As Brodhead's successor, General William Irvine, observed, among the western Pennsylvania militia "a great majority have no other views than to acquire lands." The lack of mention of such "views" from the pension narratives is striking yet consistent with a pattern emphasizing Indian culpability for provoking war and its consequences. Deponents projected their own aggression onto "the Indians."[6]

In addition to omitting such perspectives in their pension depositions and lumping all Indians together, veterans also skillfully employed language that implicated Natives as dishonorable foes. Revolutionaries commonly described themselves as "killing" the enemy, while stating that Indians committed "murders" or "massacres." Soldiers went out of their way to portray Indian warfare as murderously cruel. Benjamin Lewis noted the "many massacres committed by the savages in the neighborhood of Northumberland." Northampton County militiamen framed their actions in much the same terms: Christian Acker fought "against the Indians who were at that time murdering the inhabitants"; Peter Wolf accused Indians of "murdering" and in battle of having "slaughtered a number of our troops"; John Miller guarded "the citizens against the cruelties of the Indians who occasionally visited and committed murders and depredations." Bedford County's John Dean fought to "save the lives of the defenseless inhabitants from the cruelty of the savages," and John Elder, a volunteer Northumberland County ranger, recalled how at the "Massacre of Wyoming . . . Captains Boon and Dougherty and nearly the whole of their command were put to death." George Vanzant of Bedford County served to "prevent the savages from murdering and plundering the inhabitants on the frontiers." Similarly, Andrew Myers of Washington County condemned Indian "outrages on the frontier inhabitants." Lawrence Konkle of Westmoreland County recalled that Indians committed "many murders and depredations." Thomas Rees decried the "great number of murders by the Indians."[7]

The linking of such terms as *outrages, murder, massacre,* and *savages* with *the Indians* was crucial during a period when narratives of murder in the United States no longer attributed the perpetrators' culpability to the general human condition of original sin. In the early nineteenth century, murderers came to be seen, in the words of historian Karen Halttunen, as "something other than human," as violent creatures lacking morals. In ascribing the term *murder* to any Indian military action, and not just the killing of nonsoldiers, veterans applied the discourse of depraved crime rather than of warfare to enemy acts. The conflation of crime, inhumanity, and Indians was powerful. The Westmoreland militia, for example, spoke fearfully in a petition of leaving "our families exposed to be again ravaged by the Indians and probably all murdered." The term *ravage* added sexual as well as economic violation to the litany of crimes charged against Indians who killed in an "inhuman manner."[8]

Although the discursive tradition of wartime "murder" tantalizingly suggests the congealing of a biological view of Indian difference, the narrative practice of referring to "the Indians" as "savage" enemies indicates that an imagined cultural inferiority may have been just as important. The racial component in the veterans' othering of Indians emerges far more plainly, however, in their penchant for describing themselves as "Whites." Pennsylvania's frontier revolutionaries constructed a binary view of the frontier war as one of "Indians" against "Whites." Significantly, color attached to only one of the elements in the binary; pension applicants referred specifically to their own perceived skin color without ascribing a similar characteristic to Native people. Thus, Northumberland County militiaman John Dougherty recalled that "the Indians were continually committing depredations against the whites," and Lancaster County soldier John Foster similarly explained that Indians "massacred the whites." Militiaman Adam Wolfe of Westmoreland County recalled that he had been a guard "between the Indians and whites during the holding of a treaty at Pittsburgh," and Andrew Myers of Washington County that "the Indians . . . [were] determined not to yield to the white people." David Freemoyer, a New Yorker who served on Sullivan's expedition, decried Indians' "predatory incursions upon the whites."[9]

The term *White* was, of course, in popular usage by the time the veterans made their pension depositions in the 1820s and 1830s. Revolutionary-era accounts indicate, however, that the word was also widely employed in describing frontier military conflict as it happened. In 1776, the *Pennsylvania Gazette* reported, "The Indians have scalped two or three white people on the Ohio." In 1779, the *Gazette* covered various frontier actions based on accounts received from the region that again specified Whiteness. On one sortie, "Captain Brady of the 8th Pennsylvania regiment, with 20 white men and a young Delaware chief, all painted like Indians," went out against hostile Indians. On one of Daniel Brodhead's expeditions, the paper described his vanguard of his troops as "consisting of 15 white men." Joseph Martin similarly drew a White-Indian polarity in a letter warning of "a plan . . . forming between the Northern and southward Indians" that had been "seen by a white man" and was directed against "whites" in general. Euro-Americans found among Indians who fought against the revolutionaries were also consistently described by perceived skin color. Lieutenant Erkuries Beatty, a Pennsylvanian on General John Sullivan's 1779 expedition into Iroquoia, noted in his campaign journal that "Captain Graham . . . had caught one squaw and killed one and had taken two or three children and one white man." In a similar fashion, a petition to Congress from Connecticut residents in the Wyoming Valley complained that "the Indians with a number of white people, enemies to these states[,] committed repeated depredations." Crucially, like those offered by the pension applicants, none of these accounts give Indians a specific color, but they make anyone of European descent White in an essentialist way.[10]

Definitions of Whiteness were of course both arbitrary and sometimes confusing.[11] The equation of cultural origins with a pale skin complexion often proved difficult to demonstrate outside of a Euro-American social context. The Reverend William Rogers reported in his journal of the Sullivan Campaign that it was difficult to tell Indians from "painted Tories" who not only decorated their bodies with war paint, but also obscured their Whiteness. Sometimes it was even more difficult to identify "White" persons. According to Erkuries Beatty, in a Seneca town "[a] young child . . . about three years old [was] found running about the houses." An officer "picked [it] up and found it to be a white child but it was so much tanned and smoked that we could hardly distinguish it from a[n] Indian child and was exceedingly poor, scarcely able to walk." Beatty and his comrades were startled to find a "white child" so "tanned" and out of cultural context. Whiteness could be physically obscured and without cultural cues—"It could talk no English; nothing but Indian and . . . but little of that"—identity was slippery. Nonetheless, even in the absence of linguistic or other cultural reference to a European heritage, the soldiers deduced that the tanning and smoking hid white skin and that the child deserved the care and quarter dictated by the immutable biological origins signified by skin color.[12]

Another incident further suggests that pale skin had come to supersede ethnic identity as a primary mark of self-identity. George Roush enlisted as an "Indian spy." As commonly employed by revolutionary veterans, the term had dual connotations: these men had not only fully adopted "Indian" military tactics and skills in navigating the woods, but they also could move among Indians with their Whiteness disguised. As Roush recalled: "In obedience to the order of his said Captain Brady, he proceeded to tan his thighs and legs with wild cherry and white oak bark and to equip himself after the following manner, to wit, a breechcloth, leather leggings, moccasins, and a cap made out of a raccoon skin, with the feather of a hawk, painted red, fastened to the top of the cap. Declarant was then painted after the manner of an Indian warrior. His face was painted red, with three black stripes across his cheeks, which was a signification of war." Significantly, Roush and his comrades did not believe adopting the appearance and the cultural markers of an Indian warrior could be effective without "tanning" their skins. This attempt to conceal Whiteness was a crucial moment for a people who had previously discussed the relation between skin complexion and ethnic origin in only a nonsystematic way. Ordinary frontier revolutionaries were coming to see a bifurcated racial world composed simply of Whites and non-Whites.[13]

Veterans dwelled on their own skin color for several reasons. First, Whiteness united an ethnically diverse Euro-American population fighting to protect its varied communities. Before the Revolution, the increasingly heterogeneous Anglo-American frontier region was held together not by common cultures, languages, or religion but by a shared identity as British subjects. By the time of independence, such perceptions obviously no longer worked and a new definition of what it meant to be "American" was necessary. Whiteness was an intellectual construct that encapsulated the European heritage of frontier-area residents in a physical characteristic. Soldiers' discourse about the war linked Whiteness and the American cause. Euro-Americans might have various reasons for fighting in the Revolution, but they were united by their perceived skin color. In fact, this view of racial identity may have been one of the few things that large numbers of revolutionaries on Pennsylvania's frontiers shared. The Pennsylvania wartime government reinforced this sharp racial dichotomy between "Whites" and "Indians" by making all White men subject to militia service and test oaths. Thus encouraged in their self-articulation as Whites, veterans fused Whiteness, the revolutionary cause, and the full rights of citizenship in the new republic. During the nation's birth, a powerful connection between being a White male and being an American was forged on the Pennsylvania frontier.[14]

Of course, not all American Whites in the region were revolutionaries. How to describe such persons became a vital concern of local "Patriots," who tended to label them "White savages" for their alliance with Indians and their betrayal not only of "civilization" but of their presumed innate racial identity. Frontier Tories deserved particular condemnation, for, unlike "the Indians," they acted on inclination rather than nature. Such egregious treason against the imagined community of American Whites was a recurrent trope in accounts of frontier raids. The *Pennsylvania Gazette,* for example, reported on the capture of a young woman by "three Indians and twenty-seven white savages." James Dunlop of Cumberland County similarly observed that a number of local Tories "left their habitations and [were] supposed to be joined to the savages," and in 1778 the *Pennsylvania Packet* reported that word arrived from Carlisle that "33 Tories lately formed the horrid design of joining the savages in murdering and scalping their neighbors." Later the same year, the paper noted the capture in New York of the Tory John Snow, "one of those who had transformed themselves into savages." And John Piper of Bedford County characterized Tories in the region as "still more savage" than the Indians.[15]

Articulation of Whiteness also gave soldiers a way to rationalize what otherwise would appear to be a double standard regarding Indian and revolutionary military actions. Adaptation to Indian ways of fighting was fraught with peril. Nonetheless, frontier revolutionaries and their Indian opponents fought in very similar ways, and each side waged guerrilla raids on the other's settlements. When Indians carried out hit-and-run attacks against revolutionaries' communities, veterans saw them as cowardly and unmanly. William Elliott, for example, recalled how the Indians "frequently came down upon the defenseless settlers and on one occasion killed nine out of one family." Yet Pennsylvania frontier soldiers proudly declared their comparable actions heroic, as did George Reem when he recalled his participation in "destroying the cornfields and burning the Indian villages" or George Roush when he described his unit's ambush of an Indian hunting camp: "We fired and killed three, one of which was a squaw, and then approached the camp. . . . Whilst we were examining their guns, an Indian boy, which we supposed to be of the age of fifteen or sixteen years, came near and halloed to us and said, 'Unhee, what did you shoot at?' And a man by the name of Fulks answered in the Indian language and said, 'A racoon.' The Indian came across the creek, and when he came in shooting distance one of our company shot him."[16]

Each side also scalped and killed prisoners and noncombatants. Not surprisingly, such actions when committed by Indians were denounced, in the words of John Struthers, as "barbarities."[17] Yet revolutionaries extolled their ability to do the same. They saw no contradiction but instead employed an emerging logic of biological difference to render their embrace of elements of Indian warfare somehow central to their White identity. Soldiers believed that they could engage in a common frontier military culture without endangering their superiority because race rather than culture was becoming the definitive boundary between Euro-Americans and Indians. In other words, cultural convergence among Native and European Americans and the development of racist ideology mutually supported each other. The "Indianized" fighter image created by veterans thus reconciled one of the contradictory elements of an emerging American national identity: a simultaneous loathing of and desire for the Indian other. The term *White* fulfilled the longing for cultural similarity because arbitrarily constructed biological difference maintained hierarchy.[18]

The proclivity of revolutionary soldiers to kill neutral and friendly Indians as well as hostile ones further reveals the bifurcated racial universe they inhabited. As soon as conflict broke out on the frontiers of Pennsylvania, diplomats and officers had their hands full trying to prevent the widening of the war through the indiscriminate slaughter of Indians. In March 1777, George Morgan, an official at Fort Pitt, worried that local inhabitants would "massacre our known friends at their hunting camps."[19] A few months later, Colonel Edward Hand, the Continental army commander at Fort Pitt, remarked that, "the people here [Fort Pitt] are well-disposed, savage-like, to murder a defenseless unsuspecting Indian." John Gibson informed Hand that one of the revolutionaries' Delaware allies, White Eyes, was "in danger of being killed" because of recent Indian attacks and that "it was with the utmost difficulty [that] I prevented one of the men who escaped [from a recent battle] from killing the Delawares." After another hostile Indian attack killed a single militiaman, Colonel Gibson again suggested to Hand that it was "not safe for the [friendly] Delaware to pass unless you send a party down to escort them to Fort Pitt to treat." Hand passed the information on to local Indians and declared that "it would be dangerous for any Indians to come near this place [Fort Pitt] owing to the foolish conduct of the Mingos and Wyandots." Hand explained that, although he himself knew who was responsible for the raids, his men and the Anglo-American inhabitants would blame Indians in general and seek revenge against "any Indian."[20]

In September 1777, the situation deteriorated further when a militia group murdered the Shawnee leader Cornstalk, a proponent of neutrality, while he was being held as a hostage in a fort, thereby alienating the few Shawnees who did not advocate war with the United States. Captain John Stuart, who witnessed Cornstalk's murder, emphasized the militia's need for vengeance in response to Indian attacks. When the men had retrieved the body of a comrade "scalped and covered in blood, . . . the cry was raised let us kill the Indians in the fort and every man with his gun in his hand came up the [river] bank pale as death with rage."[21]

Violence against nonbelligerent Indian groups mounted as the war continued. In 1778, White Eyes died under mysterious circumstances—a Virginia militiaman probably killed him—while he was carrying messages for the revolutionaries. In the following year, troops continued to single out the Delawares as subjects for revenge for deeds committed by other Indian groups. Among the men of the Eighth Pennsylvania Regiment, a soldier disrupted discipline and diplomacy by firing "a gun at one of the friendly Delawares."[22] "So violent are the prejudices against the Indians . . . [among] the people in the back counties," Pennsylvania's Supreme Executive Council president Joseph Reed complained in 1779, it had become impossible to approve Colonel Daniel Brodhead's request to equip Delaware allies for an expedition against the Six Nations Iroquois.[23] The next year, those prejudices erupted violently when a group of pro-American Delawares directly under Brodhead's protection at Fort Pitt nearly died at the hands of Westmoreland County residents furious over attacks by other Indians. "Upwards of forty men from the neighborhood of Hannah's Town have attempted to destroy them," Brodhead reported, suspecting that "the women and children were to suffer an equal carnage with the men." Such attitudes among rank-and-file revolutionaries augmented the number of Native warriors in arms against the United States, as did Brodhead's decision in April 1781 to launch a preemptive strike against one of the last remaining significant neutral Delaware communities, Coshocton. The village—some of the residents of which had earlier served with Brodhead—was razed by Continentals, joined by militia and a few Coshocton Delawares who served as guides, including the prorevolutionary leader Killbuck. The victors executed fifteen prisoners, and the survivors of the raid retreated to Sandusky where they joined Wyandots and Delawares already fighting the revolutionaries.[24]

To some degree, at least, the tendency of those who called themselves Whites to lump all Native people together gained strength from the development of racialist discourse among eastern Indian groups. European Americans did not construct race in a vacuum. Rather, they affected and were affected by Indian views. Historian Nancy Shoemaker has found convincing evidence that in the early eighteenth-century southern nations, such as the Creeks, Cherokees, and Chickasaws, employed the term *White* to denote Euro-Americans while conceiving themselves to be *Red*. She argues that these Indians constructed their color-based identity in conjunction with southern colonists who defined Africans and African Americans as Black and themselves, in opposition, as White. Interestingly, the color red had various cultural connotations regarding identity among southern nations, especially the Cherokees, that it did not have among northern groups. Shoemaker finds that, as a result, few northeastern Indians described themselves as Red during the same period. There is, nonetheless, evidence that these groups were also creating racialized worldviews in the eighteenth century. Gregory Evans Dowd has elucidated a pattern of Indian spiritual revivals during the period 1745–75 that led to the development of a militant nativist movement. Nativist leaders "taught that all Indians were a single people, separately created," suggesting that differences between Native and European Americans were more than purely cultural. Few who lived in the region before the war could have been unaware that many Indians placed all Europeans and Euro-Americans under a rubric very similar to the category of Whiteness.[25]

The process of racial self-definition was mutually reinforcing. Indiscriminate revolutionary attacks apparently strengthened Indian notions that all Euro-Americans comprised a single potentially dangerous group. In one well-publicized 1778 incident in Bedford County, a group of Loyalists set out to join attacks on the revolutionaries but, according to one account, "the Indians suspecting some design in the white people," killed one leader and forced the other Tories to flee. The employment of racialist discourse in the letter is intriguing. It is not clear whether the author of the report, a Bedford County militia official named John Piper, was summarizing the witnesses' testimony of Indian behavior or his own impression. Some evidence does suggest, however, that the unidentified Indians indeed embraced the racial consciousness that Piper attributed to them.

Richard Weston, one of the Loyalists, testified that he "went with the company over Allegheny Mountain. That in their progress they were met by Indians and that one of them shot his brother and another of them scalped him. That after his brother was shot, McKee[?] pulled a letter out of his pocket that he had got from an English officer in Carlisle gaol and with the letter displayed a handkerchief crying peace, peace, brother, but that the savages ran off without giving attention." Although the Indians might well have expected a party of "Long Knives" to be hostile, it is striking that they fled after the attack even when the party of Euro-Americans clearly associated themselves with British authority and did not fight back or attempt to avenge the death of Weston's brother.[26]

The development of wartime White identity, then, appears to have further fostered both pan-Indian unity and a racialist self-identity that had been developing since the mid-eighteenth century. While creating unity among diverse native peoples, however, Indian racial consciousness did not preclude cooperation with Europeans. Many groups that took up arms against the United States had formidable factions of accommodationists who sought not only to ally themselves with Britain, but to embrace the system of economic exchange that had existed before the war. It was also apparent to even the most militant of Indian nativists that the war effort required assistance from the British. Thus it was never very practical to dismiss all "Whites" as exactly the same. As a result, the military violence prosecuted by such groups as the Iroquois, Delawares, Wyandots, Miamis, Mingos, and others was not nearly as racially indiscriminate as that of the revolutionaries. They could not afford to kill their Tory and British allies wholesale to rid the region of all Whites. Few, indeed, envisioned an Indian-only postwar world.[27]

Thus, although the McKee incident proved exceptional, as Indians fought in coalition with large numbers of Loyalists as well as the British, rebel authorities nonetheless made sure that it was well known to those social outsiders who still wondered if their communal interests might be best served by fighting with Indians against those defined as White. Frontier revolutionaries were not interested in cultivating Indian alliances or neutrality, even if it would serve larger strategic interests. They saw all Indians as non-White outsiders irredeemably opposed to the interests of the imagined White community. Frontier Loyalists thus became communal traitors, "savage whites" who turned their back on their race to fight alongside Indian and British enemies.[28]

Figure 13 King George III shares a feast of his former White American subjects. Indians are portrayed as cannibals while an Anglican bishop rushes to join in. *The Allies,* 1780. John Carter Brown Library, Providence, Rhode Island.

The behavior and discourse of ordinary frontier revolutionaries suggested that many envisioned a postwar world purged of Indians. In 1783 when the Treaty of Paris formally ended hostilities between the United States and the British, General William Irvine lamented that some Native Americans were still fighting. "I presume," he continued, that "this conduct will give force to a temper already pretty prevalent among the back settlers, never to make peace with the Indians; and, indeed, I am almost persuaded it will [be] next to impossible to insure peace with them till the whole of the western tribes are driven over the Mississippi and lakes, entirely beyond American lines."[29]

The consequences of this "temper" proved tragic. In spring 1782, the *Pennsylvania Gazette* reported news of farms being attacked in the west, resulting in several casualties and captives.

> These different parties of Indians, striking the settlements so early in the season greatly alarmed the people, and but too plainly

evinced their determination to harass the frontiers and nothing could save them but a quick and spirited exertion. They [the local militia] therefore determined to extirpate the aggressors, and, if possible, to recover the people that had been carried off. And having received intelligence from a person who was taken prisoner last fall (but had made his escape, and came home a few days before) that the Indian towns on the Muskingum were not moved, as they had been told, a number of men, properly provided, collected and rendezvoused on the Ohio, opposite Mingo Bottom with a design to surprise the above towns. . . . When they got over, officers were chosen; and they proceeded to the towns on the Muskingum, where the Indians had collected a large quantity of provisions, to supply their war parties. They arrived at the town in the night undiscovered, attacked the Indians in their cabins, and so completely surprised them, that they killed and scalped upwards of ninety (but a few making their escape) about forty of whom were warriors, the rest old men, women, and children. About eighty horses fell into their hands, which they loaded with the plunder, the greatest part furs and skins and returned to the Ohio without the loss of one man.[30]

What the story does not fully reveal is that this "expedition" was the infamous March 1782 Gnadenhütten Massacre. The Indians were mostly Christian Delawares (along with a few Shawnees), who had been converted by Moravian missionaries in the Ohio country. Not only were they pacifist neutrals, they also, to a large extent, had adopted numerous aspects of Euro-American material culture. Additionally, Moravian missionaries in the area had been passing intelligence on hostile Indian military dispositions to the revolutionary authorities. As a result of this activity, the Moravian Indians were removed from their villages in 1781 by northern Indian neighbors who viewed them as potentially dangerous. The movement was so sudden that many Moravian Delawares left corn crops in their fields and were conducted back to their towns when winter food supplies ran low. This was when the Pennsylvania militia struck. Near the town of Gnadenhütten, in the Muskingum Valley of present-day Ohio (named for the Lehigh Valley mission community destroyed in an earlier war), the métis Joseph Shabosh, son of a Moravian missionary, first encountered the revolutionaries. After attempting to identify himself as a friend, he was literally cut to pieces by the militia. Upon arriving at the village, the Pennsylvania troops informed the other Indians that they intended to move them closer to Fort Pitt to protect them from Native groups allied with the British. Other Pennsylvania soldiers invited Moravian Delawares from the nearby town of Salem to join those at Gnadenhütten to prepare for the same move. The militiamen then deliberated among themselves and decided to execute the Moravian Indians, whom they deemed enemy warriors. There were, of course, no warriors in the pacifist community. The men and women of Gnadenhütten prepared for their grim fate by singing hymns until the soldiers conducted the Indians to their "cabins" and proceeded to bludgeon them to death with mallets. Some of the victims were scalped while still living; the corpses of others were cut up by a number of soldiers.[31]

That the Indians at Gnadenhütten were not only Christian but also dressed, farmed, and used land in European style did not mitigate their fate. Instead, these affronts to racial assumptions only sealed that fate. The massacre marked the apotheosis of White racialist identity and its effects on the brutalization of war on the frontier. Obviously, Indians in the region, the British, and Loyalists all vehemently decried the incident as coldblooded, unjustified, and mindless murder. Significantly, a number of revolutionary authorities criticized the action as a "massacre" as well. General William Irvine denounced the actions of the militia, informing George Washington that "they found about ninety men, women, and children all of whom they put to death, it is said, after cool deliberation and considering the matter for three days." Congress delegate David Howell also openly criticized "the Massacring of the Moravian Indians." In response, some western Pennsylvanians attempted to defend their militia's acts by arguing that the attack was necessitated by the popular belief that the Moravians were harboring hostile war parties in their communities. In support of this belief, the militiamen claimed that one of the Moravian women was wearing the dress of a White captive. Finally the soldiers themselves argued that the presence of metal utensils, china, and pots was clear evidence that these Delawares were dealing in war spoils from hostile raids; surely Indians could not have acquired them through legitimate participation in the Atlantic economy.[32]

The situation was considerably more complex, however. Defenders of the killings at Gnadenhütten only made such facile rationalizations when speaking to their eastern and elite critics. The Washington County militia party led by Colonel David Williamson was more fully aware of the complicated economic, cultural, and military position of the Moravian Delawares than they openly admitted. They understood that these Christian people lived on the spatial and cultural boundary between communities of revolutionaries and of Indians at war with the Euro-Pennsylvanians. Although the Gnadenhütten Delawares remained neutral in the war, their missionaries, such as David Zeisberger, had been actively forwarding intelligence to Americans at Fort Pitt. Nevertheless, the Moravians had to respect the power and wishes of Indian neighbors who sent war parties through their villages. Still, in the end, most militiamen knew that the Moravian Indians were not a serious military threat and that killing them would only further alienate neutrals. The logic employed by the militia at Gnadenhütten grew from the weltanschauung of White frontier racial identity. The militiamen asserted that they were seeking revenge against generalized "Indians" who raided White communities.[33]

The choice of the Moravian Delawares as the target of vengeance was significant. In some ways, they were more "civilized" than the militiamen who attacked them. They were pacifists who offered no resistance, they were Christians, they employed a European-style gendered division of labor in their agriculture, they used European goods. The militiamen, meanwhile, had adapted many aspects of Indian military culture. They wore leggings, used tomahawks, and scalped their victims. Much like their predecessors the Paxton Boys, the militia at Gnadenhütten were probably subconsciously troubled in their own racial and gendered identity by this cultural inversion. They assuaged those concerns by embracing the paradox, by violently acting out the supposed immutable, noncultural differences between Whites and non-White Indians.[34] The missionary John Heckewelder recalled in horror that the militiamen torturously beat the nonresisting, hymn-singing people of Gnadenhütten with mallets and then took "off their scalps." Some, Heckewelder said, wanted to burn the Indians alive, inflicting what they believed to be the customary torture among Indians. As Heckewelder described the incident, based on Delaware witnesses' testimony, Gnadenhütten resembled the staple Anglo-American narratives of Indian barbarity against Whites in warfare with the roles simply inverted. The revolutionaries were the savages and the Delawares the stoic Christian victims.[35]

What Heckewelder portrayed as tragic irony, the militia saw as their intentional assertion of region-specific American racial identity. The soldiers viewed themselves as White and therefore superior to any Indian regardless of the ironic blurring of cultural identity among the Delawares and the Euro-Americans. They proudly utilized such Indian traditions as torture and scalping of the enemy to show their mastery of frontier warfare and to celebrate their victory over foes. It did not matter that their victims were pacifist Christians. They were inferior beings and generally culpable for enemy attacks, as were all Indians. Race was innate, unaffected by cultural intermixing. In one interesting exchange between the two groups, as the Moravian Delawares pleaded their friendliness toward the revolutionaries, the militia responded by pointing out that pots, kettles, tools, and other implements that they had were "things as were made use of by White People and not by Indians." Although this appears to be a rationale for attributing the Delawares' possession of these goods to theft, involvement in raids, or trade with hostile Indians, the soldiers knew that these people did indeed "make use" of them and had done so for a long time even before the war. Yet only "White People" could properly use them. Identity was not so much formed by the use of the implements as by *who* used them. Indians could utilize a plow and still be Indians. It would not mitigate their fate at the hands of White enemies. White people could wield a tomahawk and still be White people. It did not diminish what the militia saw to be the fundamental marker of superiority: Whiteness, not culture. The revolutionary troops were intentionally declaring and prosecuting race war.[36]

Also, according to historian Dowd, it was clear that the attack on Gnadenhütten was "no spontaneous outbreak of frontier frenzy" regarding recent hostile Indian attacks. In 1781, the local militia had planned an assault on the Moravian towns and had been opposed by Continental authorities, such as Colonel John Gibson, who asserted that the Christian Delawares were helpful to the revolutionary cause. Additionally, as Irvine pointed out in his letter to Washington, the militiamen discussed at length what to do with the Moravians. They purposefully deceived the Delawares by stating that they meant only to move them closer to Fort Pitt to protect them from British-allied Indians. Some militiamen went to another Moravian village, Salem, and brought the inhabitants back to Gnadenhütten. The methodical slaughter of the captives that followed was premeditated and meant to send a message to all Indians in the region regarding the intentions of the rank-and-file revolutionaries.[37]

The militia explicitly demonstrated that they would use the common military culture of the frontier against all Indians. Laden with spoils, the militiamen were not finished even as they neared Fort Pitt. According to Heckewelder, "having in those parts no further opportunity of killing innocent people and no stomach to engage with warriors," the militiamen "set off [for] home with their horses and plunder they had taken and afterwards falling upon the peaceable Indians on the north side of the Allegheny River opposite Pittsburgh, killed several of those." These "peaceable Indians" were in fact Killbuck and his party of Coshocton Delawares who had remained allied to the United States, even participating in the 1781 raid on Coshocton. The militia party's genocidal behavior marked the full expression of frontier racial "American" identity. As Whites they were simultaneously making war on the Indian enemy they had racially imagined and turning all actual Native Americans into very real foes. By 1783, the year that the Treaty of Paris was signed, most Indians in the Ohio Valley and Great Lakes region were actively at war, having secured a significant victory over United States troops at Sandusky in June of the previous year and ostentatiously torturing to death Colonel William Crawford in retaliation for Gnadenhütten. The consolidation of White revolutionary identity and its racist brutalization of the war fostered pan-Indian alliance, thereby reinforcing many Euro-Americans' notions that "the Indians" were all their enemies.[38]

The importance that Whiteness assumed in veterans' retrospective early nineteenth-century accounts of the American Revolution is difficult to overestimate. As Gordon Wood has argued, the Revolution paved the way for the then-radical notion of universal White manhood suffrage. Veterans were aware that their military service was a basis from which to claim full citizenship. Because their sacrifices helped found the republic, many believed that they should be enfranchised. Clearly, the most important change in national identity in the United States from the end of the Revolution to the 1830s was the profound shift from a gendered economic basis of citizenship to a gendered biological one. White manhood replaced male property-holding as the prerequisite for participation in the formal public sphere. Not surprisingly, veterans offered narratives that proudly recounted their claims to political inclusion by emphasizing the "White race" in contrast to Indians. These discussions were superfluous to the requirements of the pension but obviously important to the deponents, who gained the satisfaction of recounting how they came to see themselves as Americans, through a revolution that defined the White race against non-Whites. This emphasis on self-identity helps to explain the initially puzzling absence of references to Indians' skin color being "Red," despite the wide use of that color term in the early nineteenth century. Ordinary soldiers of the Revolution chose to invoke color only in terms of their own identities, reaffirming their claims to the privileges of Whiteness.[39]

The veterans' forthright articulation of a seeming double standard of combat behavior was critical to their identity as White Americans as well. The frontiersman who mixed elements of Indian and European culture, especially methods of warfare, was a staple of literature and popular culture in the early republic, for the one thing that apparently made Americans distinct from Europeans was adaptation to the American environment. While audiences in the courts might have wished for stories of George Washington, veterans would have been untroubled by the contradiction of lauding patriot frontier military culture while characterizing comparable Indian acts as "savagery." Whites who adopted some Indian ways were the very embodiment of a powerful strain of early national identity: "Americans" as biologically superior to Indians and culturally superior to Europeans.[40]

The attitudes of ex-soldiers who came largely from the lower and middling ranks of society also help explain the support of many ordinary Americans for the federal Removal policy of the 1830s. Cherokees and others of the "civilized tribes" who had republican government, Christianity, farming, livestock, European gender roles, and a written language could no more be entitled to the rights of Whites than had the Moravian Delawares at Gnadenhütten. Despite a variety of Indian strategies to preserve their independence, including assimilation, accommodation, and armed resistance, imperial expansion could always be justified racially. Even those more sympathetic to Native peoples than ordinary veterans had difficulty placing independent Indians within a world that included the American nation. Thomas Jefferson offered inclusion to Indians not only at the cost of their cultural identity but also through imagined biological transformation through intermarriage with Whites.[41]

Few Indians desired full incorporation into the U.S. body politic, but their theoretical racial exclusion had sweeping consequences. It bolstered the concept of the White male nation. Most members of the other major group defined as racial others, African Americans, did in fact actively seek citizenship. The denial of Indian fitness to be "American" undoubtedly informed a general assumption among most Whites that African Americans were not qualified to be citizens because of perceived biological difference. Indeed, the soldiers' narratives were being collected during a period when states in both the North and the South were enacting new legal restrictions on the political and civil rights of free Blacks. Pennsylvania itself was in the process of formalizing its denial of franchise to free Black males in the late 1830s after years of informal discrimination. Contemporary public affirmations of the Revolution as a war to defend the interests of Whites against those of Indians would have certainly spoken directly to an evolving racially exclusive concept of citizenship.[42]

The frontier veterans' descriptions of the American Revolution revealed an increasingly dominant perception of national subjectivity. Although the early United States was diverse, conflict-prone, and competitive, the potential for serious contention was mitigated by the construct of biological citizenship premised in White male supremacy. Competitive White males could contend with each other within the body politic. Those defined as biologically unfit to be political subjects of the republic—Indians, African Americans, and women—were formally excluded. Such a biological and racial formulation fulfilled the additional function of muting class conflict among White men because of their shared commitments to White male supremacy. The pervasiveness of the White male nation reached its zenith by the 1830s when many of the pension narratives were given, an era in which universal White male suffrage was largely attained. The roots of the White male nation were set firmly in the American Revolution, and nowhere were they more visible than in the frontier war and its memory among veterans who based their claims for citizenship on the White male status they had asserted in their revolutionary war against the Indian other.[43]

AFTERWORD

JAMES H. MERRELL

Twenty-five years ago Douglas Greenberg, surveying scholarship on the Middle Colonies of Pennsylvania, New Jersey, and New York, reported that the Native peoples of that region were forgotten folk. In colonial times, "Indians prompted far more curiosity among their white contemporaries," Greenberg observed, "than they have among later historians." Concluding that "there is much yet to be done in this field," he hoped that "perhaps . . . the next generation of Middle Colonies specialists" would "pursue the Indian response to European colonization more systematically than their predecessors have."[1]

It has taken more than one scholarly generation, but the essays in this volume herald the arrival of that hoped-for flock of historians, hard at work on the Native experience in and around "Penn's Woods." Given the riches they have found, it is surprising that it has taken so long for scholars in any numbers to start poking around those parts. True, they are not the first to have a look. In the early twentieth century, Charles A. Hanna and C. Hale Sipe compiled a wealth of information on area Natives, albeit information suffused with the prejudices and myopia of that time.[2] Around midcentury, Paul A. W. Wallace and his son Anthony F. C. Wallace wrote more sophisticated, more sensitive studies of the Pennsylvania frontier.[3] In more recent times, Francis Jennings published classic accounts of diplomacy between Natives and colonists, accounts in which Pennsylvania-Indian relations figured largely.[4] Nonetheless, it seems fair to say that Penn's Woods has remained relatively unexplored. Over the past thirty years, students of the Indian experience during the colonial era have ranged far and wide, from Canada through New England to Iroquoia, from the Chesapeake through Carolina to Florida, even leaping the Appalachians to explore the Great Lakes, Louisiana, and the Southwest. Yet this omnivorous scholarly curiosity somehow passed right by Pennsylvania. It is necessary, and instructive, to ask why.

Some of the neglect is a matter of what might be called historical timing. Pennsylvania, founded in 1682, was second to last of the English provinces planted in North America. (That colonies of Finns, Swedes, and Dutch were living beside the Delaware River well before William Penn showed up are not likely to catch the eye or kindle the imagination of a collective American memory that is Anglocentric to a fault.) Coming near the end is inherently less interesting: who remembers what baseball team finished next to last? Moreover, as latecomers, Penn's people could learn from their colonial predecessors' mistakes. Hence no lost colony to add an aura of mystery to Penn's Woods, no starving time that would have the desperation and death guaranteed to fascinate subsequent generations. And if no starving time, then no Native coming to the rescue: Virginia had its Pocahontas, New England its Squanto; and Pennsylvania . . . ?[5]

Similarly, New England had its Pequots and Wampanoags, New York its Iroquois, Virginia its Powhatans, Carolina its Cherokees and Creeks, and Pennsylvania . . . its scattered, battered bands of Lenapes (Delawares). This very lack of powerful Natives in the vicinity has also helped deflect scholarly attention away from Penn's Woods.[6] Moreover, because Penn's Lenape neighbors—few in number, already well versed in the boisterous, sometimes brutal ways of European colonists—were welcoming rather than threatening, and because their approach matched his own, the Proprietor and his heirs long managed to avoid the frontier warfare that so devastated many English colonies and has so entranced scholars since. Historians are an intellectually bloodthirsty bunch: war is not only more compelling and more dramatic; its causes, course, and consequences also seem to demand more study. And Indian raids, long a staple of American lore, exert a particularly powerful magnetic attraction. With scalping knives sheathed and muskets aimed at deer rather than people, Pennsylvanians and their Native neighbors offer too little gore until after 1750, leaving scholars' attention to wander toward colonial combat with Powhatan and Opechancanough, Pequots and King Philip, Tuscaroras and Yamasees.

Nor can someone who, against the odds and against the grain, becomes interested in Pennsylvania's relations with its Indian neighbors find ready to hand great colonial chroniclers of that chapter in American history. Once again a look at other English colonies reveals the disparity: New England has Roger Williams and William Wood, Virginia John Smith and William Strachey, Carolina John Lawson and James Adair; and Pennsylvania . . . ? The richest sources on Natives of this region, compiled by the Swedish naturalist Pehr Lindeström in the 1650s and the German missionaries John Heckewelder and David Zeisberger more than a century later, are not nearly as famous, perhaps (again) because of our Anglocentric mind set.

Whatever the cause of this neglect, the effect is a striking lacuna in our rapidly growing knowledge of the confluence and collision of cultures in early America. Many today will have heard of William Penn's friendship with Indians, at least as refracted by Benjamin West's famous 1771 painting and one hundred more by Edward Hicks fifty years later. Some will know of the Walking Purchase, one more link in that tarnished chain of Euro-American chicanery against North America's Natives. A few might have vague notions about the Paxton Boys' slaughter of peaceful Conestogas in December 1763. Beyond these impressions, however, Pennsylvania's Indian history is largely terra incognita.

This is unfortunate, but not because there is a crying need to color in this empty spot on the colonial canvas. History is not (or should not be) some vast fill-in-the-blanks form, and scholars do not (or should not) scurry about plugging "gaps" in our knowledge. Rather, the experience of Indians and colonists in Penn's Woods merits scrutiny because it has much to teach about early America—and indeed about America as a whole.

Take the very lack of frontier wars there before 1755: all of the scholarly (and colonial) attention to such hostilities tends to obscure the fact that, while friction was common as peoples from different worlds bumped and jostled one another, all-out combat was in fact occasional and isolated. Examining how Indians and Pennsylvanians worked out ways to live together, without the distraction of looking for the causes of this war or the aftershocks of that one, enables scholars better to attend to those more frequent, everyday, forgotten threads of the American encounter.

Or consider the lack of powerful Native groups in or near Penn's

Woods. Here again, the colony's experience was more typical than might be thought. Despite the European colonial (and modern scholarly) tendency to lump Indians together into Cherokees, Iroquois, and the like, most Natives in eastern North America—including Cherokees and Iroquois—thought more in terms of town or kin than nation or empire.[7] Hence Pennsylvania's contacts with Natives—first with Lenape bands along the Delaware, later with Shawnees, Conoys, Tuscaroras, Tutelos, and other small refugee groups in the Susquehanna River valley as well as various Iroquois peoples in the Susquehanna's upper reaches—properly direct our gaze toward the small-scale, intimate encounters between Indian and colonial settlers.

Think, finally, about the dearth of big-name colonial authorities on this corner of early America. In fact, this can be a benefit rather than a burden. Scholars of early Virginia or early Carolina, by necessity and by choice, rely heavily on one or two men for the bulk of their information about Indians. Such texts yield a wealth of evidence, but they are also colored (and, yes, tainted) by that colonist's own particular experience and point of view. The very lack of such a colossus commanding (and, yes, obscuring) our view of Pennsylvania compels scholars to cast their nets widely, to glean bits and pieces from a wide array of texts. The opportunity is therefore greater for what Daniel K. Richter calls "triangulation": the use of various sources to fix a particular point or theme in Native history.[8] Who would not wish for a Pennsylvania version of Roger Williams, John Smith, or John Lawson? Yet there are dangers here, too. The light cast by these chroniclers is so bright that it can blind us to the pitfalls of relying too heavily on one man's opinion.

No single volume—not even one with two editors and thirteen authors—can hope to cure the case of historical amnesia afflicting Pennsylvania's frontier. But what these authors have done, by fanning out into what was made into Penn's Woods, is to offer fascinating glimpses of the historical bounty there. They do so by willfully, creatively, and productively defying convention in any number of ways, thereby opening up new vistas while also placing the familiar in a new light. Against the conventional celebration of William Penn, James Spady paints a portrait of the Founder in darker hues.[9] Against the standard scrutiny of the Walking Purchase itself, Steven Harper follows its aftermath among disgruntled Delawares. Against the usual, almost casual condemnations of the Paxton Boys, Krista Camenzind insists upon exploring the forces that set these men on the road to infamy.

As these essays deepen and complicate understanding of the legendary high (and low) points of Pennsylvania's Indian past, so they also defy conventional geographical and chronological limits. Recognizing that provincial boundaries were ill defined (if defined at all), and that in any case neither Natives nor colonists confined themselves to one colony, the chapters range far beyond Pennsylvania, from Massachusetts and Pine Plains, New York, through Iroquoia to the Ohio country. Replacing the usual opening scene (Penn's arrival) and the standard closing act (the frontier wars of 1755–65), the authors here insist that, from the Native point of view at least, William Penn's arrival was nothing new; he was only the latest in a long line of uninvited guests from faraway lands to show up on the banks of the Delaware. Similarly, for Natives neither 1765 nor 1776 marked a terminus. If few Indians remained within Pennsylvania's borders except as visitors, Paul Moyer and Gregory Knouff reveal that the Native continued to exert a powerful grip on White Pennsylvanians' behavior and their thought, their imagination and their memory.

Even as these essays expand the chronological and geographical horizons, they also explore beyond the well-trodden precincts of the treaty council ground. Those congresses at Philadelphia and Easton, Logstown and Lancaster, Onondaga and Albany have drawn a great deal of scholarly attention, and no wonder. Not only are the minutes of council speeches abundant and accessible (that bright evidential light again), but these diplomatic encounters, often involving hundreds of people, were compelling dramas vital to the continent's transfer from Native to European hands.[10] Yet just as too much devotion to the study of frontier wars can distort understanding of frontier life, so lingering too long at these treaty councils can hinder appreciation of the American encounter's full richness. Like wars, treaties punctuated everyday intercourse between Native and newcomer; they did not dominate it. Just as no study of modern America would be complete if it only examined World War II, Korea, and Vietnam, only visited summit meetings, SALT talks, and Camp David accords, so no study of the Pennsylvania borderlands can confine itself to the Seven Years' War and the treaty councils.

Adopting this line of sight, examining what Alison Duncan Hirsch terms "more personal frontiers," brings to light a host of startling scenes, scenes evocative of that powerful, overlooked current of contact. An imaginary tour of Penn's Woods, with these chapters as guide, offers glimpses of that larger confluence and concordance across the cultural divide. In one town, a *métis* woman gives a German man a prescription to cure what ails him. In another, German women tend their Indian sisters during childbirth or sit with them to compare the state of their souls. And in a third, a Conestoga woman regales Quakers and Natives with her recent dream about visiting William Penn in London. One day on the Pennsylvania frontier a Seneca man and an English colonist sit down beside a campfire to trade. Another, Pennsylvanians invite two Nanticokes to Sunday dinner. And yet another, an Iroquois sits drinking with some Irishmen. Here Natives celebrate the Christmas season with colonists. There, a Native helps Europeans at harvest time or rents land to them. Over there, an Indian and a Swede are strolling along a path, chatting. And still farther along, White Pennsylvanians are donning leggings, breech cloths, and moccasins, then tanning their legs and painting their faces. The great Pennsylvania naturalist John Bartram captured this dimension of frontier life—the permeable boundaries, the casual borrowing and sharing—when he reported that many Natives were "allmost dayly familiars at thair [colonists'] houses[,] eat drank cursed and swore together[,] were even intimate playmates."[11]

These and the many other remarkable moments in this volume would seem to make Penn's Woods a candidate for inclusion in the growing list of sites that can be termed "a middle ground," a physical place (and cultural space) where different peoples somehow managed to forget or overlook their differences in order to get along. During the past decade or so, scholars inspired by Richard White's brilliant study of Indian-colonial relations in the Great Lakes region have scoured the early American countryside, searching for similar configurations of contact.[12] Since no all-out warfare bloodied Pennsylvania for so long, and since scenes of concord and easy interaction are so thick on the ground there, Penn's Woods might seem a likely spot.

In fact, however, the authors in this volume are careful not to go too far toward the end of the contact spectrum awash in light, peace, and understanding.[13] It was, as Carla Gerona concludes, at best "a troubled middle ground." That Seneca swap session and that Nanticoke invitation to dinner found their way into the records, after all, because shortly after trading began the colonist killed the Seneca, and shortly after the Nanticokes showed up to dine, their hosts hauled one of them off to jail for molesting a Pennsylvania girl. Similarly, that chat the Swede and Native were having as they ambled along actually ends badly: they come upon a snake and, despite (or, rather, because of) the Indian's insistence that they leave the creature alone because it "was sacred to him," his fellow traveler beats it to death with a stick. So, too, with the war that came in 1755: Natives often targeted the very people who once had been their neighbors and "playmates."

Distance, strangeness, and misunderstanding were particularly prominent at the beginning of colonization, of course. Michael Mackintosh, noting the "visible congruences" between Lenape and Finnish or Swedish ways—woodcraft and hunting, huts and boats, even sweat lodges— nonetheless suggests that these "probably seemed much more like ephemera" compared with their views on snakes, land, and other elements of the natural world. The English arrival, both Mackintosh and James Spady argue, did nothing to improve the situation. All of the treaty talk between Natives and the Founder about understanding and unity, brotherhood and friendship, might have been "keenly felt," Spady notes. However, it was "also tactical," divided as these peoples were by profoundly different notions about land, leadership, and gender. Friendship there might be, but for Europeans it was, in the long run, friendship on colonial terms.

Nor did things get better when newcomers and Natives had spent more time together. Gerona's fascinating sketch of the resemblance between Quaker and Indian dream cultures nonetheless makes clear that dreams, like trade or treaties, could contain deep misunderstandings, could be a handy tool of empire. Even the close, intimate correspondence Amy Schutt finds between Native and German women of the Moravian faith was short-lived, as after 1760 fewer colonial women went into mission work. Equally brief were the rental agreements David Preston treats. Colonial tenants on Indian land were heirs to the Finns, Swedes, and early English colonists Mackintosh and Spady brought to light. Glad as they were to lease farms from Natives, these tenants considered the arrangement temporary, a means to the ultimate end: ownership of the soil. Small wonder that, when war came, their Indian landlords, feeling betrayed, often singled out these farms for attack. Reciprocity, a balance of power, remained the Native goal, subordination the European aim. Gregory Knouff's Revolutionary War soldiers as well as Paul Moyer's Susquehanna settlers carried on this tradition: even as they borrowed dress and tactics from their Delaware or Iroquois neighbors, they were not "going native," but rather further driving the Indian not only from Penn's Woods but from American memory.

Plotting the trajectory of how Native America became Penn's Woods, from "Peoples in Conversation" through "Fragile Structures of Coexistence" and on "Toward a White Pennsylvania," it is hard not to wind up in a dark, bleak place, with Indian-haters in full cry and Indians themselves in full retreat. Whatever the ignorance and arrogance in William Penn's hopes and plans, whatever the stresses and strains in competing, clashing ways of seeing justice done, whatever the fate of peacemakers, nonetheless we should not let an unhappy ending ruin the pageant of Penn's Woods. If this volume closes with the demolition of that colonial place and time, its other theme, the "cultural construction" that went on there, bears keeping in mind. Especially in our own dark, bleak times, it is worth remembering that there was a day when alien peoples found ways to get past their fundamental differences in order to carry on a conversation about any number of topics, to swap dreams and goods, to share a confidence or a bottle.

It is worth remembering, too, that while no paragon of modern multiculturalism, William Penn was comparatively flexible in his dealings with Natives. Of England's other colony founders in the seventeenth century, only Roger Williams in Rhode Island comes close to matching Penn's fascination with (and respect for) Indian ways, his interest in forging friendships, his vision of an America that might contain Natives as well as newcomers. John Smith? An English conquistador, full of bluff and bluster, threats and warnings. William Bradford or John Winthrop? No Smith, to be sure, but in their eagerness to keep Indians at arm's length (if not rule them outright), no Penn or Williams either. The faceless, forgotten founders of other provinces in that era—in Carolina and Maryland, New Netherland and New Jersey—were closer to Smith, Winthrop, and Bradford than to Williams and Penn.

Or compare Pennsylvania's Indian relations with other corners of the frontier on the eve of Penn's arrival. A quick tour reveals that eastern America in those times was a dark and bloody ground indeed. Forget the terrible clashes that almost annihilated Virginia in 1622 and then, in 1644, almost annihilated Virginia's Native neighbors.[14] Set aside New England's brutal (and nearly successful) campaign to exterminate Pequots in the

1630s as well as the ferocious wars between Dutch and Indians in the 1640s and 1650s.[15] Merely surveying the scene from the mid–1670s forward reveals a frontier awash in carnage. In New England, a pan-Indian uprising since called "King Philip's War" devastated colonial and Native settlements alike.[16] The Chesapeake, meanwhile, was rocked by Indian raids after Virginia and Maryland troops in 1675 killed Susquehannock headmen who had come to parley under a flag of truce.[17] Farther south in Carolina, a decade's strife culminated in the Westo War of 1680, an operation so efficient that by 1683, it was said, only fifty Westoes survived.[18] Those fifty, like defeated Natives up and down the East Coast, were prey for victorious Englishmen hunting fresh slaves.

Given these dark passages, perhaps William Penn was not engaging in hyperbolic self-promotion when he promised a new, brighter day. Writing from England in 1681, he told his soon-to-be Indian neighbors that "I am very sensible of the unkindness and Injustice that hath been too much exersised towards you by the People of thes[e] Parts off the world, who have sought . . . to make great Advantages by you, rather then by examples of Justice and Goodness unto you, which I hear, hath been [a] matter of trouble to you, and caused great Grudgeings and Animosities. . . . [B]ut," Penn concluded, "I am not such a Man." Perhaps he was not being duplicitous, conniving, or hypocritical when he went on to say that he wanted to "enjoy it [this land on the Delaware] with your Love and Consent, that we may always live together as Neighbours and freinds." Maybe he really did look forward to his arrival, when he and the Indians "may more largely and freely confer and discourse of thes[e] matters."[19]

If it pays to be skeptical about Penn's warm words, to keep in mind the imperial enterprise beneath them, it pays not to be too cynical about them, either. It pays, too, to remember them. Certainly the Indians did. As Jane Merritt and others have shown, soon after Penn left his province for the last time in 1701, Native diplomats from many nations began talking up (and embellishing) their memories of him.[20] At treaty after treaty through the eighteenth century, Conestogas and Conoys, Iroquois and Delawares fondly recalled for their colonial audience how the Founder "had at his first Coming amongst them made an agreement with them that they should always Live as friends and Brothers, and be as one Body, one heart, one mind, and as one Eye and Ear; . . . and that there should be nothing but Love and friendship between them and us forever."[21] Keeping the bright flame of Penn's words alive, Natives shrewdly used the Proprietor as a tool for insisting that his literal and figurative descendants (his sons, Quakers, and Pennsylvanians in general) live up to the high hopes, the shining ideals of the Indians' "old friend and brother," William Penn.

Natives, forgetting neither Penn's words nor the promise that was Penn's Woods, were also insisting that they, too, be remembered, and respected, "from Generation to Generation" for "as long as the Sun it self."[22] Somewhere between their day and our own, amnesia arrived: Natives, out of sight in Pennsylvania, were also out of mind. The essays here, and the larger scholarly projects each represents, hold out the hope that Pennsylvania's Native friends and foes, landlords and trading partners, neighbors and "playmates," will be forgotten folk no more.

ABBREVIATIONS

Handbook	William C. Sturtevant, ed., *Handbook of North American Indians*, vol. 15, *Northeast*, ed. Bruce G. Trigger (Washington, D.C.: Smithsonian Institution, 1978)
HSP	Historical Society of Pennsylvania, Philadelphia
JAH	*Journal of American History*
LCP	Library Company of Philadelphia
MAB	Archives of the Moravian Church, Bethlehem, Pa.
MPCP	[Samuel Hazard, ed.], *Minutes of the Provincial Council of Pennsylvania, from the Organization to the Termination of the Proprietary Government,* 10 vols. (Harrisburg, Pa., 1838–52)
NEP	Albert Cook Myers, ed., *Narratives of Early Pennsylvania, West New Jersey, and Delaware, 1630–1707* (New York: Charles Scribner's Sons, 1912)
NNN	J. Franklin Jameson, ed., *Narratives of New Netherland, 1609–1664* (New York: Charles Scribner's Sons, 1909)
NYCD	E. B. O'Callaghan and B. Fernow, eds., *Documents Relative to the Colonial History of the State of New York,* 15 vols. (Albany, 1853–87)
PA	Samuel Hazard et al., eds., *Pennsylvania Archives* (title varies), 9 series, 122 vols. (Harrisburg and Philadelphia, 1852–1935)
PH	*Pennsylvania History*
PHMC	Pennsylvania Historical and Museum Commission, Harrisburg
PMHB	*Pennsylvania Magazine of History and Biography*
PSA	Pennsylvania State Archives, Harrisburg
PWJ	James Sullivan et al., eds., *The Papers of Sir William Johnson,* 14 vols. (Albany: State University of New York, 1921–65)
PWP	Richard S. Dunn and Mary Maples Dunn, eds., *The Papers of William Penn,* 5 vols. (Philadelphia: University of Pennsylvania Press, 1981–86)
QCHC	Quaker Collection, Haverford College, Haverford, Pa.
RMM	*Records of the Moravian Mission Among the Indians of North America,* microfilm (New Haven, Conn.: Research Publications, 1970)

RPRG   Records of Pennsylvania's Revolutionary Governments, 1775–90, Record Group 27, microfilm, Pennsylvania Historical and Museum Commission, Harrisburg

RWPF   Revolutionary War Pension Application Files, National Archives, Washington, D.C.

SCP   Julian P. Boyd and Robert J. Taylor, eds., *The Susquehannah Company Papers,* 11 vols. (Wilkes-Barre, Pa., and Ithaca, N.Y.: Cornell University Press, 1930–71)

WMQ   *William and Mary Quarterly,* 3d ser.

NOTES

Introduction

1. James H. Merrell, *Into the American Woods: Negotiators on the Pennsylvania Frontier* (New York: W. W. Norton, 1999), 37.

2. William A. Hunter, "Documented Subdivisions of the Delaware Indians," *Bulletin of Archaeological Society of New Jersey* 35 (1978): 20–40; Marshall J. Becker, "Cultural Diversity in the Lower Delaware River Valley, 1550–1750: An Ethnohistorical Perspective," in Jay F. Custer, ed., *Late Woodland Cultures of the Middle Atlantic Region* (Newark: University of Delaware Press, 1986), 90–101; Robert Steven Grumet, "'We Are Not So Great Fools': Changes in Upper Delawaran Socio-Political Life, 1630–1758" (Ph.D. diss., Rutgers University, 1979).

3. Laurence M. Hauptman, "Refugee Havens: The Iroquois Villages of the Eighteenth Century," in Christopher Vecsey and Robert W. Venables, eds., *American Indian Environ-ments: Ecological Issues in Native American History* (Syracuse: Syracuse University Press, 1980), 128–39; Peter C. Mancall, *Valley of Opportunity: Economic Culture Along the Upper Susque-hanna, 1700–1800* (Ithaca: Cornell University Press, 1991), 27–70; Michael N. McConnell, *A Country Between: The Upper Ohio Valley and Its Peoples, 1724–1774* (Lincoln: University of Nebraska Press, 1992), 6–60.

4. Francis Jennings, "'Pennsylvania Indians' and the Iroquois," in Daniel K. Richter and James H. Merrell, eds., *Beyond the Covenant Chain: The Iroquois and Their Neighbors in Indian North America, 1600–1800* (Syracuse: Syracuse University Press, 1987), 75–91; Richter, *The Ordeal of the Longhouse: The Peoples of the Iroquois League in the Era of European Coloni-zation* (Chapel Hill: University of North Carolina Press, 1992), 241–44.

5. Merrell, *Into the American Woods*, 34–38. See also Jane T. Merritt, *At the Crossroads: Indians and Empires on a Mid-Atlantic Frontier, 1700–1763* (Chapel Hill: University of North Carolina Press, 2003), which appeared too recently to have had the impact it deserves on the chapters below.

6. See Wilbur Zelinsky, "Geography," in Randall M. Miller and William Pencak, eds., *Pennsylvania: A History of the Commonwealth* (University Park: The Pennsylvania State Uni-versity Press, 2002), 389–94; William Cronon, *Changes in the Land: Indians, Colonists and the Ecology of Colonial New England* (New York: Hill and Wang, 1983); and Timothy Silver, *A New Face on the Countryside: Indians, Colonists and Slaves on the South Atlantic Frontier, 1500–1800* (Ithaca: Cornell University Press, 1990).

7. Peter C. Mancall, *Valley of Opportunity: Economic Culture Along the Upper Susque-hanna, 1700–1800* (Ithaca: Cornell University Press, 1991), 29–85; Tim H. Blessing, "The Upper Juniata Valley," in John B. Frantz and William Pencak, eds., *Beyond Philadelphia: The American Revolution in the Pennsylvania Hinterland* (University Park: The Pennsylvania State University Press, 1998), 153–70; Merritt, *At the Crossroads*, 19–49.

8. James H. Merrell, "Shamokin, 'the Very Seat of the Prince of Darkness': Unsettling the Early American Frontier," in Andrew R. L. Cayton and Fredrika J. Teute, eds., *Contact Points: American Frontiers from the Mohawk Valley to the Mississippi, 1750–1830* (Chapel Hill: University of North Carolina Press, 1998), 16–59.

9. See Jane T. Merritt, "Metaphor, Meaning, and Misunderstanding: Language and Power on the Pennsylvania Frontier," in Cayton and Teute, eds., *Contact Points*, 60–87; Mer-ritt, "Cultural Encounters Along a Gender Frontier: Mahican, Delaware, and German Women

in Eighteenth-Century Pennsylvania," *Pennsylvania History* 67 (2000): 523–52; and Natalie Zemon Davis, "Iroquois Women, European Women," in Margo Hendricks and Patricia Parker, eds., *Women, "Race," and Writing in the Early Modern Period* (New York: Routledge, 1994), 243–58.

10. Irene Silverblatt, *Sun, Moon, and Witches; Gender Ideologies and Class in Inca and Colonial Peru* (Princeton: Princeton University Press, 1987); Karen Anderson, *Chain Her by One Foot: The Subjugation of Women in Seventeenth-Century New France* (London: Routledge, 1991).

11. William McLoughlin, "Cherokee Anomie, 1794–1840: Red Men, Red Women, Black Slaves," in Richard L. Bushman and Stephan Thernstrom, eds., *Uprooted Americans: Essays in Honor of Oscar Handlin* (Boston: Little, Brown, 1997); Peter Mancall, *Deadly Medicine: Indians and Alcohol in Early America* (Ithaca: Cornell University Press, 1995).

12. For another example, see David Hsiung, "Death on the Juniata: Delawares, Iroquois, and Pennsylvanians in a Colonial Whodunit," *Pennsylvania History* 65 (1998): 445–77. A classic study of alcohol excusing Native American crime is William Taylor, *Drinking, Homicide, and Rebellion in Colonial Mexican Villages* (Stanford: Stanford University Press, 1979). See also Richter, *Ordeal of the Longhouse*, 86, 263–68.

13. Gregory Evans Dowd, "Thinking and Belonging: Nativism and Unity in the Age of Pontiac and Tecumseh," *American Indian Quarterly* 16 (1992): 309–35; Dowd, *War Under Heaven: Pontiac, the Indian Nations, and the British Empire* (Baltimore: Johns Hopkins University Press, 2002).

14. Peter Kolchin, "Whiteness Studies: The New History of Race in America," *Journal of American History* 89 (2002): 154–73. For a provocative discussion of these issues for Pennsylvania, see Peter Rhoads Silver, "Indian-Hating and the Rise of Whiteness in Provincial Pennsylvania" (Ph.D. diss., Yale University, 2000).

15. *Minutes of the Supreme Executive Council of Pennsylvania, from Its Organization to the Termination of the Revolution*, 16 (Harrisburg: Theo. Fenn and Co., 1853), 404.

Chapter 1

1. Pehr Kalm, *Peter Kalm's Travels in North America: The English Version of 1770*, ed. Adolph B. Benson (New York: Wilson-Erickson, 1937).

2. Raymond Williams, *Keywords: A Vocabulary of Society and Culture* (New York: Oxford University Press, 1976), 184; Williams, *Problems in Materialism and Culture: Selected Essays* (London: Verso, 1980), 70.

3. Williams, *Problems in Materialism and Culture*, 67, assumes that there is a unified mankind that has a shared, monolithic understanding of nature.

4. The account of this incident is from "David De Vries's Notes," *NEP*, 5.

5. Ibid., 17.

6. Ibid., 5.

7. In the American colonies, domesticated animals were often at the root of tensions between Indians and colonists. European animals (especially pigs) tended to thrive in the woods, breeding rapidly, eating away undergrowth, contributing to soil erosion, and outcompeting native animal species. Domestic animals often caused conflicts by wandering into Indian crops. Natives tended to be displeased by the damage the animals caused and defended their crops by killing the offending animal; animal owners rarely recognized Indian rights in such matters and often exacted retribution with little restraint. See William Cronon, *Changes in the Land: Indians, Colonists, and the Ecology of New England* (New York: Hill and Wang,

1983), 82–107; Virginia DeJohn Anderson, "King Philip's Herds: Indians, Colonists, and the Problem of Livestock in Early New England," *WMQ* 51 (1994): 601–24; and Stephen Aron, "Pigs and Hunters: 'Rights in the Woods' on the Trans-Appalachian Frontier," in Andrew R. L. Cayton and Fredrika J. Teute, eds., *Contact Points: American Frontiers from the Mohawk Valley to the Mississippi, 1750–1830* (Chapel Hill: University of North Carolina Press, 1998), 175–204. The issues described above were less important at Swanendael than they would be in later colonial encounters; the small size, the newness, and the brief existence of the station seem to have prevented such conflicts from developing. However, the Americans there reacted to European animals strongly and violently nonetheless.

8. Near present-day Lewes, Delaware.

9. The "Delaware Valley" in this essay refers to the lands surrounding the Delaware River and Bay and their tributaries; in present-day terms: southern New Jersey, northeastern Delaware, and southeastern Pennsylvania.

10. The classic study of New Sweden is Amandus Johnson, *Swedish Settlements on the Delaware, Their History and Relation to the Indians, Dutch and English, 1638–1664* (New York: Appleton, 1911).

11. Amandus Johnson, trans., *The Instructions for Johan Printz, Governor of New Sweden* (Philadelphia: Swedish Colonial Society, 1930), article 18.

12. The strongest statement of this position is Marshall Joseph Becker, "Lenape Archaeology: Archaeological and Ethnological Considerations in Light of Recent Excavations," *Pennsylvania Archaeologist* 50, no. 4 (1980): 19–30. Becker asserts that the Lenape had little, if any, subsistence reliance on agriculture before contact in "A Summary of Lenape Socio-Political Organization and Settlement Patterns at the Time of European Contact: The Evidence for Collecting Bands," *Journal of Middle Atlantic Archaeology* 4 (1988): 79–83.

13. See C. A. Weslager, *The Delaware Indians: A History* (New Brunswick, N.J.: Rutgers University Press, 1972); Herbert C. Kraft, ed., *A Delaware Indian Symposium* (Harrisburg: PHMC, 1974); and Kraft, *The Lenape: History, Archaeology, and Ethnography* (Newark: New Jersey Historical Society, 1986). There is abundant room for further study of the Lenapes both before and after contact.

14. Alfred Crosby, "Virgin Soil Epidemics as a Factor in the Aboriginal Depopulation of America," *WMQ* 33 (1976): 289–99.

15. Arguments and estimates range quite broadly regarding the numbers of Natives killed by foreign diseases. See Henry Dobyns, *Their Number Became Thinned: Native American Population Dynamics in Eastern North America* (Knoxville: University of Tennessee Press, 1983); Wilbur R. Jacobs, "The Tip of an Iceberg: Pre-Columbian Indian Demography and Some Implications for Revisionism," *WMQ* 32 (1974): 123–32; John W. Veran and Douglas H. Ubelaker, eds., *Disease and Demography in the Americas* (Washington, D.C.: Smithsonian Institution Press, 1992). Also, different Native groups were affected by diseases at different times. The restructuring of the human landscape of the American southeast may have been initiated by the incursion of the De Soto expedition in the 1540s, whereas the Iroquois in the lower Great Lakes region were relatively isolated from disease until the mid-seventeenth century. See Patricia Galloway, *Choctaw Genesis, 1500–1700* (Lincoln: University of Nebraska Press, 1995), 128–43, and Daniel K. Richter, *The Ordeal of the Longhouse: The Peoples of the Iroquois League in the Era of European Colonization* (Chapel Hill: University of North Carolina Press, 1992), 58–60.

16. Pehr Lindeström, *Geographia Americae, or a Description of Indiae Occidentalis,* 165.

17. See Alfred W. Crosby, Jr., *The Columbian Exchange: Biological and Ecological Consequences of 1492* (Westport, Conn.: Greenwood, 1972), 187–88.

18. See J. H. Elliott, *The Old World and the New, 1492–1650* (Cambridge: Cambridge

University Press, 1970); Stuart Schwartz, ed., *Implicit Understandings: Observing, Reporting, and Reflecting on the Encounters Between Europeans and Other Peoples in the Early Modern Era* (Cambridge: Cambridge University Press, 1994); and Anthony Grafton, *New Worlds, Ancient Texts: The Power of Tradition and the Shock of Discovery* (Cambridge: Harvard University Press, 1992).

19. Genesis 1:26–29. Lynn White, Jr., famously found in these passages the blame for all the modern world's ecological problems in "The Historical Roots of Our Ecological Crisis," in White, *Dynamo and Virgin Reconsidered: Essays in the Dynamism of Western Culture* (Cambridge: MIT Press, 1971). This analysis does not argue for such broadly realized consequences but still acknowledges the real and meaningful significance of such ideas in shaping the thoughts and practices of colonizing Europeans.

20. Useful reconstructions of Native understandings of spiritual relations within the natural world are found in Catherine Albanese, *Nature Religion in Early America: From the Algonkian Indians to the New Age* (Chicago: University of Chicago Press, 1990), chap. 1, and Gregory Evans Dowd, *A Spirited Resistance: The North American Indian Struggle for Unity, 1745–1815* (Baltimore: Johns Hopkins University Press, 1992), chap. 1.

21. See Cronon, *Changes in the Land*, esp. chap. 4. On landholding patterns in New Sweden, see "Returns of Inhabitants and Lands Owned and Improved in Portions of Philadelphia County in 1684," in Henry D. Paxon, *Where Pennsylvania History Began: Sketch and map of a trip from Philadelphia to Tinicum Island . . .* (Philadelphia: George H. Buchanan, 1926), 217–18.

22. See Weslager, *Delaware Indians*, 36–40.

23. Keith Thomas examines how these ideas were important in early modern England in *Man and the Natural World: Changing Attitudes in England, 1500–1800* (London: Allen Lane, 1983), chap. 1.

24. Johnson, trans., *Instruction for Johan Printz*, 88.

25. Ibid.

26. Johan Printz, "Report to the Right Honorable West India Company in Old Sweden, sent from New Sweden, February 20, 1647," in Johnson, trans., *Instruction for Johan Printz*, 129.

27. See Alfred Crosby, *Ecological Imperialism: The Biological Expansion of Europe, 900–1900* (Cambridge: Cambridge University Press, 1986).

28. Printz, "Report, 1647," 135.

29. Johan Papegoja to Pehr Brahe, 15 July 1644, in Johnson, trans., *Instructions for Johan Printz*, 159.

30. The prospect of an archaeological examination of Tinicum Island is detailed in Robert E. King, "Tinicum Island: A Swedish Legacy" (Master's thesis, University of Pennsylvania, 1973).

31. Printz, "Report, 1647," 131.

32. King, "Tinicum Island," 14.

33. Brahe to Printz, 9 Nov. 1643, in Johnson, trans., *Instruction for Johan Printz*, 156.

34. Printz to Axel Oxenstierna, 26 Apr. 1653, in ibid., 187–89.

35. For New England, the standard account of the Pequot War is Alfred A. Cave, *The Pequot War* (Amherst: University of Massachusetts Press, 1996). For a broader context, see Alden T. Vaughan, *New England Frontier: Puritans and Indians, 1620–1675* (New York: W. W. Norton, 1965); and Neal Salisbury, *Manitou and Providence: Indians, Europeans, and the Making of New England, 1500–1643* (New York: Oxford University Press, 1982). An interesting interpretation of Kieft's War in New Netherland is Evan Haefeli, "Kieft's War and the Cultures of Violence in Colonial America," in Michael A. Bellesiles, ed., *Lethal Imagination:*

Violence and Brutality in American History (New York: New York University Press, 1999). For a broader history of the colony, see Oliver A. Rink, *Holland on the Hudson: An Economic and Social History of Dutch New York* (Ithaca: Cornell University Press, 1986). For Virginia, see Karen Ordahl Kupperman, *Indians and English: Facing off in Early America* (Ithaca: Cornell University Press, 2000), 183–86; and Edmund S. Morgan, *American Slavery, American Freedom: The Ordeal of Colonial Virginia* (New York: W. W. Norton, 1975), 92–107.

36. Israel Acrelius, "Account of the Swedish Churches in New Sweden," *NEP*, 72–73.

37. Ibid.

38. Printz to Oxenstierna, 1 Aug. 1651, in Johnson, trans., *Instruction for Johan Printz*, 179–84.

39. Ibid., 182.

40. Johnson, trans., *Instruction for Johan Printz*, 80.

41. Ibid., 80–81.

42. The climate of the Delaware Valley was too cold for the best tobacco and too warm for the thickest, most valuable beaver pelts. Johan Printz, "Relation to the Noble West India Company in Old Sweden, despatched from New Sweden on June 11, Anno 1644," in Johnson, trans., *Instruction for Johan Printz*, 121.

43. Christopher L. Miller and George R. Hamell, "New Perspectives on Indian-White Contact: Cultural Symbols and Colonial Trade," *JAH* 73 (1986): 311–23.

44. Lindeström, *Geographia Americae*, 211.

45. Ibid., 237.

46. Ibid., 357.

47. Ibid., 162–63.

48. See James H. Merrell, *Into the American Woods: Negotiators on the Pennsylvania Frontier* (New York: W. W. Norton, 1999), for analysis of how these tensions influenced Indian-colonial relations in eighteenth-century Pennsylvania.

Chapter 2

1. The "each . . . branches" and "spread . . . ground" quotations are from Thomas Clarkson, *Memoirs of the Public and Private Life of William Penn* (London, 1813), 339–40; all others are from Thomas F. Gordon, *The History of Pennsylvania* (Philadelphia, 1829), 75. Gordon's account drew heavily from Clarkson's, which was the first in print and was mainly a description of Benjamin West's painting. See Helmut von Erffa and Allen Staley, *The Paintings of Benjamin West* (New Haven: Yale University Press, 1986), 207. Benjamin West's "conquest . . . dagger" statement is as quoted in Laura Rigal, "Framing the Fabric: A Luddite Reading of Penn's Treaty with the Indians," *American Literary History* 12 (2000): 557.

2. For an example of a more critical perspective and a bibliography of the debate and consensus on the alleged benevolence of Penn's policy, see Thomas J. Sugrue, "The Peopling and Depeopling of Early Pennsylvania: Indians and Colonists, 1680–1720," *PMHB* 116 (1992): 3–31 and nn1–2. See also Daniel K. Richter, "Onas, the Long Knife: Pennsylvanians and Indians, 1783–1794," in Frederick E. Hoxie, Ronald Hoffman, and Peter J. Albert, eds., *Native Americans and the Early Republic* (Charlottesville: University Press of Virginia, 1999), 126–61; James H. Merrell, *Into the American Woods: Negotiators on the Pennsylvania Frontier* (New York: W. W. Norton, 1999), 28–30; and J. William Frost, "William Penn's Experiment in the Wilderness: Promise and Legend," *PMHB* 107 (1983): 577–605.

3. Ann Uhry Abrams, "Benjamin West's Documentation of Colonial History: William Penn's Treaty with the Indians," *Art Bulletin* 64 (1982): 60; *PWP*, 2:128–29.

4. This chapter's approach is partly drawn from Daniel K. Richter, *The Ordeal of the Longhouse: The Peoples of the Iroquois League in the Era of European Colonization* (Chapel Hill: University of North Carolina Press, 1992); Richard White, *The Middle Ground: Indians, Empires, Republics in the Great Lakes Region, 1650–1815* (Cambridge: Cambridge University Press, 1991); and Patricia Seed, *Ceremonies of Possession in Europe's Conquest of the New World, 1492–1640* (Cambridge: Cambridge University Press, 1995). This approach is also similar to other recent scholarship reflecting the influence of the new cultural history, itself influenced by cultural studies and its linguistic and semiotically inflected approach to resistance, ceremonies, memory, and visual artifacts. See Hoxie et al., eds., *Native Americans and the Early Republic;* Colin G. Calloway, "Introduction: Surviving the Dark Ages," in Calloway, ed., *After King Philip's War: Presence and Persistence in Indian New England* (Hanover, N.H.: University Press of New England, 1997), 1–28; and Jean M. O'Brien, "'Divorced' from the Land: Resistance and Survival of Indian Women in Eighteenth-Century New England," ibid., 144–61.

5. Merrell, *Into the American Woods,* 35–37, 61–62, 106–7; Hannah Benner Roach, "The Planting of Philadelphia: A Seventeenth Century Real Estate Development," *PMHB* 92 (1968): 3–47; T. J. C. Brasser, "The Costal Algonkians: People of the First Frontiers," in Eleanor Burke Leacock and Nancy Oestreich Lurie, eds., *North American Indians in Historical Perspective* (New York: Random House, 1971), 66–78.

6. Ives Goddard, "The Delaware Jargon," in Carol E. Hoffecker et al., eds., *New Sweden in America* (Newark: University of Delaware Press, 1999), 137–39.

7. Robert Juet, *Juet's Journal: The Voyage of the Half Moon from 4 April to 7 November 1609,* ed. Robert M. Lunny (Newark, N.J.: n.p., 1959), 28; David Pietersz De Vries, "From the 'Korte Historiael Ende Journaels Aenteyckeninge,'" *NEP,* 7–8; Amandus Johnson, *The Swedish Settlements on the Delaware: Their History and Relation to the Indians, Dutch and English: 1638–1664,* 2 vols. (New York: Appleton, 1911), 170–71.

8. Thomas Campanius Holm, *Description of the Province of New Sweden,* trans. Peter S. Du Ponceau (Philadelphia, 1834), 144; Goddard, "Delaware Jargon," 142–44.

9. De Vries, "Korte Historiael," *NEP,* 7–49; Amandus Johnson, trans., *The Instruction for Johan Printz, Governor of New Sweden* (Philadelphia: Swedish Colonial Society, 1930), 231, 273–75; Gunlög Fur, "Cultural Confrontation of Two Fronts: Swedish-Lenape and Swedish-Saamis Relations in the Seventeenth Century" (Ph.D. diss., University of Oklahoma, 1993), 46; "Affidavit of Four Men from the Key of Calmar" *NEP,* 87–88. On use rights, see Peter Thomas, "In the Maelstrom of Change, The Indian Trade and Cultural Process in the Middle Connecticut River Valley: 1635–1665" (Ph.D. diss., University of Massachusetts, Amherst, 1979), 133–44.

10. Francis Jennings, "Glory, Death, and Transfiguration: The Susquehannock Indians in the Seventeenth Century," *Proceedings of the American Philosophical Society* 112 (1968): 17–20. See also Thomas, "In the Maelstrom of Change," 285–329.

11. Johnson, *New Sweden,* 408; Johnson, ed., *Instruction for Printz,* 272.

12. Johnson, ed., *Instruction for Printz,* 273.

13. Johnson, *New Sweden,* 375–76; Johnson, ed., *Instruction for Printz,* 78–80; Stellan Dahlgren and Hans Norman, *The Rise and Fall of New Sweden: Governor Johan Risingh's Journal 1654–1655 in Its Historical Context* (Stockholm: Uppsala University, 1988), 66–67.

14. Johnson, *New Sweden,* 436–37.

15. Regula Trenkwalder Schonenberger, *Lenape Women, Matriliny, and the Colonial Encounter, Resistance, and Erosion of Power (c. 1600–1876): An Excursus in Feminist Anthropology* (Bern: P. Lang, 1991), 161–68, 172–73; Barry C. Kent, *Susquehanna's Indians* (Harrisburg: PHMC, 1984), 34–35; Jennings, "Glory, Death, and Transfiguration," 15–53; Marshall Becker, "Lenape Population at the Time of European Contact: Estimating Native Numbers in the

Lower Delaware Valley," *Proceedings of the American Philosophical Society* 133 (1989): 112–19; Dahlgren and Norman, *Rise and Fall*, 207; Goddard, "Delaware Jargon," 213–39; Anthony F. C. Wallace, "Women, Land, and Society: Three Aspects of Aboriginal Delaware Life," *Pennsylvania Archaeologist*, no. 17 (1947): 1–35; Robert Steven Grumet, "Sunksquaws, Shamans, and Tradeswomen," in Mona Etienne and Elenor Leacock, eds., *Women and Colonization: Anthropological Perspectives* (New York: Praeger, 1980), 43–62; C. A. Weslager, *Delaware Indians: A History* (New Brunswick, N.J.: Rutgers University Press, 1972), 63; Holm, *Description of New Sweden*, 145–46.

16. Schonenberger, *Lenape Women*, 154–83; Thomas Young, "The Relation of Thomas Young," *NEP*, 43; Wallace, "Women, Land, and Society," 13; Kathleen M. Brown, "The Anglo-Algonquian Gender Frontier," in Nancy Shoemaker, ed., *Negotiators of Change: Historical Perspectives on Native American Women* (New York: Routledge, 1995), 27–31.

17. Dahlgren and Norman, *Rise and Fall*, 175.

18. Peter Lindeström, *Geographia Americae with an Account of the Delaware Indians*, ed. and trans. Amandus Johnson (Philadelphia: Swedish Colonial Society, 1925), 126–29 175, 177, 179 (quotation p. 129).

19. Ibid., 128–31.

20. *NEP*, 112n; Johnson, *New Sweden*, 30–35.

21. Hans Norman, "The New Sweden Colony and the Continued Existence of Swedish and Finnish Ethnicity," in Hoffecker et al., eds., *New Sweden in America*, 189–90; William Whitehead et al., eds., *Documents Relating to the Colonial, Revolutionary, and Post-Revolutionary History of the State of New Jersey* (publisher varies, 1880–1945), 1st ser., 1:72–73; Victor Hugo Paltsits, ed., *Minutes of the Executive Council of the Province of New York: Administration of Francis Lovelace, 1668–1673* (Albany: State of New York, 1910), 2:5, 502; Jennings "Glory, Death, and Transfiguration," 30.

22. Norman, "New Sweden Colony," 189–90; Leiby, *Dutch and Swedish Settlements*, 91.

23. For biographical information and activities of Peter Rambo, Peter Cock, Lars Cock, Israel Helme, and Henry Jacob Falkinburg, see Johnson, *New Sweden*, 462–63; Smith, *History of West New Jersey*, 94; Whitehead et al., eds., *Documents Relating to New Jersey*, 1st ser., 1:114–15, 182–83, 21:399, 403, 412, 431, 513, 649, 671, 684, 23:221–22; Charles T. Gehring, ed., *New York Colonial Manuscripts: Dutch*, vols. 20–21, *Delaware Papers (English Period): A Collection of Documents Pertaining to the Regulation of Affairs on the Delaware, 1664–1682*, New York Historical Manuscript Series (Baltimore: Genealogical Pub. Co., 1977), 273; Frank H. Stewart, *Indians of Southern New Jersey* (Port Washington, N.Y.: Kennikat Press, 1973), 60; Goddard, "Delaware Jargon," 144–45; *PWP*, 2:264, 268; Smith, *History of New Jersey*, 94; John Frederick Lewis, Jr., *The History of an Old Philadelphia Land Title: 208 South Fourth Street* (Philadelphia: Patterson and White, 1934), 42, 45.

24. Paltsits, ed., *Minutes of Executive Council of New York*, 2:501–2; Jennings, "Glory, Death, and Transfiguration," 30, 39–42; Whitehead, ed., *Documents Relating to the Colonial History of the State of New Jersey*, 182–83.

25. Francis Jennings, "Miquon's Passing: Indian-European Relations in Colonial Pennsylvania, 1674 to 1755" (Ph.D. diss., University of Pennsylvania, 1965), 54; Dahlgren and Norman, *Rise and Fall*, 121.

26. Barry Levy, "From 'Dark Corners' to American Domesticity: The British Social Context of the Welsh and Cheshire Quakers' Familial Revolution in Pennsylvania, 1657–1685," in Richard S. Dunn and Mary Maples Dunn, eds., *The World of William Penn* (Philadelphia: University of Pennsylvania Press, 1986), 215–39; Bartlett Burleigh James and J. Franklin Jameson, eds., *Journal of Jasper Danckaerts, 1679–1680* (New York: C. Scribner's Sons, 1913), 156; P. Richard Metcalf, "Who Should Rule at Home? Native American Politics and Indian-White

Relations," *JAH* 61 (1974): 651–65; Erik Johnson, "Some by Flatterings Others by Threatenings" (Ph.D. diss., University of Massachusetts, Amherst, 1993), 43, 69–73, 78–85, 189–96.

27. Hugh Barbour and Arthur O. Roberts, eds., *Early Quaker Writings: 1650–1670* (Grand Rapids, Mich.: Eerdmans, 1973), 425–26 (quotation from p. 495); C. A. Weslager, *The English on the Delaware: 1610–1682* (New Brunswick, N.J.: Rutgers University Press, 1967), 231–32; Samuel Smith, *The History of the Colony of Nova-Caesaria, or New-Jersey* (Burlington, N.J., 1765), 92–105; Thomas Budd, *Good Order Established in Pennsylvania & New Jersey* ([Philadelphia], 1685); Stewart, *Indians of Southern New Jersey*, 60–61.

28. Budd, *Good Order Established*, 32–33.

29. James and Jameson, eds., *Journal of Danckaerts*, 139, 149, 159.

30. Gabriel Thomas, "An Historical and Geographical Account of Pensilvania and of West-New-Jersey 1698," *NEP*, 342–43; James and Jameson, eds., *Journal of Danckaerts*, 159–60.

31. *The True Account of the Dying Words of Ockanikon* (London, 1682), reprinted in *Journal of the Friends Historical Society* 9 (1909): 164–66.

32. Budd, *Good Order Established*, 29–32; Gehring, ed., *Delaware Papers*, 75, 79, 273; Frank H. Stewart, *Notes on Old Gloucester County, New Jersey* ([Camden]: New Jersey Society of Pennsylvania, 1917), 262–63; *PWP*, 2:263, 264.

33. *Dying Words of Ockanikon*, 166.

34. Budd, *Good Order Established*, 32.

35. William Penn, "To the Kings of the Indians," 18 Aug. 1681, *PWP*, 2:128–29; Penn, "Additional Instructions to William Markham," 28 Oct. 1681, ibid., 129; "Penn to The Committee of Trade," 14 Aug. 1683, ibid., 435.

36. [Edward Byllynge], "Present State of West-Jersey," *NEP*, 191–92; William Penn, "Some Account of Pennsylvania," *NEP*, 202–6; Dahlgren, "The Crown of Sweden and the New Sweden Company," in Hoffecker et al., eds., *New Sweden in America*, 54–55; Peter Laslett, *The World We Have Lost* (New York: Scribner's, 1965), 22–52; Charles Wilson, *England's Apprenticeship, 1603–1763* (New York: St. Martin's Press, 1965), 226–39; David Armitage, *The Ideological Origins of the British Empire* (Cambridge: Cambridge University Press, 2000), 3–4, 146–49, 168–69.

37. Penn, "Letter to the Free Society of Traders," *NEP*, 230.

38. Endy, *William Penn and Early Quakerism*, 324 (quotation); Beatty, *William Penn*, 268–69; Anthony F. C. Wallace, "New Religious Beliefs Among the Delaware Indians, 1600–1900," *Southwestern Journal of Anthropology* 12 (1956): 1–21.

39. *PA*, 4th ser., 1:21–22.

40. Pennsylvania deeds, *PWP*, 2:261–69 (quotations); James and Jameson, eds., *Journal of Danckaerts*, 156; Weslager, *Delaware Indians*, 162.

41. Penn, "A Further Account of Pennsylvania," *NEP*, 260; Carl Bridenbaugh, "The Old and New Societies of the Delaware Valley in the Seventeenth Century," *PMHB* 100 (1976): 162–63; "Letter of Thomas Paschall," *NEP*, 254.

42. Nicholas More to Penn, 1 Dec. 1684, *PWP*, 2:608; *PA*, 1st ser., 1:66.

43. William Penn to Thomas Holme, 8 June 1685, in Weslager, *Delaware Indians*, 169; *PA*, 1st ser., 1:62.

44. Penn, "Further Account," 276.

45. "A Humble Remonstrance & Address of several, the Adventurers, Free holders & Inhabitants and others therein concerned" in Roach, "The Planting of Philadelphia," *PMHB* 92 (1968): 187.

46. *PWP*, 3:106–7, 112–13; *MPCP*, 1:162, 181–82, 187–88; Robert Proud, *History of Pennsylvania*, 337–38, notes rumors of a similar incident in 1688 that was resolved without bloodshed by a conference.

47. Penn, *Some Proposals for a Second Settlement* (London, 1690), quoted in Jennings, "Miquon's Passing," 89 ; Weslager, *Delaware Indians,* 169–70.

48. *PA,* 1st ser., 1:88, 91–92, 92–93, 95, 116–17, quotation from pp. 116–17 (italics added).

49. "Letter of Paschall," 250–54; Penn, "Further Account," 276.

50. Francis Daniel Pastorius, "Circumstantial Geographical Description of Pennsylvania . . . 1700," *NEP,* 409–10; "Letter of Paschall," 250–54; William Markham to William Penn, 22 Aug. 1686, *PWP,* 3:107; Esposito, "Indian-White Relations," 234–35; Marshall Joseph Becker, "Hannah Freeman: An Eighteenth-Century Lenape Living and Working Among Colonial Farmers," *PMHB* 114 (1990): 249–69; William Markham to Penn, 25 June 1696, *PWP,* 3:451, 453; Marshall Joseph Becker, "Lenape Population at the Time of Contact: Estimating Native Numbers in the Lower Delaware Valley," *Proceedings of the American Philosophical Society* 133 (1989): 112–22; "John Ladd's Account with Jeremy the Indian" in Stewart, *Indians of Southern Jersey,* 16–18; Smith, *History of New Jersey,* 95–96.

51. See Henry J. Cadbury, "Caleb Pusey's Account of Pennsylvania," *Quaker History* 64 (spring 1975): 49, for a memoir by a man acquainted with Penn who mentions an early meeting with Lenape leaders.

52. *PWP,* 4:51.

53. *PA,* 1st ser., 1:364, 370–71, 392, 393, 413.

54. Ibid., 431, 442–45, 467–68.

Chapter 3

1. Peter Lindeström, *Geographia Americae with an Account of the Delaware Indians, Based on Surveys and Notes Made in 1654–1656,* trans. Amandus Johnson (Philadelphia: Swedish Colonial Historical Society, 1925), 207–9.

2. On Quaker dreams, see Carla Gerona, "Stairways to Heaven: A Cultural Study of Early American Quaker Dreams" (Ph.D. diss., Johns Hopkins University, 1998); Gerona, "Mapping Ann Moore's Secrets: Dream Production in Late-Eighteenth-Century Quaker Culture," *Journal of Feminist Studies in Religion* 16 (fall 2000): 43–70; and Phyllis Mack, *Visionary Women: Ecstatic Prophecy in Seventeenth-Century England* (Berkeley: University of California Press, 1992). For a Quaker perspective, see Howard Brinton, "Dreams of Quaker Journalists," in Brinton, ed., *Byways in Quaker History: A Collection of Historical Essays by Colleagues and Friends of William I. Hull* (Wallingford, Pa: Pendle Hill, 1944), 230. On Quaker spirituality in general, see J. William Frost, *The Quaker Family in Colonial America* (New York: St. Martin's Press, 1973), and Howard H. Brinton, *Friends for 300 Years: The History and Beliefs of the Society of Friends Since George Fox Started the Quaker Movement* (Wallingford, Pa: Pendle Hill, 1994).

3. On dreams in Iroquois society, see esp. Anthony Wallace, "Dreams and the Wishes of the Soul: A Type of Psychoanalytic Theory Among the Seventeenth Century Iroquois," *American Anthropologist* 60 (1958): 234–48. For a comparative discussion of dreams among Indians and Europeans, see Natalie Zemon Davis, "Iroquois Women, European Women," in Margo Hendricks and Patricia Parker, eds., *Women, "Race," and Writing: In the Early Modern Period* (New York: Routledge, 1994), 243–58.

4. On Indian and Quaker relations, see Rayner W. Kelsey, *Friends and the Indians, 1655–1917* (Philadelphia: Associated Committee of Friends on Indian Affairs, 1917); and Diane Brodatz Rothenberg, "Friends Like These: An Ethnohistorical Analysis of the Interaction Between Allegany Senecas and Quakers, 1798–1823" (Ph.D. diss, City University of New York, 1976). On Indian and Euro-American relations in Pennsylvania, see James Merrell, *Into the*

American Woods: Negotiators on the Pennsylvania Frontier (New York: W. W. Norton, 1999). On Quaker pacifism, see Peter Brock, *Pioneers of the Peaceable Kingdom* (Princeton: Princeton University Press, 1972).

5. See, e.g., Phyllis Mack, *Visionary Women: Ecstatic Prophesy in Seventeenth-Century England* (Berkeley: University of California Press, 1992); Mechal Sobel, *Teach Me Dreams: The Search for Self in the Revolutionary Era* (Princeton: Princeton University Press, 2000); Sobel, "The Revolution in Selves: Black and White Inner Aliens," in Ronald Hoffman, Mechal Sobel, and Fredrika J. Teute, eds., *Through a Glass Darkly: Reflections on Personal Identity in Early America* (Chapel Hill: University of North Carolina Press, 1997), 163–205; and Morton Kelsey, *God, Dreams, and Revelation: A Christian Interpretation of Dreams* (1968; Minneapolis: Augsburg-Fortress, 1991).

6. See Calvin Martin, "The Metaphysics of Writing Indian-White History," in Martin, ed., *The American Indian and the Problem of History* (New York: Oxford University Press, 1988). Other overviews of Native American historiography include James Merrell, "Some Thoughts on Colonial Historians and American Indians," *WMQ* 46 (1989): 94–119; and Daniel K. Richter, "Whose Indian History?" *WMQ* 50 (1993): 379–93. Some of the most important recent work on America in the European consciousness includes Tzvetan Todorov, *The Conquest of America: The Question of the Other*, trans. Richard Howard (New York: Harper, 1984); Anthony Pagden, *The Fall of Natural Man: The American Indian and the Origins of Comparative Ethnology* (Cambridge: Cambridge University Press, 1982); and Stephen Greenblatt, *Marvelous Possessions: The Wonder of the New World* (Chicago: University of Chicago Press, 1991). A useful collection of essays is Karen Ordahl Kupperman's *America in European Consciousness, 1493–1750* (Chapel Hill: University of North Carolina Press, 1995). A good collection of articles that focuses on cultural exchanges is Andrew R. L. Cayton and Fredrika Teute, eds., *Contact Points: American Frontiers from the Mohawk Valley to the Mississippi, 1750–1830* (Chapel Hill: University of North Carolina Press, 1998).

7. See Anthony F. C. Wallace, "Revitalization Movements," *American Anthropologist* 58 (1956): 264–81; and Wallace, *The Death and Rebirth of the Seneca* (New York: Alfred A. Knopf, 1972).

8. Richard White, *The Middle Ground: Indians, Empires, and Republics in the Great Lakes Region, 1650–1815* (Cambridge: Cambridge University Press, 1991), 330, xi; Jane Merritt, "Dreaming of the Savior's Blood: Moravians and the Indian Great Awakening in Pennsylvania," *WMQ* 54 (Oct. 1997): 723–46. See also Gregory Evans Dowd, *A Spirited Resistance: The North American Indian Struggle for Unity, 1745–1815* (Baltimore: Johns Hopkins University Press, 1992); Ruth Benedict, "The Vision in Plains Culture," *American Anthropologist* 24 (1992): 1–23; Lee Irwin, *The Dream-Seekers: Native American Visionary Traditions of the Great Plains* (Norman: University of Oklahoma Press, 1994); Barbara Tedlock, *Dreaming: Anthropological and Psychological Interpretations* (Cambridge: Cambridge University Press, 1987); and Hugh Brody, *Maps and Dreams* (New York: Pantheon, 1982).

9. I have uncovered about four hundred mentions of dreams and visions in Quaker journals, commonplace books, letters, and other texts from the late seventeen hundreds to the early nineteen hundreds. More than half of these are detailed narratives of visionary dreams, but only about twenty concern Native Americans. In describing dreams or visions this chapter follows the language of the sources. If a source describes a "dream," I call it a dream. If a source describes a "vision," I call it a vision.

10. In addition to Mechal Sobel's and my own work, see Ann Kirschner, "'Tending to Edify and Instruct': Published Narratives of Spiritual Dreams in the Early Republic," *Early American Studies* 1, no. 1 (spring 2003): 198–229. For other studies of dreams in early American culture, see Merle Curti, "The American Exploration of Dreams and Dreamers," *Journal*

of the History of Ideas 27 (1966): 391–416; David D. Hall, *World of Wonder, Days of Judgment: Popular Religious Beliefs in Early New England* (New York: Alfred A. Knopf, 1989), 213–38; Jesse Lemisch, "Listening to the 'Inarticulate': William Widger's Dream and the Loyalties of American Revolutionary Seamen in British Prisons," *Journal of Social History* 3 (1969–70): 1–29; Christine Heyrman, *Southern Cross: The Beginnings of the Bible Belt* (New York: Alfred A. Knopf, 1997); Jon Butler, *Awash in a Sea of Faith: Christianizing the American People* (Cambridge: Harvard University Press, 1990), esp. 184, 186, 222–23, and 238–39. For recent overviews of religion in early America that stress its multifaceted nature, see Butler, *Awash in a Sea of Faith;* and Charles L. Cohen, "The Post-Puritan Paradigm of Early American Religious History," *WMQ* 54 (1997): 695–722.

11. George Fox, *The Journal of George Fox,* ed. Norman Penney, 2 vols. (Cambridge: Cambridge University Press, 1911), 2:251. The vision is also in William S. Simmons, *Spirit of the New England Tribes: Indian History and Folklore, 1629–1984* (Hanover, N.H.: University Press of New England, 1986), 68. On George Fox and Indians, see Kelsey, *Friends and the Indians,* 19–23. A good secondary account of Fox's voyage is H. Larry Ingle, *First Among Friends: George Fox and the Creation of Quakerism* (New York: Oxford University Press, 1994), 231–42. First encounter dreams and prophecies can be found in Ella Elizabeth Clark, *Indian Legends of Canada* (Toronto: McClelland and Stewart, 1960), 151–52; James Axtell, *After Columbus: Essays in the Ethnohistory of Colonial North America* (New York: Oxford University Press, 1988), 129–34; Simmons, *Spirit of the New England Tribes,* 66–67, 71–72; Todorov, *Conquest of America,* 63–97; George Henry Loskiel, *History of the Mission of the United Brethren Among the Indians in North America,* trans. George Ignatius La Trobe (London, 1794), 123–24; and James P. Ronda, "Generations of Faith: The Christian Indians of Martha's Vineyard," *WMQ* 38 (1980): 369–70.

12. Roger Williams provides an interesting comparison. Although he details the Indian practice of visionary dreaming, he does so in a factual and descriptive (even ethnographic) manner that does not accord divine "truth" to dreams (*A Key into the Language of America* [London, 1643], 19–20). A more typical view is that of the Rev. Joseph Fish, who thought that Indians who paid attention to visions were simply misguided. See William S. Simmons and Cheryl L. Simmons, eds., *Old Light on Separate Ways: The Narragansett Diary of Joseph Fish, 1765–1776* (Hanover, N.H.: University Press of New England, 1982), 93–94.

13. For the view that Indians were poor, see [John Burnyeat], *The Truth Exalted in the Writings of that Eminent and Faithful Servant of Christ John Burnyeat Collected Into this Ensuing Volume as a Memorial to his Faithful Labours in and for the Truth* (London, 1691), 45. On Delaware Indians, see C. A. Weslager, *The Delaware Indians: A History* (New Brunswick, N.J.: Rutgers University Press, 1972), and Paul A. W. Wallace, *Indians in Pennsylvania* (Harrisburg: PHMC, 1964).

14. Fox, *Journal,* 2:250–51. [Burnyeat], *Truth Exalted,* 49. For George Bishop's account, see Bishop, *New England Judged by the Spirit of the Lord* (1703; Philadelphia: T. W. Stuckey, 1885), 36–38.

15. Thomas Thompson Jr., A Vision, 28 Nov. 1702, Manuscripts, Friends Historical Library, Swarthmore College, Swarthmore, Pa.

16. Usually attributed to Samuel Clarke, one commonplace book identified it as N. Davis's dream, "A Friend in New England." See [Samuel Clarke], *Strange and Remarkable Swanzey Vision* (Salem, Mass., 1776), 5. The manuscript version attributed to N. Davis is "A Dream or Vision of a Friend in New England the 21st Day of the 11th Month 1734," in Milcah Martha Moore, Notebook of Milcah Martha Moore, QCHC.

17. For an example of how Puritans believed Indian wars represented God's judgment, see Increase Mather, *A Brief History of the Warr with the Indians,* in Richard Slotkin and

James K. Folsom, eds., *So Dreadfull a Judgement: Puritan Responses to King Philip's War, 1676–1677* (Middletown, Conn.: Wesleyan University Press, 1978), and Mary Rowlandson, *The Sovereignty and Goodness of God*, ed. Neal Salisbury (Boston: Bedford Books, 1997).

18. The best study of Quakers in Massachusetts is Carla Gardina Pestana, *Quakers and Baptists in Colonial Massachusetts* (Cambridge: Cambridge University Press, 1991). For an account of the historiographical tradition following the Quaker executions, see Pestana, "The Quaker Executions as Myth and History," *JAH* 80 (1993): 441–69.

19. William Penn, "To the King of the Indians," in Jean Soderlund, ed., *William Penn and the Founding of Pennsylvania* (Philadelphia: HSP, 1983), 86–88. See also chapter 2, above.

20. [Thomas Chalkley], *Journal* (Philadelphia, 1749), 49–50. On Conestoga during this period, see Merrell, *Into the American Woods*, 83, 106–27.

21. Wallace, "Dreams and Wishes of the Soul," 235.

22. [Chalkley], *Journal*, 49–50.

23. Ibid., 50. A good account of this period is Francis Jennings, *The Ambiguous Iroquois Empire: The Covenant Chain Confederation of Indian Tribes with English Colonies from Its Beginnings to the Lancaster Treaty of 1744* (New York: W. W. Norton, 1984), 223–367. Also see Sydney V. James, *A People Among Peoples: Quaker Benevolence in Eighteenth-Century America* (Cambridge: Harvard University Press, 1963), 89.

24. On Weiser, see Joseph S. Walton, *Conrad Weiser and the Indian Policy of Colonial Pennsylvania* (New York: Arno Press, 1971); and Paul A. W. Wallace, *Conrad Weiser: Friend of Colonist and Mohawk* (Philadelphia: University of Pennsylvania Press, 1945); Conrad Weiser to Christopher Sau[e]r, Dec. 1746, *PMHB* 1 (1877): 319; Conrad Weiser, Memorandum, 1:33, Conrad Weiser Papers, HSP.

25. For an account of this dream, see Walton, *Conrad Weiser and Indian Policy*, 385; and Wallace, *Conrad Weiser*, 151–52.

26. In New York, for example, William Johnson supposedly exchanged a scarlet uniform for five hundred acres of Mohawk Chief Hendrick's land based on their dream exchanges. See Samuel G. Drake, *The Book of the Indians of North America* (Boston, 1833), 24–25. Richard Peters, a Penn family secretary, said that if an Indian dreamed of some impending disaster and requested rum as a preventative, the request should be met (Merrell, *Into the American Woods*, 271).

27. For the reformation of Quaker religion during the Seven Years' War, see Jack Marietta, *The Reformation of American Quakerism, 1748–1783* (Philadelphia: University of Pennsylvania Press, 1984), esp. 150–86.

28. Ann Whitall, Diary, 16 Mar. 1760, QCHC.

29. Substance of conferences between several Quakers in Philadelphia and the heads of the six Indian Nations, QCHC. For an account of the Seven Years' War as it affected the Quakers and Indians, see Francis Jennings, *Empire of Fortune: Crown, Colonies, and Tribes in the Seven Years War in America* (New York: W. W. Norton, 1988); and Theodore Thayer, *Israel Pemberton: King of the Quakers* (Philadelphia: University of Pennsylvania Press, 1943). On the Friendly Association, see Theodore Thayer, "The Friendly Association," *PMHB* 67 (1943): 356–76.

30. John Churchman, *An Account of the Gospel Labours and Christian Experiences of a Faithful Minister of Christ John Churchman, Late of Nottingham in Pennsylvania, Deceased* (Philadelphia, 1779), 185–86.

31. Churchman, *Account*, 183–84. For discussions of treaties, see Merrell, *Into the American Woods*, 225–30; and Jennings, *Empire of Fortune*, 341–48. On Teedyuscung, see Anthony F. C. Wallace, *King of the Delawares: Teedyuscung, 1700–1763* (Philadelphia: University of Pennsylvania Press, 1949).

32. Churchman, *Account,* 186.

33. Ibid.

34. Phillips P. Moulton, ed., *The Journal and Major Essays of John Woolman* (Richmond, Ind.: Friends United Press, 1989), 297–98, 124–37.

35. John W. Jordan, ed., "Journal of James Kenny, 1761–63," *PMHB* 37 (1913): 1–47, 152–201, esp. pp. 163, 169, 184; James Kenny, "Journal to the Westward, 1758–59," ed. Jordan, ibid., 395–449.

36. Kenny, "Journal to the Westward," 434; Kenny, "Journal," 153.

37. Kenny, "Journal," 176–77.

38. On Neolin, see White, *Middle Ground,* 283; Dowd, *Spirited Resistance,* 128–29; Charles Hunter, "The Delaware Nativist Revival of the Mid-Eighteenth Century," *Ethnohistory* 18 (1971): 39–49; and Kenny, "Journal," 176.

39. Kenny, "Journal," 184. See also Dowd, *Spirited Resistance,* 1.

40. Kenny, "Journal," 191, 40, 191–92.

41. Ibid., 193.

Chapter 4

1. Gunlög Fur, " 'Some Women Are Wiser Than Some Men': Gender and Native American History," in Nancy Shoemaker, ed., *Clearing a Path: Theorizing the Past in Native American Studies* (New York: Routledge, 2002), 84–85.

2. Granville John Penn presented the belt to the Historical Society of Pennsylvania in 1857, where it remained until the HSP transferred its artifacts to Philadelphia's Atwater Kent Museum in 2001 (Nicholas B. Wainwright, *One Hundred Years of Collecting by the Historical Society of Pennsylvania, 1824–1974* [Philadelphia: HSP, 1974], 6).

3. In 1711, Isabelle Montour and her kin produced six hundred wampum belts in New York. Vetch Account, Aug. 1711, Peter Van Brugh and Hendrick Hansen, Account Book for the Vetch Expedition Against Canada, Aug. 1711, New-York Historical Society, New York.

4. Here I follow the method of reconstructing women's work found in Helen C. Rountree, "Powhatan Indian Women: The People Captain John Smith Barely Saw," *Ethnohistory* 45 (1998): 17–18. See also Barbara A. Mann, "The Fire at Onondaga: Wampum as Proto-Writing," *Akwesasne Notes,* n.s. 1, no. 1 (1995): 40–48. For an archaeologist's imaginative use of evidence to reconstruct Native women's work, see Janet D. Spector, *What This Awl Means: Feminist Archaeology at a Wahpeton Dakota Village* (St. Paul: University of Minnesota Press, 1993).

5. For the recent evolution of historians' conceptions about the Anglo-American frontier, see James H. Merrell, "Indians and Colonists in Early America," in Bernard Bailyn and Philip D. Morgan, eds., *Strangers Within the Realm: Cultural Margins of the First British Empire* (Chapel Hill: University of North Carolina Press, 1991), 125; and Kathleen M. Brown, "Brave New Worlds: Women's and Gender History," *WMQ* 50 (1993): 317–21. I have expanded Brown's notion of a gender frontier to include social and personal interaction in general.

6. Laurel Thatcher Ulrich describes patterns of work and social interaction, primarily among Euro-American women, in *Good Wives: Image and Reality in the Lives of Women in Northern New England, 1650–1750* (New York: Alfred A. Knopf, 1982); and *A Midwife's Tale: The Life of Martha Ballard, Based on Her Diary, 1785–1812* (New York: Alfred A. Knopf, 1990).

7. Historians of the gender frontier have dealt with intermarriage. See Jennifer S. H. Brown, *Strangers in Blood: Fur Trade Company Families in Indian Country* (Vancouver: University of British Columbia Press, 1980); Jacqueline Peterson, "Métis Society and Culture in

the Great Lakes Region" (Ph.D. diss., University of Chicago, 1981); Jacqueline Peterson and Jennifer S. H. Brown, *The New Peoples: Being and Becoming Métis in North America* (Lincoln: University of Nebraska Press, 1985); Lucy Eversvald Murphy, "To Live Among Us: Accommodation, Gender, and Conflict in the Great Lakes Region, 1769–1832," in Andrew R. L. Cayton and Fredrika I. Teute, eds., *Contact Points: American Frontiers from the Mohawk Valley to the Mississippi, 1750–1830* (Chapel Hill: University of North Carolina Press, 1998), 270–303; Susan Sleeper-Smith, "Women, Kin, and Catholicism: New Perspectives on the Fur Trade," *Ethnohistory* 47 (2000): 423–52.

8. Nancy Shoemaker, "Categories," in Shoemaker, ed., *Clearing a Path*, 55–57.

9. Joan Kelly, "Did Women Have a Renaissance?" in Renate Bridenthal and Claudia Koonz, eds., *Becoming Visible: Women in European History* (New York: Houghton Mifflin, 1977); Joan Hoff-Wilson, "The Illusion of Change: Women and the American Revolution," in Alfred F. Young, ed., *The American Revolution: Explorations in the History of American Radicalism* (DeKalb: Northern Illinois University Press, 1976); Richard White, *The Middle Ground: Indians, Empires, and Republics in the Great Lakes Region, 1650–1815* (Cambridge: Cambridge University Press, 1991).

10. Rountree, "Powhatan Indian Women," 2.

11. Laurel Thatcher Ulrich provides a model for such imaginative use of interdisciplinary tools. She writes of a seventeenth-century Algonkian basket and the story behind its acquisition by an English family: "Interpreting such an object requires both imagination and skepticism, imagination to see new possibilities in an old story, but skepticism about its placid surface." *The Age of Homespun: Objects and Stories in the Creation of an American Myth* (New York: Alfred A. Knopf, 2001), 43–44.

12. John W. Jordan, ed., "Spangenberg's Notes of Travel to Onondaga in 1745," *PMHB* 2 (1878): 429; Journal of Martin Mack, 19 Sept. 1745, 28: 217: 12b, MAB.

13. I have told her story more fully in "The 'Celebrated Madame Montour': 'Interpretress' Across Early American Frontiers," *Explorations in Early American Culture* 4 (2000): 81–112.

14. Jacqueline Peterson has traced the "ethnogenesis" of the *métis* in the Great Lakes region of the late seventeenth and early eighteenth centuries. The roots of the *Métis* nation of Canada lay there, but descendents of these early *métis* "became" entirely French or entirely Indian, especially those within the United States ("Prelude to Red River: A Social Portrait of the Great Lakes Métis," *Ethnohistory* 25 [1978]: 47).

15. Besides her two documented marriages, Isabelle Montour was rumored to have had liaisons with two other French men and an Ottawa chief, Outoutagan or Jean Le Blanc. Her sisters married French traders and interpreters; one sister, Marguerite, may later have married a Miami. Their older brother married a Sokoki woman and, later, an Algonquin; the younger brother married an Abenaki. Michel Germaneau, Isabelle's son by her first marriage, married the daughter of a French trader. Her son Andrew, whose father was probably Carandowana, married first a Lenape and then an Oneida woman. Catherine and Esther Montour, who were sometimes called Madame Montour's granddaughters, married Lenape and Seneca chiefs, respectively. James P. LaLone, "Montour Family," unpaginated typescript in author's possession, 1989; Alison Duncan Hirsch, "Madame Montour," 87–90, 93, 97, 101.

16. Cadwallader Colden, "Letters on Smith's History of New York," in *Collections of New York-Historical Society* 1 (1868): 200; Robert Hunter to Kilian van Rensalaer, 15 May 1712, Hunter MSS, New-York Historical Society, New York.

17. *NYCD*, 5:268, 273.

18. See James Hijiya, "Why the West Is Lost," *WMQ* 51 (1994): 279n; and the response by Paul Boyer et al., ibid., 721.

19. Nancy Hagedorn, "'A Friend to Go Between Them': Interpreters Among the Iroquois, 1664–1775" (Ph.D. diss., College of William and Mary, 1995).

20. *PA*, 2d ser., 1:231; *MPCP*, 3:176, 200.

21. Evelyn A. Benson, "The Huguenot Letorts: First Christian Family on the Conestoga," *Journal of the Lancaster County Historical Society* 65 (1961): 92–105; *MPCP*, 1:396–97; Penn Letters and Ancient Documents, 1:248, American Philosophical Society, Philadelphia, Pa.; Simone Vincens, "French Pioneers in Lancaster County," *Journal of the Lancaster County Historical Society* 85 (1981): 152–57; *PWP*, 4:154–57.

22. Joseph H. Coates, ed., "Journal of Isaac Zane to Wyoming, 1758," *PMHB* 30 (1906): 419; Jordan, ed., "Spangenberg's Notes," 424; William C. Reichel, ed., *Memorials of the Moravian Church* (Philadelphia: J. B. Lippincott, 1870), 1:133.

23. *MPCP*, 2:388.

24. John Richardson, *An Account of the Life of . . . John Richardson* (Philadelphia: Friends' Book Store, 1880), 132–40.

25. *MPCP*, 3:129.

26. Petition to the Governor and Council and Accounts of James Le Tort, October 1704, Logan Papers, 11:4, HSP; *PWP*, 4:49–53, 98–99.

27. "The Journal of Christian Frederick Post" [Oct. 1758–Jan. 1759], in Reuben Gold Thwaites, ed., *Early Western Travels, 1748–1846* (Cleveland: A. H. Clark, 1904), 1:238.

28. Cadwallader Collection–George Croghan Section, box 2, 1768 Accounts, folder 1; box 3, 1773 Accounts, folder 1; Accounts, n.d., folder 11, HSP.

29. *MPCP*, 3:172, 200.

30. Ibid., 116–17.

31. Mack, Journal, 19 Sept. 1745. The woman known in Pennsylvania as Marguerite Montour, or "French Margaret," was probably Marguerite Fafard, who appears in the church records of Detroit and the province of Quebec. Her mother was Marguerite Couc Montour of Trois Rivières and St. Joseph, the older sister of Isabelle Couc Montour. No matter what their baptismal names, both male and female relatives in this widespread family adopted the name "Montour," which was well known in the world of Native-Euro-American trade (Hirsch, "Madame Montour," 92, 97).

32. For instance, Charles Hanna's lengthy list of "Pennsylvania Indian Traders" is an all-male one. He includes both Jacques and James Le Tort but does not mention Anne Le Tort, who actually ran the family's trading post much of the time. Another list transcribed by Hanna is a census of the civilian inhabitants of Fort Pitt in the 1760s, which includes the names of many women. "Nearly all the male inhabitants of Pittsburgh were Indian Traders," he writes, but he says nothing about the work women there were doing. *The Wilderness Trail* (New York: G. P. Putnam's Sons, 1911), 2:326–43, 360–61.

33. James H. Merrell, *Into the American Woods: Negotiators on the Pennsylvania Frontier* (New York: Alfred A. Knopf, 1999); Eric Hinderaker, *Elusive Empires: Constructing Colonialism in the Ohio Valley, 1673–1800* (Cambridge: Cambridge University Press, 1997); Michael N. McConnell, *A Country Between: The Upper Ohio Valley and Its Peoples, 1724–1774* (Lincoln: University of Nebraska Press, 1992).

34. Merrell, "Indians and Colonists," 137–38.

35. John Heckewelder, *History, Manners, and Customs of the Indian Nations Who Once Inhabited Pennsylvania and the Neighboring States* (1881; repr., New York, 1971), 157.

36. Ibid., 158; Petition and Accounts of Le Tort, HSP.

37. Benson, "Huguenot Letorts," 92–105; *MPCP*, 1:396–97; Penn Letters and Ancient Documents, 1:248; Vincens, "French Pioneers," 152–57; *PWP*, 4:154–57.

38. Cadwallader Collection–George Croghan Section, box 2, 1768 Accounts, folder 1; box 3, 1773 Accounts, folder 1; Accounts n.d., folder 11, HSP.

39. Peter Wraxall, *An Abridgment of the Indian Affairs Contained in Four Folio Volumes, Transacted in the Colony of New York, from the Year 1678 to the Year 1751*, ed. Charles H. McIlwain (Cambridge: Harvard University Press, 1915), 144.

40. Albany Indian Commissioners' Minutes, 19 June 1725, reel 1220, vol. 1, f. 137a, National Archives of Canada, Ottawa. Jean Montour was Isabelle's and Marguerite's younger brother, Jean-Baptiste Couc. Jean-Baptiste Fafard, known as Maconce, was Marguerite's son, and Joseph Montour was her nephew, the son of her older brother.

41. For the difficulties of travel across Pennsylvania, see Paul A. W. Wallace, *Indian Paths of Pennsylvania* (Harrisburg: PHMC, 1987), 2–3 and passim; and Merrell, *Into the American Woods*, 128–56.

42. Journal of Thomas Chalkley, quoted in Hanna, *Wilderness Trail*, 1:78. The name "Canatowa" is in *MPCP*, 2:73.

43. Merrell, *Into the American Woods*, 138; Journal of Martin Mack; "A Missionary's Tour to Shamokin and the West Branch of the Susquehanna, 1753," *PMHB* 39 (1915): 442.

44. Le Tort Account; *PWP*, 4:51.

45. Weynepeeweyta was "Cousin to Savannah," the Shawnee chief (*MPCP*, 3:148). Her testimony at the Provincial Council hearing of the case (*MPCP*, 3:149–50) seems to be the longest recorded speech by a Native woman from Pennsylvania during this early period. A brief account of the case from her perspective is in Alison Duncan Hirsch, "Women and the Fur Trade in Eighteenth-Century Pennsylvania," in Louise Johnston, ed., *Aboriginal People and the Fur Trade: Proceedings of the Eighth North American Fur Trade Conference, Akwesasne* (Cornwall, Ontario, and Rooseveltown, N.Y.: Mohawk Council of Akwesasne and Mohawk Nation Council of Chiefs, 2001), 204.

46. For more on the Moravians and hospitality, see chapter 5, below.

47. *PWP*, 4:98–99; Alison Duncan Hirsch, "Instructions from a Woman: Hannah Penn and the Pennsylvania Proprietorship" (Ph.D. diss., Columbia University, 1991), 185–86.

48. Hannah Penn to James Logan, 12 Mar. 1719, Penn Family to James Logan, Penn Papers, HSP, 1:76.

49. Paul A. W. Wallace, *Conrad Weiser, 1696–1760, Friend of Colonist and Mohawk* (Philadelphia: University of Pennsylvania Press, 1945), 80, 139–40, 188, 196, 219; Journal of Martin Mack, 15, 17, 23 Oct. 1745.

50. Hanna, *Wilderness Trail*, 1:304.

51. *PWP*, 4:597, 605.

52. Hanna, *Wilderness Trail*, 305.

53. *PA*, 1:254–55. James Le Tort translated and Edmund Cartlidge transcribed the message about the incident, sent by Lenape leaders to the governor. Eight years after his trial and conviction, Cartlidge was just as active in the trade as ever. It is tempting to imagine that the Shawnee woman here was Weynepeeweytah, reprising her role in this archetypal frontier drama. But, unlike that of the Cartlidge brothers, her name never reappears in the record.

54. *MPCP*, 3:39.

55. Ibid., 383.

56. Ibid., 6:149. Peter Mancall writes, "Indian women often played a pivotal role in this Indian rum trade." He gives other examples of both European and Native men blaming Indian women for the trade. *Deadly Medicine: Indians and Alcohol in Early America* (Ithaca: Cornell University Press, 1995), 60.

57. *MPCP*, 3:426.

58. Journal of Martin Mack, 16, 21, 23 Oct. 1745.

59. Ann Firor Scott, *Making the Invisible Woman Visible* (Chicago: University of Illinois Press, 1984).

60. Gerda Lerner, *The Majority Finds Its Past: Placing Women in History* (New York: Oxford University Press, 1979), 145–59.

61. Gary B. Nash, "The Hidden History of Mestizo America," *JAH* 82 (1995): 941–64. For Pennsylvania's historical marker program, the first established in the nation, see George R. Beyer, *Guide to the State Historical Markers of Pennsylvania* (Harrisburg: PHMC, 2000) and http://www.phmc.state.pa.us, which includes a searchable guide to the markers. Hannah Freeman's marker is in Beyer, *Guide*, 105. Marshall Becker has written about her in "Hannah Freeman: An Eighteenth-Century Lenape Living and Working Among Colonial Farmers," *PMHB* 114 (1990): 249–69. The Montour women are in Beyer, *Guide*, 70, 73, 239, 246, 274, although the markers omit Esther's last name.

62. Beyer, *Guide*, 107, 137, 188, 215, 218, 261. The Moravian women named were Ester Brodhead, Catharine Hillman, Helen Haines, Rebecca Jones, Mary Clark, Catherine Holly, Hannah McMichael, and Mary Solathe.

63. Beyer, *Guide*, 59, 73, 113, 115, 118, 176, 177, 202, 224, 225, 246, 279, 280, 282, 283, 331, 346, 385. For Benigna Zinzendorf, see Katherine M. Faull, *Moravian Women's Memoirs: Their Related Lives, 1750–1820* (Syracuse, N.Y.: Syracuse University Press, 1997).

64. Beyer, *Guide*, 94, 225, 226, 240, 244, 246, 329, 337, 354, 387.

Chapter 5

1. Martin Mack, Diary of a journey to New England (German and English), 17 and 18 Feb. 1743, items 1 and 3, folder 3, box 111 (hereafter written as 1 and 3: 3: 111), *RMM*, reel 1. All mission diaries listed below come from the *RMM* microfilm collection. These records are nearly all in German. Unless otherwise noted, translations into English are my own. Jeannette Mack was also known as Anna and "Jannetje." For variants of her name, see William C. Reichel, *Memorials of the Moravian Church* (Philadelphia: J. B. Lippincott, 1870), 1:34n, 53n; and Carl John Fliegel, comp., *Index to the Records of the Moravian Mission Among the Indians of North America* (New Haven, Conn.: Research Publications, 1970), 2:594.

2. Fliegel, *Index*, 2:594, 464, 703; Mack, Diary of a journey, 18 Feb. 1743 (quotations).

3. Catalogs of Indian converts, 1: 2, 3, and 5: 313, *RMM*, reel 33; Ted J. Brasser, *Riding on the Frontier's Crest: Mahican Indian Culture and Culture Change* (Ottawa: National Museums of Canada, 1974), 7; Ives Goddard, "Delaware," *Handbook*, 213–16, 221; Franz Laurens Wojcie-chowski, *Ethnohistory of the Paugussett Tribes: An Exercise in Research Methodology* (Amsterdam: De Kiva, 1992), 14–16, 85–88.

4. John Ettwein and David Zeisberger, "Kurze Nachricht von den Missionen der Evangelischen-Brüder-Kirche unter den Heiden in North-America," 1: 8: 313; John Heckewelder, *A Narrative of the Mission of the United Brethren Among the Delaware and Mohegan Indians, from Its Commencement in the Year 1740, to the Close of the Year 1808* . . . (Philadelphia: McCarty and Davis, 1820; repr. [New York]: Arno Press, 1971), 19–31; Joseph Mortimer Levering, *A History of Bethlehem, Pennsylvania, 1741–1892* . . . (Bethlehem, Pa.: Times Publishing, 1903), 394–404.

5. The story of the Moravian missions contributes significantly to the debates about Native American women's responses to Christianity. Some scholars argue that Indian women primarily resisted or faced subjugation to an essentially patriarchal Christianity presented by missionaries: Carol Devens, *Countering Colonization: Native American Women and Great Lakes Missions, 1630–1900* (Berkeley: University of California Press, 1992); Karen Anderson,

Chain Her by One Foot: The Subjugation of Women in Seventeenth-Century New France (London: Routledge, 1991); Regula Trenkwalder Schönenberger, *Lenape Women, Matriliny and the Colonial Encounter: Resistance and Erosion of Power (c. 1600–1876): An Excursus in Feminist Anthropology* (Bern: Peter Lang, 1991). Like my own study, however, many works note the importance of Indian women adopting and adapting Christianity. Michael Harkin and Sergei Kan note that "in most cases there is clear evidence of [Indian] women adapting to the missionary message," and they ask, "why were women in many cases the earliest and/or most enthusiastic converts?" (Harkin and Kan, "Introduction" to special issue on Native American Women's Responses to Christianity, *Ethnohistory* 43 [1996]: 563–71 [quotation on 565]). For more on adaptive approaches to Christianity among Indian women, see Harkin, "Engendering Discipline: Discourse and Counterdiscourse in the Methodist-Heiltsuk Dialogue," ibid., 643–61; Kan, "Clan Mothers and Godmothers: Tlingit Women and Russian Orthodox Christianity, 1840–1940," ibid., 613–41; Nancy Shoemaker, "Kateri Tekakwitha's Tortuous Path to Sainthood," in Shoemaker, ed., *Negotiators of Change: Historical Perspectives on Native American Women* (New York: Routledge, 1995), 49–71; Jane T. Merritt, "Cultural Encounters Along a Gender Frontier: Mahican, Delaware, and German Women in Eighteenth-Century Pennsylvania," *PH* 67 (2000): 502–31; and James P. Ronda, "Generations of Faith: The Christian Indians of Martha's Vineyard," *WMQ* 38 (1981): 369–94.

6. Catherine A. Brekus, *Strangers and Pilgrims: Female Preaching in America, 1740–1845* (Chapel Hill: University of North Carolina Press, 1998), 26 (quotation). See also Susan Juster's discussion of eighteenth-century Baptist revivalists' dilemma "of creating a sense of community among individuals who thought themselves beyond the bounds of conventional social categories" (*Disorderly Women: Sexual Politics and Evangelicalism in Revolutionary New England* [Ithaca: Cornell University Press, 1994], 79).

7. Katherine M. Faull, trans., *Moravian Women's Memoirs: Their Related Lives, 1750–1820* (Syracuse, N.Y.: Syracuse University Press, 1997), xxviii (first and second quotations); Beverly Prior Smaby, "Female Piety Among Eighteenth-Century Moravians," *PH* 64 (supplemental issue, 1997): 155–58 (third quotation on 155). On the choir system, see Beverly Smaby, *The Transformation of Moravian Bethlehem: From Communal Mission to Family Economy* (Philadelphia: University of Pennsylvania Press, 1988), 10–11; and Jacob John Sessler, *Communal Pietism Among Early American Moravians* (New York: Henry Holt, 1933), 94–105.

8. David Zeisberger, "History of the Northern American Indians," ed. Archer Butler Hulbert and William Nathaniel Schwarze, *Ohio Archaeological and Historical Publications*, vol. 19 (Columbus, 1910), 77; Samuel Hopkins, "Historical Memoirs Relating to the Housatonic Indians," *Magazine of History with Notes and Queries* 5, no. 17 (1911): 63–64; "Letter from William Penn to the Committee of the Free Society of Traders, 1683," *NEP*, 231; "Letter of Isaack de Rasieres to Samuel Blommaert, 1628 (?)," *NNN*, 107; M. R. Harrington, "A Preliminary Sketch of Lenápe Culture," *American Anthropologist*, n.s., 15 (1913): 215; Goddard, "Delaware," *Handbook*, 219.

9. Zeisberger, "History," 13 (first quotation), 16 (third quotation); John Heckewelder, *History, Manners, and Customs of the Indian Nations Who Once Inhabited Pennsylvania and the Neighbouring States* (Philadelphia: HSP, 1876), 156 (second quotation).

10. Heckewelder, *History*, 158, 116–17 (first and second quotations), 215 (third quotation), 245–46 (fourth and fifth quotations), 247 (sixth quotation); M. R. Harrington, "Religion and Ceremonies of the Lenape," *Indian Notes and Monographs*, Museum of the American Indian, Heye Foundation, no. 19 (n.p., n.d.), 63. For a more general discussion of such rituals, see Margaret Connell Szasz, *Indian Education in the American Colonies, 1607–1783* (Albuquerque: University of New Mexico Press, 1988), 15–17.

11. Indian Conference, Gnadenhütten, 31 Oct. 1747, 2: 1: 119, *RMM*, reel 6; Gnadenhütten diary, 17 May 1748, 1: 3: 116, *RMM*, reel 4.

12. Indian Conference, Gnadenhütten, 31 Oct. 1747; Gnadenhütten diary, 21 May 1747, 1: 1: 116 (first quotation); ibid., 15 June 1747, 1: 1: 116 (second quotation); Friedenshütten diary, 17, 18 July 1767, 1: 4: 131, *RMM*, reel 7 (third quotation); ibid., 18 July 1771, 1: 8: 131. On the range of foods eaten, see Fliegel, *Index*, 3: 1121. Women commonly prepared a corn-based food called *Agridges:* Friedenshütten diary, 18 Sept. 1770, 1: 7: 131; Fliegel, *Index*, 3: 1115; Friedenshütten diary, 21 Nov. 1770, 1: 7: 131. Making hemp bags was a very old practice; see the seventeenth-century account of David Pietersz de Vries, "From the 'Korte Historiael Ende Journaels Aenteyckeninge,' " in *NNN*, 219. For another view of the changing agricultural roles of Native men and women in the eighteenth century, see Merritt, "Mahican, Delaware, and German Women," 522–25.

13. Gnadenhütten diary, 7 Feb. 1749, 1: 5: 116 (first quotation); Fliegel, *Index*, 3: 943; 2: 464, 557–58; Gnadenhütten diary, 20 Dec. 1748, 1: 4: 116 (second quotation); ibid., 6 July 1747, 1: 1: 116 (third quotation). For other examples of missionary women meeting in conversation with Indian women, see ibid., 31 July, 1, 5 Aug., 1 Sept. 1747, 1: 2: 116; ibid., 4 Jan. 1749, 1: 5: 116; Pachgatgoch diary, 11 Aug. 1752, 1: 7: 114, *RMM*, reel 3; Friedenshütten diary, 1, 8 Oct. 1769, 17 June 1770, 1: 6 and 7: 131. Merritt, "Mahican, Delaware, and German Women," 517–18, 522, 529, also considers female relationships.

14. Shekomeko diary (English), 12 Mar. 1744, 2: 1: 112, *RMM*, reel 2 (first quotation, emphasis added); Pachgatgoch diary, 12 Nov. 1758, 9, 16 Feb. 1759, 10 June 1760, 1: 8 and 9: 115, *RMM*, reel 4; Wechquetank diary, 19 Mar. 1761, 1: 2: 124, *RMM*, reel 6; ibid., 22 Mar. 1761, 1: 2: 124 (second quotation). On Grube's health, see Fliegel, *Index*, 2: 521–22.

15. Wechquetank diary, 5 Mar. 1762, 1: 3: 124; ibid., 6 Mar. 1762 (quotation); Catalog of Indian converts, 1: 4: 313.

16. Gnadenhütten diary, 12/1 Sept. 1747, 1: 2: 116 (first quotation); ibid., 7 May 1747, 1: 1: 116 (second quotation); ibid., 18 Aug. 1747, 1: 2: 116 (third quotation). On Esther's later influences on Native women, see Friedenshütten diary, 12 Jan. 1766, 1: 2: 131. For additional examples of Native women holding spiritual conversations with other Native women, see Gnadenhütten diary, 8 Mar. 1750, 1: 7: 116; Friedenshütten diary, 23 Feb. 1767, 1: 4: 131.

17. Gnadenhütten diary, 5 Feb. 1747, 1: 1: 116.

18. Gnadenhütten diary, 20 Apr. 1754, 1: 1: 118, *RMM*, reel 5 (first long quotation); ibid., 19 May 1754, 1: 1: 118 (second long quotation). See also ibid., 6 April 1754, 1: 1: 118. On Moravian bands, see Sessler, *Communal Pietism*, 98.

19. Gnadenhütten diary, 21 June 1747, 1: 1: 116 (Sarah's delivery); ibid., 3 Feb. 1749, 1: 5: 116 (Beata's delivery); ibid., 8 Dec. 1747, 1: 2: 116 (Lydia's delivery).

20. Pachgatgoch diary, 16 June 1753, 1: 8: 114 (first quotation); ibid., 20 Mar. 1754, 1: 9: 114 (second quotation); Gnadenhütten diary, 7/18 Dec. 1750, 1: 1: 117, *RMM*, reel 5 (third quotation).

21. Salem diary, 28 Aug. 1781, 1: 1: 148, *RMM*, reel 10; Goshen diary (English), 18 Feb. 1801, 1: 8: 171, *RMM*, reel 19 (quotation); Schechschequanunk diary, 8 and 10 Aug. 1771, 1: 3: 133, *RMM*, reel 8; Memoir of Gottlob Sensemann, MAB; Zeisberger, "History," 80.

22. Shekomeko diary, 12 Mar. 1744, 2: 1: 112; Fliegel, *Index*, 2: 594; Gnadenhütten diary, 19 Dec. 1753, 1: 4: 117; ibid., 29, 30 May 1751, 1: 2: 117; Pachgatgoch diary, 1 Dec. 1755, 1: 3: 115; Heckewelder to Seidel, 21 Mar. 1781, 14: 3: 215.

23. Friedenshütten diary, 22 May 1768, 1: 5: 131 (first quotation); ibid., 7 June 1767, 1: 4: 131 (second quotation); ibid., 3 June 1770, 1: 7: 131; Gnadenhütten diary, 2 Jan., 10, 28 Feb. (third quotation), 29 Mar. 1747, 1: 1: 116; ibid., 3 Aug. 1747, 1: 2: 116; Anthony F. C. Wallace, "Woman, Land, and Society: Three Aspects of Aboriginal Delaware Life," *Pennsylvania Ar-*

chaeologist 17 (1947): 6–7; Brasser, *Riding*, 6–7; Gary Steven Kinkel, *Our Dear Mother, the Spirit: An Investigation of Count Zinzendorf's Theology and Praxis* (Lanham, Md.: University Press of America, 1990), 74, 10.

24. Nain diary, 29 Dec. 1758, 14: 1: 125, *RMM*, reel 7; Pachgatgoch diary, 13 Mar. 1763, 1: 12: 115; Gnadenhütten, Ohio, diary, 5 July 1773, 1: 1: 144, *RMM*, reel 9; Gnadenhütten diary, 9 Dec. 1747, 1: 2: 116. See also Merritt, "Mahican, Delaware, and German Women," 518–19.

25. Gnadenhütten diary, 3 Mar. 1748, 1: 3: 116.

26. Gnadenhütten diary, 3 May, 26 July 1747, 1: 1 and 2: 116; Pachgatgoch diary, 28 Jan. 1753, 1: 7: 114; Shekomeko diary, 6 Mar. 1746, 1: 1: 111; Philadelphia Barracks diary, 25 May 1764, 1: 2: 127, *RMM* (quotation), reel 7; Gnadenhütten diary, 23 Jan. 1752, 1: 3: 117; Friedenshütten diary, 29 May, 26 Dec. 1768, 1: 5: 131; ibid., 2 Feb. 1770, 1: 7: 131; Sessler, *Communal Pietism*, 101–2.

27. Gnadenhütten diary, 28 Apr. 1747, 1: 1: 116 (first quotation); Bethlehem diary, 25 Feb./ 8 Mar. 1746, microfilm copy, reel 2, MAB (second quotation); Smaby, *Transformation*, 146; Bethlehem diary, 27 Feb./10 Mar. 1746. On views of pregnancy during the colonial period, see Catherine M. Scholten, *Childbearing in American Society, 1650–1850* (New York: New York University Press, 1985), 16–21.

28. Memoir of Johann Georg Jungmann, MAB; Fliegel, *Index*, 2:557–58; Mabel Haller, *Early Moravian Education in Pennsylvania* (Nazareth, Pa.: Moravian Historical Society, 1953), 45; Faull, *Memoirs*, xxix.

29. Shekomeko diary, 13 Nov. 1743, 1: 1: 111; Gnadenhütten diary, 14 Jan. 1752, 1: 3: 117; Langundo Utenunk diary, 18 Nov. 1770, 1: 1: 137, *RMM*, reel 8; Fliegel, *Index*, 2: 464, 557–58.

30. Gnadenhütten diary, 18 Oct. 1751, 1: 2: 117.

31. For an overview of the work of these women, see Fliegel, *Index*, vol. 2; Carl John Fliegel's translation of catalog of Indians, 2 and 4: 3191, *RMM*, reel 34; and Merritt, "Mahican, Delaware, and German Women," 531.

32. The Moravian emphasis on female leadership seemed radical in eighteenth-century America, raising hostility and suspicion against the church. As Smaby writes, male Moravian leaders after 1760 "had tired of the unending criticism of the Moravian Church and resolved to bring their religious practice into line with that of other Protestant churches." By 1760, male leaders were ready to move closer to mainstream attitudes and practices. During the 1760s leaders prevented women from holding churchwide offices and strengthened male authority (Smaby, "Female Piety," 160–61 [quotation on 160]).

33. Fliegel's catalog of Indians.

34. The linguistic ability of Jungmann was certainly an ongoing help in her relations with Indian women. Moravian records are probably not a good indicator of the range of the activities of Schmick and Jungmann in the post–1765 period. No doubt these women were even more involved than extant mission records suggest. We might know more about their activities had one of them been married to David Zeisberger, who dominated Moravian work among the Delawares and Mahicans in this time period and kept many, though not all, mission records. A bachelor until 1781, he did not have a spouse to inform him of women's activities and his writings do not provide rich accounts of the work of missionary women. Zeisberger often appears primarily interested in male activities, and he sometimes aroused opposition from Indian women. Goschgoschunk diary, 4, 6 July 1768, 1: 1: 135, *RMM*, reel 8; Merritt, "Mahican, Delaware, and German Women," 531–32; Zeisberger to Seidel, 11 June 1781, 1: 5: 229, *RMM*, reel 32.

35. John Ettwein to Zeisberger and William Edward, 10 Mar. 1778, no. 1251, Ettwein Papers, MAB.

36. One of the most successful leaders was Esther who was instrumental in inspiring a

revival among the female population at Friedenshütten in 1765–66 when there was no Euro-American woman at the Susquehanna mission. Indian *Arbeiterinnen* reported that many Indian women requested baptism during this revival. Zeisberger acknowledged Esther's role in the conversions: "We have become aware of a new working again of the Savior among the women, especially among several, among whom one had not noticed anything before. They declared to Esther they wanted from now on to become totally the Savior's." Indians in the Ohio country later recognized Esther as an important figure. Wyalusing diary, 5 and 12 Jan. 1766, 1: 2: 131, *RMM*, reel 7; Zeisberger to Seidel, 20 Jan. 1766, 15: 2: 229. When she died in 1780, many Indians from the vicinity of the Ohio missions honored her by attending her funeral. Gnadenhütten, Ohio, diary, 21, 22 Aug. 1780, 1: 11:144. Other Indian leaders from the later period were Anna Caritas, Anna Salome, and Anna. Anna Caritas was a "Saaldienerin" and "Helferin" in the Ohio country. The renowned midwife Anna Salome was also a member of the Helpers Conference at Schönbrunn, as was Anna. Petquottink diary, 28 Mar. 1789, 1: 2: 155, *RMM*, reel 10; Schönbrunn diary, 3 Mar. 1774, 1: 5: 141; ibid., 21 Sept. 1775, 1: 7: 141; ibid., 8 Apr. 1776, 1: 7: 141; ibid., 27 Apr. 1776, 1: 8: 141.

37. Goshen diary (English), 2 Feb. 1801, 1: 8: 171, *RMM*, reel 19.

Chapter 6

1. The evidence for Sawantaeny's death is found in *MPCP*, 3:148–56; and "An Indian Council held at Philadelphia, 21 March 1721/2," Society Miscellaneous Collections, Indians, 1682–1900, box 11C, folder 2, HSP. Pages 10–12 of the latter manuscript are labeled "Depositions of Jonathan Swindel and William Wilkins" and provide the fullest account of the incident. In the manuscript of the March 1722 council, Logan indicated that he thought the crime had been committed on 9 January. According to the date written at the top of p. 10, Swindel's and Wilkins's depositions were taken before Governor Sir William Keith on 22 March 1722. Less useful depositions given by witnesses George Rescarrick and Richard Satler, Jr., can be found in Indian Treaties, Du Simitière Collection, folder 2, LCP. Satler's deposition, given on 10 March 1722, dates Sawantaeny's death in the last week of February, which contradicts Logan's account and the depositions of Swindel and Wilkins. Sawantaeny's death has also been discussed in Francis Jennings, "Miquon's Passing: Indian-European Relations in Colonial Pennsylvania, 1674 to 1755" (Ph.D. diss., University of Pennsylvania, 1965), 198–206; Jennings, *The Ambiguous Iroquois Empire: The Covenant Chain Confederation of Indian Tribes with English Colonies* (New York: W. W. Norton, 1984), 290–91; Daniel K. Richter, *The Ordeal of the Longhouse: The Peoples of the Iroquois League in the Era of European Colonization* (Chapel Hill: University of North Carolina Press, 1992); Eric Hinderaker, *Elusive Empires: Constructing Colonialism in the Ohio Valley, 1673–1800* (New York: Cambridge University Press, 1997), 123–24; and James H. Merrell, *Into the American Woods: Negotiators on the Pennsylvania Frontier* (New York: W. W. Norton, 1999), 115–21.

2. Although the recorded council minutes for these meetings describe Tanachaha as a representative of the "Five Nations" of the Iroquois, the appellation may be incorrect. Given that the Tuscaroras became the sixth member of the Iroquois League at some point during 1721 or 1722, it is difficult to fit the change from the Five to the Six Nations into the chronology of Sawantaeny's death and its aftermath told here. To avoid confusion, I have used the terms "Iroquois nations" or "Iroquois Confederacy" instead of either the Five or Six Nations.

3. For Merrell's use of this metaphor, see *Into the American Woods*, 116, 121.

4. This term is taken from Robert Cover, "The Folktales of Justice: Tales of Jurisdiction," in Martha Minow, Michael Ryan, and Austin Sarat, eds., *Narrative, Violence, and the Law: The Essays of Robert Cover* (Ann Arbor: University of Michigan Press, 1992), 173–203.

5. For discussions of "jurisgenerative" and "jurispathic," see Robert Cover, "Nomos and Narrative," in Minow, Ryan, and Sarat, eds., *Narrative, Violence, and the Law*, 95–172, esp. 155–59.

6. I do not mean to suggest by this sentence that the Pennsylvanians' position was monolithic nor that there was a single "Indian" stance toward Sawantaeny's death. The distinctions among Pennsylvanians and Indians, respectively, will be treated along with the distinctions between various Pennsylvanians and Indians, below. For an account of early provincial-Indian relations that emphasizes William Penn's role in constructing the myth of his own benevolence toward the Indians, see James Spady, "Friendly Meetings: The Art of Conquest and the Mythical Origins of Pennsylvania, ca. 1620–ca. 1730" (master's thesis, College of William and Mary, 1996); and his essay in this volume.

7. The Sawantaeny case is discussed in Jennings, "Miquon's Passing," 198–206; and Merrell, *Into the American Woods*, 115–21. For explorations of the comparative treatment of Europeans and Indians under colonial law, see Francis Jennings, *The Invasion of America: Indians, Colonialism, and the Cant of Conquest* (Chapel Hill: University of North Carolina Press, 1975), 45, 49, 77–81, 132; Alden T. Vaughan, "Tests of Puritan Justice," in Vaughan, *Roots of American Racism: Essays on the Colonial Experience* (New York: Oxford University Press, 1995), 200–211; Lyle Koehler, "Red-White Power Relations and Justice in the Courts of Seventeenth-Century New England," *American Indian Culture and Research Journal* 3 (1979): 1–31; Glenn W. LaFantasie, "Murder of an Indian, 1638," *Rhode Island History* 38 (1979): 67–77; Yasuhide Kawashima, *Puritan Justice and the Indian: White Man's Law in Massachusetts, 1630–1763* (Middletown, Conn.: Wesleyan University Press, 1986); James P. Ronda, "Red and White at the Bench: Indians and the Law in Plymouth Colony, 1620–91," *Essex Institute Historical Collections* 110 (1974): 200–215; James W. Springer, "American Indians and the Law of Real Property in Colonial New England," *American Journal of Legal History* 30 (1986): 25–58. For an interpretation of intercultural homicides that emphasizes reciprocity, not equality, as the normative standard that Indians and colonists aspired to, see Katherine Hermes, "'Justice Will Be Done Us': Algonquian Demands for Reciprocity in the Courts of European Settlers," in Christopher L. Tomlins and Bruce M. Mann, eds., *The Many Legalities of Early America* (Chapel Hill: University of North Carolina Press, 2001), 123–49.

8. Vaughan, "Tests of Puritan Justice," 212.

9. See, e.g., Vaughan's discussion of colonists' increasingly harsh legal treatment of Indians, "Tests of Puritan Justice," 210–12; and Kawashima, *Puritan Justice and the Indian*, 149–79. Jennings's explanation of Sawantaeny's death also falls into this category; he has argued that the Cartlidges' arrest and eventual freedom were the result of a power struggle between Logan and Pennsylvania Governor Sir William Keith (*Ambiguous Iroquois Empire*, 291–93). One major exception to this trend is Alan Taylor's comparative study of intercultural killings between Euro-Americans and Iroquois in Canada and upstate New York following the American Revolution: Taylor, "Covering the Grave," unpub. seminar paper presented at the Massachusetts Historical Society, September 2000, cited with permission of the author.

10. My notion of "national characters," individuals who embody the "national character" of the state, is drawn from David Waldstreicher, *In the Midst of Perpetual Fetes: The Making of American Nationalism, 1776–1820* (Chapel Hill: University of North Carolina Press, 1997), 108–76, esp. 124–26.

11. See James Axtell, *After Columbus: Essays in the Ethnohistory of Colonial North America* (New York: Oxford University Press, 1988), 9–44.

12. Kawashima, *Puritan Justice and the Indian*, 150, 154, argues that equality under the law was the nominal basis for justice under Puritan legal codes. Kawashima does not deny

that equality was limited by race, religion, and gender, but does indict the Massachusetts Puritans for failing to live up to their own code.

13. Daniel K. Richter, *Facing East from Indian Country: A Native History of Early America* (Cambridge: Harvard University Press, 2001).

14. I use the term "our" advisedly here. Just as I hope to stress the diversity of perspectives among Europeans and Indians—rendering the terms "European" and "Indian" useful heuristics more than accurate descriptors—I do not mean to deny alternative readings of this event by speaking in the "we." As shall become clear in the conclusion, I hope that this chapter might provide an example of the ways in which mediating between multiple historical moral narratives may help mediate moral narratives in the present.

15. For the treaty, see "Treaty with the Susquehannah Indians, 12 Sept. 1700," George Vaux Collection of Correspondence and Documents, QCHC. Determining the "identity" of the "Susquehanna Indians," as that term was used in colonial Pennsylvania's diplomatic records, is an admittedly problematic task, given that the ethnic or tribal terms used by colonial clerks often appear on close inspection to have a haphazard relation to the ethnic or tribal designations ethnohistorians use to describe eastern indigenous peoples. In this case, I am following Francis Jennings's assertion that early eighteenth-century Susquehanna Valley Indians were "an ethnic mixture [of] Iroquois, Shawnees, Conoys, Nanticokes, Delawares, Tuscaroras, and Tutelos apparently intermingled and intermarried with the Susquehannock-Conestoga" peoples who had moved there after the Susquehannock tribe was dissolved in the 1670s and re-formed as the Conestoga tribe in the 1690s (Jennings, "Susquehannock," *Handbook*, 362–67, quotation from p. 366; see also Jennings, "Glory, Death, and Transfiguration," *Proceedings of the American Philosophical Society* 109 [1968]: 15–33).

16. On William Penn's early attempts to force outsiders to carry physical tokens of their good character, such as passes or seals, see John Smolenski, "Friends and Strangers: Religion, Diversity, and the Ordering of Public Life in Colonial Pennsylvania, 1681–1764" (Ph.D. diss., University of Pennsylvania, 2001), 101–6.

17. On the often paradoxical relation between indigenous agency and authority and the limits of colonial law more generally, see Lauren F. Benton, "Colonial Law and Cultural Difference: Jurisdictional Politics and the Formation of the Colonial State," *Comparative Studies in Society and History* 41 (1999): 563–88.

18. See Smolenski, "Friends and Strangers," chap. 3.

19. On the rapidly changing nature of treaty councils during the colonial period, see Merrell, *Into the American Woods*, 253. Even the most famous treaty council outside of Philadelphia—Penn's Great Treaty of 1701—took place at the proprietor's mansion at Pennsbury, not at an Indian or a neutral site.

20. I am using "periphery" here as a relative term, of course. After all, Philadelphia itself was a "periphery" of Indian "cores" to the west; see Jeanne Chase, "Porous Boundaries and Shifting Borderlands: The American Experience in a New World Order," *Reviews in American History* 26 (1998): 54–69; and James H. Merrell, "The Customes of Our Countrey" in Bernard Bailyn and Philip D. Morgan, eds., *Strangers Within the Realm: Cultural Margins of the First British Empire* (Chapel Hill: University of North Carolina Press, 1991), 117–56.

21. For a discussion of wampum in establishing authority at the outset of conferences, see Merrell, *Into the American Woods*, 32, 189.

22. *MPCP*, 2:245.

23. Ibid., 386–90.

24. Ibid., 472.

25. My discussion of the communicative role of wampum relies here partially on Merrell's discussion of wampum's meaning (*Into the American Woods*, 187–93 and passim) and

on Gordon M. Sayre's analysis of the relation between wampum and writing (Sayre, *Les Sauvages Américains: Representations of Native Americans in French and English Colonial Literature* [Chapel Hill: University of North Carolina Press, 1997], 144–218, esp. 162–63, 186–88, 213). As I hope my discussion will show, I think that the functional differences between wampum and alphabetic script in colonial political, legal, and diplomatic relations were smaller than Sayre suggests.

26. *MPCP*, 1:372.

27. Ibid., 447.

28. Ibid., 2:403.

29. Ibid., 386–90.

30. Ibid., 471.

31. Ibid., 511–12.

32. Ibid., 200, 204.

33. Ibid., 510.

34. Logan Papers, 11:2, HSP. This event may well have renewed the desire of many Indians for the provincial government to license traders more effectively, as evidenced by the September 1700 treaty Logan negotiated with the Susquehanna Indians, discussed above.

35. *MPCP*, 2:247 (emphasis added).

36. Ibid., 403–5.

37. Ibid., 512.

38. Ibid., 45–46.

39. "Articles of Agreement Between William Penn and the Susquehannah, Shawoneh, and North Patomack Indians," 23 Apr. 1701, *PA*, 1st ser., 1:144–47.

40. *MPCP*, 2:247.

41. Penn Manuscripts, Indian Affairs, 1:34, HSP.

42. *MPCP*, 1:372–73, 2: 244–48, 469–72.

43. The quotation is from Connessoa of the Onondaga (Penn Manuscripts, Indian Affairs, 1:34, HSP). For a similar comment from Gookin, see *MPCP*, 2:516.

44. *MPCP*, 2:45–46, 244–48.

45. Ibid., 3:148–49.

46. Ibid., 149. As Jennings has pointed out, Logan failed to include the depositions of Swindel and Wilkins in his official report. Jennings's speculation that Logan suppressed these testimonies because they showed Cartlidge's culpability is more dubious, however. The very manuscript account that Logan "suppressed" notes that Keith was present at the depositions; this raises the question of who, exactly, Logan was trying to hide the depositions from. See "An Indian Council held at Philadelphia, 21 January 1721/2," Society Miscellaneous Collections, Indians, 1682–1900, box 11C, folder 2, pp. 10–12, HSP.

47. This fact was in some dispute, as one witness claimed not to have seen Sawantaeny with his gun, while four witnesses claimed that he did have his gun. Since one of these witnesses was Sawantaeny's wife, who claimed she was in the cabin when he left with his gun, I believe that he actually did retrieve his gun.

48. The testimony can be found in *MPCP*, 3:150–52.

49. Ibid., 155.

50. Ibid..

51. For a further discussion of these laws, see Smolenski, "Friends and Strangers," 103–4.

52. The most recent interracial death was that of Francis LaTore, at the hands of a group of Indians (probably Shawnee warriors). LaTore, a servant, had run away from his master, who then hired local Indians to capture or kill him. They killed him. See *MPCP*, 2:533–34.

53. The only indirect evidence that Logan, at least, may have been aware of this statute

is his long association with William Penn as the proprietor's agent. Logan arrived in 1699—when the mixed-jury statute was still on the books although not enforced—and was in all likelihood aware of Penn's unusual and progressive ideas on diplomatic and legal relations with Indians.

54. Weynepeeweyta was, as noted above, a Shawnee who had close ties to the Seneca on the Pennsylvania frontier (Charles Callender, "Shawnee," *Handbook,* 622–23). It is difficult to know whether Sawantaeny's place of residence and status were defined by his tribal background and lineage or Weynepeeweyta's; although the Shawnees were at this time both patrilineal and patrilocal (ibid., 626–27), the Senecas were matrilocal and matrilineal, as were the Delaware and Conestoga people living in the region. This confluence of different political lineage systems in one community makes determining Sawantaeny's political affiliation in death even more problematic.

55. *MPCP,* 2:608.

56. Ibid., 3:24.

57. Smolenski, "Friends and Strangers," 218–77; Jennings, *Ambiguous Iroquois Empire,* 291–92.

58. Jennings, *Invasion of America,* 45, 49, 77–81, 132.

59. Indian Treaties, Du Simitière Collection, folder 4, LCP. This Indian Council was not recorded in the official minutes of the Provincial Council. See *MPCP,* 3:160–61.

60. The Cartlidges, in their petition for bail to the Provincial Council on 22 Mar., had implied that Sawantaeny might still be alive, noting that they were "heartily sorry for the Death of the Indian (if He be really dead)" (*MPCP,* 3:156).

61. Indian Treaties, Du Simitière Collection, folder 4, LCP. Although this manuscript does not say which treaty Civility was referring to when he held "a Parchment in his Hand," it was most likely the "Treaty with the Susquehannah Indians" from September 1700 that prohibited unlicensed traders from selling alcohol to those Indians; see note 15, above. This treaty became an issue in 1735, see below.

62. *MPCP,* 3:163–65.

63. Ibid., 168.

64. See Keith's message to the Iroquois nations (ibid., 194); and his reiteration of the same theme at a September meeting in Philadelphia (ibid., 197).

65. Keith quoted Satcheechoe's message at the September council at Albany; see ibid., 198.

66. Ibid., 200.

67. Jennings sees this as the true beginning of Pennsylvania's participation in the Covenant Chain, arguing that Penn had largely ignored the Iroquois in his dealings, making treaties primarily with the Delaware and the Susquehanna (Conestoga) Indians. (*Ambiguous Iroquois Empire,* 290–94).

68. This point is also made by Jennings, *Ambiguous Iroquois Empire,* 293–94. In one critical respect, however, Keith did reject the Iroquois claim to sovereignty over the region. He gladly took control of the lands around Conestoga that the Iroquois ceded, but, he told those assembled at Albany, "You know very well that the Lands about Conestogoe, upon the River Susquehannah, belong to your old friend and kind Brother William Penn." Keith had managed to accept their gift without recognizing their authority to give it (*MPCP,* 3:202).

69. On narrative contextualization and fact-making, see Clifford Geertz, "Local Knowledge: Fact and Law in Comparative Perspective," in Geertz, *Local Knowledge: Further Essays in Interpretive Anthropology* (New York: Basic Books, 1983), 167–234.

70. Jane T. Merritt and Nancy Shoemaker have recently argued for the significance of familial and body language, respectively, as structuring metaphors in Indian-colonial diplo-

macy in Pennsylvania. See Merritt, "Metaphor, Meaning, and Misunderstanding: Language and Power on the Pennsylvania Frontier," in Andrew R. L. Cayton and Fredrika J. Teute, eds., *Contact Points: American Frontiers from the Mohawk Valley to the Mississippi, 1750–1830* (Chapel Hill: University of North Carolina Press, 1998), 60–87; Nancy Shoemaker, "Body Language," in Janet Moore Lindman and Michelle Lise Tartar, eds., *A Centre of Wonders: The Body in Early America* (Ithaca: Cornell University Press, 2001), 211–22. I do not intend to suggest here that familial or body language is insignificant to Civility's speech, or in any other Indian-colonial interactions for that matter. I am suggesting, however, that although Civility employs these metaphors in describing the relationship between his people and the provincial government, his normative statements regarding how the provincials should act are grounded in a history of alliance, friendship, and reciprocity. In this case—where Civility is making claims on the colonial government—normative folktales of justice are used in combination with descriptive metaphors of connection.

71. *MPCP*, 3:46.

72. Ibid., 2:599–600, 607–8. For other examples of Pennsylvania's Indians invoking Penn's example, see ibid., 3:46, 123; "Acount of Indian Council held at Philadelphia 15 Sept. 1718," Logan Papers, 9:7; "James Logan's Report on Meeting with Indians," *Memoirs of the Historical Society of Philadelphia* (Philadelphia: Historical Society of Pennsylvania, 1858), 6:254–57. James Spady has discussed Keith's (and later, Patrick Gordon's) references to Penn's history with the Indians as a continuation of a myth propagated by the proprietor himself about his own benevolence. See Spady's "Friendly Meetings" (1996) and his chapter in this volume. I would argue from the evidence presented here that Civility and other negotiators for the Conestoga and Delaware Indians were more instrumental in making the mythic relationship between Penn and provincial Indians central to colonial-Indian treaty discourse in the 1720s than was Penn's earlier propaganda. It seems likely that Keith's and Gordon's mentions of the Penn myth were more directly related to Indians' repeated invocation of the Penn-Indian relationship in the 1710s and 1720s than they were to anything Penn said or wrote about his relations with local Natives.

73. Both "Miquon" and "Onas" are Indian puns. Each word means, in its respective language, "quill" or "pen," thus working as cognates for Penn.

74. The discussion here is influenced by Robert A. Williams, Jr.'s analysis of Native American treaties as stories. See Williams, *Linking Arms Together: American Indian Treaty Visions of Law and Peace, 1600–1800* (New York: Oxford University Press, 1997).

75. *MPCP*, 3:221.

76. Merrell suggests that Civility conspired with the Cartlidges to bury Sawantaeny immediately both to keep the peace and to keep the Iroquois out of Pennsylvania, although he does not develop the question of whether or not any Indians in Pennsylvania would have desired that the Cartlidges be tried under English law for murder (Merrell, *Into the American Woods*, 117).

77. I should make clear that I do not intend by this passage to further the "myth" of the Iroquois Empire, or to suggest that the Iroquois attempt to bring the Indians on the Susquehanna under their influence was the equivalent of the colonial expansion of Pennsylvania's government and authority. As Jennings and Matthew Dennis have argued, the notion that the Iroquois nations functioned as an imperial or colonial power in any way comparable to European colonialism is inaccurate. See Jennings, *Ambiguous Iroquois Empire*, 10–24; Jennings, "'Pennsylvania Indians' and the Iroquois," in Daniel K. Richter and James H. Merrell, eds., *Beyond the Covenant Chain: The Iroquois and Their Neighbors in Indian North America, 1600–1800* (Syracuse, N.Y.: Syracuse University Press, 1987), 75–92; Dennis, *Cultivating a Landscape of Peace: Iroquois-European Encounters in Seventeenth-Century America* (Ithaca:

Cornell University Press, 1993), 6, 67, 229, 256, 257–58. Hinderaker, on the other hand, may go too far in this direction; his discussion of the settlement of Sawantaeny's death ignores the fact that non-Iroquois Indians were affected by the agreements reached between the Iroquois and Keith. He thus misses the fact that many Indians living on Pennsylvania's borders did consider the Iroquois unwanted intruders, if not "imperial" in the sense discussed above (*Elusive Empires*, 125–28).

78. *MPCP*, 3:302–3; *PA*, 1st ser., 1:215–21; "James Logan's Report," 258–63; Merrell, *Into the American Woods*, 158–64; Jennings, *Ambiguous Iroquois Empire*, 247; Hinderaker, *Elusive Empires*, 123–24.

79. "James Logan's Report," 258–63.

80. *MPCP*, 3:313.

81. Ibid., 329–31.

82. Ibid., 337.

83. *PA*, 1st series, 1:303–4; *MPCP*, 3:605.

84. *MPCP*, 3:435–52. Critically, however, whereas Gordon described this agreement on harboring fugitive slaves as implying that all Pennsylvania laws would be upheld on the frontier—including those punishing those guilty of intercultural assault or homicide—his Iroquois counterparts were silent on that issue.

85. *MPCP*, 3:500–505.

86. Ibid., 4:90–95.

87. Jennings, *Invasion of America*, 128–45.

88. My understanding of how assertions of jurisdiction transform space into territory—a particular kind of space under the domain of a single sovereign authority—is influenced by Christopher L. Tomlins, "The Legal Cartography of Colonization, the Legal Polyphony of Settlement: English Intrusions on the American Mainland in the Seventeenth Century," *Law and Social Inquiry* 26 (2001): 315–72. I should note that my argument here implicitly disagrees with the emphasis Tomlins places on colonial charters in mapping colonial rule; I argue here that ongoing practices of sanction and ratification, not the initial jurisdictional chartering, play the key role in producing territorial sovereignty. This is particularly true with respect to Tomlins's analysis of Pennsylvania. My disagreement is more a matter of emphasis and priority, however, than a rejection of Tomlins's fundamental argument, which is quite accurate.

89. *MPCP*, 3:330–31.

90. Ibid., 448–49. See also *MPCP*, 3:331.

91. Civility's attempts to retrospectively incorporate the Shawnees into the 1700 and 1701 treaties suggests that these two weaker Indian groups had made common cause in their efforts to stem the expansion of Iroquois influence to the south.

92. *MPCP*, 3:606.

93. Michael Meranze, "Even the Dead Will Not Be Safe: An Ethics of Early American History," *WMQ* 50 (1993): 373.

94. Ibid., 375, 378.

95. My argument here is heavily influenced by Daniel K. Richter's trenchant critique of the contemporary uses of this kind of early American victimology ("Whose Indian History?" *WMQ* 50 [1993]: 379–93).

96. My thinking here is deeply influenced by Cover, "Nomos and Narrative," and Axtell, *After Columbus*, 34–44.

97. Nor should we assume that Sawantaeny would necessarily have wanted to describe himself in a single, unifying narrative. As Richard White has pointed out, many Native American cultures were far more likely to employ multiple—and potentially contradictory—narratives of self to convey their social and political identity; see White, "'Although I am

dead, I am not entirely dead. I have left a second of myself': Constructing Self and Persons on the Middle Ground of Early America," in Ronald Hoffman, Mechal Sobel, and Fredrika J. Teute, eds., *Through a Glass Darkly: Reflections on Personal Identity in Early America* (Chapel Hill: University of North Carolina Press, 1997), 404–18. On identity as a product of personal narratives, see Charlotte Linde, *Life Stories: The Creation of Coherence* (New York: Oxford University Press, 1993). This discussion of cultural position and the interpretation of narratives is influenced by Arnold Krupat's discussion of the difficulties of an "authentic" indigenous literary criticism and the problems of Native American autobiography (*Ethnocriticism: Ethnography, History, Literature* [Berkeley: University of California Press, 1992], 153, 201–31).

98. For a discussion of the process by which dissenters or otherwise marginalized individuals—such as Sawantaeny—can have their "true Americanness" ratified and become symbolically incorporated into the national fold, see Waldstreicher, *In the Midst of Perpetual Fetes*, 349–52.

Chapter 7

1. "Proceedings Against John Toby at Paxton, February 15–17 [1751]," Weiser Collection, HSP. This consists of the two depositions and Weiser's account of events. There are two copies of each item, both in Weiser's hand, one of which is noticeably neater, suggesting that it was copied from the rougher version, which was probably the original. Another copy of the series is found at the Lancaster County Historical Society.

2. Alden T. Vaughan, "Frontier Banditti and the Indians: The Paxton Boys' Legacy, 1763–1775," *PH* 51 (1984): 19–20.

3. See Harold E. Driver, *Indians of North America* (Chicago: University of Chicago Press, 1969), 309–29, for contrasting Indian customs about killing. For the Paxton Boys' assumption that the war with Indians was continuous, see *MPCP*, 9:138–42.

4. James Axtell, *The European and the Indian: Essays in the Ethnohistory of Colonial North America* (New York: Oxford University Press, 1981), 152–53, 181–83, 194. A recent work that is in agreement on the basic point that Indian males did not routinely molest white female prisoners is Sharon Block's "Coerced Sex in British North America, 1700–1820" (Ph.D. diss., Princeton University, 1995), 235–39. Block, however, believes some captive women were forced to marry Indians when given the alternative of acceptance or death (239–41).

5. P. A. W. Wallace, *Conrad Weiser, 1696–1760: Friend to Mohawk and Colonist* (Philadelphia: University of Pennsylvania Press, 1945), 294–97, 333–35.

6. "Proceedings Against John Toby."

7. John and Edmund Cartlidge and Sawantaeny, for instance, had been drinking prior to their fateful argument; see chapter 6, above, and James H. Merrell, *Into the American Woods: Negotiators on the Pennsylvania Frontier* (New York: W. W. Norton, 1999), 115–16.

8. "Proceedings Against John Toby." Assuming there had been consistent spacing by the original penman, the crossed-out portion of the sentence is too narrow to have accommodated the thirteen character spaces of "private parts" yet too wide for the four letters in "cock." The language in Weiser's report is suspiciously similar to a victim's statement in a rape case heard in an English court, in the Lent session of 1759, suggesting that a very standardized wording was expected in rape indictments. "He had thrown her to the ground and 'lay with me, and entered his —— into my ——. I cried out murder as long as ever I was able; he stopt my mouth with my apron; I had hardly breath, and was near almost gone. He hurt me very much.'" Quoted in J. M. Beattie, *Crime and the Courts in England, 1660–1800* (Princeton: Princeton University Press, 1986), 125.

9. Conrad Weiser to Nanticoke Indians, 17 Feb. 1751, RG–21, Records of the Provincial Council, 1682–1776 (microfilm roll B2, item 564), PSA.

10. Weiser to [Gov. James Hamilton], 20 Feb. 1751. PHMC, Conrad Weiser Homestead, Womelsdorf, Pa.

11. David Hackett Fischer, *Albion's Seed: Four British Folkways in America* (New York: Oxford University Press, 1989), 194, 304; Hugh F. Rankin, *Criminal Trial Proceedings in the General Court of Colonial Virginia* (Williamsburg, Va.: Colonial Williamsburg, 1965), 222. Block quantifies and analyses the different systems applied to black and to white males but does not compare treatment of accused Indians because of paucity of examples ("Coerced Sex in British North America," 125–78).

12. Act of 27 Nov. 1700, chap. 4, James T. Mitchell and Henry Flanders, comps., *The Statutes at Large of Pennsylvania from 1682 to 1801*, 17 vols. (Harrisburg: State Printer, 1896–1915), 2:7; Act of 12 Jan. 1706, chap. 120, ibid., 2:178; Act of 31 May 1718, chap. 236 at sec. 4, ibid., 3:202. Separate statutes pertaining to Negroes offending white females were passed on 27 Nov. 1700 (ibid., 2:77) and 12 Jan. 1706 (ibid., 2:233).

13. Negley K. Teeters, *Scaffold and Chair: A Compilation of Their Use in Pennsylvania, 1682–1962* (Philadelphia: privately printed, 1963), 62–65.

14. *The King v. Patrick Kennedy, The King v. James DeWar, The King v. Thomas Fryer,* and *The King v. Neal McCarriher,* March 1772 session of oyer and terminer court, Chester County. RG–33, Records of the Supreme Court, Eastern District, oyer and terminer courts, papers 1757–1787, Chester County, PSA.

15. Examination of Patrick Kennedy and Neal McCarriher, 3 Dec. 1771; Examination of Thomas Fryer, 2 Dec. 1771; Examination of James DeWar, 2 Dec. 1771; Examination of Jane Walker in the presence of Thomas Fryer and James DeWar, 2 Dec. 1771, ibid.

16. *MPCP,* 4:280–82, 5:277; *PA,* 1st ser., 1:547–48. For Samuel Bethel and his tavern, see Franklin Ellis and Samuel Evans, *History of Lancaster County, Pennsylvania* (Chicago: Everts and Peck, 1883), 362–63; Jerome Wood Jr., *Conestoga Crossroads* (Harrisburg: PHMC, 1976), 11, 12, 50.

17. *MPCP,* 4:420–21, 447, 573–74.

18. Merrell, *Into the American Woods,* 42–55; Wallace, *Conrad Weiser,* 175–83. Basic documents about the murders can be found in *MPCP,* 4:675–84, and *PA,* 1st ser., 1:643–44, 646.

19. G. S. Rowe, *Embattled Bench: The Pennsylvania Supreme Court and the Forging of a Democratic Society, 1684–1809* (Newark: University of Delaware Press, 1994), 88–89; Act of 19 Oct. 1744, chap. 362, *Statutes at Large,* 5:5–6. The text of the Treaty of Lancaster is printed in Julian P. Boyd, ed., *Indian Treaties Printed by Benjamin Franklin, 1736–1762* (Philadelphia: HSP, 1938), 41–79; Wallace, *Conrad Weiser,* 181.

20. *MPCP,* 5:543–45.

21. Ibid.; C. A. Weslager, *The Nanticoke Indians, Past and Present* (Newark: University of Delaware Press, 1983), 150–52; Christian F. Feest, "Nanticoke and Neighboring Tribes," *Handbook,* 246. The Nanticokes' reputation for sorcery, poison, and treachery was so well established that it is also possible they assumed Pennsylvania would prefer that they live far away. They originally moved to Pennsylvania in the 1740s after the partially substantiated belief arose in Maryland that in 1742 the tribe had plotted, with Shawnee support, an uprising (Weslager, *Nanticoke Indians,* 97–99, 135–47).

22. *PA,* 8th ser., 4:3479.

23. *MPCP,* 9:328–32; Oscar J. Harvey and Ernest G. Smith, *A History of Wilkes-Barre, Luzerne County, Pennsylvania,* 6 vols. (Wilkes-Barre, Pa.: Raeder Press, 1909–30), 1:443. Harvey was convinced that "ore" meant anthracite coal. For Anderson, see *SCP,* 3:xvn.

24. Merrell, *Into the American Woods,* 312–13.

25. *MPCP*, 9:619–20; *SCP*, 3:165–66.

26. Although horse theft had long carried a death sentence in England, it did not in early American colonial history. There was no comprehensive branding system, so ownership was difficult to prove and any unguarded horse could be assumed to be an available natural object. Owners of missing horses could usually describe them only as "strayed or stolen." Indians had developed a reputation for being habitual horse thieves, but the problems of proving that a particular Indian had taken a particular horse were daunting. In Pennsylvania, the crime was more seriously punished after the Act of 21 Feb. 1767, and Toby and Turbutt Francis may have intended this to be French's fate. See *MPCP*, 7:172; ibid., 9:384, 698; Act of 31 May 1718, chap. 236, *Statutes at Large*, 2:199 (at 211–12); Act of 24 Feb. 1721, chap. 241, ibid., 240; Act of 9 May 1724, chap. 279, ibid., 3:422; Act of 21 Feb. 1767, chap. 557, ibid., 7:90; "Strayed or Stolen away from the Borough of Wilmington . . . ," *Pennsylvania Gazette*, 2 May 1751.

Chapter 8

1. Witham Marshe, "Journal of the Treaty Held with the Six Nations by the Commissioners of Maryland, and Other Provinces, at Lancaster, in Pennsylvania, June 1744," *Collections of the Massachusetts Historical Society*, 1st ser., 7 (1801): 179.

2. Daniel G. Brinton, *The Lenape and Their Legends; with the Complete Text and Symbols of the Walam Olum, a New Translation, and an Inquiry into Its Authenticity* (Philadelphia: D. G. Brinton, 1884), 121; Paul A. W. Wallace, *Conrad Weiser, 1696–1760, Friend of Colonist and Mohawk* (Philadelphia: University of Pennsylvania Press, 1945), 73, 126; Francis Jennings, *The Ambiguous Iroquois Empire: The Covenant Chain Confederation of Indian Tribes with the English Colonies from Its Beginnings to the Lancaster Treaty of 1744* (New York: W. W. Norton, 1984), 362.

3. Donald A. Grinde Jr., "Iroquois Political Theory and the Roots of American Democracy," in Oren R. Lyons and John C. Mohawk, eds., *Exiled in the Land of the Free: Democracy, Indian Nations, and the U.S. Constitution* (Santa Fe: Clear Light Publishers, 1992), 241, 251. See also Grinde, *The Iroquois and the Founding of the American Nation* (San Francisco: Indian Historian Press, 1977); and Bruce E. Johansen, *Forgotten Founders: Benjamin Franklin, the Iroquois, and the Rationale for the American Revolution* (Ipswich, Mass.: Gambit, 1982). The most to-the-point refutations are found in Elisabeth Tooker, "The United States Constitution and the Iroquois League," *Ethnohistory* 35 (1988): 305–36; and William A. Starna and George R. Hamell, "History and the Burden of Proof: The Case of Iroquois Influence on the U.S. Constitution," *New York History* 77 (1996): 427–52.

4. Canasatego plays a role in a number of authoritative studies of the period. See, e.g., Wallace, *Conrad Weiser*; Jennings, *Ambiguous Iroquois Empire*; William N. Fenton, *The Great Law and the Longhouse: A Political History of the Iroquois Confederacy* (Norman: University of Oklahoma Press, 1998); and James H. Merrell, *Into the American Woods: Negotiators on the Pennsylvania Frontier* (New York: W. W. Norton, 1999).

5. William M. Beauchamp, ed., *Moravian Journals Relating to Central New York, 1745–66* (Syracuse, N.Y.: Dehler Press, 1916), 22; Hanni Woodbury, personal communication, 1994.

6. See Fenton, *Great Law*, 193.

7. Beauchamp, ed., *Moravian Journals*, 13.

8. Fenton, *Great Law*, 411.

9. John Bartram, *A Journey from Pennsylvania to Onondaga in 1743* (Barre, Mass.: Imprint Society, 1973), 58–59; Wallace, *Conrad Weiser*, 160.

10. Beauchamp, ed., *Moravian Journals*, 46.

11. Ibid., 56, 58.

12. Ibid., 46.

13. Ibid., 14; *MPCP*, 4:662, 665, 668.

14. *MPCP*, 5:401.

15. Daniel K. Richter, *The Ordeal of the Longhouse: The Peoples of the Iroquois League in the Era of European Colonization* (Chapel Hill: University of North Carolina Press, 1992), 255, 256, 270.

16. *NYCD*, 5:485–87; Richter, *Ordeal*, 232; John Duffy, *Epidemics in Colonial America* (Baton Rouge: Louisiana State University Press, 1953), 81.

17. *NYCD*, 6:362.

18. Quoted in Wallace, *Conrad Weiser*, 88.

19. Ibid., 126.

20. *MPCP*, 4:564.

21. Beauchamp, ed., *Moravian Journals*, 85.

22. Ibid., 94–95.

23. Ibid., 94–97.

24. Ibid., 70.

25. Ibid., 73–74.

26. Ibid., 75.

27. Ibid., 79; Richter, *Ordeal*, 263–66.

28. Richter, *Ordeal*, 266; *NYCD*, 5:275, 487–88; 9:1041, 1083–85, 1090.

29. Jennings, *Ambiguous Iroquois Empire*, 307; Richter, *Ordeal*, 271.

30. Jennings, *Ambiguous Iroquois Empire*, 307; Richard White, *The Middle Ground: Indians, Empires, and Republics in the Great Lakes Region, 1650–1815* (Cambridge: Cambridge University Press, 1991), 189, and see esp. chaps. 5 and 6.

31. White, *Middle Ground*, 168.

32. Jennings, *Ambiguous Iroquois Empire*, 307.

33. Ibid., 307–8; James H. Merrell, "'Their Very Bones Shall Fight': The Catawba-Iroquois Wars," in Daniel K. Richter and James H. Merrell, eds., *Beyond the Covenant Chain: The Iroquois and Their Neighbors in Indian North America, 1600–1800* (Syracuse, N.Y.: Syracuse University Press, 1987), 115–33.

34. Francis Jennings, "Miquon's Passing: Indian-European Relations in Colonial Pennsylvania, 1674 to 1775" (Ph.D. diss., University of Pennsylvania, 1965); Richard L. Haan, "The Problem of Iroquois Neutrality: Suggestions for Revision," *Ethnohistory* 27 (1980): 317–30. The Mohawks remained uninterested in Pennsylvania and the Susquehanna lands throughout a good part of the eighteenth century. Their attention was directed toward the English in Albany, with whom they traded and to whom they were fast losing their lands. There also was the French presence in the Champlain Valley to be reckoned with. And they had lost significant numbers of their population to disease and emigration to the St. Lawrence missions, causing them to stay close to their homeland. These factors taken together explain their lack of participation in Pennsylvania treaty business. Fenton, *Great Law*, 401–3, 410; Jennings, *Iroquois Empire*, 251.

35. *MPCP*, 4:80. For an account of Shickellamy's life, political involvements, and accomplishments, see James H. Merrell, "Shickellamy, 'A Person of Consequence,'" in Robert S. Grumet, ed., *Northeastern Indian Lives, 1632–1816* (Amherst: University of Massachusetts Press, 1996), 227–57; and Merrell, *Into the American Woods*.

36. Quoted in Wallace, *Conrad Weiser*, 44.

37. Ibid.; Jennings, *Ambiguous Iroquois Empire*, 322–23.

38. Quoted in Jennings, *Ambiguous Iroquois Empire,* 324.

39. Richter, *Ordeal,* 275; Jennings, *Ambiguous Iroquois Empire,* 322–23; Wallace, *Conrad Weiser,* 67, 70.

40. Richter, *Ordeal,* 275.

41. *MPCP,* 4:80. At the 1742 treaty in Philadelphia, Canasatego observed: "This affair was recommended to you by our Chiefs at our Last Treaty [1736], and you then, at our earnest desire, promised to write a Letter to that person who has the authority over those People, and to procure Us his Answer" (ibid., 4:570). This suggests that either Canasatego had been well coached about what he was to say to the governor, or that he had been present at the 1736 treaty and was recalling what had taken place.

42. *MPCP,* 4:583–86; Wallace, *Conrad Weiser,* 126.

43. *MPCP,* 4:559–60.

44. Ibid., 561.

45. Jennings, *Ambiguous Iroquois Empire,* 328–42. See also Wallace, *Conrad Weiser;* and Anthony F. C. Wallace, *King of the Delawares: Teedyuscung, 1700–1763* (Philadelphia: University of Pennsylvania Press, 1949).

46. *MPCP,* 4:570.

47. Ibid., 573.

48. Ibid., 575.

49. Ibid., 575–76.

50. Ibid., 579.

51. Ibid., 579–80. The label "women," applied to the Delawares, has often been linked to the false notion of their defeat by the Iroquois. It is, however, perhaps more relevant in situations where the Delawares acted as mediators or agreed to let the Iroquois speak for them, at least in New York. See Francis Jennings, " 'Pennsylvania Indians' and the Iroquois," in Richter and Merrell, eds., *Beyond the Covenant Chain,* 79–80.

52. *MPCP,* 4:580. By 1742, many Delawares, perhaps the majority, had already migrated west. C. A. Weslager, *The Delaware Indians: A History* (New Brunswick, N.J.: Rutgers University Press, 1972), 173–95.

53. Jennings, *Ambiguous Iroquois Empire,* 344.

54. Ibid., 343–46; *MPCP,* 4:567.

55. *MPCP,* 4:567–69.

56. John Bartram, *Travels in Pensilvania and Canada* (Ann Arbor, Mich.: University Microfilms, 1966).

57. Wallace, *Conrad Weiser,* 147; *MPCP,* 4:644–46.

58. *MPCP,* 4:660.

59. Ibid., 661.

60. Beauchamp, ed., *Moravian Journals,* 23; Marshe, "Journal," 179–80.

61. *MPCP,* 4:644–46, 661–62; Jennings, *Ambiguous Iroquois Empire,* 354–55.

62. *MPCP,* 4:654, 641, 663.

63. Ibid., 667–68.

64. Ibid., 728.

65. Ibid., 700.

66. Ibid., 703–4.

67. Ibid., 706–7.

68. Jennings, *Ambiguous Iroquois Empire,* 357.

69. Ibid., 359–60; *MPCP,* 4:715–16, 726, 729.

70. Jennings, *Ambiguous Iroquois Empire,* 361–62.

71. Wallace, *Conrad Weiser,* 221; *MPCP,* 4:778.

72. *MPCP,* 4:778.

73. Ibid., 731–32.

74. Quoted in Wallace, *Conrad Weiser,* 225.

75. Beauchamp, ed., *Moravian Journals,* 13–14.

76. *NYCD,* 6:300; *MPCP,* 5:18, 22–23.

77. See Timothy J. Shannon, *Indians and Colonists at the Crossroads of Empire: The Albany Congress of 1754* (Ithaca: Cornell University Press, 2000), 33–35.

78. *NYCD,* 6:289; *MPCP,* 5:9; Julian P. Boyd, ed., *Indian Treaties Printed by Benjamin Franklin, 1736–1762* (Philadelphia: HSP, 1938), 309–10.

79. Jennings, *Ambiguous Iroquois Empire,* 307, 335.

80. Boyd, ed., *Indian Treaties,* 309.

81. Wallace, *Conrad Weiser,* 229.

82. *MPCP,* 5:24.

83. Ibid., 18.

84. Boyd, ed., *Indian Treaties,* 310.

85. *MPCP,* 5:8–9.

86. Ibid., 4:735, 5:19.

87. See Tooker, "United States Constitution and the Iroquois League," 321–22.

88. Conrad Weiser to Richard Peters, 8 May 1749, Conrad Weiser Correspondence, 1741–66, HSP (1st quotation); Wallace, *Conrad Weiser,* 277–85 (2d quotation from p. 279). This account of the 1749 conference was written in collaboration with David Preston.

89. Quoted in Wallace, *Conrad Weiser,* 278–79.

90. Ibid.

91. Ibid., 281.

92. Quoted in ibid., 282.

93. Quoted in ibid.

94. *MPCP,* 5:395–410 (quotation from p. 400).

95. *MPCP,* 5:408, 477.

96. Ibid., 5:399.

97. Ibid., 399–400.

98. Beauchamp, ed., *Moravian Journals,* 46–47.

99. Ibid., 49–50.

100. Ibid., 53.

101. Christian Daniel Claus, *Daniel Claus' Narrative of His Relations with Sir William Johnson and Experiences in the Lake George Fight* (New York: Society of Colonial Wars, 1904), 5.

102. Helga Doblin and William Starna, trans. and eds., *The Journals of Christian Daniel Claus and Conrad Weiser: A Journey to Onondaga, 1750,* Transactions of the American Philosophical Society 84, pt. 2 (Philadelphia: American Philosophical Society, 1994), 16. Compare: "They informed me further that Mr Camerhoff went from Onontago, to the Cajuger and Sinicker Country and told the Indians there that he had bought a great piece of Land of Canasatego and paid him with Silver Ornaments (I doubt the Truth of this Last article and beliefe it was invented to blaken Canasategos Caracter) but it was currently reported at Onontago, and perhaps occasioned his Canasategos Death" (quoted in Wallace, *Conrad Weiser,* 314).

103. *MPCP,* 5:467.

104. Doblin and Starna, trans. and eds., *Journals,* 14–15; see Wallace, *Conrad Weiser,* 314.

105. Doblin and Starna, trans. and eds., *Journals,* 15; see Wallace, *Conrad Weiser,* 314.

106. Beauchamp, ed., *Moravian Journals,* 54–56, 95–97.

107. Ibid., 54. The historical record does not contradict any of Cammerhoff's statements. See Wallace, *Conrad Weiser*, 313–15; *RMM*, reel 34, box 317, folder 1, items 3 and 4.

108. Beauchamp, ed., *Moravian Journals*, 60.

109. Wallace, *Conrad Weiser*, 343–46.

110. Doblin and Starna, trans. and eds., *Journals*, 15; Wallace, *Conrad Weiser*, 314.

111. Claus's version of Canasatego's death was probably written twenty-five or more years after the fact. He had little reason to misrepresent what had happened. See Jennings, *Iroquois Empire*, 363n.

112. *MPCP*, 5:480. The word is "buried" in the original document. Francis Jennings, personal communication, 1994.

113. Jennings, *Ambiguous Iroquois Empire*, 364–65.

114. Doblin and Starna, trans. and eds., *Journals*, 13; *MPCP*, 5:467, 475.

115. Doblin and Starna, trans. and eds., *Journals*, 17.

Chapter 9

1. Delawares to Jeremiah Langhorne, Smithfield, 3 Jan. 1741, Penn Manuscripts, Indian Affairs, vol. 4, Indian Walk, 30, HSP.

2. Francis Jennings, "Miquon's Passing: Indian-European Relations in Colonial Pennsylvania, 1674 to 1755" (Ph.D. diss., University of Pennsylvania, 1965), 380–84.

3. Charles Thomson, the Pennsylvania schoolmaster and later secretary of the Continental Congress, witnessed negotiations between Delawares and King George's representatives. He investigated the causes of Delaware alienation and published his findings in *An Enquiry into the Causes of the Alienation of the Delaware and Shawanese from the British Interest* (Philadelphia, 1759). John Heckewelder, the Moravian missionary who learned Delaware ways firsthand and from his predecessor David Zeisberger, wrote an *Account of the History, Manners, and Customs of the Indian Nations Who Once Inhabited Pennsylvania* (Philadelphia: HSP, 1876). Like Thomson, Heckewelder documented Delaware dissatisfaction with the Walking Purchase. The later Moravian chronicler William Reichel relied on them.

4. Heckewelder, *History*, 66–69.

5. Penn Manuscripts, Indian Affairs, Indian Walk, 4:43, HSP.

6. Account of the Walking Purchase by Moses Tetamie, Friendly Association Papers, 1:407, QCHC.

7. William J. Buck, *History of the Indian Walk, Performed for the Proprietaries of Pennsylvania in 1737* ([Philadelphia]: privately printed, 1886), 43.

8. Ibid., 205–6.

9. William C. Reichel, ed., *Memorials of the Moravian Church*, vol. 1 (Philadelphia: J. B. Lippincott, 1870), 218.

10. "Affair of Nicholas Depue," *[Pennsylvania] Department of Internal Affairs Monthly Bulletin* 21, no. 1 (October 1953): 32.

11. William Allen to John Penn, 17 Nov. 1739, Penn Manuscripts, Official Correspondence, 3:91, HSP.

12. Delawares to Jeremiah Langhorne, Smithfield, 3 Jan. 1741, Penn Manuscripts, Indian Affairs, vol. 4, Indian Walk, HSP.

13. George Thomas to Delaware Indians, 21 Mar. 1741, Penn Manuscripts, vol. 4, Indian Walk, HSP.

14. Thomas Penn to Richard Peters, 17 July 1752, HSP.

15. Thomas Penn to Richard Peters, 12 Apr. 1759, Penn Manuscripts, Supplementary Saunders Coates, 17:92, HSP.

16. Quoted in Ralph Grayson Schwarz, *Bethlehem on the Lehigh* (Bethlehem, Pa.: Bethlehem Area Foundation, n.d.), 5.

17. Pennsylvania Land Records, Patent Books, F6, 102, PSA; Northampton County Deed Books, C1, 156–64, Northampton County Courthouse, Easton, Pa.; Buck, *History of the Indian Walk,* 45; Schwarz, *Bethlehem on the Lehigh,* 5.

18. Elizabeth L. Myers, *The Upper Places: Nazareth, Gnadenthal, and Christian's Spring* (Easton, Pa.: Northampton County Historical and Genealogical Society, 1929), 4.

19. Heckewelder, *History,* 47–70; Joseph M. Levering, *A History of Bethlehem, Pennsylvania, 1741–1892* (Bethlehem, Pa.: Times Publishing, 1903), 50–52, 153–56.

20. Quoted in Buck, *History of the Indian Walk,* 46.

21. Anthony F. C. Wallace, *King of the Delawares, Teedyuscung, 1700–1763* (Philadelphia: University of Pennsylvania Press, 1949), 38.

22. Jane Merritt, "Dreaming of the Savior's Blood: Moravians and the Indian Great Awakening in Pennsylvania," *WMQ* 54 (1997): 746.

23. Sereno Edwards Dwight, ed., *Memoirs of the Reverend David Brainerd* (New Haven, Conn.: S. Converse, 1822), 176.

24. Ibid., 151, 168, 174–78.

25. James Steel to John Chapman, 17 May 1733, James Steel Letterbook, HSP.

26. "Count Zinzendorf and the Indians, 1742," in Reichel, ed., *Memorials of the Moravian Church,* 1:26–27.

27. Pennsylvania Land Records, Applications, 1732–33:17, PSA; Pennsylvania Land Records, Patent Book A8:405–6, PSA; Patent Book A9:530–32, PSA. The fullest treatment of Tatamy is William A. Hunter, "Moses (Tunda) Tatamy, Delaware Indian Diplomat," in Robert S. Grumet, ed., *Northeastern Indian Lives, 1632–1816* (Amherst: University of Massachusetts Press, 1996), 258–73.

28. Zinzendorf, as quoted in Reichel, ed., *Memorials of the Moravian Church,* 1:26–27.

29. *MPCP,* 4:624–25.

30. Richard Peters to Thomas Penn, 21 Nov. 1742, Peters Letterbook, vol. 5, HSP. Penn replied, "I hope the Governor has given such an answer to the Fork Indians as you say he intended, their assurance is indeed astonishing, you have not informed me how they [be]-came converted to Calvinism and I suppose they are not acquainted with much of their doctrines" (Penn to Peters, Penn Letterbooks, 2:25, HSP).

31. David Brainerd, *Mirabilia Dei Inter Indicos; or The Rise and Progress of a Remarkable Work of Grace Amongst a Number of the Indians in the Provinces of New-Jersey and Pennsylvania* (Philadelphia, 1746), 8.

32. Ibid.

33. Ibid., 9.

34. Dwight, ed., *Memoirs of Brainerd,* 178.

35. Brainerd, *Mirabilia Dei Inter Indicos,* 9–10, emphasis in original.

36. Ibid., 10–14.

37. He was so designated by the 1738 patent that granted him full rights to his farm. Pennsylvania Land Records, Patent Book A8:405–6, PSA.

38. Quoted in Hunter, "Moses (Tunda) Tatamy," 264.

39. Bernhard Adam Grube, Diarium von Meniowolagamekah, 14, 17 May, 14 June 1752, MAB; *MPCP,* 8:463–72; *PA,* 3:707–9; Samuel Parrish, *Some Chapters in the History of the Friendly Association for Regaining and Preserving Peace with the Indians by Pacific Measures* (Philadelphia: Friends Historical Association, 1877), 117.

40. Steven C. Harper, *Promised Land: The Holy Experiment, the Walking Purchase, and*

Dispossession of the Delawares, 1600–1763 (Bethlehem, Pa.: Lehigh University Press, forthcoming).

41. Resolution requesting a warrant for two hundred acres for Tatamy, an Indian, 1769, Pennsylvania Land Papers, Moore Collection, HSP.

42. Hunter, "Moses (Tunda) Tatamy," 258–72; James H. Merrell, *Into the American Woods: Negotiators on the Pennsylvania Frontier* (New York: W. W. Norton, 1999), 145; Marshall J. Becker, "The Boundary Between the Lenape and Munsee: The Forks of the Delaware as a Buffer Zone," *Man in the Northeast* 26 (1983): 1–20.

43. Quoted in Merritt, "Dreaming of the Savior's Blood," 730.

44. Quoted in Reichel, ed., *Memorials of the Moravian Church,* 1:119–20.

45. Moses Tatamy, Account of Indian Complaints, Friendly Association Papers, 1:65, QCHC.

46. Reichel, ed., *Memorials of the Moravian Church,* 1:192.

47. Ibid., 1:193–94.

48. Peters to Thomas Penn, 4 Aug. 1756, Peters Letterbook, 1755–57, HSP.

49. Reichel, ed., *Memorials of the Moravian Church,* 1:200; Buck, *History of the Indian Walk,* 222–23.

50. Buck, *History of the Indian Walk,* 222–29, 236–38.

51. Reichel, ed., *Memorials of the Moravian Church,* 1:207.

52. Robert Hunter Morris to Moravian Indians, 4 Dec. 1755, in Reichel, ed., *Memorials of the Moravian Church,* 1:211.

53. Edward Shippen to William Allen, 16 Dec. 1755, HSP.

54. Richard Peters to Thomas Penn, 4 Jan. 1757, HSP.

55. Richard Peters to Thomas Penn, 7 Jan. 1757, HSP.

56. Conrad Weiser to Thomas Penn, 28 Feb. 1757, HSP.

57. Friendly Association Papers 1:63, QCHC.

58. *MPCP,* 7:109.

59. Thomas Penn to William Peters, 7 July 1756, HSP.

Chapter 10

1. Richard Peters identified the Stuarts as illegal settlers in 1750: see *MPCP,* 5:444.

2. Beverley W. Bond, ed., "The Captivity of Charles Stuart, 1755–57," *Mississippi Valley Historical Review* 13 (1926): 58–81.

3. Bond, ed., "Captivity of Charles Stuart," 61–62. Alan Taylor's review of James Merrell's *Into the American Woods* calls for an investigation of ordinary settlers' relations with Natives ("The Bad Birds," *New Republic* 9 [August 1999]: 45–49).

4. I am defining "ordinary settlers" as the middling to poor farmers, tavern keepers, rural artisans (blacksmiths, millers, carpenters, weavers, etc.), and squatters living on small tracts of frontier land with their families. I also use the term to denote ordinary Indian settlers or villagers who are often neglected at the expense of well-known Indian sachems and warriors.

5. *PWJ,* 10:645.

6. For a detailed analysis of land tenure arrangements between Natives and colonists on the New York–Pennsylvania–Six Nations borders, see David L. Preston, "The Texture of Contact: European and Indian Settler Communities on the Iroquoian Borderlands, 1720–1780" (Ph.D. diss., College of William and Mary, 2002).

7. Thomas Penn to James Hamilton, 31 July 1749, Thomas Penn Letterbooks, 2:272–73,

Thomas Penn Papers, HSP; Richard Peters to the Proprietors, 25 April 1749, Richard Peters Letterbooks, 1737–50, Richard Peters Papers, 348, HSP.

8. New York Council Minutes, 3 Mar. 1722, 13, 14 May 1746, New York Council Minutes, 1668–1783 (A1895), 12:250, 21:91–92, New York State Archives, Albany.

9. The proprietors launched three expeditions in 1748, 1750, and 1768 to eject squatters from disputed lands within their charter claims.

10. Jeremy Adelman and Stephen Aron, "From Borderlands to Borders: Empires, Nation-States, and the Peoples in Between in North American History," *American Historical Review* 104 (1999): 814–41. For an exploration of the "Iroquoian borderlands" surrounding the Six Nations, see Preston, "Texture of Contact," 2–17.

11. See James T. Lemon, *The Best Poor Man's Country: A Geographical Study of Early Southeastern Pennsylvania* (Baltimore: Johns Hopkins University Press, 1972); and D. W. Meinig, *The Shaping of America: A Geographical Perspective on Five Hundred Years of History*, vol. 1, *Atlantic America, 1492–1800* (New Haven: Yale University Press, 1986), 131–44.

12. Rowland Berthoff and John M. Murrin, "Feudalism, Communalism, and the Yeoman Freeholder: The American Revolution Considered as Social Accident," in Stephen G. Kurtz and James H. Hutson, eds., *Essays on the American Revolution* (New York: W. W. Norton, 1973), 256–88; Lemon, *Best Poor Man's Country*, chap. 2; Alan Tully, *William Penn's Legacy: Politics and Social Structure in Pennsylvania, 1726–1755* (Baltimore: Johns Hopkins University Press, 1977), 3–15.

13. The proprietors' land purchases at the 1749 Philadelphia treaty, the 1754 Albany Conference, and the 1768 Fort Stanwix treaty encompassed the Susquehanna and Juniata valleys and much of the Ohio country. For explanations of the treaties, see William N. Fenton, *The Great Law and the Longhouse: A Political History of the Iroquois Confederacy* (Norman: University of Oklahoma Press, 1998).

14. James Anderson, quoted in Patrick Griffin, "The People with No Name: Ulster's Migrants and Identity Formation in Eighteenth-Century Pennsylvania," *WMQ* 58 (2001): 587–614; *MPCP*, 9:509 (2d quotation); Lucy Simler, "Tenancy in Colonial Pennsylvania: The Case of Chester County," *WMQ* 43 (1986): 542–69; James T. Lemon and Gary B. Nash, "The Distribution of Wealth in Eighteenth Century America: A Century of Change in Chester County, Pennsylvania, 1693–1802," *Journal of Social History* 2 (1968): 1–24.

15. Richard Maxwell Brown, "Backcountry Rebellions and the Homestead Ethic in America, 1740–1799," in Richard Maxwell Brown and Don E. Fehrenbacher, eds., *Tradition, Conflict, and Modernization: Perspectives on the American Revolution* (New York: Academic Press, 1977), 73–99; Daniel Vickers, "Competency and Competition: Economic Culture in Early America," *WMQ* 47 (1990): 3–29; Stephen Aron, *How the West Was Lost: The Transformation of Kentucky from Daniel Boone to Henry Clay* (Baltimore: Johns Hopkins, 1996), 79–81.

16. *PA*, 1st ser., 2:14 (1st quotation), 8th ser., 4:3325 (2d quotation); *MPCP*, 6:218–19 (3d quotation), 4:445 (4th quotation); Phillip W. Hoffman, "Simon Girty: His War on the Frontier," in Nancy L. Rhoden and Ian K. Steele, eds., *The Human Tradition in the American Revolution* (Wilmington, Del.: Scholarly Resources, 2000), 221–40; Griffin, "People with No Name," 587–614.

17. Richard White, *The Middle Ground: Indians, Empires, and Republics in the Great Lakes Region, 1650–1815* (Cambridge: Cambridge University Press, 1991), 341; Aron, "Rights in the Woods," 175–204; Aron, *How the West Was Lost*, chaps. 1 and 2; John Mack Faragher, *Daniel Boone: The Life and Legend of an American Pioneer* (New York: Henry Holt, 1992), 19–23; Daniel H. Usner, *Indians, Settlers, and Slaves in a Frontier Exchange Economy: The Lower Mississippi Valley Before 1783* (Chapel Hill: University of North Carolina Press, 1992). See also chapter 11, below.

18. Pennsylvania Provincial Council Minutes, 1 Sept. 1728, in Francis Jennings, William N. Fenton, Mary A. Druke, and David R. Miller, eds., *Iroquois Indians: A Documentary History of the Diplomacy of the Six Nations and Their League*, 50 microfilm reels (Woodbridge, Conn.: Research Publications, 1984), reel 10; *MPCP*, 3:599.

19. David Landy, "Tuscarora Among the Iroquois," in *Handbook*, 520; *MPCP*, 8:722–23; Barry C. Kent, Janet Rice, and Kakuko Ota, "A Map of Eighteenth Century Indian Towns in Pennsylvania," *Pennsylvania Archaeologist* 51, no. 4 (1981): 1–18, esp. 8–9, 12; Henry Harbaugh, *The Life of Rev. Michael Schlatter* (Philadelphia: Lindsay and Blakiston, 1857), 172–73.

20. George Armstrong, warrant no. 40, 3 Feb. 1755, Original Warrants, Cumberland County, Records of the Land Office (RG–17) (microfilm reel no. 3.46), PSA; New Purchase Register, entries 3793, Records of Land Office, PSA (microfilm reel 1.9); John W. Jordan, *A History of the Juniata Valley and Its Peoples*, 3 vols. (New York: Historical Publishing, 1913), 1:30–31 (quotations).

21. *MPCP*, 5:544 (1st quotation); "Diary of J. Martin Mack's, David Zeisberger's and Gottfried Rundt's Journey to Onondaga in 1752," in William M. Beauchamp, ed., *Moravian Journals Relating to Central New York, 1745–66* (Syracuse, N.Y.: Dehler Press, 1916), 151 (2d quotation), 179; *MPCP*, 7:676 (3d quotation). See also chapter 9, above, on Teedyuscung's role in intercultural diplomacy during the Seven Years' War.

22. Marshall J. Becker, "Hannah Freeman: An Eighteenth-Century Lenape Living and Working Among Colonial Farmers," *PMHB* 114 (1990): 249–70; *PA*, 8th ser., 2:1701; 1st ser., 1:239; 2d ser., 19:626; *MPCP*, 3:48–49, 4:656–58, 8:198–99, 247; "Journey to Onondaga in 1752," in Beauchamp, ed., *Moravian Journals*, 151; William Cronon, *Changes in the Land: Indians, Colonists, and the Ecology of New England* (New York: Hill and Wang, 1983); Virginia DeJohn Anderson, "King Philip's Herds: Indians, Colonists, and the Problem of Livestock in Early New England," *WMQ* 51 (1994): 601–24; Timothy Silver, *A New Face on the Countryside: Indians, Colonists, and Slaves in the South Atlantic Forests, 1500–1800* (Cambridge: Cambridge University Press, 1990).

23. *PA*, 1st ser., 1:205–6 (1st quotation); *MPCP*, 3:507 (2d quotation); Jonathan Edwards, *The Life of David Brainerd*, ed. Norman Pettit, vol. 7 of *The Works of Jonathan Edwards* (New Haven: Yale University Press, 1985), 347; Edmund Berkeley and Dorothy Smith Berkeley, *The Correspondence of John Bartram, 1734–1777* (Miami: University Press of Florida, 1992), 400 (4th quotation); Preston, "Texture of Contact," chaps. 1–4. On the Delaware Jargon, see chapter 2, above. On friendly relations between Euro-American settlers and the Conestoga Indians see also Rhoda Barber, Journal, HSP.

24. U. J. Jones, *History of the Early Settlement of the Juniata Valley* (Harrisburg: Telegraph Press, 1940; orig. pub. Philadelphia, 1856), 64–65.

25. See James H. Merrell, "Shikellamy, 'A Person of Consequence,'" in Robert S. Grumet, ed., *Northeastern Indian Lives, 1632–1816* (Amherst: University of Massachusetts Press, 1996), 227–57.

26. Abraham H. Cassell, ed., "Notes on the Iroquois and Delaware Indians," *PMHB* 1 (1877): 165–66; *PA*, 1st ser., 2:319–20.

27. *PA*, 8th ser., 4:3327; Merrell, "Shikellamy," 227–57; *MPCP*, 4:648, 561.

28. *PA*, 1st ser., 2:24 (1st quotation); *MPCP*, 5:389 (2d quotation); *MPCP*, 5:391–92; Warren Hofstra, "'The Extension of His Majesty's Dominions': The Virginia Backcountry and the Reconfiguration of Imperial Frontiers," *Journal of American History* 84 (1998): 1281–312.

29. *PA*, 1st ser., 2:15; Paul A. W. Wallace, *Conrad Weiser, 1696–1760: Friend of Colonist and Mohawk* (Philadelphia: University of Pennsylvania Press, 1945), 277–79; idem, *Indian Paths of Pennsylvania* (Harrisburg: PHMC, 1965), 49–53, 168–70; *MPCP*, 5:394–95 (quotation).

30. *PA*, 1st ser., 2:15; John W. Jordan, ed., "The Journal of James Kenny, 1761–1763," *PMHB* 37 (1913): 177.

31. *PA*, 1st ser., 2:24. Weiser later informed the Shamokin Indians that Scaroyady "had given liberty (with what right I could not tell) to setle."

32. James Lynch, "The Iroquois Confederacy and the Adoption and Administration of Non-Iroquoian Individuals and Groups Prior to 1756," *Man in the Northeast*, no. 30 (fall 1985): 83–99; Kathleen J. Bragdon, *Native People of Southern New England, 1500–1650* (Norman: University of Oklahoma Press, 1996), 43, 137–39; Anthony F. C. Wallace, "Woman, Land, and Society: Three Aspects of Aboriginal Delaware Life," *Pennsylvania Archaeologist*, no. 17 (1947): 1–35.

33. Michael N. McConnell, "Peoples 'In Between': The Iroquois and the Ohio Indians, 1720–1768," in Richter and Merrell, eds., *Beyond the Covenant Chain*, 93–114; Paul A. W. Wallace, *Indians in Pennsylvania*, 2d ed. (Harrisburg: PHMC, 1993), 181; Daniel K. Richter, *The Ordeal of the Longhouse: The Peoples of the Iroquois League in the Era of European Colonization* (Chapel Hill: University of North Carolina Press, 1992), 275.

34. *MPCP*, 5:407–8.

35. Richard Peters to the Proprietors, 5 July 1749, Richard Peters Letterbooks, 1737–50, 363, HSP; Wallace, *Conrad Weiser*, 297; Joseph S. Lucas, "The Course of Empire and the Long Road to Civilization: North American Indians and Scottish Enlightenment Historians," *Explorations in Early American Culture* 4 (2000): 166–90.

36. Conrad Weiser to Richard Peters, 7 Feb. 1754, Berks and Montgomery Counties Miscellaneous Manuscripts, 1693–1869, HSP.

37. Richard Peters to the Proprietors, 16 May, 5 July 1749, Richard Peters Letterbooks, 1737–50, 357, 363; "Letter from Thomas Penn to James Tilghman, November 7, 1766," *Western Pennsylvania Historical Magazine* 57 (1974): 239–48 (quotation p. 242); Woody Holton, "'Rebel Against Rebel': Enslaved Virginians and the Coming of the American Revolution," *Virginia Magazine of History and Biography* 105 (1997): 157–92.

38. Thomas Penn to James Hamilton, 9 Oct. 1749, Thomas Penn Letterbooks, 2:390; Richard Peters to the Proprietors, 11 Sept. 1749, Richard Peters Letterbook, 1737–50, 381; Peters to the Proprietors, 5 May 1750, Penn Manuscripts, Official Correspondence, 5:9; Conrad Weiser to Peters, 7 Feb. 1754, Berks and Montgomery Counties Manuscripts. For Indian-settler tenant relations, see New Purchase Applications, 1769, Land Records, PSA (microfilm reel 1.9) [Arthur Auchmuty, no. 46]; William Henry Egle, ed., *Minutes of the Board of Property*, *PA*, 2d ser., 1:239–43. Periodic famines and food shortages also may have induced some Susquehanna Indians to negotiate land tenure relationships that involved payment-in-kind: see "An Account of the Famine Among the Indians of the North and West Branch of the Susquehanna, in the Summer of 1748," *PMHB* 16 (1892): 430–32; and James H. Merrell, "Unsettling the Early American Frontier," in Andrew R. L. Cayton and Fredrika Teute, eds., *Contact Points: American Frontiers from the Mohawk Valley to the Mississippi, 1750–1830* (Chapel Hill: University of North Carolina Press, 1998), 23, 28. For Andrew Montour's role, see Merrell, "'The Cast of His Countenance': Reading Andrew Montour," in Ronald Hoffman et al., eds., *Through a Glass Darkly: Reflections on Personal Identity in Early America* (Chapel Hill: University of North Carolina Press, 1997), 13–39.

39. "The Report of Richard Peters," *PA*, 8th ser., 4:3321–32. For other narratives of Peters's expedition, see Wallace, *Conrad Weiser*, 277–78, 294–97.

40. Richard Peters to the Proprietors, 12 July 1750, Penn Manuscripts, Official Correspondence, 5:29; Thomas Penn to Peters, 27 Aug. 1750, Thomas Penn Letterbooks, 3:20; Abraham Slack (or Schlechl) never applied for a survey of his Path Valley tract. He lived there in the early 1760s but had relocated to the Wyoming Valley by 1769: Original Warrants, no. 167,

Cumberland County (microfilm reel 3.51); New Purchase Register, 1769, application no. 2580, Land Records, PSA (microfilm reel 1.9).

41. *PA*, 8th ser., 4:3321–32 (quotations pp. 3323, 3331, 3324).

42. *MPCP*, 5:452–55, 468–69.

43. Ibid., 4:3324–25.

44. Using the households in the Peters's report as a sample, I was able to identify definitively forty-four of the sixty-one squatter households using the Pennsylvania Land Records, Minutes of the Board of Property, and Cumberland County tax lists from the 1750s and 1760s. For references to William and Mary White, see *PA*, 3d ser., 24:776; 20:567; for Peters's promises to settlers, see *Minutes of the Board of Property* in *PA*, 3d ser., 1:140, 152, 234, 241, 346, 2:248–49; and *Pennsylvania Gazette*, 16 December 1763.

45. Richard Peters to the Proprietors, 20 July 1750, Penn Manuscripts, Official Correspondence, 5:39.

46. Thomas Penn, quoted in Francis Jennings, *Empire of Fortune: Crowns, Colonies, and Tribes in the Seven Years War in America* (New York: W. W. Norton, 1988), 101–6; *Pennsylvania Gazette*, 18 March 1756 (Delawares). On the 1754 Albany Congress, see Wallace, *Conrad Weiser*, 350–63; Jennings, *Empire of Fortune*, 104; and Timothy J. Shannon, *Indians and Colonists at the Crossroads of Empire: The Albany Congress of 1754* (Ithaca: Cornell University Press, 2000).

47. *PA*, 2d ser., 2:684; Charles Desmond Dutrizac, "Local Identity and Authority in a Disputed Hinterland: The Pennsylvania-Maryland Border in the 1730s," *PMHB* 115 (1991): 35–62; Paul B. Moyer, "Wild Yankees: Settlement, Conflict, and Localism Along Pennsylvania's Northeast Frontier, 1760–1820" (Ph.D. diss., College of William and Mary, 1999).

48. Dorothy V. Jones, *License for Empire: Colonialism by Treaty in Early America* (Chicago: University of Chicago Press, 1982), xii.

49. "Journal of James Kenny," 199; *MPCP*, 9:481–82, 507.

Chapter 11

1. Reports at the time disagree as to the exact number of Paxton Boys who attacked the Lancaster jail. On 27 Dec. 1763 both Sheriff John Hay and David Henderson estimated the size of the group at approximately fifty men. Edward Shippen, Sr., reported "upwards of a hundred men" riding into town (Hay to John Penn, *MPCP*, 9:103; David Henderson to Joseph Galloway, Friendly Association Papers, QCHC; Shippen to Penn, *MPCP*, 9:10).

2. Henry's description appears in John Dunbar, ed., *The Paxton Papers* (The Hague: Martinus Nijhoff, 1957), 29.

3. Benjamin Franklin, "A Narrative of the Late Massacres, in Lancaster County, of a Number of Indians," in Leonard Labaree, ed., *The Papers of Benjamin Franklin* (New Haven: Yale University Press, 1967), 11:53.

4. Penn to Assembly, 3 Jan. 1764, *MPCP*, 9:109.

5. *Pennsylvania Gazette*, 9 Feb. 1764.

6. For a full text of the *Declaration* and *Remonstrance*, see Dunbar, ed., *Paxton Papers*, 101–10.

7. Brooke Hindle, "The March of the Paxton Boys," *WMQ* 3 (1946): 461–86. Dunbar, ed., *Paxton Papers*, introduction. Although his article is more narrative than analytical, Hubertis Cummings agrees with the contention that the Euro-American frontiersmen acted out of a democratic motive against an autocratic Philadelphia government ("The Paxton Killings," *Journal of Presbyterian History* 44 [1966]: 219–43).

8. James Kirby Martin, "The Return of the Paxton Boys and the *Historical* State of the Pennsylvania Frontier, 1764–1774," *PH* 38 (1971): 117–33.

9. James Crowley, "The Paxton Disturbance and Ideas of Order in Pennsylvania Politics," *PH* 37 (1970): 317–39; George Franz, *Paxton: A Study of Community Structure and Mobility in the Colonial Pennsylvania Backcountry* (New York: Garland Publishing, 1989).

10. Alden T. Vaughan, "Frontier Banditti and the Indians: The Paxton Boys' Legacy, 1763–1775," *PH* 51 (1984): 2.

11. Richard Slotkin pioneered the proposition that violence against Indians was a constructive force in the development of an early American identity. He argued that the relation between White men and Indians and the wilderness was fundamentally violent and that that violence formed the root of the American identity (*Regeneration Through Violence: The Mythology of the American Frontier, 1600–1860* [Middletown Conn.: Wesleyan University Press, 1973]).

12. The most thorough and impressive treatment of Washington's skirmishes with the French and the subsequent global conflict is Fred Anderson, *Crucible of War: The Seven Years' War and the Fate of Empire in British North America, 1765–1766* (New York: Alfred A. Knopf, 2000).

13. Although it is impossible to know the exact number of Euro-Pennsylvanians killed and captured during the war, historian Matthew Ward estimates that Delaware warriors and their French allies killed more than 1,500 Euro-Americans and took another 1,000 captive along the Virginia and Pennsylvania frontiers. See Ward, "La Guerre Sauvage: The Seven Years War on the Virginia and Pennsylvania Frontier" (PhD. diss., College of William and Mary, 1992), appendix C.

14. When the first wave of Scots-Irish settlers arrived in the 1720s and 1730s, Provincial Secretary James Logan explicitly supported their settlement in frontier regions because he believed that the people who "had so bravely defended Derry and Inniskillin" in Ireland would be suitable to defend provincial boundaries from potential Native American attacks (quoted in Franz, *Paxton*, 95).

15. Daniel Vickers, "Competency and Competition: Economic Culture in Early America," *WMQ* 47 (1990): 3–29.

16. My understanding of patriarchy and manhood as constructions shaped by age, a desire for economic independence, a need to control labor, and a sense of duty to protect and support family members has been informed by a number of scholars of early American history, including Kathleen M. Brown, *Good Wives, Nasty Wenches, and Anxious Patriarchs: Gender, Race, and Power in Colonial Virginia* (Chapel Hill: University of North Carolina Press, 1996); Anne Spencer Lombard, "Playing the Man: Conceptions of Masculinity in Anglo-American New England, 1675–1765" (Ph.D. diss., University of California, Los Angeles, 1998); Daniel Vickers, *Farmers and Fishermen: Two Centuries of Work in Essex County, Massachusetts, 1630–1850* (Chapel Hill: University of North Carolina Press, 1994); and Lisa Wilson, *Ye Heart of a Man: The Domestic Life of Men in Colonial New England* (New Haven: Yale University Press, 1999).

17. Weiser to Morris, 19 Nov. 1755, *PA*, 1st ser., 2:504–5.

18. Ibid.

19. Ibid.

20. For a discussion of the hierarchy among patriarchs, see Stephanie McCurry, *Masters of Small Worlds: Yeoman Households, Gender Relations, and the Political Culture of the Antebellum South Carolina Low Country* (New York: Oxford University Press, 1995), chap. 3.

21. Lurgan Township, Cumberland County, petition to Governor Robert Morris, 1 Aug. 1755, *MPCP*, 6:533; Lancaster County petition to Morris, 1 Nov. 1755, *PA*, 1st ser., 2:450; Cumberland County petitions to Morris, 7 Aug. 1755, 21 Aug. 1756, ibid., 385–86, 757–58.

22. Morris to the Assembly, 15 Oct. 1754, *MPCP*, 6:166.

23. Paul Gilje, *The Road to Mobocracy: Popular Disorder in New York City, 1763–1834* (Chapel Hill: University of North Carolina Press, 1987), 17.

24. Petition of York inhabitants to Morris, n.d., *MPCP*, 7:233–34.

25. Petition of Derry Township to Denny, 16 May 1757, *PA*, 1st ser., 3:159.

26. Hoops to Morris, 3 Nov. 1755, *PA*, 1st ser., 2:462–63.

27. Earl P. Olmstead, *David Zeisberger: A Life Among the Indians* (Kent, Ohio: Kent State University Press, 1997), 96.

28. "A Brief Narrative of the Incursions and Ravages of the French and Indians in the Province of Pennsylvania," 29 Dec. 1755, *MPCP*, 6:768.

29. James Burd to Edward Shippen, 2 Nov. 1755, *PA*, 1st ser., 2:455.

30. Potter to Peters, *MPCP*, 6:673–74.

31. Michael Roup to William Parsons, 24 Apr. 1757, *MPCP*, 7:493–94.

32. According to William Hunter, settlers typically selected an existing building, such as a well-built barn, church, house, or mill, for modifications to become a fort (*Forts on the Pennsylvania Frontier, 1753–1758* [Harrisburg: PHMC, 1960], 549).

33. Michael Roup to William Parsons, 24 Apr. 1757, *MPCP*, 7:493.

34. General Council for Cumberland County, 30 Oct. 1755, Lamberton Scotch-Irish Collection, box 1, folder 23, HSP.

35. Burd to Edward Shippen, 2 Nov. 1755, *PA*, 1st ser., 2:455.

36. Jacob Morgan to William Denny, 4 Nov. 1755, *PA*, 1st ser., 3:30–31.

37. Groups such as these fit the model of rural crowds advanced by Thomas Slaughter, who maintains that rural crowds were distinct from the urban mobs historians have described in the revolutionary period because of "their interpersonal violence, their lack of respect for institutions, and their intolerance for lawful authority." Frontier crowds in Pennsylvania from the first days of the war to the Paxton Boys fit this model ("Crowds in Eighteenth-Century America: Reflections and New Directions," *PMHB* 115 [1991]: 14).

38. Weiser to Morris, 30 Oct. 1755, *MPCP*, 6:657–59, quotation from p. 657.

39. Parsons to Peters, 31 Oct. 1755, *PA*, 1st ser., 2:443.

40. I use the term *metonym* instead of *metaphor* to emphasize the cathartic power of Euro-American frontiersmen's activities. The actions frontiersmen engaged in were not simple acts of substitution where an external or independent thing stood as a metaphor or substitute for the central object or objective. Further, analyzing frontiersmen's actions as metonyms for war helps to explain otherwise irrational acts. Wasting ammunition in a time of war and scarcity was not an efficient strategy for waging war, but for frightened Euro-Americans, engaging in limited warlike actions was a way of participating in the larger processes of war without exposing themselves to additional danger. For an anthropological use of *metonymy*, see Pamela Wright, "The Timely Significance of Supernatural Mothers or Exemplary Daughters: The Metonymy of Identity in History," in Jane Schneider and Rayna Rapp, eds., *Articulating Hidden Histories: Exploring the Influence of Eric R. Wolf* (Berkeley: University of California Press, 1995): 243–61. Roman Jakobson explores the linguistic relation between *metonymy* and *metaphor* in "The Metaphoric and Metonymic Poles," in *Selected Writings*, vol. 2, *Word and Language* (The Hague: Mouton, 1971), 254–59.

41. James H. Merrell, *Into the American Woods: Negotiators on the Pennsylvania Frontier* (New York: W. W. Norton, 1999), 24–25.

42. In his study of George Robert Twelves Hewes, Alfred Young documents how participation in crowd activity could alter an individual's understanding of his society and its conflicts. Hewes's participation in such events as the Boston Massacre and the Boston Tea Party not only politicized him, but also accelerated his movement toward a more democratic view of society. Thus, a mob could shape and legitimate a particular ideology, whether democracy

or the racialization of Indians (*The Shoemaker and the Tea Party: Memory and the American Revolution* [Boston: Beacon Press, 1999], 52–56).

43. The eastern Delaware leader Teedyuscung exemplified the porousness of the boundary between friend and enemy during the war. At the beginning of the war Teedyuscung, a man who had been baptized by the Moravians, led raids against Euro-American settlers. By 1756, however, he presented himself to the Pennsylvania government as a spokesman for the Delawares and the Six Nations and participated actively in the peace conferences at Easton. See Anthony F. C. Wallace, *King of the Delawares: Teedyuscung, 1700–1763* (Philadelphia: University of Pennsylvania Press, 1949), 39–40, 83–86, 103–6.

44. Dunbar, ed., *Paxton Papers*, 107.

45. For a detailed discussion of the conferences, see Steven Auth, *The Ten Years' War: Indian-White Relations in Pennsylvania, 1755–1765* (New York: Garland Publishing, 1989), chap. 4.

46. Horsfield to Morris, 7 July 1756, *MPCP*, 7:190–91.

47. Extract from William Parson's diary, 26 July 1756, *PA*, 1st ser., 2:725.

48. Spangenberg to Morris, 26 June 1756, *MPCP*, 7:173.

49. The disruptive settlers were subsequently released with a warning to behave better in the future (Weiser to Denny, 18 July 1757, *PA*, 1st ser., 3:221–22).

50. For the Moravians' efforts on behalf of the Indians, and their concerns about the danger inherent in hosting so many Indians in Bethlehem, see Augustus Gottlieb Spangenberg to Israel Pemberton, 28 June 1756, Friendly Association papers, 1:137, QCHC; same to William Denny, 29 Nov. 1756, 23 Apr. 1757, *PA*, 1st ser., 3:69, 141; and same to Richard Peters, 31 July 1758, ibid., 500–501.

51. Jack Marietta, *The Reformation of American Quakerism, 1748–1783* (Philadelphia: University of Pennsylvania Press, 1984), chap. 7.

52. For a narrative summary of the activities of the Friendly Association during its eight-year life span (1756–64), see Theodore Thayer, "The Friendly Association," *PMHB* 67 (1943): 356–76. Francis Jennings resurrected the role of the Friendly Association from the dustbin of history when he credited the Quakers with "the rebuilding of British credit among Indians" (*Empire of Fortune: Crowns, Colonies, and Tribes in the Seven Years War in America* [New York: W. W. Norton, 1988], 339). The anger the Paxton Boys felt toward pacifist Quakers generally, and the Friendly Association particularly, was apparent in the eighth point of the *Remonstrance* they submitted to the governor, which cited Israel Pemberton "for not only abett[ing] our Indian Enemies, but [keeping] up a private intelligence with them" (Dunbar ed., *Paxton Papers*, 109). Pemberton so feared the wrath of the Paxton Boys that he fled Philadelphia as they approached the city in winter 1764 (James Pemberton to John Fothergill, Mar. 7, 1764, Pemberton Papers, 34:127–28, HSP).

53. The construction of an Indian racial identity was not a one-way process. While Euro-American settlers increasingly pointed to a singular Indian race, Native spiritual leaders also sought to build a pan-Indian unity in opposition to Euro-Americans; see Gregory Evans Dowd, *A Spirited Resistance: The North American Indian Struggle for Unity, 1745–1815* (Baltimore: Johns Hopkins University Press, 1992), chap. 2. Daniel K. Richter points to 1763 as a crucial turning point in the evolution of racial thinking and antagonism on the part of both European and Native Americans: "In parallel ways, Pontiac and the Paxton Boys preached the novel idea that all Native people were 'Indians,' that all Euro-Americans were 'Whites,' and that all on one side must unite to destroy the other" (*Facing East from Indian Country: A Native History of Early America* [Cambridge: Harvard University Press, 2001], 207). Richter and I agree that 1763 was a crucial turning point in the process of mutual racialization and that the events of that year did not mark the end of that process.

54. Joseph S. Lucas, "Conquering the Passions: Indians, Europeans, and the Idea of Cultural Change in Early American Social Thought, 1580–1830" (Ph.D. diss., Pennsylvania State University, 1999), 137–38, 158–65.

55. The Conestogas signed their first treaty of alliance with the Pennsylvania government in 1701 (*MPCP*, 2:10).

56. Morris to John Ross, 8 Mar. 1756, *PA*, 1st ser., 2:595.

57. Elder to Peters, n.d. Nov. 1755, *MPCP*, 6:704–5.

58. Same to same, 30 July 1757, *PA*, 1st ser., 3:251.

59. "Some Account of the Missions in Pennsylvania, &c., delivered at a Convention of the Clergy of that Province at Philadelphia," 2 May 1760, in William Stevens Perry, ed., *Historical Collections Relating to the American Colonial Church*, 5 vols. (Hartford, Conn.: Church Press, 1870–78), 2:316.

60. Murray to the Secretary for the Society for the Propagation of the Gospel, 19 Apr. 1763, in Perry, ed., *Historical Collections Relating to American Colonial Church*, 2:346.

61. Hamilton to James Burd, 22 Feb. 1760, Shippen Papers, 5:15, HSP.

62. Edward Shippen to James Burd, 1 Sept. 1762, Burd-Shippen Papers, Miscellaneous Items, American Philosophical Society, Philadelphia.

63. McKee to Burd, 9 July 1763, Shippen Papers, 6:41.

64. David Crockett, *Narrative of the Life of David Crockett of the State of Tennessee* (Knoxville: University of Tennessee Press, 1973); Michael A. Lofaro, ed., *Tall Tales of Davy Crockett: The Second Natville Series of Crockett Almanacs, 1839–1841* (Knoxville: University of Tennessee Press, 1987); Frank M. Meola, "A Passage Through 'Indians': Masculinity and Violence in Francis Parkman's *The Oregon Trail,*" *American Transcendental Quarterly* 13 (1999): 5–25.

Chapter 12

1. For a more thoroughgoing description of this event, see James H. Merrell, "'The Cast of His Countenance': Reading Andrew Montour," in Ronald Hoffman, Mechal Sobel, and Fredrika J. Teute, eds., *Through a Glass Darkly: Reflections on Personal Identity in Early America* (Chapel Hill: University of North Carolina Press, 1997), 13–17. See also Examination of Moravians, 2 Nov. 1755, *PA*, 1st ser., 2:459–60; and John Harris to Governor Robert Morris, 28 Oct. 1755, *MPCP*, 6:654–55.

2. Proclamation of Reward for the Perpetrator of the Murder of Edward Gobin, August 11, 1804, *PA*, 4th ser., 4:535–36.

3. Several recent studies have noted frontier insurgents' use of Indian disguise; more important, they have shed light on the fact that between 1750 and 1800 America's hinterlands were the scene of numerous disputes over land and authority that pitted White settlers, government officials, and land speculators against one another. See Alan Taylor, *Liberty Men and Great Proprietors: The Revolutionary Settlement of the Maine Frontier, 1760–1820* (Chapel Hill: University of North Carolina Press, 1990); idem, "Agrarian Independence: Northern Land Rioters After the Revolution," in Alfred F. Young, ed., *Beyond the American Revolution: Explorations in the History of American Radicalism* (DeKalb: Northern Illinois University Press, 1993): 221–45; Michael Bellesiles, *Revolutionary Outlaws: Ethan Allen and the Struggle for Independence on the Early American Frontier* (Charlottesville: University Press of Virginia, 1993); and Paul B. Moyer, "Wild Yankees: Settlement, Conflict, and Localism Along Pennsylvania's Northeast Frontier, 1760–1820" (Ph.D. diss., College of William and Mary, 1999).

4. Some of the more recent studies that discuss Indian-European relations and the impact of colonization on Pennsylvania's Indians include Peter C. Mancall, *Valley of Opportu-*

nity: Economic Culture Along the Upper Susquehanna, 1700–1800 (Ithaca: Cornell University Press, 1991); and James H. Merrell, *Into the American Woods: Negotiators on the Pennsylvania Frontier* (New York: W. W. Norton, 1999).

5. For narratives of the Wyoming dispute, see *SCP*, passim.

6. Alan Taylor, "'A Kind of Warr': The Contest for Land on the Northeast Frontier, 1750–1820," *WMQ* 46 (1989): 4–5, 11; Bellesiles, *Revolutionary Outlaws*, 27–32; Thomas L. Purvis, "Origins and Patterns of Agrarian Unrest in New Jersey, 1735–1754," *WMQ* 39 (1982): 602–10; William Cronon, *Changes in the Land: Indians, Colonists and the Ecology of New England* (New York: Hill and Wang, 1983), 54–81.

7. William E. Price, "A Study of a Frontier Community in Transition: The History of Wilkes-Barre, Pennsylvania, 1750–1800" (Ph.D. diss., Kent State University, 1979), 9; Robert J. Taylor, *Colonial Connecticut: A History* (Millwood, N.Y.: KTO Press, 1979), 29, 56–59; *SCP*, 1:lviii–lxii.

8. Julian P. Boyd, "Connecticut's Experiment in Expansion: The Susquehannah Company, 1753–1803," *Journal of Economic and Business History* 27 (1931): 40–41; Price, "Frontier Community in Transition," 23–25; *SCP*, 1:lviii–lxiv.

9. *SCP*, 1:xxxii–xxxiii, lxxiv–lxxv; Boyd, "Connecticut's Experiment in Expansion," 42–43. For more on New England's seventeenth-century town corporations, see John Frederick Martin, *Profits in the Wilderness: Entrepreneurship and the Founding of New England Towns in the Seventeenth Century* (Chapel Hill: University of North Carolina Press, 1991).

10. Susquehannah Company meeting minutes, 18 July 1753, 1 May, 20 Nov. 1754, *SCP*, 1:28–29, 86–87, 168; Boyd, "Connecticut's Experiment in Expansion," 42.

11. Susquehannah Company meeting minutes, 18 July, 6 Sept. 1753, *SCP*, 1:28–29, 40–41.

12. Richard Peters to the Pennsylvania Proprietors, 27 Nov. 1753, *SCP*, 1:42; Thomas Penn to Richard Peters, 1 Feb. 1754, *SCP*, 1:51–52.

13. James Hamilton to Roger Wolcott, 4 Mar. 1754, *SCP*, 1:56; Anthony F. C. Wallace, *King of the Delawares: Teedyuscung, 1700–1763* (Philadelphia: University of Pennsylvania Press, 1949), 47–53.

14. Richard Peters to Sir William Johnson, 18 May 1761, *SCP*, 2:98.

15. For a comprehensive examination of the Albany Congress and its impact, see Timothy J. Shannon, *Indians and Colonists at the Crossroads of Empire: The Albany Congress of 1754* (Ithaca: Cornell University Press, 2000).

16. *SCP*, 1:lxxxi–lxxxix, Deed from Indians of the Six Nations to the Susquehannah Company, 11 July 1754, *SCP*, 1:101–21; Shannon, *Indians and Colonists*, 108–9.

17. Shannon, *Indians and Colonists*, 161–71; Francis Jennings, "'Pennsylvania Indians' and the Iroquois," in Daniel K. Richter and James H. Merrell, eds., *Beyond the Covenant Chain: The Iroquois and Their Neighbors in Indian North America, 1600–1800* (Syracuse, N.Y.: Syracuse University Press, 1987), 75–91.

18. For a more detailed account of Delaware attitudes, their involvement in the Seven Years' War, and how their decision to go to war was connected with the Wyoming dispute, see *SCP*, 2:i–xvi; Memorandum of Conrad Weiser's Conversations with Moses Tetamy and Others, 26 Nov. 1756, *SCP*, 2:2–5; Thomas Penn to William Logan, 21 June 1757, *SCP*, 2:11; and Francis Jennings, *Empire of Fortune: Crowns, Colonies, and Tribes in the Seven Years War in America* (New York: W. W. Norton, 1988), 263–81.

19. A good description of the process by which the Delawares made peace with the English and the Six Nations can be found in Jennings, *Empire of Fortune*, 274–81, 342–48, 396–403.

20. Richard Peters to Lewis Gordon, 15 Sept. 1760, *SCP*, 2:24; Memorandum of a Confer-

ence with Teedyuscung, 18 Sept. 1760, *SCP*, 2:25; Minutes of the Indian Conference at Easton, Aug. 1761, *SCP*, 2:111–12.

21. Susquehannah Company meeting minutes, 19 May, 27 July 1762, *SCP*, 2:130–31, 145–46.

22. Wallace, *King of the Delawares*, 254–58; *SCP*, 2:xxvi–xxvii; Conference with Teedyuscung, 19 Nov. 1762, *SCP*, 2:180–83.

23. For an overview of Teedyuscung's efforts to resist the Connecticut claim, see *SCP*, 2:xvii–xxxii; for an account of Teedyuscung's death and the circumstances that surrounded it, see Wallace, *King of the Delawares*, 258–61.

24. For an examination of the imperial government's involvement in the Wyoming dispute, see *SCP*, 2:xxxiii–xlii; and Instructions from the Privy Council to Thomas Fitch, 15 June 1763, *SCP*, 2:256.

25. Wallace, *King of the Delawares*, 261–66; Frederick J. Stefon, "The Wyoming Valley," in John B. Frantz and William Pencak, eds., *Beyond Philadelphia: The American Revolution in the Pennsylvania Hinterland* (University Park: The Pennsylvania State University Press, 1998), 134–36.

26. Dorothy V. Jones, *License for Empire: Colonialism by Treaty in Early America* (Chicago: University of Chicago Press, 1982), 21–35, 58–63, 75–92; Michael N. McConnell, "Peoples 'In Between': The Iroquois and the Ohio Indians, 1720–1768," in Richter and Merrell, eds., *Beyond the Covenant Chain*, 93–112; Peter Marshall, "Sir William Johnson and the Treaty of Fort Stanwix, 1768," *Journal of American Studies* 1 (1967): 149–79.

27. *SCP*, 3:i–xvi; Susquehannah Company meeting minutes, 28 Dec. 1768, *SCP*, 3:43–47; Instructions to Charles Stewart and Others, 1769, *SCP*, 3:331–32; James Kirby Martin, "The Return of the Paxton Boys and the *Historical* State of the Pennsylvania Frontier, 1764–1774," *PH* 38 (1971): 126.

28. Oscar Jewell Harvey, *A History of Wilkes-Barre* (Wilkes-Barre, Pa.: Raeder Press, 1909), 2:640–44; Stewart Pearce, *Annals of Luzerne County* (Philadelphia: J. B. Lippincott, 1866), 100–119; Deposition of John Philip De Hass, September 26, 1770, *MPCP*, 9:682–84.

29. Harvey, *History of Wilkes-Barre*, 2:640–41; Pearce, *Annals of Luzerne County*, 101.

30. Alexander Graydon to James Burd, October 16, 1763, *SCP*, 2:272; extract from the *Pennsylvania Gazette*, 27 Oct. 1763, *SCP*, 2:277; George W. Franz, *Paxton: A Study of Community Structure and Mobility in the Colonial Pennsylvania Backcountry* (New York: Garland Publishing, 1989), 66–67.

31. For an overview of the Paxton Boys' massacres and Pennsylvania's frontier crisis, see Alden T. Vaughan, "Frontier Banditti and the Indians: The Paxton Boys' Legacy," *PH* 51 (1984): 1–29, and Brooke Hindle, "The March of the Paxton Boys," *WMQ* 3 (1946): 461–86.

32. Robert G. Crist, "Cumberland County," in Franz and Pencak, eds., *Beyond Philadelphia*, 112–13; Eleanor M. Webster, "Insurrection at Fort Loudon in 1765, Rebellion or Preservation of the Peace?" *Western Pennsylvania History Magazine* 47 (1964): 125–40; Dorothy Fennell, "From Rebelliousness to Insurrection: A Social History of the Whiskey Rebellion, 1765–1802" (Ph.D. diss., University of Pittsburgh, 1981), 10; Lt. Col. Reid to General Gage, 1 June 1765, 4 June 1765, *MPCP*, 9:268–69; General Gage to John Penn, 16 June 1769, *MPCP*, 9:267–68.

33. Crist, "Cumberland County," 113–15; Martin, "Return of the Paxton Boys," 121–23; Deposition of William Blyth, 19 January 1768, *MPCP*, 9:414.

34. Richard M. Brown, "Back Country Rebellions and the Homestead Ethic in America, 1740–1799," in Richard M. Brown and Don E. Fehrenbacher, eds., *Tradition, Conflict, and Modernization: Perspectives on the American Revolution* (New York: Academic Press, 1977), 76–79.

35. *SCP*, 3:xv–xviii; Edmund Physick to Thomas Penn, 19 Apr. 1769, *SCP*, 3:101–2, 103n2; Edmund Physick to Thomas Penn, 28 Sept. 1769, *SCP*, 3:185; Martin, "Return of the Paxton Boys," 126–27.

36. *SCP*, 4:vi–vii; Petition of Lazarus Young and Others, 11 Sept. 1769, *SCP*, 3:176–77; Executive Committee to John Montgomery and Lazarus Young, 15 Jan. 1770, *SCP*, 4:5–6; Martin, "Return of the Paxton Boys," 120, 128–30.

37. John Penn to Thomas Penn, March 10, 1770, *SCP*, 4:42–43.

38. *SCP*, 3:xxiii–xxvi; Susquehannah Company meeting minutes, 12 Apr. 1769, *SCP*, 3:96–98.

39. For narratives of the first Pennamite-Yankee war, see James R. Williamson and Linda A. Fossler, *Zebulon Butler: Hero of the Revolutionary Frontier* (Westport, Conn.: Greenwood Press, 1995), 18–25; Harvey, *History of Wilkes-Barre*, 2:625–796; and Stefon, "Wyoming Valley," 133–52.

40. Eliphalet Dyer and Others to Jonathan Trumbull, 27 Mar. 1771, *SCP*, 4:192, 194–95n; Zebulon Butler's Memorandum Book, February–May 1770, *SCP*, 4:81–82; Warrant for the Arrest of Lazarus Stewart and Others, 20 March 1770, *SCP*, 4:50–51.

41. For an overview of the Paxton Boys' involvement in the Wyoming dispute and of Pennamite-Yankee violence, see *SCP*, 4:i–xxv; and Moyer, "Wild Yankees," 25–37.

42. Charles Stewart to John Penn, 21 Jan. 1771, *SCP*, 4:153–54; Deposition of William Sims, 21 Jan. 1771, *SCP*, 4:155–56; Deposition of William Nimens, 25 Jan. 1771, *SCP*, 4:156–57; Deposition of Peter Kachlein, 31 Jan. 1771, *SCP*, 4:163–64.

43. Act of the Connecticut General Assembly Erecting the Town of Westmoreland, Jan. 1774, *SCP*, 5:268–69. For an account of the relation between the Wyoming dispute and revolutionary loyalties, see Ann M. Ousterhout, "Frontier Allies: Indians and Tories," in *A State Divided: Opposition in Pennsylvania to the American Revolution* (Westport, Conn.: Greenwood Press, 1987), 231–45, and idem, "Frontier Vengeance: Connecticut Yankees vs. Pennamites in the Wyoming Valley," *PH* 62 (1995): 330–63.

44. *SCP*, 5:l–lii; extract from *Connecticut Courant*, 22 Jan. 1776, *SCP*, 6:422–25; Sheriff William Scull and Others to Governor Penn, 30 Dec. 1775, *SCP*, 6:425–26.

45. *SCP*, 7:xvi–xvii; Ousterhout, "Frontier Vengeance," 336–37. For information on Vanderlip, see Minutes of a Meeting of the Proprietors and Settlers Held in Wilkes-Barre, 14 Sept. 1773, *SCP*, 5:167–68; Minutes of a Meeting of the Proprietors and Settlers in Wilkes-Barre, 22 Nov. 1774, *SCP*, 6:292–93; Ousterhout, *State Divided*, 272–73n.

46. Mancall, *Valley of Opportunity*, 130–59; Gregory Knouff, "'An Arduous Service': The Pennsylvania Backcountry Soldiers' Revolution," *PH* 61 (1994): 45–74; Colin G. Calloway, *The American Revolution in Indian Country* (Cambridge: Cambridge University Press, 1995), 26–64.

47. Harvey, *History of Wilkes-Barre*, 2:951–52; 3:1254–55, 1277–79; Mancall, *Valley of Opportunity*, 139.

48. David Craft, *History of Bradford County, Pennsylvania* (Philadelphia: L. H. Everts, 1878), 101–3; James Edward Brady, "Wyoming: A Study of John Franklin and the Connecticut Settlement into Pennsylvania" (Ph.D. diss., Syracuse University, 1973), 20–22, 146–86.

49. Proclamation Announcing the Trenton Decree, 6 Jan. 1783, *SCP*, 7:247–49. A detailed account of the events leading up to the Trenton Decree can be found in *SCP*, 7:xxii–xxxiii, 144–246.

50. Moyer, "Wild Yankees," 50–88; *SCP*, 7:xxxiii–xxxix, 8:xvi–xxii.

51. Knouff, "'Arduous Service,'" 68; *SCP*, 9:209–10.

52. Deposition of William Brink, 27 July 1784, *SCP*, 8:7–8; Deposition of Henry Brink, 15 Aug. 1784, *PA*, 10:651; Deposition of Wilhelmus Van Gordon, 15 Aug. 1784, *PA*, 10:652; Deposi-

tion of Catherine Cortright, 11 Aug. 1784, *PA*, 10:642; John Franklin to William Samuel Johnson, Eliphalet Dyer, and Jesse Root, 11 Oct. 1784, *SCP*, 8:109–10.

53. John Franklin's Diary, 3 July to 7 Dec. 1784, *SCP*, 8:155–56.

54. Deposition of James Moore, 14 Sept. 1784, *PA*, 10:656–57; Deposition of John Stickafoos, 24 Sept. 1784, *PA*, 10:667–68; Deposition of Harmon Brink, 22 Sept. 1784, *PA*, 10:661.

55. Alexander Patterson to John Armstrong Jr., 28 Sept. 1784, *SCP*, 8:85; Deposition of Henry Shoemaker, 28 Sept. 1784, in Harvey, *History of Wilkes-Barre*, 3:1438–39.

56. John Franklin to Frederick Antes, Daniel Montgomery, and William Bonam, 23 Oct. 1784, *SCP*, 8:130–31; John Armstrong, Jr., to John Dickinson, 25 Oct. 1784, *SCP*, 8:135; Deposition of John Armstrong, Jr., 28 July 1784, *PA*, 10:623–24.

57. Deposition of Henry Brink, 14 Jan. 1785, *SCP*, 8:200.

58. Calloway, *American Revolution in Indian Country*, 39.

59. Charles W. Upham, *The Life of Timothy Pickering*, 2 vols. (Boston: Little, Brown, 1873), 2:381–82; Samuel Wallis to Samuel Meredith, 11 Oct. 1792, *SCP*, 10:161; Deposition of Thomas Smiley, 15 July 1801, in Craft, *History of Bradford County*, 45–46.

60. For insights into the character of popular protest in early modern Europe, see Buchanan Sharp, "Popular Protest in Seventeenth-Century England," in Barry Reay, ed., *Popular Culture in Seventeenth-Century England* (London: Croom Helm, 1985), 271–308; Martin Ingram, "Ridings, Rough Music and Mocking Rhymes in Early Modern England," ibid., 166–97; and William Pencak, Matthew Dennis, and Simon P. Newman, eds., *Riot and Revelry in Early America* (University Park: The Pennsylvania State University Press, 2002). For an exploration of the links between European popular protest and backcountry unrest in America, see Paul B. Moyer, "A Riot of Devils: Indian Imagery and Popular Protest in the Northeastern Backcountry, 1760–1845" (master's thesis, College of William and Mary, 1994), 10–18.

61. Moyer, "Riot of Devils," 32–41; Peter Shaw, *American Patriots and the Rituals of Revolution* (Cambridge: Harvard University Press, 1981), 204–20; Philip Deloria, *Playing Indian* (New Haven: Yale University Press, 1998), 10–37.

62. Moyer, "Riot of Devils," 18–31; Bellesiles, *Revolutionary Outlaws*, 91; Alan Taylor, "Agrarian Independence," 222–23; idem, *Liberty Men*, 185–205.

63. For an account of the decline of Wild Yankee resistance and the settlement of the Wyoming dispute, see Moyer, "Wild Yankees," 241–71.

64. Taylor, *Liberty Men*, 185–89.

Chapter 13

1. On the general early colonial English tendency to comment on Indian cultural differences rather than skin color, see Alden T. Vaughan, "From White Man to Redskin: Changing Anglo-American Perceptions of the American Indian," *American Historical Review* 86 (1982): 917–53. On the development of racial ideology among Pennsylvanians in the era of the Seven Years' War, see chapter 11, above, and Jane T. Merritt, *At the Crossroads: Indians and Empires on a Mid-Atlantic Frontier, 1700–1763* (Chapel Hill: University of North Carolina Press, 2003).

2. Dana D. Nelson, *National Manhood: Capitalist Citizenship and the Imagined Fraternity of White Men* (Durham, N.C.: Duke University Press, 1998); David Roediger, *The Wages of Whiteness: Race and the Making of the American Working Class* (New York: Verso, 1999); Alexander Saxton, *The Rise and Fall of the White Republic: Class Politics and Mass Culture in Nineteenth-Century America* (New York: Verso, 1990); and Caroll Smith-Rosenberg, "Discovering the Subject of the 'Great Constitutional Discussion,' 1786–1789," *JAH* 79 (1992):

841–73. On the movement toward universal White manhood suffrage beginning in the Jeffersonian era and continuing through the 1830s and 1840s, see Joyce Appleby, *Inheriting the Revolution: The First Generation of Americans* (Cambridge: Harvard University Press, 2000), 28–29. On the consolidation of racism in the wake of postrevolutionary northern emancipation, see, e.g., Gary B. Nash, *Forging Freedom: The Formation of Philadelphia's Black Community* (Cambridge: Harvard University Press, 1988), 246–79. On the varied yet complementary ways that the racial Othering of Indians and African Americans served to bolster the power of dominant Euro-Americans, see Patrick Wolfe, "Land, Labor, and Difference: Elementary Structures of Race," *American Historical Review* 106 (2001): 866–905.

3. RWPF, R11329; R11329; (M804); John C. Dann, ed., *The Revolution Remembered: Eyewitness Accounts of the War for Independence* (Chicago: University of Chicago Press, 1980), 283, 310–11.

4. *Pennsylvania Evening Post,* 17 Oct. 1778. On Indian motives for fighting in the Revolution as a defense of their own communities and independence, see Gregory Evans Dowd, *A Spirited Resistance: The North American Indian Struggle for Unity, 1745–1812* (Baltimore: Johns Hopkins University Press, 1992), 65–89; Colin G. Calloway, *The American Revolution in Indian Country* (Cambridge: Cambridge University Press, 1995); and Richard White, *The Middle Ground: Indians, Empires, and Republics in the Great Lakes Region, 1650–1815* (Cambridge: Cambridge University Press, 1991), 366–412.

5. *Pennsylvania Packet,* 8 Apr. 1777; Calloway, *American Revolution in Indian Country,* 26–64, quotation from p. 46. On settler intrusions on Indian land and murders of Indians straining neutrality, see Dowd, *Spirited Resistance,* 65–78.

6. Daniel Brodhead to Captain Clark, 11 Oct. 1779, Order Book of Daniel Brodhead, Darlington Memorial Library, University of Pittsburgh, Pittsburgh, Pa.; Orderly Book of the Eighth Pennsylvania Regiment, Draper Manuscript Collection, microfilm, 2 NN 33, State Historical Society of Wisconsin, Madison, Wis.; William Irvine to George Washington, 20 Apr. 1782, in C. W. Butterfield, ed., *Washington-Irvine Correspondence* (Madison, Wis., 1882), 109. The Eighth Pennsylvania (Continental Army) Regiment was largely recruited from the frontier regions of the state; see John B. B. Trussell in *The Pennsylvania Line: Organization and Operations* (Harrisburg: PHMC, 1993), 106.

7. RWPF, S13746; S22073; S7963; R7207; S12751; W24117; S23042; W5155; S22341; S7377.

8. Karen Halttunen, "Early American Murder Narratives: The Birth of Horror," in Richard Wrightman Fox and T. J. Jackson Lears, eds., *The Power of Culture: Critical Essays in American History* (Chicago: University of Chicago Press, 1993), 67–101, quotation from p. 85; Petition of Westmoreland Militia, 23 Jan. 1781, *SCP,* 7:79–80.

9. RWPF, S12779; S23637; S4731; W5155; Dann, *Revolution Remembered,* 304.

10. *Pennsylvania Gazette,* 13 Mar. 1776, 14 July, 20 Oct. 1779; Joseph Martin to Col. B. Logan, 20 Feb. 1783, Draper Manuscript Collection, 46 J 74; Erkuries Beatty, "Journal of an Expedition to Onondaga," *PA,* 2d ser., 15:223; "Petition of the Inhabitants of Westmoreland to the Continental Congress," 12 Mar. 1778, *SCP,* 8:38. On the Wyoming Valley region and the conflict between "Yankees" and Pennamite "Tories," see Paul B. Moyer, "Wild Yankees: Settlement, Conflict, and Localism Along Pennsylvania's Northeast Frontier, 1760–1820" (Ph.D. diss., College of William and Mary, 1999); Anne M. Ousterhout, *A State Divided: Opposition in Pennsylvania to the American Revolution* (Westport, Conn.: Greenwood Press, 1987), 5, 230–70; William E. Price, "A Study of a Frontier Community in Transition: The History of Wilkes-Barre, Pennsylvania, 1750–1800" (Ph.D. diss., Kent State University, 1979), 131–32; and chapter 12, above.

11. Given such imprecise and historically evolving understandings of Whiteness, it is no surprise that historians themselves have difficulty defining the term. For a critique of recent

"Whiteness studies scholarship" that takes its practitioners to task for definitional vagueness and elusive discussions of causality and power, see Eric Arneson, "Whiteness and the Historians' Imagination" *International Labor and Working Class History Journal,* no. 60 (fall 2001): 3–32. For an effective response to Arneson that acknowledges such limitations but defends the utility of the field, see Eric Foner, "Response to Eric Arneson," ibid., 57–60.

12. William Rogers, "Journal of Reverend William Rogers, D.D.," *PA,* 2d ser., 15:270; Beatty, "Journal of Expedition to Onondaga," ibid., 242.

13. Quoted in Dann, *Revolution Remembered,* 259. Equations of certain ethnic groups with specific skin colors was varied and unsystematic as reported in the popular Pennsylvania press of the mid-eighteenth century. On 25 July 1775, the *Pennsylvania Gazette* ran an advertisement regarding a runaway "English servant man," Stephen Archer, who was described as having a "brown complexion." On other occasions, the same paper referred to a runaway Irish servant's "yellow complexion" (30 July 1766), a "Negroe Man, named Tony" who was "of a very yellow complexion" (7 May 1767), and an Irish servant, Brian Roony with a "black complexion" (10 Apr. 1766).

14. On the ethnic, religious, and local disputes that divided European Americans on the Pennsylvania frontier both before and during the Revolution, see the essays in John B. Frantz and William Pencak, eds., *Beyond Philadelphia: The American Revolution in the Pennsylvania Hinterland* (University Park: The Pennsylvania State University Press, 1998); Gregory Knouff, "The Common People's Revolution: Race, Class, Masculinity, and Locale in Pennsylvania, 1775–1783" (Ph.D. diss., Rutgers University, 1996), 314–25; and Liam Riordan, "Identity and Revolution: Everyday Life and Crisis in Three Delaware River Towns," *PH* 64 (1997): 56–101. On the ethnic heterogeneity and conflict in the greater Ohio Valley, see Elizabeth A. Perkins, *Border Life: Experience and Memory in the Revolutionary Ohio Valley* (Chapel Hill: University of North Carolina Press, 1998), 81–115. On the 1777 Pennsylvania militia law that made "every white male person" liable for militia service, see *Pennsylvania Gazette,* 26 Mar. 1777. On the White male status as a prerequisite for loyalty oaths and the militia law in Pennsylvania, see Theodore C. Tappert and John W. Doberstein, eds. and trans., *The Notebook of a Colonial Clergyman: Condensed from the Journals of Henry Melchior Muhlenberg* (Philadelphia: Muhlenberg Press, 1959), 171–74.

15. *Pennsylvania Gazette,* 19 May 1779; James Dunlop to Jonathan Hoge, 22 June 1778, RPRG, reel 14, frame 309; *Pennsylvania Packet,* 6 May, 13 Aug. 1778; John Piper to President Wharton, 4 May 1778, RPRG, reel 13, frame 1287.

16. RWPF, S16378; R8633, R1638; Dann, *Revolution Remembered,* 260–61.

17. Quoted in Dann, *Revolution Remembered,* 254.

18. For more specifics on the common military culture of torture, killing prisoners, and scalping that emerged via cultural exchange among both revolutionaries and Indians, see Gregory T. Knouff, "Soldiers and Violence on the Pennsylvania Frontier," in Frantz and Pencak, eds., *Beyond Philadelphia,* 171–93. On the role of race and simultaneous and contradictory desire and repulsion toward the other in the construction of early American national subjectivity, see Smith-Rosenberg, "Dis-Covering the Subject," 843–48.

19. Quoted in Dowd, *Spirited Resistance,* 75.

20. Edward Hand to Jasper Yeates, 2 Oct. 1777, in Reuben Gold Thwaites and Louise Phelps Kellogg, eds., *Frontier Defense on the Upper Ohio, 1777–1778* (Madison: Wisconsin Historical Society, 1912), 119; John Gibson to Edward Hand, 1 Aug. 1777, ibid., 35; John Gibson to Edward Hand, 1 Aug. 1777, Edward Hand Correspondence, 1777–1785, Darlington Memorial Library, University of Pittsburgh; Edward Hand to the Delawares, 17 Sept. 1777, in Thwaites and Kellogg, eds., *Frontier Defense,* 86. On the alliance of Delawares with the revolutionaries and the latter's increasing reluctance to differentiate between friendly, neutral, and

hostile Delawares, see Carola Wessel, "'We Do Not Want to Introduce Anything New': Transplanting the Communal Life from Herrnhut to the Upper Ohio Valley" in Hartmut Lehmann, Hermann Wellenreuther, and Renate Wilson, eds., *In Search of Peace and Prosperity: New German Settlements in Eighteenth-Century Europe and America* (University Park: The Pennsylvania State University Press, 2000).

21. "Portion of the Narrative of Captain John Stuart," in Thwaites and Kellogg, eds., *Frontier Defense,* 159.

22. Dowd, *Spirited Resistance,* 77–78; Orders, 29 July 1779, Orderly Book of the Eighth Pennsylvania Regiment, Draper Manuscripts Collection, 2 NN 108.

23. Quoted in Randolph C. Downes, *Council Fires on the Upper Ohio* (Pittsburgh: University of Pittsburgh Press, 1989 [orig. pub., 1940]), 250.

24. Daniel Brodhead to Joseph Reed, 2 Nov. 1780, RPRG, reel 16, frame 1273; Dowd, *Spirited Resistance,* 81–83.

25. Nancy Shoemaker, "How Indians Got to Be Red," *American Historical Review* 102 (1997): 625–44; Dowd, *Spirited Resistance,* 47–89, quotation from p. xiii.

26. John Piper to President Wharton, 4 May 1778, RPRG, reel 12, frame 1286; Examination of Richard Weston, 22 May 1778, ibid., reel 14, frame 93–94.

27. Dowd, *Spirited Resistance,* 47–89.

28. John Piper to President Wharton, 4 May 1778, RPRG, reel 12, frame 1286.

29. William Irvine to George Washington, 16 Apr. 1783, in Butterfield, ed., *Washington-Irvine Correspondence,* 149.

30. *Pennsylvania Evening Post,* 16 Apr. 1782.

31. Solon J. Buck and Elizabeth Hawthorn Buck, *The Planting of Civilization in Western Pennsylvania* (Pittsburgh, Pa.: University of Pittsburgh Press, 1939), 197–98; Dowd, *Spirited Resistance,* 85–87; Thomas P. Slaughter, *The Whiskey Rebellion: Frontier Epilogue to the American Revolution* (New York: Oxford University Press, 1986), 75–78.

32. William Irvine to George Washington, 20 Apr. 1782 in Butterfield, ed., *Washington-Irvine Correspondence,* 99; David Howell to Moses Brown, 6 Nov. 1782, in Paul H. Smith, ed., *Letters of Delegates to Congress, 1774–1789* (CD-Rom edition, Summerfield, Fla.: Historical Database, 1998), 18:448. On the rationalizations for killing the Moravian Delawares, see Buck and Buck, *Planting of Civilization,* 197, and White, *Middle Ground,* 390.

33. Slaughter, *Whiskey Rebellion,* 75–77.

34. See chapter 11, above. My interpretation of what transpired at Gnadenhütten builds upon Thomas Slaughter's theoretical perspective in his analysis of the Paxton Boys' massacre of the Conestoga in 1764 in "Crowds in Eighteenth Century America: Reflections and New Directions," *PMHB* 115 (1991): 3–34.

35. Paul A. W. Wallace, ed., *Thirty Thousand Miles with John Heckewelder* (Pittsburgh: University of Pittsburgh Press, 1958), 189–99; quotation from p. 195.

36. Ibid., 193.

37. Slaughter, *Whiskey Rebellion,* 76; White, *Middle Ground,* 190–91.

38. Wallace, *Thirty Thousand Miles,* 197; Dowd, *Spirited Resistance,* 86–89.

39. Gordon S. Wood, "Equality and Social Conflict in the American Revolution," *WMQ* 51 (1994): 703–16. The pension applications were recorded in the 1820s and 1830s, a period in which, according to Alden Vaughan in "From White Man to Redskin," 917–53, the term *Red* was popularly used to describe Indians and their supposed complexions. The veterans preferred to imply that Indians were non-White rather than having any specific skin color of their own.

40. Jill Lepore, "Remembering American Frontiers: King Philip's War and the American Imagination" in Andrew R. L. Cayton and Fredrika J. Teute, eds., *Contact Points: American*

Frontiers from the Mohawk Valley to the Mississippi, 1750–1830 (Chapel Hill: University of North Carolina Press, 1998), 327–60; Richard Slotkin, *Regeneration Through Violence: The Mythology of the American Frontier, 1600–1860* (Middletown, Conn.: Wesleyan University Press, 1973), 313–516; White, *Middle Ground*, 368–75; and Philip J. Deloria, *Playing Indian* (New Haven: Yale University Press, 1998), 10–37.

41. Theda Perdue and Michael D. Green, eds., *The Cherokee Removal: A Brief History with Documents* (Boston: St. Martin's Press, 1995); John Mack Faragher, "More Motley Than Mackinaw: From Ethnic Mixing to Ethnic Cleansing on the Frontier of the Lower Missouri, 1783–1833" in Cayton and Teute, eds., *Contact Points*, 304–26; Bernard W. Sheehan, *Seeds of Extinction: Jeffersonian Philanthropy and the American Indian* (Chapel Hill: University of North Carolina Press, 1973).

42. Larry E. Tise, *The American Counterrevolution: A Retreat from Liberty, 1783–1800* (Mechanicsburg, Pa.: Stackpole Books, 1998), 453–80; Nash, *Forging Freedom*, 246–79; Lois E. Horton "From Class to Race in Early America: Northern Post-Emancipation Reconstruction," *Journal of the Early Republic* 19 (1999): 629–49; Roediger, *Wages of Whiteness*, 58–59.

43. Smith-Rosenberg, "Dis-Covering the Subject," 841–73; Joan R. Gundersen, *To Be Useful to the World: Women in Revolutionary America, 1740–1790* (New York: Twayne, 1997), 167–84; Susan Scheckel, *The Insistence of the Indian: Race and Nationalism in Nineteenth-Century American Culture* (Princeton: Princeton University Press, 1998), 3–14, 151.

Afterword

1. Douglas Greenberg, "The Middle Colonies in Recent American Historiography," *WMQ* 36 (1979): 416.

2. Charles A. Hanna, *The Wilderness Trail; Or, The Ventures and Adventures of the Pennsylvania Traders on the Allegheny Path, with Some New Annals of the Old West, and the Records of Some Strong Men and Some Bad Ones* (New York: G. P. Putnam's Sons, 1911); C. Hale Sipe, *The Indian Chiefs of Pennsylvania; Or, A Story of the Part Played by the American Indians in the History of Pennsylvania, Based Primarily on the Pennsylvania Archives and Colonial Records, and Built Around the Outstanding Chiefs* (Butler, Pa.: Ziegler Printing, 1927); Sipe, *The Indian Wars of Pennsylvania: An Account of the Indian Events, in Pennsylvania, of the French and Indian War, Pontiac's War, Lord Dunmore's War, the Revolutionary War and the Indian Uprising from 1789 to 1795* (Harrisburg: Telegraph Press, 1929).

3. Paul A. W. Wallace, *Conrad Weiser, 1696–1760: Friend of Colonist and Mohawk* (Philadelphia: University of Pennsylvania Press, 1945); Paul A. W. Wallace, *Indians in Pennsylvania*, rev. ed. by William A. Hunter (Harrisburg: PHMC, 1986 [orig. pub. 1961]); Anthony F. C. Wallace, *King of the Delawares: Teedyuscung, 1700–1763* (Philadelphia: University of Pennsylvania Press, 1949).

4. Francis Jennings, *The Ambiguous Iroquois Empire: The Covenant Chain Confederation of Indian Tribes with English Colonies from Its Beginnings to the Lancaster Treaty of 1744* (New York: W. W. Norton, 1984); Jennings, *Empire of Fortune: Crowns, Colonies, and Tribes in the Seven Years War in America* (New York: W. W. Norton, 1988). Since Jennings's work, a handful of other scholars have examined the Pennsylvania frontier. See, e.g., Peter C. Mancall, *Valley of Opportunity: Economic Culture Along the Upper Susquehanna, 1700–1800* (Ithaca: Cornell University Press, 1991), esp. chaps. 1–4; James H. Merrell, *Into the American Woods: Negotiators on the Pennsylvania Frontier* (New York: W. W. Norton, 1999); Jane T. Merritt, *At the Crossroads: Indians and Empires on a Mid-Atlantic Frontier, 1700–1763* (Chapel Hill: Uni-

versity of North Carolina Press, 2003). An excellent overview of the literature up to 1990 and a useful interpretation of Indian history in this region is Daniel K. Richter, "A Framework for Pennsylvania Indian History," *PH* 57 (1990): 236–61.

5. This sentence is inspired by Edmund S. Morgan, "Conflict and Consensus in the American Revolution," in Stephen G. Kurtz and James H. Hutson, eds., *Essays on the American Revolution* (Chapel Hill: University of North Carolina Press, 1973), 309. Morgan, himself echoing Patrick Henry's 1765 speech that "Charles had his Cromwell," wrote of "a society where a Hamilton had his Jefferson, a Hoover his Roosevelt, and a Nixon—might profit by their example."

6. It might also be that the dearth of Native groups in the state today, when Indians are visible and vocal in other states up and down the eastern seaboard, could further limit interest in Pennsylvania's Indian past.

7. William N. Fenton, "Locality as a Basic Factor in the Development of Iroquois Social Structure," in idem, ed., *Symposium on Local Diversity in Iroquois Culture,* Smithsonian Institution, Bureau of American Ethnology, Bulletin 149 (Washington, D.C., 1951), 39–54.

8. Daniel K. Richter, *The Ordeal of the Longhouse: The Peoples of the Iroquois League in the Era of European Colonization* (Chapel Hill: University of North Carolina Press, 1992), 5.

9. He is not the first to do so. See Thomas J. Sugrue, "The Peopling and Depeopling of Early Pennsylvania: Indians and Colonists, 1680–1720," *PMHB* 116 (1992): 3–31. Nonetheless, it seems fair to say that that Founder's reputation remains, in most minds, untarnished. An excellent survey is J. W. Frost, " 'Wear the Sword as Long as Thou Canst': William Penn in Myth and History," *Explorations in Early American Culture* 4 (2000): 13–45.

10. Merrell, *Into the American Woods,* chap. 7.

11. Quoted in chapter 10, above.

12. Richard White, *The Middle Ground: Indians, Empires, and Republics in the Great Lakes Region, 1650–1815* (Cambridge: Cambridge University Press, 1991).

13. White himself was careful to say that his middle ground "was not an Eden, and it should not be romanticized. Indeed, it could be a violent and sometimes horrifying place" (ibid., x). Those following in his footsteps have been less careful about offering a balanced, nuanced view of intercultural relations.

14. James Axtell, *After Columbus: Essays in the Ethnohistory of Colonial North America* (New York: Oxford University Press, 1988), 182–221.

15. Neal Salisbury, *Manitou and Providence: Indians, Europeans, and the Making of New England, 1500–1643* (New York: Oxford University Press, 1982); Allen W. Trelease, *Indian Affairs in Colonial New York: The Seventeenth Century* (Ithaca: Cornell University Press, 1960), chaps. 2 and 6.

16. Jill Lepore, *The Name of War: King Philip's War and the Origins of American Identity* (New York: Alfred A. Knopf, 1998).

17. The classic accounts of this conflict are Wilcomb E. Washburn, *The Governor and the Rebel: A History of Bacon's Rebellion in Virginia* (Chapel Hill: University of North Carolina Press, 1957); and Stephen Saunders Webb, *1676: The End of American Independence* (Cambridge: Harvard University Press, 1984), bk. 1.

18. Verner W. Crane, *The Southern Frontier, 1670–1732* (Durham, N.C.: Duke University Press, 1928), 17–21.

19. *PWP,* 2:128–29.

20. Jane T. Merritt, "Metaphor, Meaning, and Misunderstanding: Language and Power on the Pennsylvania Frontier," in Andrew R. L. Cayton and Fredrika J. Teute, eds., *Contact Points: American Frontiers from the Mohawk Valley to the Mississippi, 1750–1830* (Chapel Hill:

University of North Carolina Press, 1998), 84–85; Frost, "William Penn," 23–24; Merrell, *Into the American Woods,* 122–27, 275, 277.

21. *MPCP,* 2:553; "At a Council held at Philad[elph]ia ye 15th of 7ber 1718 in ye Court house," Papers of James Logan, box 11, folder 7, HSP.

22. *MPCP,* 2:607; Council at Philadelphia, 15 Sept. 1718, Logan Papers, box 11, folder 7, HSP.

CONTRIBUTORS

KRISTA CAMENZIND received her Ph.D. from the University of California, San Diego, in 2002. Her dissertation is entitled "From the Holy Experiment to the Paxton Boys: Violence, Manhood, and Race in Pennsylvania During the Seven Years' War." She thanks Catherine Forslund, René Hayden, Michael Meranze, and Sarah Schrank for their helpful comments. Her chapter is recipient of third prize in the 2003 Colonial Essay competition, sponsored by the Colonial Society of Pennsylvania, in cooperation with the McNeil Center for Early American Studies.

CARLA GERONA teaches at the University of Texas at Dallas and is completing a book titled *Night Journeys: The Power of Dreams in Transatlantic Quaker Culture*. Versions of her chapter were presented at the Newberry Library in 2001 and the Organization of American Historians annual meeting in 1998. For their comments, she thanks the participants in those sessions as well as Matthew Dennis, Toby Ditz, Gregory Dowd, Jerry Frost, Jack Greene, Christopher Grasso, Frederick Hoxie, Carol Karlsen, James Merrell, Carla Pestana, and Mechal Sobel. She especially acknowledges Alden Vaughan, who inspired her to become an early Americanist while she was an undergraduate at Columbia University.

STEVEN C. HARPER teaches Church history and doctrine at Brigham Young University and is a volume editor of the Joseph Smith Papers. He completed his Ph.D. at Lehigh University, where he was Lawrence Henry Gipson Dissertation Fellow in 2000. He thanks Jean R. Soderlund for her substantial shaping of his chapter.

ALISON DUNCAN HIRSCH (Ph.D., Columbia University, 1991) is the editor of the forthcoming *Early American Indian Documents: Treaties and Laws*, vol. 3: *Pennsylvania Treaties, 1756–1776*, and author of several articles on early American women's history. She has taught history, American studies, and women's studies for twenty years, most recently at Susquehanna University.

GREGORY T. KNOUFF completed his Ph.D. in early American history at Rutgers University in 1996. He is a member of the history department at Keene State College and the author of *The Soldiers' Revolution: Pennsylva-*

nians in Arms and the Forging of Early American Identity (Penn State University Press, 2004).

MICHAEL DEAN MACKINTOSH is a Ph.D. candidate in history at Temple University and has been a Friends of the MCEAS fellow at the McNeil Center for Early American Studies. His chapter is recipient of second prize in the 2003 Colonial Essay competition, sponsored by the Colonial Society of Pennsylvania, in cooperation with the McNeil Center.

JAMES H. MERRELL is the Lucy Maynard Salmon Professor of History at Vassar College. His works include *The Indians' New World: Catawbas and Their Neighbors from European Contact Through the Era of Removal*, and *Into the American Woods: Negotiators on the Pennsylvania Frontier*.

PAUL MOYER is a member of the history department at the State University of New York College at Brockport. He received his doctorate from the College of William and Mary and has previously taught at William and Mary and the University of Central Arkansas. He is completing a book on frontier settlement and agrarian unrest in revolutionary-era northeastern Pennsylvania.

WILLIAM A. PENCAK, professor of history at Penn State University, was the founding editor of *Explorations in Early American Culture* (now *Early American Studies*) and was the editor of *Pennsylvania History* from 1994 to 2002. His coedited volumes include *Beyond Philadelphia: The American Revolution in the Pennsylvania Hinterland; Making and Remaking Pennsylvania's Civil War; Riot and Revelry in Early America;* and *Pennsylvania: A History of the Commonwealth*, all published by Penn State University Press. He is writing a book on the Jewish communities of early America.

DAVID L. PRESTON teaches early American history and American Indian history at the Citadel. He completed his graduate studies at the College of William and Mary and is at work on a book tentatively titled "The Texture of Contact: European and Indian Settler Communities on the Iroquoian Borderlands, 1720–1780." He thanks James Axtell, Mike McGiffert, Bob Gross, Paul Moyer, James Spady, and the attendees of a colloquium of the Omohundro Institute of Early American History and Culture in March 2001 for their comments on his chapter.

DANIEL K. RICHTER is the Richard S. Dunn Director of the McNeil Center for Early American Studies and professor of history at the University of Pennsylvania. He is author of *Facing East from Indian Country: A Native History of Early America* (2001), and *The Ordeal of the Longhouse: The Peoples of the Iroquois League in the Era of European Colonization* (1992). With James H. Merrell, he is coeditor of *Beyond the Covenant Chain: The Iroquois and Their Neighbors in Indian North America, 1600–1800*, recently published in paperback by Penn State University Press.

AMY C. SCHUTT is a postdoctoral researcher with the McNeil Center for Early American Studies and the National Park Service. She gratefully acknowledges support from a Spencer Foundation Small Research Grant and from a Garrison Fellowship/Major Grant from Colgate University, which enabled her to complete the research for her chapter. She expresses her thanks to Vernon Nelson of the Moravian Archives, Bethlehem, for his assistance.

JOHN SMOLENSKI is a member of the history department at the University of California, Davis. He was educated at Yale University and the University of Pennsylvania, where he received his Ph.D. in 2001. His chapter is drawn from his current book project, entitled "Friends and Strangers: The Evolution of a Creole Civic Culture in Colonial Pennsylvania." Earlier versions of his chapter were presented at the 1998 meeting of the Organization of American Historians and the 1999 Roundtable on Law and Semiotics. He thanks Matthew Dennis, Carol Karlsen, Michael Zuckerman, Kathleen Brown, Alan Taylor, Stephanie Dyer, and Ken Miller for their comments, suggestions, and assistance.

JAMES O'NEIL SPADY is a Ph.D. candidate in American studies at the College of William and Mary, where he is writing a dissertation on colonialism and the cultural politics of education in Georgia and South Carolina from 1700 to the 1820s. He acknowledges the contributions of friends and mentors to early drafts of his chapter, beginning with his master's thesis committee: James Axtell, Robert A. Gross, and Michael McGiffert. He also thanks Sharon Block, Wendy Gonaver, Grey Gundaker, Leisa Meyer, Richard Price, and David Preston for their criticism and encouragement.

WILLIAM A. STARNA is professor of anthropology emeritus at the State University of New York, Oneonta, and lives in Bremen, Germany. He has published widely on the Iroquoian and Algonquian Indian populations of the eastern United States and Canada, in addition to contemporary state-federal-Indian relations. He is grateful for the prodding of Elisabeth Tooker and the late Francis Jennings in the development of his essay, and thanks Corinna Dally-Starna and Martha D. Shattuck for their comments on early drafts. Portions of his chapter appear in William A. Starna and George R. Hamell, "History and the Burden of Proof: The Case of Iroquois Influence on the U.S. Constitution," *New York History* 77 (1996): 427–52, and are reprinted here with permission.

LOUIS M. WADDELL received his Ph.D. from the University of North Carolina in 1971 and has been an associate historian on the staff of the Pennsylvania Historical and Museum Commission since 1973. He was the last editor of *The Papers of Henry Bouquet* and is employed in the Core Services Section of the State Archives in Harrisburg.

INDEX

Acker, Christian, 241
agriculture, 10
    increasing role of Indian men in, 93–94
Albany Congress, 225–26
alcohol, hospitality and, 79–80
Allen, William, 168, 170, 171, 175, 178
Andros, Edmund, 26, 30
Armstrong, George, 187
Armstrong, Jack, 138–39
Axtell, James, 106, 130

baptismal ceremonies, sharing of, by Indian
    and Euro-American women, 99
Barton, Reverend Thomas, 218
Bartram, John, 189
Beatty, Erkuries, 243
Bechtel, Anna Margaretha, 95
Bezaillon, Martha, 69, 82
Blanchard, Benjamin, 234
Boehler, Peter, 170
Brahe, Pehr, 13
Brainerd, David, 171, 173–74, 189
Brink, Henry, 234
Brodhead, Daniel, 168, 240, 242–43, 247
Bruce, David, 69
Buchanan, Arthur, 187
Burd, James, 211
Burd, John, 210
Burd, Sarah Shippen, 82
Burnyeat, John, 47, 48
Butler, Zebulon, 231, 232
Büttner, Anna Margaretha, 88, 95
Byllynge, Edward, 27

Calvinists. See Puritans
Camenzind, Krista, 262–63
Cammerhoff, John, 146, 160, 161–62
Canasatgo, 144–63, 183, 190, 193
Cartlidge, Edmund, 104–5, 115–16
Cartlidge, John, 78, 104–5, 115–16, 119
Chalkley, Thomas, 50–52, 77
Chapman, John, 172
childbirth, Indian and Moravian women
    sharing experiences of, 97–98

Choir organizations, Moravian, 90
Christianity, Indian women and, 102–3
Churchman, John, 54–55
Civility, 115, 125
    role of, in Sawantaney's death case,
        118–22
Clayton, Asher, 229
Cock, Lars, 26, 33
Cock, Peter, 25–26, 26
colonial courts, 116–17. See also legal systems
colonial women. See women, colonial
Conestoga Indians, 125, 217
Conestoga Town, burning of, 201–92
Congregationalists, 49
Connecticut, Wyoming Valley land disputes
    and, 223–25
county courts, 109. See also legal systems
Crawford, William, 255
Croghan, George, 69, 75–76, 185, 190, 192, 195
crowds, collective and symbolic nature of,
    212

Danckaerts, Jasper, 28–29
Dean, John, 241
Delaware Indians, 125, 185–87, 188, 251–52
    Christian, 251–54
    effects of Walking Purchase on, 175–79
    gender separation by, 90–92
    kinship bonds of, 98–99
    Walking Purchase and, 167–70, 171–72
Delaware Jargon, 21
    colonial translators of, 25–26
Delaware Valley, Quaker colonization of, 19–
    20, 26–28
Denny, William, 211
devils, Quakers and, 61–62
de Vries, David, 5
diplomacy, Native American women and, 65
diplomatic councils. See treaty councils
diseases
    impact of, on Lenapes, 37
    Native Americans and, 7–8
Doughtery, John, 242
Dowed, Gregory Evans, 248, 254

dreams
  belief in, by Quakers and Indians, 61–62
  of benevolence of Penn, 50–52
  centrality of, in American Quaker cul-
    ture, 45–46
  of John Churchman, 54–56
  as fantasy for Indians and Quakers,
    43–44
  of George Fox, 46–47
  importance of, 41
  importance of, for Quakers, 41–42
  of James Kenny, 57–61
  Native Americans and, 44–45
  problem of defining, 45
  recorded by Thomas Chalkley, 50–52
  spiritual force of Indian, 41–42
  thought of as foolish, by Conrad Weiser,
    52
  use of, by Quakers, 61–62
  use of, for orchestrating truces, 53–54
  of Ann Whitall, 54
  of John Woolman, 56–57
Dunlop, James, 245
Durkee, John, 230
Dutch
  conflicts with Swedes and, 22
  conquering of New Sweden by, 25
  gendered property rights and, 23
Dyck, Gregorios van, 24–25

Easton, Treaty of (1758), 226
Edmund, Cartlidge, 78
Elder, Reverend John, 218
Elliott, William, 245
Euro-American women. See women, colo-
  nial
Europeans
  effect of contact with new world on, 8–9
  marriage to Native Americans and, 81
  role of nature in shaping relationships
    with Native Americans and, 3–4
Evans, John, 79–80, 109, 111, 112, 113
exchange economies, on frontiers, 185

Fafard, Jean, 76
Falconer, Peter, 198
Falkinburg, Jacob, 29–30
Farmer, Jasper, 79
Fenton, William N., 145

Ferrée, Marie, 82
Finns, in Delaware Valley, 16
Fischer, David Hackett, 135
Fletcher, Benjamin, 109–11
Forbes, John, 204, 218
Fort Stanwix Treaty of 1768, 227–28
Foster, John, 242
Fox, George, 27
  Indian visions and, 46–47
Francis, Turbot, 187
Franklin, Benjamin, 201–2
Franklin, John, 233–34, 236–37
Freeman, Hannah (Indian Hannah), 82
Freemoyer, David, 242
French, John, 104–5, 115, 116
frontiers. See also multiple frontiers
  in colonial Pennsylvania, 183
  exchange economies on, 185

Garret, Elisha, 234
gender, Lenape property rights and, 22–23
Gerona, Carla, 264, 265
Gibson, John, 246, 254
Gilje, Paul, 209
Girty, Ann, 75
Girty, Mary, 75
Girty, Simon, Sr., 184–85
Gnadenhütten, 89, 93, 96–97, 177
  female relationships at, 99–102
  massacre at, 251–53
  sex-segregated religious meetings at,
    99–100
Gobin, Edward, 221, 236
Gookin, Charles, 109, 112
Gordon, Patrick, 39, 122–25, 188
Great Treaty Wampum Belt, 63–64, 64f. See
  also wampum belts
Greenberg, Douglas, 259
Grube, Margaretha Elisabeth, 95–96, 100, 101
Grube, Martin, 78

Hagen, Margaretha, 101
Halttunen, Karen, 241–42
Hamilton, James, 193, 195, 218, 224–25
Harper, Steven, 262
Harris, Esther, 69, 73
Harris, John, 221
Heckewelder, John, 73–74, 92, 168, 171, 253–
  54, 261

Heckewelder, Sarah, 101
Helme, Israel, 26
Henderson, Andrew, 234
Henry, William, 201
Hetaquantegechty, 147
Hicks, Edward, 261
Hirsch, Alison Duncan, 263
Holme, Thomas, 35
homicides, on North American frontiers,
    106, 129–30
Hoops, Adam, 210
Horsfield, Timothy, 214
hospitality
    alcohol and, 79–80
    among colonists and Native Americans,
        78–79
Howell, David, 252
Hunter, Ann, rape case of, 129, 142–43

illegal settlements, 193, 199. See also squatters
Indian Esther, 96–97, 99
Indian Hannah (Hannah Freeman), 82
Indians. See Native Americans
Irish, Nathaniel, 170
Ironcutter, John, 229
Iroquois League, 125, 147. See also Six Na-
    tions
    case of Sawantaney's death and, 119–20
    Wyoming Valley land disputes and, 224
Irvine, William, 241, 250, 252

Jemison, Mary, 882
Jennings, Francis, 167, 259–60
Jennings, John, 228, 230
Jungman, Anna Büttner, 95, 100–101, 102
juries, 116. See also legal systems
justice, folktales of, 106–7. See also legal sys-
    tems

Kalm, Pehr, 3, 17
Keiser, Peter, 239
Keith, Governor William, 80, 105, 117–20, 135
Kennedy, Patrick, 135–36
Kenny, James, 57–61
Kieft, Willem, 14
King Philip's War, 49
Knouff, Gregory, 234, 263, 265
Konkle, Lawrence, 241

Lancaster, Penn., massacre at, 201

Lancaster, Treaty of (1744), 139
land disputes, 183–84
land ownership. See also property rights;
    squatters
    before and after Seven Years' War, 181–82
    Native American vs. European views of,
        9–10
legal systems, 105–6
    colonial courts and, 116–17
    colonial magistrates and, 108
    county courts, 109
    death of Sawantaeny as test of colonial,
        117–22
    folktales of justice and, 106–7
    juries and, 116
Lenape Indians
    advice to colonists on relations with, 27
    clashes with Swedish views of nature
        and, 13–14
    conceptions of land by, and Swedish
        views, 14–15
    encounters with colonists and, 28–29
    impact of early colonists on, 37–40
    land dealings of, 21–22
    massacre at Swanendael and, 4–6
    nature and, 16–17
    New Sweden and, 22–24
    origins of, 7
    Penn's attitude toward, 30–32
    property rights and, 22–23
    relationships with Swedes and, 22–25
    sharing of dream work with Quakers
        and, 43
Lerner, Gerda, 81–83
Le Tort, Anne, 69, 73, 74–75, 78
Le Tort, Jacques, 74–75, 78
Lewis, Benjamin, 241
Lindström, Pehr, 8, 16, 41, 42
Logan, James, 104–5, 108, 110f, 115, 116, 117,
    136, 147
Lycon, Andrew, 197, 198

Mack, Anna, 78, 97, 101
Mack, Jeannette, 66, 69, 87–88, 94, 95, 96–97,
    100, 101
Mack, Martin, 66, 69, 78, 87–88, 95
Mackintosh, Michael, 265
magistrates, colonial, 108. See also legal sys-
    tems

Mahicans
　gender separation by, 90–92
　kinship bonds of, 98–99
　marriage, between Europeans and Indians,
　　81
Marshall, Edward, 168, 177
Marshe, Witham, 144–45
massacres, 219—220
　at Gnadenhütten, 251–53
　at Lancaster, Pa., 201
　memorials to, 83
　of Moravian Delawares, 251–54
　Paxtown Boys' and, 83, 201–4, 229
　at Swanendael, 4–6
Mathers, John, 168
McCoy, Angus, 239
McDonner, John, 231
McKean, Thomas, 221
McKee, Thomas, 69, 195, 219
men, Native American
　gender-specific responsibilities of, 92–93
　increasing role of, in agriculture, 93
Merrell, James, 212
Merritt, Jane, 44, 267
métis women, 76
Miller, John, 241
Montour, Andrew, 81
Montour, Isabelle, 81
　as example of multiple frontiers of
　　women, 66–68
　hospitality of, 77, 78
　markers memorializing, 82
Montour, Jean, 76
Montour, Lewis, 80
Montour, Marguerite, 72, 73, 77
Moravian Delawares, massacre of, 251–54
Moravians
　choir organizations of, 90
　conversations between women about
　　spiritual matters and, 94–95
　female relationships and, 99–102
　gender and, 89–90
　gender boundaries of, 93–94
　Indian women and, 95
　missionary activities of, 88
　missionary relationships with Indians
　　and, 87–88
　schooling and, 100–101
Morgan, George, 246

Morgan, Jacob, 211
Morris, Robert, 209
motherhood, 98–99
Moyer, Paul, 263
multiple frontiers. *See also* frontiers
　example of Isabelle Montour, 66–68
　of Native American women, 64–66
Mushemeelin, 138–40
Myers, Andrew, 241

Native Americans. *See also* women, Native
　　American; specific tribe
　belief in dreams by, 62
　conception of Reds by, 248
　diseases and, 7–8
　dreaming and, 44–45
　generosity of, 77
　importance of dreams for, 41–42
　marriage to Europeans and, 81
　massacre at Gnadenhütten and, 251–52
　racism and, 238–40
　role of nature in shaping relationships
　　with Europeans and, 3–4
　separateness of gender by, 90–92
　similarities between Swedes and, 16
　views on land ownership by, 9–10
nature
　ambivalence between Swedes and Indi-
　　ans on understanding, 16–17
　role of, in shaping relationships between
　　Europeans and Native Americans,
　　3–4
　views of, 3–4
Neolin, 58–60, 58f
New Gothenburg, 13
New Sweden, 6–7, 11–13. *See also* Swedes
　conquered by Dutch, 25
　conquering by Dutch of, 25
　importance of establishing legitimacy of,
　　15
　importance of trade for, 15
　Lenapes and, 22–24
　practice of woodcraft and, 16
Ninichican, 35, 39
Nitschman, David, 170
Notike, 23, 25

Ockanikon, 29–30
Ogden, Amos, 228, 231
Ogden, Nathan, 231

Paine, Chester, 234
Paris, Treaty of, 250
Parsons, William, 211
Paschall, Thomas, 33
Patterson, James, 189
Paxton Boys' massacre and march, 83, 201–4,
     217–18, 229
   legacy of, 219–20
Pemberton, Israel, 57
Peminaka, 23
Penn, John, 170, 202, 228, 229
Penn, Thomas, 170, 178, 182, 195, 198, 229
Penn, William, 18–20, 267–68
   attitude toward Lenapes by, 30–32
   conflicts with Lanapes and, 35–37
   desire of, to punish colonizers who
      harmed Indians, 113
   Great Treaty of, 70, 71f
   Great Treaty Wampum Belt and, 63–64
   hospitality of, 79
   implementation of legal system by, 116
   Indian dream on benevolence of, 50–52
   narrative of Pennsylvania's founding by,
      38–39
   as ruler, 49–50
   visit to Conestoga by, 77
Penn, William, Jr., 79–80
Penn's Treaty, 18–19, 20f
Penn's Woods, 212–13
   scholars and, 260–62
Pennsylvania
   factors contributing to transformation of
      frontier of, 222
   frontier in, 183
   narrative founding of, 38–39
   Penn's colonization of, 33–37
   Provincial Council of, 114–17
   Wyoming Valley land disputes and,
      223–25
Pequot War of 1636–37, 14
Peters, Richard, 173, 175, 177, 186f, 194, 195–
     98, 224, 225
Pickering, Timothy, 235–36
Piper, John, 245, 248
Plunket, William, 232
Post, Christian Frederick, 61, 69, 71
Potter, John, 210
Powhatan coup of 1622, 14
Preston, David, 265

Printz, Johan, 11–13, 14–15, 16–17
property rights, 37–38. See also land owner-
     ship
   different views of, by Europeans and
      Lenapes, 22–23
Provincial Council of Pennsylvania
   legals issues of Sawantaney's death and,
      116–17
   sanctions and, 114–15
Puritans, Quakers and, 48–49

Quakers
   attention to Indian visionary experiences
      and, 46
   belief in dreams by, 62
   benevolence of, 49–50
   centrality of dreams in culture of Ameri-
      can, 45–46
   colonization of Delaware Valley by,
      19–20
   Congregationalists and, 49
   devils and, 61–62
   importance of dreams for, 41–42
   Puritans and, 48–49
   settling of Delaware Valley by, 26–28
   sharing of dream work with Lenapes
      and, 43
   use of dreams by, 61–62

racialization, 216. See also Whiteness; Whites
racial self-definition, process of, 248–49
racism, 238–39
Rambo, Peter, 25–26, 26, 35
Rankin, Hugh F., 135
rape, 130–31. See also Hunter, Ann
   in colonial Pennsylvania, 135–36
Rau, Jeannette. See Mack, Jeannette
Red, conception of, by Native Americans,
     248
Reed, Samuel, 234
Reem, George, 245
Rees, Thomas, 241
revolutionary soldiers
   importance of Whiteness of, 255–56
   language of, in pension depositions,
      241–42
   proclivity of killing neutral Indians by,
      246–47
   wartime behavior of, 240–41

Revolutionary War. *See* War for Indepen-
dence
Rising, Johan, 23–24
Robeson, David, 80
Roth, Marie Agnes, 101
Rountree, Heln, 66
Roush, George, 243–44, 245
importance of skin color for, 244
rum, trade in, by Native American women,
80

Saghsidowa, 52–53
Sauer, Christopher, 52
Sawantaeny
death of, 104–6, 115–16
death of, as test case of colonial legal sys-
tem, 117–22
folktales about death of, 126–28
legal issues and death of, 116–17
scalping, practice of, 246
Scaroyady, 192–93
Schlatter, Rev. Michael, 187
Schmick, Johanna, 97, 100, 101, 102
schools, Moravian, 100–101
Schutt, Amy, 265
Scull, Nicholas, 137
Sensemann, Anna Catharina, 88, 100, 101
Sensemann, Anna Maria, 101
Seven Years' War, 180–81, 204–7
Shawnee Indians, 125, 185–87
Shebosch, John Jacob, 69
Shickellamy, 52–53, 78, 138–39, 147, 190, 191
Shippen, Edward, 178
Shoemaker, Nancy, 248
Six Nations, 183, 190–91. *See also* Iroquois
League
Wyoming Valley land disputes and,
227–28
Smiley, Thomas, 236
Smith, John, 266
Sobel, Mechal, 43–44
Sophia, 102–3
Spady, James, 265
Spangenberg, Augustus Gottlieb, 214–15
Spangenberg, Joseph, 66
squatters, 180, 182, 184, 189–90, 196–97
Indian war parties and, 190–91
quest for land and property rights by,
197–98

Squaw Campaign, 83
Stager, Baltzer, 230–31
Star, Frederick, 190–91
Steel, James, 172
Stewart, Charles, 228
Stewart, Lazarus, 228–31
Struthers, John, 246
Stuart, Charles, 180–81, 197, 198
Stump, Frederick, 229
Sullivan, John, 233, 243
Susquehanna Company, 223–25
Susquehanna Indians, 185–87
Swain, Hannah, 75
Swampisse, 37, 38, 39
Swanendael, 9
massacre at, 4–6
Swanson, Swan, 35
Swanzey Vision, 49
Swedes. *See also* New Sweden
clashes with Lenape views of nature and,
13–14
conceptions of land by, and Lenape
views, 14–15
conflicts with Dutch and, 22
gendered property rights and, 23
importance of maintaining purity of language and, 13
nature and, 16–17
relationships with Lenape Indians and,
22–25
similarities between American Natives
and, 16
views of world by, 9
views on land ownership by, 9–10

Tammanend, 35, 39
Tatamy, Tunda, 172–75
Teedyuscung, 54, 56, 176, 177, 237
assassination of, 226–27
Wyoming Valley land disputes and, 226
Thomas, Gabriella, 29–30
Thomas, George, 137, 139, 149, 151, 168
Thomas, Richard, 189
Thompson, James, 239
Thompson, John, 187–88
Thompson, Thomas, Jr., 48–49
Toby, John, 129, 132, 140–42
Tohaswuchdioony, 161–62

trade
    colonial women and, 75–76
    Native American women and, 76
    role of women in, 72–74
    in rum, by Native American women, 80
treaty conferences, Native American women
    at, 65
treaty councils, 108–9
    political rituals at, 112–13
    role of wampum at, 109–12
Trenton Decree, 233–34
*A True Account of the Dying words of Ockani-
    kon* (Falkinburg), 29–30

Upshall, Nicholas, 48

Van Gordeon, Wilhelmus, 234
Vanzant, George, 241
Vaughan, Alden T., 139, 203
violence, culture of
    effect of War for Independence on, 233
    on Pennsylvania frontier, 235–36
    Wyoming Valley land disputes and, 228
visions. *See* dreams

Walker, Jane, rape case of, 135–36
Walking Purchase of 1737, 149–52, 185
    Delawares and, 167–70, 171–72
    effect of, on Delawares, 175–79
Wallace, Anthony F. C., 259
Wallace, Paul A., 259
wampum belts, 63–64, 64f, 109–12
    as messages, 111
    as signifiers of authority, 111–12
War for Independence, effect of, on culture
    of violence, 228
Washington, George, 204
Webb, Henry, 137–38
Weiser, Conrad, 52, 66, 78, 140, 142, 146, 148,
    152–56, 158, 159, 159f, 178, 190, 191, 192,
    193, 194, 195–98, 207–8, 211, 215,
    216–17
    rape of Ann Hunter and, 130–35
Wertz, George, 239
Weshichagechive, 176
West, Benjamin, 18, 20f, 40, 70, 261
Weston, Richard, 249
Weynepeeweyta, 73–74, 78
Whitall, Ann, 54

White, Richard, 44, 264
Whitefield, George, 170
Whiteness
    articulation of, 245
    importance of, for revolutionary soldiers,
    255–56
Whites
    construction of race by, 248
    definitions of, 243
    development of wartime identity of, 249
    self-identity and, 243–44
    usage of term, 242–43
Wild Yankees, 221–22
    resistance to state of Pennsylvania by,
    236–37
    use of disguise and Indian imagery by,
    236
Williams, Raymond, 3–4
Williams, Roger, 266
Williamson, David, 252
Winter, John, 122–23
Winter, Walter, 122–23
Wolf, Peter, 241
Wolfe, Adam, 242
women
    colonial: cross-cultural interactions of,
    76–77; impact of choir organization
    on Moravian, 90; importance of lin-
    guistic ability for, 69; as missionaries,
    87–88; missionary, and relationships
    with Indian women, 89; sharing bap-
    tismal ceremonies with Indian
    women and, 99; support of treaty
    conferences and military expeditions
    by, 71–72; trade and, 72–74, 75–76
    métis, 76
    Moravian, relationships with Indian
    women and, 96–98
    Native American: Christianity and,
    102–3; creation of wampum belts by,
    64; cross-cultural interactions of,
    76–77; gender specific occupations
    of, 92–93; Moravian missionaries
    and, 95–96; multiple frontiers of,
    64–66; relationships with Euro-
    American missionary women and,
    89; relationships with Moravian
    women and, 96–98, 99–102; sharing
    baptismal ceremonies with colonial

women (*continued*)
women and, 99; sharing experiences of childbirth with Moravian women and, 97–98; spiritual conversations by, 96; trade and, 76; trade in rum by, 80; at treaty conferences, 65, 69–72
Pennsylvania's historical market program of, 82–83
roles of: in diplomatic and political affairs, 50–51; as healers, 79
woodcraft, 16
Woodhouse, Ann, 75
woods, Euro-American fears about, 212–13
Woolman, John, 56–57

Wyoming Valley land disputes, 222–28, 223–25
Albany Congress and, 225–26
American Revolution and, 231–33
battles for control of, 230–31
culture of violence and, 228
forces shaping violence of, 235

Young, Thomas, 21

Zeisberger, David, 90–92, 92, 146, 160, 161–62, 252, 261
Zeisberger, Susanna, 102
Zinzendorf, Count Nikolaus Ludwig von, 78, 81, 170–71, 172